From The Women's Press Ltd
34 Great Sutton Street, London EC1V 0DX

ABOUT THE AUTHORS

Sheila Ernst *(left)* and Lucy Goodison

Sheila Ernst was educated at Dartington Hall School and Newnham College, Cambridge. She has worked as a primary school teacher, social worker, student counsellor and has done research on abortion. Her increasing involvement with the women's liberation movement and socialist politics enabled her to make changes in her personal life and her work.

Coming from a family of psychotherapists, she has moved back into therapy work herself only through Red Therapy and the development of a politically conscious approach. She is now a therapist at the Women's Therapy Centre in London and has done further training in counselling and group work. This book was being finished shortly before the birth of her third child.

Lucy Goodison was educated at Bushey Grammar School and Newnham College, Cambridge. She started work as a journalist and scriptwriter, and spent five years at the BBC where she researched and directed documentary films. Influenced by libertarian politics and the women's movement after 1968, she left the BBC and has since been involved in community and educational work. She helped start the Red Therapy group and trained in massage which she now does professionally. At the Women's Therapy Centre in London she runs groups on dance and dreams, and works with migraine sufferers. Recent publications include 'Divide and Rule – Never!', an anti-racist booklet for schools, and the pamphlet, 'Women and Migraine'. She has one child.

SHEILA ERNST & LUCY GOODISON

In Our Own Hands

A Book of Self-Help Therapy

 The Women's Press

First published by The Women's Press Limited 1981
A member of the Namara Group
34 Great Sutton Street, London EC1V 0DX

Reprinted 1981, 1982, 1984, 1985, 1986, 1988

A complete list of titles published by
The Women's Press is available from the
above address. Please send a large SAE
with all enquiries.

In Our Own Hands has been
designed by Stephanie Dowrick & Suzanne Perkins
typeset by BSC Typesetting Limited, London
Printed in Great Britain by
Hazell Watson & Viney Limited
Member of BPCC plc
Aylesbury, Bucks, England

British Library Cataloguing in Publication Data
Ernst, Sheila
   In our own hands.
 I. Self-realisation
 I. Title
 II. Goodison, Lucy
 158'.1 BF637.S4
 ISBN 0-7043-3841-6

DEDICATION

To the Red Therapy group
without whose courage and conviction
this book could not have been written

THANKS

Many people contributed to the writing of this book. All the members of Red Therapy, past and present, contributed their experience and have given us support and encouragement. In particular, Jo Ryan read large sections of the book as we wrote it and we had continuing and helpful discussions where she generously shared her special knowledge and communicated her confidence in us even when we lacked confidence in ourselves. Margaret Barnes, Linda Dove and Barbara Mound took trouble to give us valuable advice based on their experience of certain techniques, and have also let us quote from their personal writings on therapy. Marie Maguire and Sue Morrison have assisted us with their knowledge and enthusiasm. We were encouraged by several chapters being read by Tricia Bickerton and Barbara Mound who latterly were taking responsibility for starting new self-help groups. Jane Foot came in at a crucial stage when the book was nearly finished and assisted us with the writing of the introduction.

From outside the Red Therapy group, Martin Richards helped to clarify the ideas in Chapter Eight and Sue Gerry read the whole manuscript in the final stages and with a fresh eye was able to trim and tighten many sections in a warm and tactful way. The Laurieston Hall group, with their initiative in organising self-help therapy conferences, helped us to realise the relevance of the Red Therapy experience and in particular Katriona Stamp, Linda Mallet, Alice Simpson and Dave Treanor wrote up their experiences in groups which we have used.

Lucy would like to thank her parents, Betty and Robin Goodison, whose patient and generous help in looking after her daughter Corey freed her on many occasions for writing; similarly Joyce and David Morrison gave much-appreciated help by looking after their granddaughter. Apart from her women friends in the Red Therapy group, Lucy has felt most consistently supported by Paul Morrison who has weathered anxieties and tension about the book, has read and commented perceptively on many chapters, and has consistently inspired us with his belief in the importance of this book and the politics it expresses. Corey has continued to love a working and at times fraught mother.

Sheila would like to thank everyone at the Women's Therapy Centre for their daily support and for their constant confirmation that there is a need for this book. Her everyday life while writing was made possible by the consistent and patient collective sharing in her house of responsibility, money and childcare and by her household's acceptance of the inevitable remoteness of living with someone who is writing a book. Jonathan Trustram, and Sheila's daughters Sarah and Emma, tolerated her absence and pre-occupations, expressed interest and provided help at different stages and, most importantly, gave her the warmth and love which enabled her to persevere with this project.

We owe a special debt to Stephanie Dowrick at The Women's Press. This book was her brainchild and she has been far more than an editor. From her own interest in therapy she has taken issue with many of the ideas in this book and we have had an ongoing and enriching debate with her. She has offered constant encouragement, honest, stringent and often humorous criticism, and has done painstaking detailed work editing and shaping the manuscript.

Contents

Introduction
Unconsciousness Raising

The Aims of This Book
This is a book for those who want to learn to do self-help therapy for themselves, whether in a group, with a friend, or alone. It is also for those who want to be informed, active participants in the process of professional therapy.

We know that therapy is often used in mindless and reactionary ways. We are offering here an informed critique of different disciplines, pointing out their dangers but also what is *positive* in them so that a person wanting to do therapy has knowledge, and therefore power, over her choices, and so that those wanting to do self-help therapy have access to practical techniques which come from these disciplines and can use them for themselves. Too often these theories, and especially the techniques, are inaccessible within the confines of privileged professions or expensive training programmes. Demystifying them and making them available to whoever is interested seems an important contribution to the process of taking charge of our own mental health.

The therapy we write about is therapy by us and for us. We take techniques, adapt them and use them for ourselves. Most of the methods we describe were developed by men and, as feminists, we approach them critically. Unfortunately it is a fact that producing theory has been the almost exclusive province of men. It would be absurd to discount this. The point of writing from a feminist perspective is not to pretend that no previous theories exist but to use them as a basis for constructing a theory and practice which adequately reflect the experience of the other fifty per cent of the population: women.

We have been eclectic in our approach. We have had a wide range of experience and want to share it. We have not attempted to be comprehensive and our selection of techniques has been underwritten by certain assumptions such as the relationship between emotional and physical experience and the

1

significance of historical and social factors. The theory and practice of feminist therapy are still embryonic and feminists are only beginning to develop our own theories about how the personality is constructed and how we can hope to change. We have selected those approaches which are most consistent with our political ideas, giving particular attention to the theories and practice which we think contribute most to the development of a coherent feminist therapy.

We have gained a great deal from therapy and have written this book hoping that others will gain as much. Many people will read it because they are deeply unhappy, confused, frustrated, depressed; suffer physical symptoms such as migraine; observe recurrent self-destructive patterns they cannot change; feel unable to take active control over their lives; experience their emotions as overwhelming or fear they have no emotions. The ending of an important relationship, the loss of a job, a birth or a death, eviction, racist attack, rape or a striving for greater self-understanding may be among the reasons pushing you towards therapy.

Therapy can either appear to be a painful or terrifying process, or people may have unreal expectations as to how it will change their lives. We are sure that the extent of our capacity to change is limited by the nature of the society we live in. The inner changes we make through therapy need to be combined with taking action to change our material situation outside the therapy group. Nevertheless, the gains to be made through therapy are real and quite distinct from what can be gained by the 'discussion' of problems within friendship or an intimate relationship. Women in our group benefited in different ways. Some describe how they used to have sudden and incomprehensible outbursts of feelings and now, through familiarity with their anger, fear, hatred or jealousy, can accept these 'forbidden' feelings and direct them more effectively. Far from uncovering an uncontrollable mass of feelings, or a black pool of madness, women find themselves extending their *conscious* awareness, enabling them to exercise greater choice rather than to feel controlled. We have become better able to deal with contradictory desires: between wanting to be active and independent and wanting to be cared for; wanting to be intimate with others but not wanting to be swallowed up. Many women have found this increased self-awareness has enabled them to be more emotionally alive in their relationships, to bring more energy into their contact with the world. In a society which is not geared towards human relationships therapy can help us more actively to give and receive love. Through self-exploration we can begin to learn to focus less on our image as reflected in others and more on the resources we have within ourselves. We can begin to know and enjoy our bodies as they are. As women we have been taught to think of ourselves as second-best, to see difficulties arising from this as 'our fault'. Accepting ourselves more, we can begin to feel that taking care of ourselves can be a valid and necessary activity. Therapy can be a powerful tool helping us to understand what is happening in our lives, and to deal effectively with the issues and problems we face.

The Women's Liberation Movement, Therapy and Politics

One of the keystones of the new and stronger women's liberation movement which re-emerged in the radical upsurge of the late sixties was the small, informal consciousness-raising group. Here women met to talk and learned that what had previously seemed an individual problem (not being able to cope with others' demands, feeling powerless or depressed, taking anger out on children) was, in fact, a common problem shared by many. We learned that these experiences were the product not of individual failure but of the contradictory demands society makes on all women. We identified the institutions which shape female experience in a patriarchal society: schools, the family, the church, hospitals and the welfare system. We saw a clear link between our 'personal' feelings as women and the political structure we live in. These realisations gave us the strength to act together. Phyllis Chesler has described how women's liberation was, initially, far more therapeutic than therapy.[1] Women involved in the movement were generally happier, more confidently active, braver and more angry. We believed that direct struggle against oppression in the home and outside it, together with solidarity with other women, would lead to rapid change. Since the late sixties increasing numbers of women have been active in setting up refuges for battered women, fighting for better health services, housing and nurseries, for better pay and work opportunities, for changes in the media presentation of women, for changes in the legal decisions on abortion and rape and for sexual self-definition. Women have set up feminist bookstores, publishing houses, cafés and bands; some women decided to work exclusively with other women, independently of men.

Many of us tried to work out different ways of living in order to undercut the sexism, competitiveness, possessiveness and authoritarianism fostered by the family within capitalist society. Some of us started to live collectively or altered traditional sex-roles and patterns of childcare, or tried to open out our sexual relationships. We did this in the belief that by altering the structures of personal relationships we would also alter the feelings people had within them. We hoped that if we could understand how certain attitudes are socially determined, we could, by a conscious act of will, choose to change or banish them. But even within a growing and effective movement active in the world, and with a radical restructuring of domestic life, our feelings and relationships did not change easily. Women were gaining new power but continued to feel depressed, inadequate and confused.

We began to recognise the historical dimension of our oppression: the depth of our gender conditioning which would continually hinder our efforts to change. As women we have been brought up to be submissive and supportive to others, to be seductive, manipulative and passive. We have rarely been encouraged to decide what we want and to go for it openly, to be angry, powerful, demanding; nor to value our own needs as equal to other people's, especially those of men and children. Unconscious feelings formed by our childhood conditioning would continue to sabotage our conscious choices for liberation.

Recognising that we needed to unlearn this conditioning, we started to bring to the surface some of our repressed feelings. This process should, perhaps, have been called 'unconsciousness raising'. It is a pity that we called it therapy. Therapy suggests male therapists telling women they are sick; it suggests a process aimed at adjusting women to conventional and restrictive roles; it suggests drug treatment to passify us, shock treatment to frighten and silence us. What we did was very different. We started to do therapy in small groups, without leaders, using our feminist understanding to help us develop in ways which we value, to increase our strength, creativity and confidence – in ourselves and in other women. As one member of Red Therapy put it, 'I'm not sick. Deep down I'm a healthy person trying to find my power – the power I need to live my life to the full and to confront this sick society.' We hoped that by making the unconscious conscious we would reveal the ways in which we had absorbed and internalised the prevailing ideology. We could then uncover, root out and deal with those recalcitrant feelings to gain control of our emotional lives and direct them more effectively. Our experience showed us that real change would come from *combining* our political activity in the world with the ideas and experience coming from discussion and consciousness-raising groups *and* with the feelings and emotional energy we can tap through therapy.

It has taken a long time for people to accept that we need and can have a therapy which we control ourselves. Critics within the women's liberation movement point to the growth movement's emphasis on self-absorbed individualism and the adjustment role played by conventional therapy. Many women fear that therapy, with its focus on the inner world, could immobilise us from taking action in the material world. Yet misery and so-called mental illness already immobilise one in nine women in Western countries within a mental hospital for some part of her life. Therapy which can preserve our sanity in a crazy world is actually helping us to remain active, enabling us to keep and extend the control we have over our lives. We do not see therapy as a substitute for political organising. We do think there is a level at which therapy can be an integral part of the process of revolutionary change. Therapy can help us to reach beneath our conditioning to contact the power locked in ourselves and the deep love which energises us to act in our own and common interests. The revolution we want seeks a change not just in the ownership of production but in the reclamation of our sexuality, our feelings, our relationships, our working and living conditions, our creativity.

It is clear that therapy can help not only women but men too. Men are often brought up to be dominating and emotionally suppressed. The implication of our comments about the socialisation of women is that men will have to become their own women. As part of changing the sexual division of labour men must learn to give each other some of the caring, loving emotional and practical support which traditionally they have expected from women. They may then be able to be more nurturing to women and to children and to play new roles in their work and political activity which are compatible with our goal of a more caring and equal society. While we do not advocate separatism, we do see the formation of men's groups as important and hope that men will read this book. Much of what we say is directly relevant to mixed and men's therapy groups.

Different issues come up in therapy for women and for men, and these vary too according to class and race. Areas of tension may arise from taboos on the expression of certain feelings, the position of women in the family, attitudes to the body and sexuality, which are specific to particular cultures. People from racial groups which have suffered persecution may have particular fears, and also feelings of guilt if they escape that persecution. We see the policy of mental hospitals in which working-class people are often selected out as 'unsuitable' for therapy and more suitable for shock or drug treatment as an expression of class prejudice and oppression. From our own experience in our self-help group, in a community counselling service and in 'compulsive eating' workshops, we have found that therapy can be helpful and relevant to people from all classes and racial backgrounds. However, our group was predominantly middle class and all white. We recognise that what we write is limited by our own class and racial experience and we hope that women with different experience will want to use this book as a starting point from which to develop their own approaches. We see this as an important direction for therapy to develop in if it is to become a tool available to everyone, instead of remaining in the hands of a professional and class élite.

Who We Are

People come to therapy from different backgrounds and with different needs. We came to therapy from activity in non-aligned socialist politics, influenced by the anti-authoritarian traditions of the student and women's movements of the sixties. We are socialists and feminists, and these factors are interwoven throughout our activity and in what we write. In 1973 we were involved in starting a mixed leaderless therapy group called Red Therapy. Those who started the group had come to feel the need for some kind of therapy either because we were personally desperate and needed help or because we more consciously felt the need for changes in ourselves that went along with wider changes we wanted to see in society. Many of us had been politically active at work. Through the women's liberation movement we were also involved in running a food co-op, a playgroup, squatting and housing actions and organising in the abortion campaign. Many of us were living in collective households.

People starting to do therapy now will find a more accepting climate than we faced. We encountered fierce criticism both from within the women's movement and from others active in left politics. Some warned us we were doing something dangerous to engage in therapy without professional training. This hostility was discouraging in our struggle to start a leaderless group with little therapy experience. So we taught each other and learned from books and by going to occasional led groups. After the mixed group had been running for two years we decided to split into a women's group and a men's group. This was because it felt safer and easier to be in a single-sex group and because women and men seemed to have different issues to deal with.

We were asked by The Women's Press to write this book in 1977. By that time our group had started to diversify. The attitude to therapy within the women's liberation movement had begun to change and we already saw part of the function of our Red Therapy group as being to help others start leaderless groups. In 1979 the women's group ceased to function as a therapy group for ourselves. We no longer needed the same level of support to do group therapy and many group members have moved on, together or separately, to specialise in different areas. Lucy now does massage, dance and dream workshops, teaches self-help skills and has become interested in spirituality. Sheila now gives individual and group psychodynamic therapy at the Women's Therapy Centre in London and is involved in setting up self-help groups for 'compulsive eaters'. Although the book reflects the new directions we have moved into, its main basis is the six years of rich collective experience in the Red Therapy group and its offshoots.

We have found it enormously difficult to write a book while working to support ourselves financially and looking after our children. Seeing the growing numbers of women interested in self-help therapy and recognising the real need for this book has kept us going through the difficulties of completing it.

How To Use This Book
This is not a book to read at one sitting. It is a manual to be *used*. For a basic understanding of what the therapy process is like we suggest you read 'A Way In'. If you are interested in the political issues read 'The Inner and the Outer'. If you are starting a self-help group you will need to read 'A Way In' and 'Starting a Self-Help Group'. If you are in a group and are interested in exploring its dynamics read 'Encountering Each Other'. After some months the issues raised in 'Keeping a Group Going' will become relevant. General issues concerning how we choose techniques, how to approach professional therapy, how we change and relate therapy to everyday life are in 'Getting

What You Need from Therapy'. In Chapters Three to Eight we examine different approaches to therapy and you may find it helpful to work through these gradually, using the exercises to become familiar with the different techniques. We have arranged them in an order which we think makes sense to follow in sequence. If there are particular topics that you need to work on, the Index of Exercises at the end of the book will help you to find relevant exercises. Throughout the book the exercises are numbered and headed in bold type, and references to them also appear in bold type for easy reference. We have credited the source of some of these exercises; some we have invented ourselves; many have become part of the everyday vocabulary of therapy and we do not know their origin.

In our experience it is not easy to take exercises from books, whether you are doing therapy alone, with one other person, or in a group. In a group situation an exercise often works best if one woman stands out to read it aloud and help the others follow the instructions. She will need to inject her own confidence into the exercise to help others participate in it fully and overcome their fears of looking silly. She will need to read it slowly and remain sensitive to what the others are experiencing. In the structure of a session it does not work simply to pick three exercises and do them consecutively without thinking how each may affect people. Nor is it helpful to follow a programme of exercises relentlessly when it becomes clear that other issues are more immediate. Stay open to what comes up in the group. Usually exercises are good for starting a session or for inserting at appropriate points, but you need to allow some flexible time during a session. Leading the exercises should be shared equally between group members.

When doing the exercises alone, or with one other person, take time to read the instructions through slowly and absorb them. Don't waste precious energy worrying about 'forgetting' the instructions as you can refer back to the book without breaking the flow. It is also possible, especially with the longer meditative exercises, to use a tape to record the instructions before actually doing the exercise. As with all the reading aloud, this should be done very slowly, with long pauses and care for the words.

Throughout this book there are many examples of therapy in action. We knew it was vital to assess and draw from the various theories of therapy but the strength of this book lies in its sharing of the practical experience of many women in the therapy situation. We do use fictitious names and details but each example is closely based on a real person and a real situation. Even with these examples, however, we feel that it is difficult to convey the highs and lows, the excitement and closeness, the rich and complex texture of therapy. We hope that you will discover these for yourselves.

NOTES

1   Phyllis Chesler, *Women and Madness*, Avon, New York, 1973.

Chapter One
A Way In

What is self-help therapy like?
How is therapy different from consciousness-raising?
What are the basic 'ground rules' of a therapy approach?
There are so many different kinds of therapy, how can I make a start?

In this chapter we will try to answer these questions. We offer a way in to understand and use the therapy process by listing the most basic assumptions which underlie almost all the different therapy approaches and which make a therapy group so different from a consciousness-raising group. Sharing some basic understandings may make the process of starting therapy less scary, whether you are doing this in a group, with one other person or alone. If you are starting to see a professional therapist, some knowledge of the ground rules may help to demystify the techniques your therapist uses. So we give here as 'Thirteen Do's and Don'ts' a distillation of the rules we have found useful to work by.

When we started our group we did not have any ground rules. We looked desperately to one another trying to grasp what was allowed and what wasn't, what worked and what didn't, in this new therapy situation. This gave power to those group members who had more confidence and experience, and they played a larger part in running the group. If assumptions are out in the open, then all group members have equal access to them and may have equal confidence to play an active part in the group. So if you are beginning self-help therapy it is worth getting familiar with these rules through the exercises we suggest. You may disagree with them or change them for yourselves, but at least you will have a concrete basis for discussion and will not repeat our mistakes.

Most therapy approaches emphasise the need to contact our emotions and, especially at first, you may find that much of your therapy work is about learning to do this. It is not easy to move from discussing to expressing feelings, from exploring the rational to exploring the irrational, from consciousness-raising to unconsciousness-raising. Many of us find it hard enough to talk about ourselves, let alone to go a stage further into showing our anger, joy or sadness in front of others. We need not only courage and honesty but some specific techniques, so you will find that many of the ground rules below are focused on facilitating this transition from *talking* to *feeling*.

Here are the thirteen basic 'Do's and Don'ts' for starting therapy.

KEEP THE CIRCLE

In a therapy session it is common to use a room free of furniture where people can sit on the floor in a circle with their shoes off. Furniture gets in the way of therapy: chairs at different heights cut people off from one another and make them feel unequal, table-edges and ornaments get in the way when you want to move freely. The circle helps each person in the group to make eye contact with the others and to participate in what goes on; this is especially important in a leaderless situation where you are trying to share responsibility for running the group. If one woman is talking or exploring her feelings during a therapy session, the attention of the whole circle serves to give her support and encouragement. Breaking the circle may distract or undermine her. So it is important during the session for the circle to remain a cohesive unit: don't withdraw for a chat, wander out for a cigarette or to make a cup of coffee. Any boredom, irritation or distress is better expressed *in* the circle, even if it seems negative:

'I'm sorry to interrupt, but you've been going on for a long time and I wonder if we could stop briefly'
'I'm getting bored and I'm dying for a cigarette'
'What you're doing is upsetting me a lot, I'd like someone to come and sit with me and talk in the next room'
'I'm getting annoyed, I'd like to answer back to what you're saying'

The group's commitment to give her attention is crucial in making a woman feel safe enough to express her feelings. One way of making sure that everyone in the circle is able to give her full attention is to arrange for each person to have some short time for herself during the session, even when it is not her turn to work at length on a problem, so that she has a chance to speak and express things that are on her mind. This is particularly useful at the beginning and end of each session.

If you are doing therapy with one other person you will probably sit facing each other on the floor, but the same principle will apply: when your partner is exploring a problem, do not distract her by answering the telephone or getting yourself a cigarette.

Here are some exercises for using the circle which encourage equal involvement by everyone present at the session. They are useful whether you are two or twelve people.

1 Opening Circle

At the start of the session, take it in turns to say briefly how you are feeling. Go round the circle in order (so it is not always the most confident who speak first) and try to arrange for each person to speak for an equal amount of time.

2 Planning Circle

If you are unsure about what to do in the session, go through the same process as above, except this time each person says in turn what she would like to do that evening and how she would like the time to be structured . . .

'I'd like to do some massage'
'Something noisy and energetic all together as a group'
'I want to learn some Gestalt techniques'
'I had an argument at work and I've been upset all day, I'd like some help over this'

3 Unfinished Business

At the end of the session, take turns again round the circle giving each woman space to say what she got from the session and how she is feeling now. This will give her a chance to express and share any good feelings or resentments which the session has brought up. It is important that people do not take regrets or grudges home with them to mull over until the next session:

'I felt very irritated with Ann and I wish I'd told her'
'I wanted to hug you but I didn't dare. I went away wondering if I should have taken the risk or not'
'I thought the group didn't know what it was doing with the bioenergetics techniques, but I didn't say anything and no one else did and I don't feel like going back'
'I was hurt by her criticisms but I didn't mention it'
'I kept thinking of things I wanted to say to Jenny but there wasn't time'

These unspoken feelings or 'unfinished business' can be a barrier between people in the group. If we bring them out into the open, however briefly, we clear the air. This often makes it easier to end the session supportively and to feel positive about coming to the next session.

GIVE ATTENTION TO ONE PERSON AT A TIME

In a group *discussion* it is usually taken as a good sign if everyone takes part, sharing their experience and opinions equally with others. In a self-help *therapy* group, it is usually better, especially at first, to concentrate attention on one person at a time. Often it will emerge that there is one person who is clearly upset or angry or has something on her mind which seems most urgent for the group to deal with. In a consciousness-raising group, things might go something like this:

Ann: I am feeling really angry at the woman I work for.

Betty: In some ways having a woman boss is hard, isn't it, because women in authority feel they have to act like men?

Claire: I got on badly with the boss at my last job, but I found it very helpful to talk to her about it.

Ann: She keeps implying that I am no good at my job.

Claire: Have you tried going to her and explaining . . .?

In a self-help therapy situation, it is better not to discuss or generalise a woman's experience in this way, but to concentrate initially on the woman's own *feelings*. So, instead of other group members talking about themselves as in the discussion above, the process might go more like this:

Ann: I am feeling really angry at the woman I work for.

Betty: Tell us more about that.

Ann: Well, she keeps putting me down in little ways. Today she . . . and she . . .

Claire: How does that make you feel?

Ann: She makes me feel that I'm no good and that . . .

Betty: What would you like to say to her if you could really speak your mind?

In this example, the other group members are pushing Ann to share more and bring more to the surface of what she is feeling. Her experience can be generalised and the other women will be able to support her by showing that they have had similar experiences later in the session, after Ann has had time and space to explore her specific anger at her boss more fully through the kind of techniques we describe in this book.

You need to be clear about who is receiving the group's attention in this way. This is her time and, though she will be helped by listening to other people's suggestions and feedback, she is in charge. Others in the room may cry, hold someone else's hand, interrupt to say they are distressed; but they should try not to distract the attention of the group away from a woman who is exploring a problem until she herself feels she has finished.

When one woman receives the support of the group in this way, it is often referred to as 'working': 'Sarah "worked" in the group tonight', 'I'd like to "work" on my relationship with my father'. It is also sometimes referred to as 'taking the hot seat'. In this book we try to avoid these expressions. We try to explain more specifically that a woman is 'exploring feelings', 'expressing her hurt', 'releasing anger', 'dealing with a problem', or whatever is actually happening in a particular situation. But often these expressions seem inadequate and sometimes we settle for the brief and convenient way of describing a therapy experience as 'working'.

Here is an exercise which provides practice in the underrated skill of giving attention:

4 Learning to Listen

This exercise is done in pairs.

Sit facing each other, preferably on the floor. Keep eye contact with each other and hold hands if you want to. You have five minutes each. Decide who will take first turn. She has five minutes to talk about what has happened to her in the last twenty-four hours, sharing as much as possible of her feelings in every situation. The other person does not say a word but keeps eye contact and concentrates on giving *total and clear attention* to her, not rehearsing replies or mentally making comparisons with her own life, but focusing completely on being receptive to the woman who is speaking. At the end of five minutes, swap roles without making any comments. Giving attention to another is a crucial skill in self-help therapy. It sound easy, but in fact focusing clearly on another person is very difficult. Be aware how often you feel the urge to jump in with advice or 'Yes, I feel that too . . .' and notice how hard it is to restrain yourself.

At the end of the exercise share, first with your partner and then with the whole group, what you each felt during the exercise, both when you were speaking and when you were listening.

This exercise, like many others suggested in this book, derives from Co-counselling (see pp 50–55).

DON'T TRY TO MAKE EVERYTHING BETTER

When someone has a problem or a difficult feeling, our immediate reaction is often to want to make it better:

Denise: I'm not feeling very cheerful today. My hair needs washing and I'm feeling ugly and unattractive.

Linda: I was just thinking how healthy and well you look.
(or)
Jenny: I've been trying to stay on top of it, but I've been feeling miserable about my miscarriage. Two in a row is too much.
Sarah: You should be glad that at least you can conceive. You are lucky, because some women cannot get pregnant at all!

In this last example, Sarah jumps in to smooth away the unhappiness, perhaps wanting to make Jenny feel more cheerful but also wanting to stop herself feeling uncomfortable about Jenny's bad feeling. Perhaps she feels guilty because she has a child of her own already. Our impulse to hug a crying woman is often to stop ourselves getting upset. In a therapy situation, the assumption is that a distressing feeling does not always just 'go away' with a bit of consolation or reassurance from a friend. It may fade for a while but it is always likely to come up again. The only way it can be resolved is by exploring and expressing it more fully. So when Jenny says she is miserable, the other group members might respond: 'Can you talk more about what hurts most?', 'Where in your body do you feel the sadness?' and ask other questions which will push Jenny to experience the feeling even more deeply. When she has traced it, expressed it (perhaps by crying deeply) and discovered some resources of her own for dealing with it, *then* will be the time for others to give her feedback or reassurance about her miscarriage. One of the understandings of therapy is that discharging emotions can be a healing process. If a hurt or pain is not discharged, it is stored, and a lot of energy is wasted in keeping it buried. This reduces the energy and clear-sightedness which a person has available to respond to new situations. Part of why Jenny is feeling bad is because she is holding her sadness in; her fear of expressing it is probably as uncomfortable as the sadness itself and after crying she may feel a sense of relief. She may even feel stronger to realise her pain is not as overwhelming as she feared. It is not 'kind' of Sarah to deny her the expression of those feelings by telling her she should feel lucky. Ironically, the most supportive response is often to recognise another woman's unhappiness and allow her to release it, rather than trying to plaster over the cracks. Here is how one woman describes this experience:

I was very unhappy in the year before I started therapy and I used to be even more desperate when people would say, 'Look how much you're doing; look how many people you know.' What I wanted was someone to say 'Yes, you *are* unhappy.' And paradoxically that's more supportive than being cheered up . . . because that's a validation of you as you, of you as a specific individual – and not the projection of the other person's desire to be surrounded by cheery people . . . To be of use to someone by letting them talk, by not denying their experience.[1]

Our most validated role as women in this society is to care for the emotions of other people, often while feeling that we have little or no right to our own separate emotions. Therapy is a good situation to change this pattern, to be 'allowed' our feelings and the space to explore them instead of having them dismissed or comforted away.

5 Exercise in Not Consoling

Get into pairs. Sit facing each other, keep eye contact and hold hands if you want. You have ten minutes each. In your ten minutes, tell your partner all the situations in the last week when you felt bad (upset, anxious, uncomfortable, frightened, angry or bored). Your partner should encourage you and make responses which help you to get into the difficult feelings more fully. For example, 'How did you feel?', 'What did you want to say to them?' and so on. The idea is that if you push a bad feeling to fuller expression, it often clears away. If you try to deny it, it can persist. Therapy is not all about 'bad' feelings, but it is important to learn to allow their expression so that they can clear and 'good' feelings come to the surface and also be expressed.

When you are in the listening role, be aware how often you need to stop a reaction which would 'make it all better', like hugging your partner or telling her 'I'm sure they didn't mean it' or making other consoling remarks. Be aware, too, how uncomfortable her difficult feelings make you. Often we want to give consolation, not for the other's good but for our own peace of mind. After ten minutes, exchange roles without any discussion in between and repeat.

At the end, give each other feedback about how it went (did she really seem to be accepting your feelings?). Then share your experience with the rest of the group, each woman speaking for a couple of minutes in turn.

A variation of this exercise is to use the time to talk about one particular distressing event in your life (for example, a loss, separation, attack or violation).

DON'T JUDGE

We have given an example of a woman coming to a group and saying she didn't feel attractive. In some feminist groups a remark like that might be met with 'But appearances don't matter', or 'You shouldn't think of yourself as a sex object', 'You shouldn't care so much about things like that', or even a hostile silence.

Different groups have different feelings which are taboo. In most conventional groups in our society it is not acceptable for women to be assertive, pushy, unmotherly, or to have any kind of 'nasty' feelings. Trying to change ourselves through the women's liberation movement, we still have some of the old taboos on certain feelings and have sometimes created new ones for ourselves:

'You shouldn't be angry with another woman, it's not sisterly'
'You shouldn't be dependent like that'
'I shouldn't feel jealous, it's bourgeois'

One of the understandings of therapy is that you cannot banish feelings by condemning them as 'nasty' or 'incorrect', any more than you can banish them by reassurance. Difficult or irrational feelings don't go away by being censored, denied or avoided; they go away by being recognised and worked through. What we feel is largely determined by our upbringing, conditioning and our position as women in society which make it, for example, very hard for *any* woman to be unaware of her appearance. We will stop being affected by such feelings only through exploring them, tracing their origin, and getting them out of our system through expressing them, then the work of slowly building new structures and ways of relating can be done on a solid basis of *feeling*, not of guilt and 'shoulds'.

In this, the approach of a feminist therapy group is different from that of traditional Psychoanalysis or of the newer growth movement. For example, in a growth movement group, a woman would be encouraged to express her anxiety about being attractive, but she would also be expected to *be* or to want to be attractive: that aspect of women's role in society would probably not be questioned or challenged. In a feminist self-help group, on the other hand, we would accept that women in our society are likely to have such feelings of anxiety about appearance and would not judge or condemn a woman for having such feelings; but we would also be committed to developing other ideas about what being a woman can mean, ways of finding our identity and a sense of our own value other than through our physical appearance. We recognise the contradictions in our experience as feminists and want to work towards building new, non-sexist ways of relating.

6 Exercise in Not Judging

Sit in pairs facing each other with eye contact. Five minutes each way. In your five minutes you speak to your (silent) partner in sentences which always begin: 'If I didn't think you'd judge me I'd tell you . . .'

The sentence should end differently each time, for example: 'If I didn't think you'd judge me I'd tell you that I'm frightened of going to the demonstration on Saturday', 'If I didn't think you'd judge me I'd tell you that I feel really stupid doing this exercise', 'If I didn't think you'd judge me I'd tell you that I can be quite nasty sometimes'.

If you get stuck thinking about things you are ashamed to tell, let yourself tell little things (which are often just as significant). This is not an honesty game to force yourself to expose huge and 'shameful' secrets to your partner, but an exercise to explore for yourself how many of your feelings are normally judged 'wrong' by various standards. After five minutes, swap roles. At the end give each other feedback (which was the hardest thing to say? was your partner's reaction what you expected?) and then share with the group.

ACCEPT RESPONSIBILITY FOR YOUR OWN FEELINGS

In a therapy group people are encouraged to recognise and to take responsibility for their own feelings. In our daily lives we have many different ways of avoiding this. One way is to *blame* our feelings onto other people: 'I had forgotten all about that unhappy love affair until you reminded me about it and brought it all back', 'I was cheerful until I talked to you and now you have really depressed me'.

If merely having contact with a person makes you feel depressed, it is almost certainly because you were depressed already. Maybe the emotion was unconscious, maybe you would prefer not to be made aware of it, but the feeling was there and what the other person has done is to put you in touch with it. So 'You've depressed me' might be more honestly expressed as 'I was depressed but keeping it down really well and now you've brought it out'.

Another way we often avoid taking responsibility for our own feelings is by projecting onto other people qualities or emotions which are in fact our own:

'You're very competitive'
'You don't seem to like me'
'You don't help the group work'
'You're acting self-indulgently'

In a therapy group, when you make remarks like these, people usually encourage you to 'own' what you are actually feeling yourself and make some statement about yourself rather than about the other person. For example, if Ann says to Betty 'You're very competitive', what she should really be saying may be '*I* feel competitive with *you*'. The woman who says 'You don't like me' often really means '*I* don't like *you*'. A remark like 'You don't help the group work' might be more honestly expressed as '*I* am jealous of the way you dominate the group'. 'You act self-indulgently' might be translated as 'I wish you and the rest of the group gave *me* more attention'.

This kind of projection is very common and these remarks change a lot when the woman speaking takes responsibility for what she feels instead of attributing it to other people. These are all negative examples, because it is usually our negative feelings which we disguise and distance in this way.

Because of our conditioning to be 'nice', women find it especially difficult to express negative feelings directly and instead we often prefer to put ourselves down ('I'm not good enough for you' is easier to say than 'I hate you for acting so superior'). But the same process happens with positive feelings too. For example, 'You are a really warm person' might, if it was owned, become 'I really like you and care about you' which is harder to say precisely because it connects the speaker with her own feelings and makes her take responsibility for them.

Another form of projection is of feelings from the past, or when emotions you have about one person are transferred onto another. For example, if Betty gets very angry at Claire in the session it might often turn out that some anger at her mother is mixed in – or even that most of the anger is at her mother and Claire is just a trigger and a useful target. This doesn't invalidate her anger at Claire – maybe Claire *is* behaving a bit like Betty's mother – but it is useful to be clear where the anger is coming from and how much of it is projection. When very strong feelings are triggered by something disproportionately small, it is very likely that projection is involved: either feelings from the past are being applied to the present (Betty's childhood rage exploding at Claire) or feelings about another person are being applied to a person in the group (Jean's frustration with her workmate explodes at Hannah who is behaving a bit like the workmate). We tend to displace feelings in this way onto almost everyone we meet or know, not just onto the members of our therapy group. A good way to check whether you are doing it is to ask yourself 'Who does this person remind me of?' You may even find that they remind you of characteristics you strongly dislike or like in yourself, or characteristics you passionately desire to have for yourself.

Because projection is so common, it is good to think carefully in a newly-formed therapy group before you leap in to 'attack' a person who is annoying you. Rather than saying 'Claire, you're a pain in the arse', Betty would do better to accept responsibility for her feelings: 'Claire, I am feeling irritated with you'. She might even add: 'I think there's something else involved in it for me'. Accusing or attacking another group member often leads to heated confrontations. These can be positive in their effect, but it is good to be familiar with therapy techniques in order to avoid merely hurting one another or getting into a deadlock. Later in this book we describe how the careful use of Encounter can be helpful for this.

Another way in which we use language to disguise our emotions from ourselves and from other people is by putting a remark as a question instead of a statement. For example, 'Do you think we're all too upset to go on with this?' really means '*I* feel too upset to go on with this'.

Many questions do not seek information, but are just an indirect way of getting others to see or do things our way: 'Do you think we need the window open?' usually equals '*I* want the window open'.

We can also avoid owning our feelings by using 'it' or 'one' or 'you' instead of 'I'. A person who says in the group 'The room feels tense' usually means '*I* feel tense', or 'One is usually irritable after a day's work' usually means '*I* feel irritable after my day's work'.

These examples may seem petty but in practice they are very useful to stop us avoiding feelings. We need to recognise our feelings as our own before we can go more deeply into exploring and expressing them.

It may sometimes feel that by owning our projections we are taking everything on ourselves, blaming ourselves for things and putting ourselves in a bad light. Betty probably feels more comfortable thinking that Claire is a pain in the arse than realising that she herself has a vat of anger boiling inside her, waiting for a chance to erupt. But, in fact, owning our own feelings helps us to own our own power. Instead of experiencing ourselves as passive victims being badly treated by other people, we recognise that we have a powerhouse of emotional energy inside us. There are strong *positive* feelings locked in with the negative ones and we can use this energy to act in the world. Recognising our projections does not invalidate our feelings or our power to act; it merely clears away debris from the past and from other situations, so that we can act clearly and appropriately in any present situation.

7 Exercise in Owning Your Feelings

This exercise can be done in pairs like those described earlier but if you are a group and are feeling confident enough to do it all together, you can also do it as a whole group. The point is to make a series of statements about how you feel at present in the group. Each statement starts 'I am feeling . . .' and ends '. . . and I own that feeling'. For example:

'I am feeling tired and lonely and I own that feeling'
'I am feeling very high and I own that feeling'
'I am feeling annoyed at Carole for being late and I own that feeling'

You may find that the statements you want to make are trivial, like 'I am feeling cold' or 'I am feeling itches in my feet' but they are, nevertheless, worth saying. The point of the exercise is to ground you in what you are experiencing in the present and to help you recognise yourself as an active agent who initiates her own perceptions. It is not what you say as much as how you say it: let yourself really *feel* that 'owning'. If you are in pairs you can take three minutes each to make these statements. If you are in a group it might be better to have each person take turns to make four of these statements. Give each other feedback afterwards if there is anything to discuss.

LISTEN TO THE BODY

Our society has consistently taught us to value our minds above our bodies. Expressions like: 'The spirit is willing but the flesh is weak', '*Be sensible!*', 'He behaved like an animal', 'You're hopelessly unreasonable', teach us to mistrust the processes of the body and to think that they need to be controlled by the superior processes of the brain and 'reason'. In all our dealings with the world, in relating to authority and in most meetings and groups (often in women's groups too) we are encouraged to behave 'reasonably' and to control our bodies tightly.

In a therapy situation we need to unlearn some of this teaching. We need to pay more attention and respect to the messages we get from the body about what is going on inside us. Breathing is a very important part of this because we often breathe very shallowly as an unconcious way of cutting off from what we are feeling. It is a good idea to start a therapy session with some breathing exercises, to relax the muscles and put us in touch with our bodies. Also, when one individual is the centre of attention, dealing with a particular problem or feeling, it is important to make sure that she continues to breathe fully and evenly throughout. Huge gasping breaths are not good, but in the early stages of a self-help group it is more likely to be light, imperceptible breathing which you have to guard against:

Alex: I'd like to talk about my friend Sally. Every time I ring her up she says she hasn't got time to see me.

Brenda: How does that make you feel?

Alex: Oh, I don't know. I suppose it doesn't really matter.
(pause)

Carol: I notice that you have almost stopped breathing. Let yourself breathe a few times into your stomach.

Alex: (*Takes several full breaths*)

Carol: What are you feeling?

Alex: I just feel really sad. I want to see her and she doesn't want to see me. I'm very unhappy about it. I want to cry.

In cases like this, full breathing is a useful way of contacting feelings which are being repressed. Another helpful approach is to pay attention to the body as a whole:

Ann: I feel stuck. I'd like to work some more on the argument I had today with my child. I've told you what happened but I don't know how to go on. I don't know how to start.

Barbara: What's happening in your body?

Ann: Well, my stomach feels tight. My head is throbbing a bit. My hands are shaking . . .

Barbara: Let them shake some more. What do they seem to be saying to you?

Ann: I think they're scared . . . I'm scared . . .

Barbara: What are you scared of?

Ann: I'm really scared of hitting him, hurting him . . .

As this example shows, when one woman is 'working', the others can often notice from the way she is holding her body clues as to what she is feeling:

'You are sitting very hunched up. Try stretching out and see if that makes it easier to express yourself'
'Are you aware that your right fist is clenched? What does it want to do?'
'The way you are sticking your chest out looks to me quite defiant. Does that link with anything you are feeling?'

Notice that none of these are 'directions'. Group members are simply asking questions or pointing out something they see in the woman's body, and she may accept or reject their interventions. Body language is very complex and we will discuss it more fully in Chapters Three and Five. At this stage all that is important is to begin to notice the body movements, and especially the breathing, of a person who is trying to express her feelings.

Because body awareness is so important to establish early on, we give here four exercises for you to try. As with all exercises, it is important to have your shoes off and clothing loose.

8 Awareness through Breathing

This is good to do at the start of a session. Lie on the floor, if possible in a circle with your heads at the centre, and have one person read aloud slowly to the others:

Become aware of your breathing . . . As you breathe out each time, imagine you are breathing out the tension in your body . . . Let it relax . . . Become aware of the parts of your body which are touching the floor . . . Let yourself feel the weight of your body on the floor . . . Breathe out the tension with each 'out' breath. Let more of your body relax and touch the ground . . . Now with each 'out' breath, make a noise like a sigh, relaxing and breathing out the tension . . . (*pause*)

Now place one hand on your belly just below your belly button. When you breathe in, breathe into your stomach so that your hand rises on the 'in' breath and falls again on the 'out' breath. Breathe out slowly, with a sigh, let

21

all the breath go right out of your lungs each time . . . Let yourself breathe for a while like this . . . Make sure your stomach lifts your hand each time on the breath in . . . (*pause*)

Now let yourself become aware of where the tension is in your body. Start with your feet. Feel the tension in your feet. As you breathe in, exaggerate the tension, let your feet tense right up; then when you breathe out, relax your feet and imagine you are breathing out all the tension in your feet. Do this a few times. Breathe in to your feet, exaggerating the tension, letting them tighten right up, then out . . . Let the tension pour right out on the 'out' breath . . .

Now your legs. Let yourself feel the tension in your legs, in your calves, knees, thighs . . . Imagine you are breathing in to those tense places, breathe in, exaggerating the tension, tensing them up . . . then when you breathe out, release the tension, let it go out with the breath, from your calves, knees, thighs . . . Do this a few times . . . (*pause*)

Now your groin. Feel the tension in your groin . . . As you breathe in, imagine you are breathing in to it, exaggerate the tension, and then out . . . release it . . . breathe it all out. Do this several more times . . . (*pause*)

Continue reading, repeating this pattern: for 'groin' now substitute 'belly', then chest, shoulders, arms, neck, head and face. Finish with relaxing the whole body together, as at the start.

It is important to read these instructions *slowly*, so that group members can really let themselves get in touch with the different parts of the body. By the end of the exercise the group should be fairly relaxed and more aware of the kind of body messages which in a therapy group we need to notice rather than ignore. At the end of the exercise, share with one another the things you noticed in your body – 'I noticed my neck is really stiff' etc.

Other breathing exercises are given elsewhere in this book.

9 Conversation without Words
Choose a partner, sit facing each other, take three minutes to have a conversation without words. You can use signs, noises, expressions, anything you like except words.

This exercise helps you to recognise your body as a wonderful vehicle of communication and to make enjoyable contact with another group member.

10 Being Moved
As we become more aware of our bodies we may begin to love and nourish them more. Here is an exercise which involves surrender to a pleasurable sensual experience.

Choose a partner and make sure your clothing is loose. One lies on the ground and breathes fully to relax her body. The other sits beside her, relaxes, and then slowly makes contact with the other's body. She then takes fifteen minutes to lift and move about her partner's arms, legs and head, working round her body and remembering to give attention to all the joints: toes, ankle, fingers, elbow, knee, hip, shoulder, neck, jaw. Experiment with your partner's body; do not force it, but see how it will move and how it won't move, where the joints will rotate, where they block. If you are the person lying, let yourself stay relaxed and be aware of how being moved by another feels different from when you move your limbs yourself. Let yourself surrender to the pleasure of the sensation.

After fifteen minutes, exchange roles. When you have both had a turn, exchange feedback about how it felt, which parts of the body were more relaxed and so on.

11   Running Commentary on Your Body

This is a body awareness exercise which can be done in pairs. Sit facing one another. Keep eye contact or, if you find this distracting, shut your eyes and hold hands so that you and your partner are in touch. You have five minutes each. Let yourself get into a regular relaxed breathing pattern, then become aware of, and tell your partner, everything that is happening in your body, however petty. The idea is to communicate all the little sensations which normally you would probably ignore or dismiss, for example, 'My shoulders feel quite tense, like they've been carrying a lot . . . I've got a spot on my forehead, it's itching . . . I can't think of anything else to say, I feel a bit silly . . . Oh, my feet are cold, my stomach is just gurgling, it feels a bit shaky . . . I can feel something like a tight band round my forehead . . .'

After five minutes, swap over. When you have both had a turn, give each other feedback on the exercise: what did you find hardest? Did your partner notice anything about the way you held your body which you missed?

STAY IN THE 'HERE-AND-NOW'

It is very easy to avoid being aware of the body by allowing the mind to wander off into discussion and digressions. There is a place for discussion in a therapy session (usually at the start and again at the end) but during the time when a person is concentrating on exploring feelings, discussion is usually very unhelpful. Long descriptions or anecdotes can also distract her. The other members of the group need to watch out for this and bring her attention back to her feelings in the 'here-and-now'.

Adrien: I'd like to do some work on my relationship with my husband. He complains that I don't give him enough attention, that I don't do enough for him.

Sue: How do you mean?

Adrien: Well, he hates it when I go out. Since he lost his job he's been depressed. He keeps things to himself a lot, he moons around the house . . . He . . . He . . . and he . . .

Sue: I think you're talking too much about *him*. Can you come back to *yourself?* How does all that make you feel? How are you feeling right now?

Adrien: Well, I feel upset and a bit guilty, I think, because I can't seem to do anything right for him. Like last night he came back from his mate's house and said 'Well, at least I can have a good time with Mick' and I said 'You mean you can't with me?' and he said 'Well, you're always too busy' so I said . . . and he said . . . and I said . . .

Carole: Can you come back to what you're feeling right now, sitting in this room with us? How do you feel about him?

Adrien: I feel really fed up with him telling me I don't do enough for him. I feel really fed up! FED UP!

In this example, the other group members brought Adrien back from two long chatty disgressions about her husband which were distracting her attention from herself and from the group. They might have done the same thing by reminding her to breathe deeply or asking her what sensations she was feeling in her body. These are all different ways of bringing the emphasis away from thinking onto feeling, away from generalisations onto the concrete fact of what emotions a person is feeling in the session.

Another way the mind takes us away from the here-and-now is to censor what is going on, moving away from certain emotions because they are not 'reasonable'.

Adrien: I feel FED UP! FED UP WITH IT! . . . But really there's no reason to get angry. It's not his fault he lost his job. He's always been good to me. I shouldn't get upset about it.

Diane: Don't worry about what you 'should' feel. You *are* feeling angry here, now, this minute, so let yourself express it for a bit. There'll be time later to work out the rights and wrongs of it all.

Adrien: I suppose so . . . It's true I do feel fed up. He makes me feel guilty the whole time. I've had enough of it. I've had ENOUGH! I feel really ANGRY!

Here is an exercise to practise focusing awareness on the here-and-now in the group.

12 Absent to Present

The idea of this exercise is that by deliberately moving your attention away from the here-and-now situation, and then coming back to it, you can become more aware and more fully present. One person in the group should read slowly, with frequent pauses:

Find a comfortable way of sitting or lying which allows you to relax. Shut your eyes. Be aware of your breathing: let it be full and regular . . . Now imagine the place where you would most wish to be in the world, your dearest fantasy, the ideal situation where you would like to be . . . (*pause*)
Imagine yourself there. Where are you? Are you outdoors or inside? Who are you with? What are you doing? What is going on around you? What is the temperature like? Be aware of sounds and smells . . . Let yourself feel what it is like, and enjoy it . . . (*pause*)
Now, slowly, start to bring yourself back from the fantasy. Be aware of what is hardest to let go . . . Gradually bring yourself back to this room . . . You are back. Be aware of what it is like, here and now: the temperature, the sounds, the smells . . . other people in the room . . . movements . . . (*pause*)
In what ways is this situation different from your fantasy? What do you like and dislike about being here? Is there anything making you uncomfortable? Anything that makes you feel happy, now, this minute, in this room? (*pause*)
Now slowly sit up if you are lying, open your eyes, and make eye contact with each person in the room . . .

After this exercise, share what you experienced.

It can be useful to do this exercise when the attention of the group is wandering, when people are feeling tired or distracted. It is based on a Gestalt therapy exercise used by Fritz Perls who believed that it is natural to move rhythmically between the two extremes of contact and withdrawal. By withdrawing deliberately in this way, and then returning to contact, he believed that we can pinpoint what is difficult or missing in the 'now' and also use the fantasy to replenish our strength for dealing with reality.

AVOID 'WHY?'

Another way we often use our heads to stop us from feeling our emotions is by getting involved in explaining things, giving reasons *why* we react in certain ways: 'I'm not really upset, it's only *because* . . .', 'I know *why* it's happening, I can see it isn't anything really'.

Sometimes we avoid expressing ourselves directly by asking rhetorical questions: 'Why did he leave me?' usually means 'I am really hurt that he left me . . .' Often when one person starts talking about a feeling she has, other

25

group members are tempted to ask her 'why' she feels that way. For example:

Ann: So when we got the eviction notice through the door, I just burst into tears.

Betty: Why did you want to cry?

Ann: Well, because I thought that it meant moving again and I didn't know whether we'd find anywhere else, and I thought that if we tried to fight it then . . .

Here the question 'why?' just pushes Ann into giving explanations and descriptions which come from her head, rather than letting herself experience what she felt emotionally about the eviction notice. If, instead of 'why?', she had been asked a question starting 'how?', she might have moved in a different direction:

Ann: So when we got the eviction notice through the door, I just burst into tears.

Betty: How did you feel?

Ann: I just felt hopeless and helpless and scared and miserable.

Betty: Let yourself feel that.

Ann: God, I just felt awful, I felt completely helpless.

Betty: You look as if you're nearly crying. Let yourself cry.

Ann: Oh, I felt so miserable . . . (*cries*)

As this example shows, questions starting with 'how' are usually good for helping emotions to surface. Ann has a chance to cry and release some of her pent-up feelings about the eviction, after which she will be calmer and stronger to discuss alternative housing and what she can actually do about her situation. Questions starting 'why?' are rarely helpful: they tend to steer the group not only towards rational explanations but sometimes into psychological interpretations of one another's feelings:

Ann: So when we got the eviction notice, I just burst into tears.

Betty: Why did you want to cry?

Ann: I don't know.

Claire: I think it's because you're an insecure person. You had to move house often when you were a child, didn't you?

Here the question 'why?' leads away from Ann's feelings and into some homespun psychoanalysis from one of the other group members. Though connections with the past often do come up in therapy, they are usually more helpful when they are *felt*, rather than coming from the head. For example, in this case, Ann might have been crying about the eviction and suddenly realised for herself that she had the same feelings as a child when she moved home. Because she made the connection emotionally, it would have more power than an intellectual realisation. It would also have more value because she made the connection for *herself*. Critics of self-help therapy often argue that it is dangerous for untrained people to play 'therapist'. One way of safeguarding against any possible danger is to make sure that the group allows the person who is 'working' to direct her own 'work', deciding how she wants to approach a problem and making connections for herself. This ensures that she is not a helpless object in therapy but learns through it what resources she has, how strong she is, how many of the answers she already knows herself. This helps her to respect herself more and realise her own power which she can then use in her daily dealings with people and the world.

In pointing out the dangers of using 'explanations' in a self-help therapy situation we are not dismissing out of hand discussions about psychological theory or about understanding why things happen in the group. Such discussions are valuable, but in our experience it works best to set aside a separate time for them.

TALK *TO* A PERSON RATHER THAN *ABOUT* HER

One very simple technique which helps us to connect with our feelings is to avoid talking in the third person, talking 'about' someone. In a therapy situation you will usually be encouraged to talk directly 'to' a person, whether they are present or not. We call this 'No gossiping', but it applies equally if we are talking about someone who is present in the room. Here's an example:

Jeannie: I feel uncomfortable in the group this evening. I feel uneasy being in the same room with Hannah. It's something to do with the way she and I behave towards each other.

Kate: Can you stop 'gossiping' about Hannah and say these things *to* her instead. *Tell* her how you feel.

Jeannie: Hannah, I feel uneasy being in the group with you. The way we behave together feels a bit unreal.

Lisa: Can you own that? Say 'I feel unreal' . . . Look at Hannah, make eye contact with her.

Jeannie: (*Looking at her*) Hannah, I feel unreal with you. We're polite to each other but I don't think we're honest. Or rather, I should say, *I'm* not honest . . .

In this example, the other women gently push Jeannie into owning and expressing her feeling more directly. To address by name, to speak and look

directly at another person in the group can be a powerful way of activating
and releasing feelings:

Kate: Jeannie, look at Hannah. What do you feel towards her?
Jeannie: I feel scared.
Kate: Tell her.
Jeannie: Hannah, I feel scared of you. I'm afraid you'll disapprove of me.
I'm scared of your strength.
Kate: Let yourself feel your fear . . .

This kind of exchange brings up a number of questions: How does Hannah
feel? Should she respond or would that interrupt Jeannie's flow? We will
discuss this more fully later, especially in Chapters Four and Nine.

What if the person with whom you have a problem is not in the group?
Often the feelings that come up in therapy sessions are to do with people who
are not in the room, or to do with people and situations in the past. The same
principle still applies. It is possible to avoid 'gossiping' or talking 'about'
these other people through the technique of talking to a cushion. At first this
may seem artificial and you may feel silly talking to a cushion as if it were a
person, but once you get over the initial embarrassment it is a very effective
method:

Mary: I am feeling really irritated by my friend Sarah. She keeps asking
me to do things for her.
Noreen: Talk *to* her. Here's a cushion, imagine it's Sarah. Look at her and
tell her what you feel.
Mary: (*To cushion*) Sarah, I feel irritated by you. You ask me to do things
for you the whole time as if you were helpless.
Noreen: How does that make you feel?
Mary: It makes me feel crowded and over-responsible.
Noreen: Tell *her* that.
Mary: Sarah, you make me feel crowded. I wish you'd stop hanging round
my skirts wanting me to look after you. I feel I've got to be
responsible for your life. Get off my back! Get off my back!

Addressing by name, looking and speaking directly, even if it's at a cushion,
helps Mary to connect with what she is feeling much more easily than if she
continued to talk 'about' her friend. Another advantage of this technique is
that it helps Mary to deal with the fear she probably feels about talking to the
real Sarah: this 'rehearsal' of what she might say opens up the possibility of
speaking directly to Sarah in real life. (We say more about techniques using

cushions, and give several simple exercises, in Chapter Five on Gestalt therapy.)

USE REPETITION

Another very simple technique for helping a person to connect directly with what she is feeling, rather than hedge around it, is to use repetition. Here's an example:

Deirdre: What did you want to say to the man who came round to evict you?
Ann: I felt I had to be polite. But really I wanted to tell him to go away.
Deirdre: Imagine he's on this cushion. Tell him to go away.
Ann: (*To the cushion*) Go away, you horrible man. I don't want you coming here throwing me out of my home. You haven't got any right to. You wouldn't like to be thrown out of your home. I don't want you here . . .
Eva: What is the *main* thing you want to tell him?
Ann: To go away.
Eva: Then just try repeating that one phrase a few times.
Ann: Go away, you horrible man.
Eva: Again.
Ann: Go away! Go away!
Eva: Again.
Ann: GO AWAY! GO AWAY! GO AWAY!

By repeating the same phrase instead of embroidering it with new points, Ann is helped to contact the basic feeling behind what she is saying, in this case, anger. Curiously enough, repetition is especially useful when the person working has said something painful and difficult which she would like to forget again as quickly as possible. For example:

Freida: Things haven't been going well between Jack and me recently. He's always late, distracted, somehow not there . . . I suppose my worst fear is that he loves her more than me now. He's treating me very strangely. He is depressed anyway, that might be half the trouble. But he spends so much time at her place . . .
Gwen: Can you just tell us again what your worst fear is?
Freida: Well . . . it's that . . . that he loves her more than me. I find it really hard to say it. It hurts my pride . . .
Gwen: Can you say it again?

Freida: He loves her more than me. He loves her more than me . . . Oh, no!
It hurts so much to say it.
Gwen: Again.
Freida: He loves her more than me . . . He loves her more than me . . .
(*cries*)

Here the other women in the group were experienced enough to pick out the one most important and emotionally loaded sentence out of a list of remarks Freida makes. By encouraging her to repeat that one sentence they help her to stay with a painful feeling until she can express it and release it.

The next and final three rules are slightly different. They are not so much about making the transition into therapy as providing conditions which will enable therapy to happen.

NO VIOLENCE

Sometimes a person talking to a cushion gets very angry and is encouraged to express that anger by hitting the cushion, or biting or twisting it, whatever helps her to let the feeling out. But when working on a relationship with someone in the room, it is important *not to attack them physically*. A situation where one person could physically hurt another rapidly becomes frightening and numbing and does not actually help the person working to experience her emotions. 'No violence' should be a clear rule established at the start. This is part of the process of building an atmosphere of safety and trust where people feel free to share feelings. Sometimes competitive feelings can be explored by two people wrestling with one another, but the group should make sure that they stay on their knees and are well buffered by cushions so that no one can get hurt.

NO DOPE

Cigarettes, alcohol, dope, coffee and tea all affect the way we feel and usually act as sedatives, numbing us and keeping emotions down to a 'safe' level. For this reason some people ban them entirely from therapy sessions. We have felt that this is very hard on regular smokers so we have no firm rules, but in practice we do not take alcohol or dope before or during a session, we do not drink tea or coffee during sessions, and smokers try to go without cigarettes. Even if you decide against rules on this, it is worth noticing *when* you reach for a cigarette or drink because this makes you more aware of what upsets you, and how you automatically react to stifle the upset.

KEEP CONFIDENTIALITY

We have put this rule last but perhaps it is one of the most important. In the early days of our group we didn't have an agreement to keep confidence about what happened in our sessions and women got upset to discover that problems and feelings they had explored were recounted to people outside the group. This felt like a betrayal of trust. We expose ourselves in a therapy group perhaps more intimately than in any other situation in our lives. This is hard enough to do without fearing that our feelings may become the subject of gossip. An agreement to keep confidence about the sessions is essential for building trust within a group or counselling relationship, and should be clearly established from the start.

NOTES

1   Ann Scott, unpublished article, London, 1976.

Chapter Two
Starting a Self-Help Group

The early days of our self-help group were often difficult. A few people, shivering in a strange environment, struggled to 'get into their feelings' and became frustrated with one another for their failure to do so. In this chapter we offer some ideas, structures and approaches which may help other groups to avoid some of the problems we faced.

BUILDING TRUST

Many of us have been brought up to feel that 'what's hardest is best for us' and when we come to do therapy we apply the same principle to therapy. We expect miracles overnight, feel that we 'should' be expressing our feelings more fully, that we must 'try harder' to change. Ambitiously we embark on the most difficult exercises which we believe will open up emotions in the most complete way, even though this prospect terrifies us. We set impossibly high standards for ourselves and others which often lead to disappointment and disillusionment. People jump in at the deep end, scare themselves and withdraw completely. Other group members become anxious, sit numbly clammed up through the sessions, or stop coming altogether. Occasional explosions make the atmosphere even more tense; more people leave and others are left to complain: 'Nobody really wanted to take any risks', 'It's all just talk, we're not getting anywhere', 'I don't trust anybody in this group'.

To avoid this kind of let-down, it is important to remember that it takes *time* to build up enough trust to explore feelings in a self-help group. Anxiety and mistrust are bound to come up at the start of a new group, and it should not be seen as a failure if you experience them. It is fine to recognise those feelings and talk about them without thinking you need to blame or attack one another. In a led group the leader provides the confidence in the group to help it get off the ground. In a self-help group we have to provide it for ourselves. So it is worth starting gradually, building up positive contact and doing what is easy and enjoyable. It helps to respect one another's defences against therapy, rather than expecting an overnight transformation. Small risks and changes need to be encouraged and appreciated so that they can blossom into bigger things. All this is not to recommend covering up negative feelings or criticism in a group. Difficult and negative feelings are bound to arise and exploring them is never easy, but paradoxically it seems more possible to be open and honest about these feelings when there is a strong basic commitment of love and trust. Criticism is much easier to accept when it comes from someone who cares about you: you do not feel defensive or hopeless but strong enough to learn from it. Love and acceptance in the group can help you to feel that you have the potential to change, that you are not just a 'lost case'. Liberating ourselves from life-long patterns is hard. We need support and impetus from other women to make the leap of faith that is going to get us there. It is important to appreciate each person's way of being in the world and the process she is going through. People can only too easily be made to feel inadequate, inferior and incapable. Our society already tends to make us feel this way and the long-term aim of therapy is to change that, to help us feel better and stronger in ourselves, not to perpetuate it by making us feel that we are a 'failure' at therapy too. In practice, this might mean starting with easy exercises before moving on to more demanding ones, structuring your sessions so that there is time for giving one another feedback and physical contact (hugs, massage), and gradually building up a commitment to one another.

KNOWING WHAT YOU HOPE TO GAIN FROM THERAPY

It's also good to start a self-help group with a clear sense of what you want to get out of it. Follow your excitement and your own sense of how you could change your life and realise yourself more fully. Go for what grabs you, what interests and gives you pleasure, not what you think you 'should' do. It can help to share in the group the kind of patterns you would like to change in your behaviour ('I'm always doing things for people and I resent it', 'I have difficulty reaching orgasm', 'I feel lonely a lot') or a particular problem you would like to deal with ('I have just separated from my husband, I want to learn to enjoy life on my own'). Have an idea what positive changes you might be able to make in your life within a certain period of time. One method is for each person to make a 'contract' in the group to work towards certain changes within a period of time; then other group members remind her of this contract and help her to keep to it. A contract might be 'To ask for what I want' or 'To recognise what is good in my life and not just what is wrong with it'.[1]

Whatever your method, it is good to hold onto the sense that therapy does not just mean difficulty and pain but a real opening out of yourself as a human being, a way to realise more fully your potential for love and self-expression. A self-help group is an ideal place to explore positive growth and to appreciate that we all have more strength in us than we dare to believe.

GETTING A GROUP TOGETHER

Who Should Be in the Group?

You may have some difficulty deciding about the membership of the group. A group of ten or more can seem unsafe and unwieldy if you are just starting. At the other end of the scale two or three people can do therapy together but you may find that you have low energy as a group and that you operate more like a co-counselling relationship. Six to eight people usually seems a good number when starting a self-help group.

We started as a mixed group and seeing men learning to express their emotions was, as one woman in the group put it, 'educational? salutory? a relief, an eye-opener, trust promoting'. But we increasingly realised there were certain issues which we found too difficult to work on in a mixed group: sexuality, self-disgust, conflicts amongst ourselves which it seemed disloyal to bring out in front of men. We then divided into a women's and a men's group. In our women's group we found the space to work seriously on our relationships with one another, which the mixed group could not provide. Groups with a common interest or motivation (as women, as compulsive eaters, as single parents) seem to hold together most strongly. It is good to talk about your motivation right at the start and see whether you have enough in common to give one another the support, validation and reassurance which is as important as the therapy you do. The group can provide a network of friends who see and accept you as you change, understand your crises and support you in being different from the person you were.

Problems may emerge if one of the members of a new group is in such a state of distress from the start that her apparently insoluble problems completely dominate the sessions. In this case it is worth asking whether she is able at this point in her life to give attention to other people in the way that is necessary for the survival of a self-help group. Maybe she needs a situation where she can get attention for herself for a while (perhaps one group member could give her counselling outside the group, perhaps she needs professional or individual therapy). An inexperienced self-help group should not feel guilty about recognising when they are out of their depth and saying 'no' when they need to.

The Time and Place

If you are feeling insecure or physically uncomfortable it is almost impossible to open up at all, let alone to open up and explore difficult repressed feelings. So, whatever your numbers, it is important to meet at clearly agreed times and in a comfortable space.

You should use a room where you can feel relaxed, where you are not likely to be interrupted, and where you feel free to make some noise without other people complaining. We have used various premises with different problems in each place: in one home neighbours called in police because of the shouting, and one noisy session in a community centre was interrupted by a bottle through the window. It is not ideal to meet in the same person's home each time as she starts to feel responsible for the group. It is often possible to use or hire a room in a growth centre, church premises or a women's centre. It is worth taking trouble to make the room as you want it (preparing cushions, putting posters on the wall, arranging sound-proofing): a friendly environment helps in the long term to make a group work more easily and fruitfully. The room must be warm and preferably carpeted so that people can sit on the floor with their shoes off. Any furniture should be put to one side to clear a space for moving around. Generally cushions are needed not just to sit on in the circle but also to use in some of the therapy exercises.

Decide clearly how often you are going to meet and for how long. Many self-help groups start with a three-hour session weekly or fortnightly but this will depend on what people need. It is good to agree what time you are going to finish, so that sessions do not drag on exhaustingly. Some groups make arrangements to provide tea or coffee before the session to avoid starting on an empty stomach after travelling to the group. Some groups find it useful to have a rotating co-ordinator responsible for arranging the time and meeting place and informing people, but who is not a leader in the sessions. Acting decisively with this kind of practical arrangement helps to create a secure framework within which self-help therapy can work more effectively.

MELTING THE ICE

Strange people can be as inhibiting as an alien environment. If you are strangers, you will need time to get to know one another and develop a sense of warm contact within the group before expecting to share feelings openly. The group might decide to devote the first few meetings to consciousness-raising, talking and learning about one another's lives. It can also be helpful to share with the group your fears about getting involved with therapy and your fantasies about what might happen in the sessions. Here are some exercises. The physical ones are especially important to release tension during early meetings. During the exercises in pairs, change partners for each exercise. This enables each person to get to know several others, and helps break down barriers between group members.

13   Say Your Name

Sitting in a circle, have people in turn say their name and one word describing how they are feeling at this moment: 'Jane – nervous', 'Sally – tired'.

Or try standing in a circle and take it in turns to say your name with a movement to express how you are feeling. Take turns round the circle three times saying your name in different ways.

A further variation is to set up a rhythm with your name and movement and all to join in in turn, setting up a kind of group chant. You can then vary or develop your sound and movement in response to others in the group.

Or you can take five minutes each to tell the group all the nicknames you have ever been called, explaining how and why they originated.

14   Introduce Each Other

Choose as a partner one of the group members you know least and take a few moments to find out the most important things about each other's lives. Then each take turns round the circle to introduce your partner to the rest of the group: 'This is Carole. She's just had a baby . . . She used to like her job . . .' The idea is to overcome the embarrassment of introducing yourself to a new group, and to encourage people to skip trivial conversation and make contact.

15   Hands Meeting

In pairs, sit facing each other with your eyes closed. Now have one of the group members give you instructions:

Let your hands explore the other's hands

Let the two pairs of hands do a dance together

Let them have a fight

Express sadness to one another

Then joy

Allow several minutes for each mood. Then part your hands and see if you can still sense any contact with your partner. Afterwards share what you experienced.

16   Drawing Your Life-Line

Each person takes coloured crayons and a big sheet of paper. On the paper she draws a line in a shape which represents her life from birth to the present day. Then she fills in on it, with the appropriate shapes, colours and words, the different events or situations which stand out during her life. Then each person takes up to ten minutes to share her 'life-line' with the rest of the group. This exercise is good for getting to know about one another's history. So is the next one.

17   Autobiography

Bring a short autobiography to a session and share it with the group. The autobiography might take the form of a written account, a picture montage, a collection of objects or a dance.

If the idea of an autobiograpy seems daunting, focus on *one important event* in your life.

18   Head and Back Massage

Divide up into pairs and sit facing each other with your hands behind your back. Let your heads touch and give each other a head-to-head massage, exploring each other's face, hair and neck. After three minutes, change to sitting back-to-back, and explore giving each other a massage with only backs touching, in a similar way.

Afterwards share with your partners how it felt.

19   Chain Massage

This exercise can be good for making physical contact as a group.

All stand or sit in a circle and each person massages the one in front of her. Give each other feedback on what feels good. Take about ten minutes and use music if it helps set the mood. You may decide to focus on vigorous, exploratory or calming strokes, depending on the group's need. The group should decide if it feels comfortable for everybody to remove any clothes.

20   Moving Freely to Music

Choose a record which suits your mood. Lie on the floor, close your eyes, let yourself breathe fully and tune in to the music. Gradually, when you feel ready, get up and, keeping your eyes closed, slowly let the music move you. Let yourselves move loosely and spontaneously and try to avoid the ways you usually move or dance. Imagine you are dancing from a place inside yourself which the music is speaking to.

Dance can be an enjoyable and relaxing activity to do together as a group. Because it starts gradually, because eyes are shut and no one is watching, this exercise can help people start to dance without self-consciousness.

21   Impromptu Lecture

Each person chooses an object in the room and delivers a two minute 'lecture' on it to the rest of the group. These lectures can be sad, funny or fantastic and the arbitrariness of the content often frees women to speak who might otherwise be nervous about doing so. This exercise can help women express their creativity in the group, and to appreciate the creativity of others.

22   'As a Woman I Am Expected to . . .'

This is a good exercise for bringing up feminist issues in a group where you have not yet spent time talking or doing consciousness-raising together. Choose a partner, sit on the floor facing each other and hold hands if you want. Keep eye contact. You have six minutes each. In your turn start by saying sentences which begin 'As a woman I am expected to . . .' For example: 'As a woman I am expected to be neat', 'As a woman I am expected not to shout', and so on. After three minutes, change to sentences which begin 'As a woman I *feel* . . .' ('As a woman I feel angry', 'As a woman I feel lonely'). When your time is up, swop roles. At the end share some feedback with your partner (which are the hardest expectations? did you have similar experiences?). Then come back into a circle and have each woman tell the group one important thing which came up for her during the exercise.

If you are a mixed group, the men can do a male version of this to explore the stereotyped roles which are required of them and how these contrast with their actual feelings.

23   Trusting the Group

Stand in a tight, close circle and take it in turns to go into the centre. The person in the centre stands straight, knees stiff, feet together, eyes closed, body relaxed. She lets herself fall and the others gently pass her back and forth around the circle. If the woman in the centre really relaxes, with her head hanging, this works as a way of learning to trust the group to take care of you. If you cannot relax, be aware of what frightens you.

24   How You'd Like to Change

Stand in a circle. Each person in turn walks into the centre and mimes a part of her personality, or a way she behaves, which she doesn't like (for example, her anxiety, jealousy or aggression). After a few minutes she switches into miming the way she would *like* to behave instead. This exercise is good to do after a physical warm-up, so that people don't feel too inhibited. It helps give the group an idea of what changes each woman wants to make for herself through the therapy sessions.

STARTING THERAPY WITH FRIENDS

If you know one another – whether as friends, work colleagues, a housing collective or a consciousness-raising group – before you start doing therapy together, you will have a different kind of ice to melt. In this case the sessions usually start against a background of accumulated likes, dislikes, hidden compromises, agreements and established patterns which have built up between people, often unconsciously, over time. Usually these patterns have developed to keep things easy in the group and they can hide quite a lot. If you want to open up relationships between group members and enable individual women to express their emotions more fully, some of these patterns will eventually have to be exposed and challenged. In Chapter Four on Encounter we give some exercises on how to do this. Here we describe some preliminary exercises which reveal the roles people play in the groups and show the possibility of changing the way you relate to each other.

25 Introducing a Hidden Personality

Stand in a circle. Give yourselves a few minutes of silence to think about a part of yourself which is not recognised in the group, an aspect of your character which you do not express and which other people do not accept or respond to. Think of a name which seems suitable for this unexpressed part of you. Then, each in turn, stand in the centre and introduce yourself to the group: 'I'm Cristabel, I'm upper-class and snobby with social airs and graces . . .', 'I'm Sylvia, I'm poetic and creative . . .', 'I'm Maureen, I'm miserable and moany and floppy . . .'

Let yourself go and enjoy getting into the part.

This exercise can be fun, but it can also make you aware of ways in which you have not been expressing yourself fully in the group. It brings into the open aspects of your personality which you are ashamed of or possessive about and which you have not wanted – or felt able – to share.

26 Picturing Relationships

You each need plenty of big wax crayons and two large sheets of paper. On one sheet draw a picture of your relationships with women, on the other a picture of your relationships with men. Allow only three minutes for each drawing. It is important to draw on impulse, not thinking about it or worrying whether your picture 'looks good'. When you have finished, have each woman in turn talk about her pictures: 'This red and brown pattern looks harmonious and happy', 'The picture is confused, there are some knotty tangled bits here'.

Then other group members can add their comments. They should not interpret the pictures, but stick to what they notice in them or feel about them: 'That blue bit looks different from the rest', 'I feel a bit frightened by that one'.

This exercise offers a framework for people to talk about themselves and their relationships more personally than they may have done previously in the group.

27 How I Put Myself Over

This exercise helps us to see whether our self-image tallies with the image our friends have of us.

Take a pencil and paper. Write down any words which describe the image you think you put over to the world ('glamorous,' 'bossy', 'tall'). Write quickly and put down anything which comes to mind, without judging. Now get into groups of three and take ten minutes each to share your list. The others will give you feedback about whether the qualities you list fit with their impression of you.

28 'I'm like you, I'm unlike you . . .'

Divide into pairs. Sit facing each other on the floor and keep eye contact. Start with three minutes each way to tell one another ways in which you are alike. Each sentence starts: 'I'm like you in . . .', 'I'm like you in that we're both capable', 'I'm like you in that we both get uptight about little things . . .' and so on. While one speaks, the other simply listens. After three minutes, exchange roles.

When you have done 'I'm like you . . .' repeat the same pattern for three minutes each way, but this time tell each other ways in which you are unlike, sentences starting 'I'm unlike you in . . .'

At the end take some time to share feedback with your partner. This is usually a fairly gentle way of opening up relationships between people, high-lighting similarities and differences which you may feel good or bad about.

If none of the exercises we give seems right, it is easy to make up your own. From this chapter alone there is plenty of material to play around with: you can use cushions, drawing, moving, talking in pairs, going round the circle, in a variety of ways to draw out the particular themes you want to explore. From the start it is good to have fun and be creative with exercises in this way. The power to decide what happens in the group rests entirely with you.

HOW TO RUN A SELF-HELP SESSION

There is a danger, when you are new to self-help therapy, that you spend a long time discussing what you are going to do in the session. This can increase any anxiety or tension because some people use talking as a way of covering over feelings they are afraid of expressing. It is usually better to *do* any exercise rather than to sit around arguing. The same issues or feelings will probably emerge anyway, whichever approach you use. When you are a new group, exercises and structures are often badly needed to help sessions get off the ground. Here is a useful plan for running a session:

1   Opening Circle

Start by allowing each person in turn to say briefly how she is feeling and what she wants from the session.

2   Warm-up

Tension often makes the atmosphere of the group flat or dead. If your body is tight or cold, your emotions usually go numb too. Here are some energetic physical exercises to loosen tension and make it easier for feelings to come to the surface.

29   Shake-out

Stand in a circle. Shake one arm, starting with the fingers then the hand, wrist, lower arm, elbow and so on until you are shaking the whole arm from the shoulder (pretend you are trying to shake it off). Stop and feel the difference between the shaken arm and the other one. Repeat with the other arm, then each leg in turn (starting with toes, ankle, lower leg and so on). Let the head move round on the neck. Finally bend forward and let the whole body shake from the hips.

This exercise should get your circulation going and leave your body feeling warmer, more open and aware. It is important to do it slowly, isolating each part of the body in turn. Have one person direct the process to prevent you rushing through it.

30   Slapping Each Other into Warmth

Get into pairs. Take it in turn to slap each other all over. Start at your partner's feet, slap thoroughly up her legs and then all over her body. Thump really hard wherever it feels right to you both, but very gently on delicate places like the throat and face.

There is a variation of this which covers only the back of the body. Ask your partner to bend over towards the floor with her knees very slightly bent. Then start from the back of her calves and work all the way up her legs and back using the sides of both hands in a vigorous 'chopping' movement.

31   Copycat

Walk in a large circle or move at random around the room. Choose one person to start doing a vigorous movement and a sound which expresses how she is feeling. Everyone copies her and exaggerates it until she tags someone else to start a different movement. Let each turn be quite long (about two minutes) so that people have time to get into the swing of each movement, which will help them to share each woman's mood.

You may also find it useful to do a breathing or awareness exercise (for example, **8** or **11**) at this stage of the group.

3   Do an Exercise Together

If no one is ready to work it may be useful to do an exploratory exercise which everyone in the group can learn something from. For example, you might choose to do a guided fantasy like **100** or **105**, a co-counselling exercise like **36** or **39**, a Gestalt exercise like **43** or **45**, or an Encounter exercise like **53** or **54**. These exercises may bring up a feeling or problem which one person would like to explore individually with the group's help. If not, you may choose to continue throughout the session with more exercises as a group or in pairs.

Sometimes it is difficult to decide which exercise to do, or there may be hesitation about who is to start one. There is a handy rule called 'Suggester starts'. If someone suggests an exercise, she starts it.

Here are some more exercises which may be useful to help feelings to surface.

32   Yes/No

Sit in pairs back to back on the floor. One shouts 'Yes!', the other shouts 'No!', and each tries with back and legs to push the other across the floor. Shout and push with all your strength. After five minutes swop so that the one who shouted 'No!' shouts 'Yes!', and repeat. At the end come back into a circle to share any feedback. (Did you push better on 'Yes' or on 'No'? Did it bring up the picture of a situation where you wanted to shout like that? Who were you shouting at?) This exercise can raise energy if you are feeling numb or depressed.

33   Happy/Sad/Angry

This exercise takes about forty-five minutes. Arrange for someone to timekeep. Choose a partner, sit facing each other on the floor, and take five minutes each way to tell each other things in the previous day and week which have made you *happy*. At the end, share feedback.

Choose another partner, and take five minutes each way to tell your partner things in the previous day and week which have made you *sad*. Share feedback.

Choose another partner, and this time use the same format to tell each other about things which have made you *angry*.

These 'scanning' exercises, which derive from Co-counselling, help you to recall events or emotions which you might like to work on in the group. They could equally be done in a threesome or foursome on the same basis of equal time each. At the end of the sequence it is a good idea to come together as a group and for each person to share the single most important thing which came up for her in the exercise. The session might then move on to one woman 'working' at length on that situation or feeling.

34 Fighting for a Cushion

This exercise can break through numbness and bring up strong feelings. One person should sit out to oversee it.

Choose a partner, sit on the floor, and place a cushion between you. Now you each imagine the cushion is something or someone very precious and important to you, something you really want. When you have pictured this clearly, find out what you are going to do about it. You can use whatever tactics you like, including force, but do not physically hurt the other person.

After about five minutes share as a pair, then in the group, how it felt. Notice if you acted directly or indirectly, whether you could enjoy getting what you wanted, or whether you felt too numb to go for it at all.

35 How You Feel about Your Body

Choose a partner. Find space in the room and have your partner touch the parts of your body which you feel good about. Then have her touch the parts you do not feel good about. Take some time to share with her your feelings about these parts of your body, the sensations, appearance, fears and memories in each part which determine how you feel about it. When you have had enough time, exchange. Come back into a circle at the end to share what you have learned in the exercise and see if material has come up for one woman to 'work' on. *This exercise can stir up strong feelings.*

4 One Person 'Works'

In a newly-formed group, it is sometimes hard to decide who should 'work'. Women may be hesitant to ask for time, nervous of being in the limelight or feel they don't deserve attention. Some groups have found it helpful to use a noticeboard on which people can write their names at the start of the session if they want to 'work' in the group. However, sometimes we are not even aware that we need attention and it takes another to point it out: 'Shirley, you seem really upset. Do you want some time in the group?'

At the other extreme, there may be two women at boiling point both wanting help to explore a problem. In this case the one who seems most troubled is usually given the time; the other is asked to wait until later on in the session, or the following week. It is worth noticing if any particular woman is often put off in this way and making sure that each person has an equal share of the group's attention over the long term. The group should decide collectively who is to work and for roughly how long, if time is a problem. Once you have decided who is working, keep the circle and give her your full attention as far as possible without interruptions; remember, this is *her* time.

What is 'working' like?

In later chapters we give many long examples of what may happen. What a woman does depends on the issue she is dealing with and the techniques she uses, whether Gestalt, Bioenergetics, Psychodrama or whatever. There is, however, a basic pattern which often underlies a piece of work, whatever the techniques used. For example, a woman often starts by talking, describing her feelings towards a particular situation or person or characteristic in herself. The other group members will make suggestions and gradually encourage her to get closer to a more direct emotional expression of those feelings, for example, by shouting, crying, laughing, making sounds and body movements. She may find this transition difficult. People do not always get straight into crying, or shouting, because of defences developed since childhood to prevent such direct expression of emotion. Most of the techniques described in this book are different ways of tackling these defences or resistances. A woman may learn a lot simply by becoming aware of her resistances ('I'm angry but I daren't express it') or she may work through them into the discharge of her feelings. Most schools of therapy recognise that the discharge of emotion, whether anger, joy or fear, is an important part of emotional healing.

Her discharge may start gently and become more intense. Other group members should not interrupt her nor try to hug or console her unless she asks for this. They will probably encourage her to persist with the discharge until the associated tension has been released as much as possible. Sometimes it may involve involuntary sounds and movements, for example, shaking or kicking. In this case the group should make sure she is protected by cushions against hitting anything hard. If she is making a lot of noise, it may be wise to check your soundproofing and station someone outside the room to reassure any well-intentioned intruders or neighbours. After a while, her movements or sounds will start to calm. She may say that she feels she has finished and would like to stop. It may take her some time to return her attention to the group and get back to normal, especially if she has been releasing very intense or painful feelings. Here are some good questions to ask her to help her gradually 're-enter' the group:

'Can you look at me?'
'What can you see in the room?'
'How do you feel towards people in the group?'
'What would you like the group to do for you now?'

If she is feeling shaky after her experience, she may be glad to curl up on her side covered with a blanket, or she might appreciate some hugs or other reassuring body contact.

Often a woman is concerned about whether she is still acceptable to the group after she has expressed her feelings, saying, 'I wish the ground would swallow me up' or 'I feel bad about taking so much time'. In this case she will need reassurance. Often she reports a tremendous feeling of relief to have let go some of her anger, joy or sadness. She may describe a sensation of peace and calm, 'I feel so much better . . .', 'I've never been able to do that before.'

Will I regain control?

Some women fear that if they start to express their feelings they may never stop, or may in some way 'go too far'. In our experience this is very rare. In the early stages of a self-help group it is far more common for a woman to allow a very slight opening up of her feelings at first. Even more likely for her to reach the brink of, say, crying, but find that her defences prevent her from shedding any tears at all. Then the group might simply help her to become more aware of her resistances. But, very occasionally, the woman who is discharging her feelings may begin to get overwhelmed by them and frightened. In this case, it is best to help her to calm and return to the group because the experience is valuable only if there is a part of her which is aware of what is happening, which can learn from the experience and can bring her back at any time. If she is breathing too deeply she may start to experience *hyperventilation* which brings a lightheaded feeling and tingling in the hands or feet. On other occasions, it may be the group members who are frightened by the discharge. They may not understand what is going on and may feel out of their depth. If so, there is no point in their pretending they can handle things (which undermines the person working). They can ask her what is going on, as she may know, or they can express their fear and ask her to stop. In any of these situations the best way to bring a person gently back to normal consciousness is to:

Ask her to breathe lightly and evenly rather than panting or gasping deeply
Ask her to count to twenty and to open her eyes and make eye contact with a group member she knows well
Ask her to put her feet on the ground and tell the group what she is experiencing
Ask her the questions we list above on p 43.

If she has been exploring particularly painful or scary feelings she might like to imagine an idyllic, peaceful scene (in a forest, lying on a beach) to nourish her while she recovers.

5   *Feedback*

Whatever has happened, allow time for feedback. This is important so that whoever works is not left stranded: she needs contact and a 'reality-check' to help her connect her experience to the world. If she was at all frightened, she may need the group to reassure her and help her recognise that she has survived her experience alive and whole. Talking about what happened will help her to learn from it and integrate what she has learned into her life. She may find that she can see an everyday problem from an entirely new perspective. Feedback is also important for the other group members. Watching someone work can stir you up and it is good to share what you are feeling rather than suppress it. If you are feeling critical or resentful about what happened she will probably pick this up anyway. It can be patronising to withhold feedback. The woman who worked has taken a big risk and exposed herself. It is important to own your feelings and be as honest about them as she has been with hers. This does not mean acting superior and offering her interpretations ('You've obviously got a problem with . . .'), or advice ('I think you should . . .', 'I can't understand why you don't . . .', 'My advice to you is . . .'). Nor is this the time to jump in to grind various axes of your own ('I was glad to see you working about losing control, I usually find you hard to relate to because you are so uptight . . .'). It does not help to tell her what she did wrong in her work, that she had the wrong feelings, that she did not 'express her feelings enough' or anything like this. Stick to sharing what you *felt* and what you *noticed* during her work:

'I felt you were very brave to show how jealous you are'

'I identified with you about feeling left out'

'I am relieved you've finished, it was too long and heavy for me'

'I noticed you kept screwing your eyes up while you were working'

'I got annoyed when you wouldn't let go'

'I was scared of you when you got angry'

'I feel like I want to hug you'

If her work has aroused difficult feelings in you, mention this but do not leap into a confrontation with her unless she wants it. This is her time, not yours. She will probably be feeling very opened up and sensitive and should be treated gently. She may have touched on a sensitive area which you need to work on separately for yourself. Don't neglect positive feedback. By the sheer fact of working, she has taken more risk than other group members and should be appreciated for what she has done. Many of us feel that our emotions are shameful and if we show them we will be rejected. It can be a revelation to learn that after expressing them we are still liked.

It often happens that one person's work stirs up another person who then wants to work straight after her.

6   Unfinished Business

After one or more people have worked, do not finish the session without allowing time to clear up any 'unfinished business' (see Exercise 3). It is important for each person to have a space to share how she is feeling before going home. It is also good to make some physical contact with each other before leaving: have a group hug or sit for a few minutes in a silent circle holding hands, imagining a flow of positive energy moving round the circle. Because we are so unused to this kind of positive contact, it may feel phony at first. Don't force it, but do give it a try.

THE FIRST SIX MONTHS

During the first six months it is worth getting familiar with some of the different therapy methods we describe, perhaps working through this book as we have put them in what seems to us an appropriate order. You may choose to spend a session on each method, or you may prefer to spend several months thoroughly learning and using one approach which suits you. Some of us did self-help Gestalt therapy for almost a year before learning about any other approach.

This may be an exciting period, almost like a religious conversion: everything becomes heightened, you do some intense therapy work and enter a state of elation which you imagine will continue. You may develop unreal expectations, believing that therapy can do magic and solve every problem of your life. Alternatively you may start very slowly and find it uphill work to do any therapy at all.

Whichever is your experience, it is likely that during this period you will face some difficulties in the organisation of the group. For example: Can someone new join? How can we stop one person running the group more than the others? How can we learn new skills? How can we go deeper in our therapy work?

Below we list some structures which can make the mechanics of the group run in a smoother and more egalitarian way over this early period.

1   Commitment

Make a clear commitment to the group. People might agree to attend four consecutive sessions at least, then to re-assess whether they want to stay in the group or leave. It can be difficult to build enough trust in a newly-started group if people drift in and out and you don't know whether you are going to see the same faces next week.

2 A Closed Group
You might decide to close the group to newcomers for a limited period so that group members have time to get to know one another without having to start again each week with new people. Some women feel that it is mean or exclusive or against the principles of self-help therapy to have a 'closed' group, but initially it is a priority to create a safe space in which self-help therapy can happen at all. In our experience it works quite well to close the group for a while and then open the doors when you feel ready, then close again. In this way new members can be integrated gradually.

3 Rotating Leadership
Take it in turns to plan, structure and run each session. This helps to equalise power in the group and enables those who might hold back to take responsibility. It can help you to avoid long gaps at the start of every session where each person waits for the other to take a lead. You might find it easier initially to take this rotating leadership in pairs.

4 Make a Six-Week Plan for Your Sessions
This might mean planning, say, three weeks of bodywork followed by three weeks of learning psychodrama techniques. Or it might involve planning a series of sessions on particular themes which group members would like to explore, such as dreams, anger, self-image. Our index will help you pick out exercises to explore such themes. This kind of planning ahead might seem unnecessarily rigid but it can help to avoid anxiety about what may happen in the group and you can be ready to abandon the plan if something more immediate arises.

5 Sharing Time
You may find you have a recurrent problem about who is to work in the group, either because no one ever comes forward or because a few people dominate the group's attention. In this case, make a habit, after warming-up, of dividing the length of the session so that each person has an equal amount of time, whether it is ten minutes or an hour. In her time each person can ask for exactly what she wants from the group: a massage; time to talk about a problem; the whole group to do some movement to music; to have feedback on her image in the group; to explore briefly a feeling which has been troubling her. Work out in which order you will take your time and have someone with a watch tell people when to stop. This structure may seem arbitrary but does make it easier for women to get what they want without having to push or compete for attention or make a big leap straight into working at length. It

also gives women valuable space to practise asking for what they need. Though the time may not be long enough to deal thoroughly with a problem, even ten minutes can be very fruitful if you use the time well. Another alternative, as you get more experienced, is to divide the group into two or three small groups so that several people can work simultaneously in different parts of the same room.

6 Having Help

Invite someone from a long-standing self-help group to help you get started. She might run a couple of sessions for you to share skills she has learned. She might help you to deal with any problems in the group by talking about her own experience of setting up a leaderless therapy situation.

7 Keep a Book

It can be very helpful for each woman to start a journal to keep account of work she does in the group. She can use it to write down dreams, peak experiences, memories which come to light, connections she makes during sessions, insights into relationships and so on. Using a journal has become, in the women's liberation movement, a recognised part of women's self-expression, and in this context it can help us to take our process of change seriously, to look from a more objective standpoint at our life and personality. Over time it is possible to see how the pieces of the jigsaw fit together and get a sense of continuity and development.

We have also found it useful to have our journals with us in group sessions, to note down feelings and impressions at the end of an exercise before sharing verbally. There is rarely time in a session to say everything you might want to. If things are down on paper they are there for you to learn from in your own time.

8 Homework

It can be very effective to back up the work you do in a therapy group by undertaking to make certain small changes in the pattern of your life between sessions. This helps to integrate the therapy work and gives you practice in behaving differently. Some examples might be:

(If you feel your life is bleak) 'To give yourself one real treat every day'
(If you have problems with a work colleague) 'To take time during the week to talk to him and initiate sorting some things out'
(If you have worked about some sexual difficulties) 'To spend at least ten minutes each day giving loving attention to your body'
(If you have worked on your self-deprecation) 'Not to say "Sorry" once all week'

(If you have just started to open up some childhood material) 'To write a short autobiography'

It is up to the group to remember the homework, check at the next meeting that the woman has done it, and give her appreciation for these steps she is taking towards change.

9   Have an 'Intensive'

If you feel stuck in your weekly or fortnightly sessions, it can help to arrange to meet differently, for a whole day, a weekend or even a week doing therapy together. This will have a pressure-cooker effect and may open up issues blocking the group. You may feel much angrier with one another and also much closer. Our group's intensives, when some of us went to the country together for a week to do therapy all day every day, stand out as milestones and catalysts in the development of the group.

10   Meet Outside the Group in Pairs

Meeting for therapy sessions in pairs outside the large group speeds up the process of getting to know and trust one another. It also provides a less intimidating situation for each person to realise and practise her ability to make suggestions and help another. You might agree to meet in this way once a week and spend one or two hours together, dividing the time equally between you. Almost any therapy method works with two people, but the one specifically developed to be used in this way is Co-counselling. So before meeting in pairs you might decide to learn the principles of this approach.

CO-COUNSELLING

Co-counselling is one of the few consciously radical therapy approaches. Since it is a well-established self-help technique it already has its own teaching structure and manuals which describe clearly how to start Co-counselling. For this reason we give here only a brief outline of the co-counselling ideas and practice. Many of its methods are similar to the 'Do's and Don'ts' listed in Chapter One, and it embraces several of the other techniques we describe in different chapters of this book. The egalitarian reciprocal structure which is the basic format of Co-counselling is invaluable in a self-help group and is used widely throughout this book.

Re-evaluation Counselling, as it is formally called, is based on the work of the American, Harvey Jackins. In several countries it has grown into a movement with its own organisation and ideology. If you arrive as a stranger in any large American or British town, you can use the co-counselling network to find someone to co-counsel with you. This kind of network can be very supportive. The movement, like any large centralised organisation, is open to the dangers of becoming a hierarchy with charismatic leaders, rigid and unresponsive to change initiated by grassroots members. There is a strong commitment to find ways to avoid these dangers, but various groups within the movement have found it necessary to split off and form their own organisation, for example, International Co-counselling. There is, in all co-counselling groups, a recognition of the links between the 'personal' and the 'political', between our individual feelings and society as a whole. Many feminists are involved in the movement and hold meetings and conferences especially for women. It is perhaps the only school of therapy which offers workshops specifically to explore, and change, patterns of sexism and racism.

The basic structure of Co-counselling is reciprocal help. The person who works is called the 'client', the person who helps her is called the 'counsellor'. They sit facing each other during the sessions and may hold hands. After an agreed time they will exchange roles for an equal amount of time. The egalitarian nature of the therapy is further ensured by an emphasis on allowing the client to direct her own work. She decides what she wants to work on and how. The counsellor is strictly discouraged from identifying or reacting emotionally. She is advised to offer clear loving attention, a powerful and validating form of support for the client. She will make as few interventions as possible, unless the client asks her to play a more active role and this is clearly agreed at the start of the session. Her interventions will be geared simply to keeping the client in touch with her feelings ('Can you repeat that?', 'Louder!', 'Who would you like to say that to?'). She offers feedback but not interpretation.

Her clear attention and sensitive interventions create the space for the client to re-experience past hurts and to allow the discharge of feeling which is central to the co-counselling therapy process. Jackins believes that we are all whole people 'inside' but have accumulated layers of garbage through our conditioning and contact with this society. If we discharge our pain, anger and other repressed feelings sufficiently then we will get back to the creative spontaneous person inside, like peeling the layers off an onion. Discharge is seen as a healing process whereby we can let go of old hurts and free ourselves to give more attention and energy to the present. Tears are a sign not of hurt, but of healing.

When expressing feelings, the client always keeps part of herself fully aware in the present situation. This 'free attention' helps her to learn from the discharge and see how it allows her to change rigid patterns of behaviour in her life. Co-counselling techniques teach the skill of 'attention-switching' which enable you to move out of any emotional state you may be in through validating yourself or describing things you are looking forward to. Instead of getting stuck in any emotion, you are able to come swiftly out of it into a positive frame of mind. Validation is seen as vital in giving the client a position of strength from which she is able to re-open childhood traumas and deal with painful feelings. Jackins points out that we are not encouraged to think well of ourselves. Any sense of self-worth is drummed out of us, so we have to take hold of any seeds we have and develop them. Co-counselling relationships can be very supportive in this way and can become a powerful source of strength for changing your life.

We have found co-counselling methods invaluable for people new to therapy. However, we do have criticisms. We find some of the movement's ideology naïve politically and feel that it gives too much weight to individual change, not enough to confronting external political realities. For example, Jews and Arabs co-counselling together in Israel seems a very worthwhile activity but should not be seen as the main way of achieving political change in that situation. We would also question the emphasis on discharge, which we feel needs to be combined with other things like understanding defences and learning new ways of relating. It is a limitation of Co-counselling that it offers no techniques for the client and counsellor to explore the relationship between them. Emotions can be hived off safely into your hour of discharge. Because interpersonal confrontation is avoided and negative feelings within it are not expressed, even that validating relationship may start to seem slightly unreal.[2]

Using Co-counselling is not the same as being in a self-help group, and you can get different things from each experience. According to co-counselling rules, you don't mix socially with your counsellor, while one of the strengths of a self-help group can be the framework it offers to bridge the gap between your therapy and your social life, offering you feedback on how you behave and helping you to develop your relationships with people in the group in new ways. We have tended to use Co-counselling very broadly, incorporating into the reciprocal structure bodywork, Gestalt and regression techniques – or whatever else has seemed appropriate. We have taken from it what is helpful and adapted that to suit our particular needs. This is typical of the breadth and strength of self-controlled self-help therapy.

Here are some co-counselling exercises. They are short, but as you get more experienced you can take longer. You can co-counsel for anything between five minutes and an hour each way and on any topic you choose. Remember to allow time for feedback after each person's turn.

36   Scanning Memories
This exercise can help you open up your past and become aware of situations in your present life which you need to work on.

In pairs, take ten minutes each way. Sit facing each other and hold hands if you want to. The counsellor should keep eye contact with the client, give attention and intervene only along the lines of 'Try repeating that' or 'How did that feel?' She should not interrupt, ask for explanation, judge or offer solutions. The client talks aloud about all the incidents or feelings she can remember on a particular theme. At the end of ten minutes, exchange roles. Here is a list of themes to choose from:

What happened today, or last week
Pleasant memories (*start from childhood and work through to the present*)
Unhappy memories (*from childhood on*)
My relationship with my father/mother
My relationship with my sister(s) or brother(s)
What happened a year ago around this time (*notice any feelings which are similar or different between then and now*)
Work
Occasions I have fully expressed my feelings
Times I have felt jealous (*from childhood on*)
Times when I have been the victim of racist or sexist violence or class discrimination
School
Sexuality
Masturbation
Ways I have dressed during my life
How I have used alcohol or drugs during my life.
My relationship with food during my life
Good and bad experiences with money

The list could be endless. Invent your own topics according to need. At the end, give each other feedback on what happened. You may find while scanning that one incident or memory looms larger than others and stirs up more feelings in you. You may decide to go on for a further period of time to work more fully on that memory.

37   'Shoulds and Shouldn'ts'
One of the first stages in the therapy process is to become aware of some of the pressures which have alienated us from our feelings. Many of these pressures can be summed up under the word 'should'. Since childhood we have been told 'You should be clean' or 'You should work hard' or 'You should behave yourself'. It is very helpful to become aware of the 'shoulds' we have heard during our life because often we are still carrying them round as a voice in our heads. When we are familiar with them we can start to recognise when they affect or inhibit us in the present and begin to lessen their grip on us.

Take twenty minutes each to tell your counsellor about all the 'shoulds and shouldn'ts' you have been told during your life, starting from childhood, covering school and jobs right up to the present day. Include 'shoulds' which you are aware of as a pressure although they are unspoken, for example, 'Every time I look at a glamorous ad, I feel it's telling me I should be beautiful' or 'My mum never said this, but she seemed to feel that I shouldn't do better at school than my brother.'

Look out especially for 'shoulds' around the areas of sexuality and control ('I should fancy my husband', 'I should keep my temper'). There may also be political 'shoulds' ('I should be more active in the abortion campaign').

At the end, share feedback.

38 Things I Like about Myself

This exercise is done in pairs, following the usual format. Take five minutes each way. In your time talk about things you *like* in yourself. Then exchange roles. Finally, share feedback.

This exercise can be distressing because we are so used to putting ourselves down that we often find it scary or painful to describe things we like about ourselves.

39 Saying the Opposite

This exercise illustrates the common co-counselling technique of saying the opposite to intensify your feelings about an issue.

Each person takes a piece of paper and writes on it a list of things she does not like in herself ('I'm stupid', 'I'm lonely'). Then she turns the paper over and writes the extreme contradiction of each one (for example, 'I'm stupid' becomes, not 'I'm not stupid' but rather '*I'm really, really clever*'). Out of this list of contradictions choose one which seems most powerful or difficult for you, then choose a partner and take about fifteen minutes each to read that contradiction aloud and explore any feelings which arise. Your partner should keep bringing you back to repeating the statement and make other interventions which keep you to the point ('Louder!', 'Who do you want to tell that you're really clever?').

The idea is that by repeating an exaggerated statement of how clever you are, your feelings of stupidity will be brought up in a very intense way and may be discharged.

40 New and Good

This is an exercise to do as a whole group.

Taking it in turns round the circle, tell the group about something new and good which has happened to you today. The idea is to start to validate the good things which are happening to you – maybe little things like having a nice breakfast – which you usually overlook and do not appreciate.

41   Poster Game

This is another exercise which reflects the co-counselling emphasis on self-validation.

Each person takes two very large sheets of paper. On both she draws her name very large in the middle, using colours which celebrate who she is. Then on one she writes around her name in colour all the things she likes about herself. She should write them boldly: not 'I can sing a bit' but 'I've got a lovely voice'. Then she places the other poster in the middle of the circle and everyone writes on each person's poster the things they like about her.

These can be lovely to hang on your bedroom wall and look at when you are feeling down.

42   Racism

With this exercise a clear instruction is given that white people should not expect help, in ceasing to be racist, from the victims of racism. They should work on their feelings of racism out of the hearing of third world people, whose experience at the receiving end of racism is painful enough without bearing the additional burden of white people's discomfort.

This exercise is based on the idea that in order to have become oppressors with racist attitudes and patterns of behaviour, we were ourselves first badly hurt: the racism masks grief. By starting from a position of pride in who we are and a sense of unity with all oppressed people (by recalling how we are or have been oppressed) we can discharge that grief and let go of the racism.

The exercise should be done in pairs. Allow five minutes for each stage. When one person has finished all four stages, exchange roles.

Stage 1   How was/am I oppressed? Get in touch with a particular incident (perhaps closing your eyes for a few minutes) then share it with your partner.
Stage 2   When was there a time I stood up against racism? (If you can't remember, make up a fantasy with yourself as heroine and tell it to your partner.)
Stage 3   When was there a time I colluded with racism and did not stand up against it? Describe a specific incident.
Stage 4   Re-tell Stage 3 as a fantasy the way it should have happened.

The listener simply gives clear attention. At the end, give each other feedback.[3]

This structure can also be used to explore sexist or class oppression.

NOTES

1   This, and several other passages in this chapter, are indebted to Hogie Wyckoff's writings in Claude Steiner (ed), *Readings in Radical Psychiatry*, Grove Press, New York, 1975.
2   *The Barefoot Psychoanalyst* (see below) does offer a way of dealing with this problem within a co-counselling format.
3   This exercise is from 'Notes for a Workshop on Racism', presented by Christopher Spence at South West London College Counselling Course, 1979.

FURTHER READING

Anne Kent Rush, *Getting Clear: Body Work for Women*, Random House, New York, and The Bookworks, Berkeley, 1973; Wildwood House, London, 1974. This book includes many fine exercises suitable for using in the early days of a self-help group.

Red Therapy, 'Red Therapy', 28 Radbourne Avenue, London N3 2BS, UK, 1978. This collectively produced pamphlet, which contains the seeds of this book, both describes the history and ideas of Red Therapy and gives practical information on how we started and worked as a group.

John Southgate & Rosemary Randall, *The Barefoot Psychoanalyst*, Association of Karen Horney Psychoanalytic Counsellors, London, 1978. Followers of Karen Horney have combined her ideas with a co-counselling format and made this available for self-help use in cartoon form.

Rose Evison & Richard Horobin, *How to Change Yourself and Your World: A Beginner's Handbook of Co-counselling*, 5 Victoria Road, Sheffield 10, England, 1978. This pamphlet describes co-counselling ideas and techniques fully and gives an idea of what a grassroots co-counselling community is like.

Harvey Jackins, *The Upward Trend*, Rational Island Publishers, Seattle, 1978. Its founder writes about Re-evaluation Counselling's ideas and techniques.

Personal Counselors Inc, *Fundamentals of Co-counseling Manual* (Elementary Counselors Manual) *for Beginning Classes in Re-evaluation Co-counseling*, Rational Island Publishers, Seattle, 1970. Brief and basic practical manual.

Chapter Three
Many Parts Make the Whole:
Gestalt Therapy

Gestalt therapy offers methods which are relevant and easy to use when starting to do self-help therapy. They are flexible, open to invention and don't involve as much technical understanding as some other therapies. They emphasise awareness in the present, helping us to become more aware of our body sensations, our emotions, our actions and the choices we are making in our lives. This is a good starting place for those new to therapy. We will explain 'talking to the cushion', a simple structure for resolving conflicts within yourself or between yourself and another person. We will also describe Gestalt techniques for exploring in detail the patterns of tension in our bodies which block us from expressing feelings directly.

WHAT IS GESTALT?

For us Gestalt has been primarily a practical approach. The name and some of the underlying ideas derive from Gestalt psychology, a theory of perception which originated in Germany. The development of the therapy itself was largely the work of Fritz Perls, who emigrated from Nazi Germany and ended up living and working on the West Coast of America. He was originally trained in psychoanalysis and was deeply influenced by both Freud and Reich but later broke with the Freudian tradition and became very critical of the lengthy psychoanalytic process which he called the 'year-decade-century-long lying on the couch'.[1] Whereas Freud emphasised the process of contacting repressed memories and experiences from the past, Perls believed that people could become healthy more quickly by focusing on what happens in the present. He was influenced by the ideas of the Existential school of philosophy (what is, is; we are who we are; what we feel, we feel). He discouraged his patients from intellectualising, rationalising or 'interpreting' their lives and behaviour in an *abstract* way. He encouraged them rather to be fully present, to become aware of their current organismic needs, to take responsibility for themselves and their actions, to recognise that they experience what they experience. He pointed out how rarely we honour our *own* experiences and perceptions. From Gestalt psychology he drew the idea of 'closure' or rounding off unfinished situations to make a whole. He emphasised the importance of dealing fully with a situation in the present so that it does not continue to preoccupy us, blocking our ability to deal with other things or fully experience anything else. The process of 'closure' also involves filling out gaps in our awareness, as when we are not concious of body tension or a repeated nervous gesture. It includes, too, the filling of holes in our personality. These 'holes' can be filled through dream work: you can identify with and act out the many disowned or rejected parts of your personality which emerge in dreams (for example, by acting the 'ogre' from your dream you realise that its strength is part of you and thus you reclaim your own power which you had projected outside yourself). The other way to fill 'holes' in the personality is by owning the projections which you put on other people, attributing them with qualities or feelings which are in fact inside you. For example, you might imagine that a friend is angry with you when actually you are angry with her or you might see her as a wonderfully kind person while completely denying your own generous qualities. By re-owning these projections you make yourself more whole. The Gestalt therapy view sees the healthy person very much as a whole organism, an organism in constant and dynamic relationship with her environment.

In practice doing self-help, this emphasis on awareness, taking responsibility for ourselves and staying in the present, would be reflected in avoiding remarks like:

'You're only doing this because . . .' (interpretation)
'It's all my mother's fault, she made me do such-and-such . . .' (blaming others and attributing them with more power than they have over our lives)
'I can't get angry . . .' (excuses)

Instead, owning our feelings in the here-and-now would be reflected in:

'I am feeling sad/put down/jealous/happy right now'
'I am tensing my stomach and shutting my eyes to stop myself crying'
'I *won't* get angry . . .'

We have many criticisms of Gestalt, but we will pick out here what we have found helpful in this approach, which does have some obvious advantages for women.

Most of us have been thoroughly conditioned to feel intellectually inferior to men and put down by the (traditionally male) world of interpretation and theory. It is validating to work with a method which challenges the normal over-estimation of the intellect and focuses instead on the bread and butter (and jam) of what we feel from moment to moment. Our immediate experience is accessible to us all and cannot easily be mystified or taken from us.

The emphasis on awareness in the present also helps us to recognise what restricts and oppresses us and *how we can act* to change our lives now. We are often immobilised by having a blur on our experience which keeps us unaware of what it is specifically we don't like in our present situation. We may also use our intuitive abilities to tune in to what others are feeling so that we can adapt ourselves to their needs in our traditionally validated role as nurturer, rather than becoming aware of what *we* feel and need. Gaining a greater awareness about our own feelings is a crucial first step towards action and change. As one Gestalt therapist puts it: 'Awareness is a way of keeping up to date with herself and her current experience. It is a preamble to lively engagement and expressive interaction in the present moment.'[2]

The idea of re-owning our projections to fill holes in the personality can also be helpful. Often we are weakened by the way we project qualities onto others. This may be expressed in different ways, like blaming people for everything that is wrong in our own lives, believing other people are so much better than ourselves that we *should* not challenge them, or feeling they are so much more powerful than us that there is no point asserting our own needs. All these attitudes lead to inactivity and a sense of powerlessness. Gestalt therapy emphasises re-owning our projections and recognising our own power. People are encouraged to take responsibility for their own lives and to see that they do have the ability to take action in the present. This is particularly helpful for women. There are very real obstacles which block us from getting what we need in this society, and we very often underestimate our own power to tackle those obstacles. By encouraging us to own our feelings, experiences and actions, Gestalt helps us to feel 'active' rather than 'passive' in our lives.

Perls rejected the 'medical' view of therapy. Instead he stressed the inborn healthiness of every individual and our ability to know what is best for ourselves. He saw therapy as a process of growing as we learn to listen more to the inner wisdom of our bodies: 'With full awareness you become aware of this organismic self-regulation, you can let the organism take over without interfering, without interrupting; we can rely on the wisdom of the organism.'[3]

In practice, this might mean that instead of branding a certain behaviour pattern as 'neurotic', we can see it as a pattern which our organism has wisely adopted in order to survive under the difficult pressures of life in our society. A Gestalt therapist would not *interpret* this behaviour or give the person directions about how to change, but instead would help her become more aware of what she is doing: how she is using the pattern (whether it is migraine, depression or agoraphobia), what she gains and loses through it, what answers or alternatives she can learn if she listens to the messages her body is sending her. Women often suffer from being defined as neurotic or hysterical, so this emphasis on the essential healthiness of our organism is strengthening and encouraging. And while we are used to (mostly male) experts apparently 'knowing what is best for us', it is important to develop a sense that *we do know what is best for ourselves*, that we do have most of the answers inside us if only we can listen.

This attitude is reflected in Perls' ideas about how people change. He believed that we cannot deliberately bring about change in ourselves or others and thought that we change by actualising ourselves, not by aiming to achieve our own or someone else's ideal of us. From this view, the therapy process is not one of setting new hurdles or expectations before us, but is more a process of *allowing* ourselves to feel, to exaggerate, to be aware, to recognise, to be stuck, to express, and in this way change and growth happen organically. Perls summed up this attitude in his 'Gestalt prayer':

I do my thing, and you do your thing.
I am not in this world to live up to your expectations
And you are not in this world to live up to mine.
You are you and I am I,
And if by chance we find each other, it's beautiful.
If not, it can't be helped.[4]

The emphasis on self-regulation rather than external regulation lends itself naturally to self-help groups and this approach can help group members to be sensitive to one another's process without pushing, bullying, or over-directing one another. In practice this can be reflected in avoiding remarks like, 'I think you're being very . . .', 'I think you should . . .', 'You always . . .', 'I can't stand the way you . . .', and instead letting the person who is actually exploring a feeling direct the process herself as much as possible, which can be helped by remarks like, 'What's happening for you now?', 'Are you aware that you're clenching your fist/twitching your eyes . . .?', 'Would it feel right for you now to do an exercise where you . . .?'

In asserting the natural drive of every organism towards health, Perls had some awareness of the role played by the pressures of society in inhibiting our healthiness and blocking our ability to live life fully. He criticised the restrictions and commodity ethic of American society where he lived most of his life:

There is a rebellion on in the United States. We discover that producing things, and the exchange of things, is not the ultimate meaning of life. We discover that the meaning of life is that it is to be lived, and it is not to be traded and conceptualised and squeezed into a pattern of systems. We realise that manipulation and control are not the ultimate joy of life.[5]

He sums it up as 'the question of *being* rather than *having*.'[6] His analysis, and that of most other Gestalt writers, does not go far beyond realising the 'anti-life' quality of much in Western society, and he does not explore the particular situation of women, but at least his is not a method geared towards 'adjusting' the individual to society as it is.

We have tried to relate this brief summary of Gestalt theory to the situation and needs of women in therapy. Now we will focus on two practical techniques which we have found most helpful: 'talking to the cushion' and using body awareness to work on blocks and resistances.

TALKING TO THE CUSHION

The word 'Gestalt' actually means a 'whole' brought together from split pieces. This therapy stresses the unity of all experience and an important part of the healing process is seen as the bringing together of splits. Perls describes how we experience unnatural splits between ourselves and the world around us, defining rigid 'ego boundaries' and feeling alien and hostile to the people and things outside us, whereas in fact:'You cannot even separate the organism and the environment. A plant taken out of its environment can't survive, and neither can a human being if you take him out of his environment . . . So we have to consider always the segment of the world in which we live as part of ourselves.'[7] In practice, one Gestalt method for bridging this split between 'us' and 'other' is to identify with and 'act out' what we experience as alien to us. This helps us to minimise the alienation, instead recognising likenesses and similarities with ourselves, and so we can relax our boundary and feel more integrated with the world. If you criticise someone for being untrustworthy, you are encouraged in Gestalt practice to act an untrustworthy person. If you feel you don't like a person, you are encouraged to play their part, talking as them and imagining being inside their skin. The theory is that often you 'project' onto other people qualities which are in fact your own. In the dialogue that develops cushions are often used, representing yourself and the other person in the dialogue. If the feelings are explored fully, there may be an integration towards the end and the two split parts may come together.

Perls pointed out that we also experience artificial splits *within* ourselves. Phrases we use such as '*I* have a *body*', '*I* dislike *myself*' or '*My headache* is stopping *me* enjoying myself', all show how little we experience ourselves as the whole organisms we actually are. One method for becoming more aware

61

of ourselves as healthy, integrated organisms is again to act out the parts
which we experience as split and develop a dialogue between them, for
example between 'head and heart', 'the dependent me and the independent
me' or 'the part which is angry and the part which thinks I shouldn't be'. If
this acting out is done with feeling and developed at some length, there can
be a coming together; the person will end up feeling more integrated and
whole. In practice, these internal splits frequently come out as a conflict
between what Perls called the 'topdog' and the 'underdog'. The 'topdog' is
something like the voice of conscience or authority: self-righteous, bullying,
full of instructions and 'shoulds'. It is the voice which asserts standards,
values, expectations and demands: 'You should work hard', 'You should
think of others first', 'You shouldn't get angry', 'You should be thinner', 'You
should behave conventionally'. The 'underdog' is the opposing voice, the
voice which doesn't want to work so hard, which wants to eat the extra piece
of chocolate, which wants to rebel against authority. It is the losing voice, so
it is defensive, wheedling, apologetic, plays the cry-baby, says 'I try my best',
'I can't help it' and so on. The two parts are usually locked in to a struggle
with each other, like parent and child, and the person is fragmented into
controller and controlled. We usually assume that the topdog is right and
expend a lot of energy on this internal conflict, torturing ourselves for not
living up to the ideals set by the topdog. In Gestalt therapy, we learn to give
more voice to the underdog, who often carries suppressed messages from the
body and emotions about what we *want* and *need* rather than what we *ought*
to do. It usually represents a submerged part of us, often a more potentially
joyful childlike part, which is squashed by the internal authority voice. Getting in touch with the losing underdog and letting it find its strength is a very
helpful process for women: 'Rooted in her submerged and disowned underdog are the seeds of change and movement . . . her own protest against the
status quo'.[8]

Here is an example where a woman explores two split parts of her personality bearing clear similarities to the topdog and underdog roles.

Sue is in a self-help group with friends. They have spent the afternoon in
the park and have come together to have a session in the evening. She tells
the group she is upset because while the others were playing football
together in the park, she sat out. She is slightly older than them and was
afraid of making a fool of herself, but part of her wanted to join in, and felt
left out when she didn't. With two cushions, she develops this into a
dialogue between a strict voice: 'Don't be silly! You'd look ridiculous
playing football! You've got better things to do anyway, you've got a good
book to read . . .', and another, more childish voice which pleaded, 'But I
want to join in! I want to be like the others! It's boring being stuck-up and
sitting reading when the others are having fun!'

The strict voice (or 'topdog') becomes contemptuous and angry, the playful voice pleads. She sits on each cushion in turn as she acts out the two voices inside her. Gradually the dialogue changes: the childish voice becomes angry, the strict 'topdog' voice softens and, finally, while sitting on this cushion, Sue beings to cry: 'I'm missing something! I've been missing something for years . . .' The two voices come closer to one another and almost merge: 'You *have* been missing something', the 'underdog' agrees. 'You need to listen more to me.' The conflict within Sue is nearer resolution. When Sue feels she has finished, she talks to the group about how difficult she found it to join in playground games as a child, and discusses how she could change that pattern of denying herself fun in her adult life. The other group members share with her what they felt during the session.

The cushion technique might seem artificial or silly at first and can feel stilted if the person does not contact the feelings involved in the conflict. To help her do this, the experience needs to be as direct and immediate as possible. For example, she should look at the cushion and address it directly, by name if possible ('Sue, you're missing out . . .', 'Hand, I wish you weren't so scarred . . .'). She should avoid descriptions and explanations *about* herself, her feelings, or other people ('My trousers were too tight to move, I'd meant to let them out . . .', 'I think I am a bit paranoid, I get it from my mother', 'Jane asked if I wanted to join in, but I think she is shy herself . . .'). Instead she should stick to direct statements in the present tense about what she feels and experiences ('Don't be silly!', 'I want to join in', 'I'm not sure if I'm wanted').

This dialogue technique can be useful for exploring contradictions we feel about changing our life-style as part of our politics within the women's liberation movement: we can act out the conflict between the part of us which wants to share and the part which doesn't, the part which feels jealous and the part which thinks it's wrong to be sexually possessive.

Here is another example of the process at work. In this case the conflict is not internal but is with another person.

Julie is complaining to the group about Simon, a man she works with. She describes how he is pompous, arrogant and drops names to impress people. The group point out to her that she is talking 'about' him, and suggest that she talks *to* him instead. They put a cushion in front of her to stand for Simon. They encourage her to look at the cushion, be aware how she feels about Simon, and address him by name, 'Simon, I feel such-and-such about you . . .' Very quickly she contacts her anger and shouts insults at him. When she seems to have run out of energy, the group suggests that she change roles and goes to sit on the 'Simon' cushion to see how it feels and to answer back to this attack. Again she is encouraged really to *be* Simon, and to talk directly to the 'Julie' cushion. As Simon, she starts out acting very superior, self-important and dismissive and as she really lets herself go into the part she realises that she is playing it very well and that is fact it is a part of her own personality which she dislikes intensely. She comments on this to the group. Swapping back she shouts again at this self-important part. Swapping again she finds the self-important character is feeling deflated and pathetic: 'I only act important and drop names to impress people. I think that otherwise they won't take me seriously', she admits. The two sides begin to understand the other's point of view, and become more integrated.

This is a clear example of bridging the split between 'me' and 'other'. As often happens, Julie ends up identifying with the person with whom she is in emotional conflict. You can begin to understand another's point of view better by playing their part and you often realise, as Julie did, that their viewpoint exists partly in you. In fact the reason you have an emotionally charged conflict with them is often that the issue *is* unresolved in yourself. If Julie had nothing in common with Simon, she would probably have seen him quite simply as a slightly pompous person and would have been able to deflate him gently and effectively without feeling churned up herself.

The integration between the two split voices does not always happen easily or magically at the end of every session. Often you may just stop when you feel finished or when you have something new to think about. Sometimes one voice may seem to lose its power rather than beoming integrated. You may need several sessions, and time to absorb what you have learned, before you can resolve a particular conflict. The secret of breaking out of stuck patterns is to allow yourself really to identify with both roles. Thus by identifying with the self-important role Julie realised that part of her acts that way because she is insecure. This understanding allows her to integrate this part of herself instead of rejecting it and separating it off as a quality she hates in other people. If she had not identified she would have been unable to embrace it as part of her character. We often project our 'unacceptable' qualities onto others and always deprive ourselves of energy and awareness when we do so. After this session, Julie is more likely to be aware when she is trying to impress people and to find more direct ways of making people take her seriously.

One way in which Julie might have moved on from this dialogue would be to use the Gestalt technique called 'Making the Rounds'. Sitting in front of each group member in turn, she would make eye contact and repeat a phrase such as 'I want you to take me seriously'. Afterwards she would share how it felt ('Scary') and others would give her feedback ('I wasn't sure you really meant it', 'I saw a new side of you which I liked'). In this way she brings the issues raised by her work directly into her relationship with other group members. In the safety of the group she tries out a new way of relating to other people which the therapy has opened up. This technique of 'Making the Rounds' can be used in a number of different ways to explore messages which you give or would like to give other people. A woman who acts with hostility to everyone might be encouraged to go round saying 'I can't stand anyone in this room'. A woman who feels hopeless might try saying 'I'm a failure' and, making eye contact with each person, might add each time something which particularly relates to them ('I just failed to get a job I wanted', 'I feel it particularly with you because you seem such a success'). The message might involve touch or face-pulling rather than words. A woman could use this exercise to explore a role she feels she is stuck in ('I'm always cheerful'), and by relating that pattern to the here-and-now, will probably intensify the feelings connected with it ('I can't stand the effort of pretending to be cheerful all the time'). She could then try going the rounds again saying the opposite ('I hurt') and thus have the chance to practise a new role. It is important to share afterwards how she and others felt during the exercise.

Julie would not have learned what she did about herself if she had had a confrontation with Simon. He would probably have hurled grievances back at her, she would have felt the need to defend herself and would probably have been inhibited by fears about the repercussions of showing her anger. The Gestalt method does not address itself to interpersonal conflicts as such, but aims to help the person who is 'working' to reach a greater awareness of herself. This may incidentally make it easier for her to resolve a conflict with another, as in the case of Julie who reached a deeper understanding of what she felt about Simon. An advantage is that you can use the cushion technique at home alone or with a partner to explore conflicts with people who might never come to a therapy group. The clarity you gain in this way can then be used to change your relationships in real life. But if you explicitly want to deal with interrelationships or the complex dynamics of what goes on between people in a group, you need to look away from Gestalt to the techniques of Encounter (Chapter Four) or Psychodrama (Chapter Seven). In Gestalt the emphasis is always on recognising what you are projecting onto other people as a way of reaching a greater wholeness in *yourself*. If you have a conflict with someone present in the same therapy group, the Gestalt approach would still be to use a cushion to stand for the person and the emphasis would continue to be on helping you to recognise that many of the feelings you direct towards her derive from your own inner conflicts and history.

Here is an example of a woman working in this way.

Christine is the organising energy behind a newly-formed group. She has been anxious about whether or not people would turn up to the session and by the time it starts she is tense and resentful. She says she would like to explore what she is feeling. She starts by explaining that she feels angry with all the other women in the group; she is always trying to persuade them to come to the group, while they act very aloof, busy and superior. She feels like a child with her enthusiasm for the group, while they are like grown-ups with possibly better things to do. At someone's suggestion she imagines putting all the women on a cushion and talks to them, telling them what a good idea the group is and how their aloofness annoys her. After a while she changes roles and sits on their cushion to answer back as the aloof people. Sitting on this cusion she gets in touch with a very cold superior part of herself, who tells the childish Christine to stop bothering her and run away to play. After a while she realises this voice sounds very like her mother. Swapping back to the 'childish' Christine, she gets cheeky, mocking, and finally very angry at the superior part: 'Get off my back you stupid superior cow! Don't tell me to go away, because without me your life would be so cold . . . *You really need me* . . . because you're dead and I'm alive and full of life!'

At the end of this session one woman suggests that Christine gets up and walks around the room to show the group how good it feels to be the 'alive child' Christine. Christine puts her hands in the pockets of her dungarees and as she moves easily and rather jauntily around the room, she experiences a sudden and intense flashback to a childhood scene, when she was walking through an orchard with her brother, feeling really happy and good in herself.

After this session, it would be important for the group to return to the initial conflict and discuss Christine's relationship with the other group members and the way the group is organised. There is a danger, because she moved into exploring an internal conflict between a 'superior' and a 'childish' part of herself, that the situation comes to be seen as 'all her problem'. In fact there is a real-life problem, about organising the group and commitment to it, in which all the group members are implicated. For Christine, the fact that she has unearthed an internal conflict will help her to understand why the situation is so charged for her and she may be able to separate off these unresolved emotions from her past which she has been projecting onto the present situation. She may still need to express some resentment or make some demands directly on other group members in the immediate situation, and this session will probably enable her to do this in a clearer and stronger way.

This example also shows something which often happens during 'talking to the cushion': Christine got in touch with a situation from her past. In our experience, where a woman explores fully the dialogue between the topdog and the underdog inside her, it often emerges that the scolding topdog is talking like one of her parents. As children we absorb and internalise our parents' controls and instructions and often we walk round as adults with these instructions still playing like tape-recorded messages inside our heads. The voice inside us which says: 'Control yourself', 'Be sensible', 'Don't be so dirty', 'Try harder', 'Don't be selfish' or other such phrases, is usually the internalised voice of one or both of our parents. Talking to cushions can be a useful method for identifying, acting out, and answering back this internalised parent voice. Here's an example:

Wendy says she is feeling depressed about herself because she keeps doing stupid things and generally making a mess of her life. The group put a cushion in front of her and suggest that she talks to herself. She starts and fairly quickly her depression changes to annoyance and then to anger at herself for being so hopeless and incompetent: 'Wendy, you're a real mess. You're completely *hopeless*. You're really incompetent!'

After a while a woman in the group asks 'Are you talking like anyone you know?' and Wendy replies, 'Yes, my father! He was always putting me down like this, telling me I was stupid and not competent enough.'

She then swaps roles and plays the underdog child: sullen, resentful, not daring to answer back. She develops the dialogue, swapping roles several times between the bullying father and the child voice inside her. The other group members encourage the 'child' to answer back: 'He won't hear you if you mumble!', 'He just told you that you're a failure. What are you going to answer to that?', 'Try looking at him and repeating that louder!', 'Take a deep breath and say it again!' They help the 'child' to avoid excuses and to find the one single important message which she wants to get over to the father. Eventually this emerges as 'No!' Wendy becomes very angry and shouts 'NO! NO! NO!' at the 'father' cushion. At this point she stops and asks for another group member to sit on the 'father' cushion and to carry on repeating several of the stock phrases her father used: 'Try harder!', 'You're so incompetent!', 'Don't be so stupid!' This helps her to go into, and explore, the child's rebellion while keeping a sense of what she is up against. She continues to shout loudly and starts to bang a cushion hard with her fists. (Lifting your arms right back over your head to take a good swipe opens up your breathing and develops the feeling.) Eventually she is physically exhausted. The woman playing the father had noticed Wendy tiring and had faded out the father's voice, letting the child 'win'. At the end Wendy says she feels very good and would like now to curl up in Ruth's arms and rest quietly for a while. The next day she has a bad sore throat. Although she had released her emotions from her stomach, her throat had still been slightly tensed against fully expressing the feelings in sound. It often happens that when tension is released in one area it highlights tension in another part of the body, showing how much our bodies do operate as a whole organism.

Notice that group members used techniques like repetition and breathing – which we describe in Chapter One – to help Wendy stay with a feeling and express it more fully. Knowing when to suggest that a person switches roles comes with practice. In general, it is good to stay put when one role is very fluent or emotionally strong, and switch over when the woman working is stuck, has nothing to say, or has said something which seems to need answering.

In our last example a woman in the group acted the role of Wendy's father to help her develop the dialogue. This kind of role-playing is similar to Psychodrama; she repeated certain phrases which Wendy had given as typical of her father. There are other techniques for group members to become more actively involved in helping a dialogue along by intervening and suggesting words and phrases. One of these techniques is called 'May I feed you a sentence?' If at some point during the dialogue Wendy seemed to be implying an attitude or message which she was not explicitly stating, a group member might touch her shoulder and say 'May I feed you a sentence? Say it and see how it feels.' For example, one might feed a line to her father: 'I am disappointed in all my children'. Wendy can use the sentence if it helps her dialogue forward, or discard it if it does not seem to fit. Feeding lines to, or playing the part of an 'adversary' like Wendy's father, might not at first seem very appealing. Thoughts like 'I couldn't act Wendy's father, I'm much too nice', 'Wendy might start to hate me if I act like him' and so on, often discourage us from stepping in to play 'unpleasant' roles for one another when it would be helpful. In fact, there is very often a woman in the group who could actually play such a part very well (possibly because she had a similar father herself) and who might learn something about herself by helping Wendy in this way. Though she might be afraid of appearing in a bad light, she would actually be giving Wendy much more positive help by playing the bossy father than by sitting quietly in the group and acting 'nice'.

This example was of an explosive session, where Wendy starts to challenge the still-powerful control of her father in a very physical and emotional way. Another woman might go through the same process differently, simply repeating one sentence several times. Each woman will find her own way. What is important is that she makes an emotional connection and *feels* what she is saying, otherwise she may go on talking or shouting at cushions for months without getting any freer of the parental voice. It is usually possible to tell when a woman is not connecting emotionally: she may sound unconvincing and other group members may find themselves getting listless or bored while she works.

This process of confronting the internalised parent is very important for women, and can help free us to make our own choices about how we want to live. It is particularly necessary because in our relationships with men we are often expected to carry on acting the submissive 'child' role. Hogie Wyckoff of the Berkeley Radical Psychiatry Group has emphasised how much we can gain by finding the child's strength to rebel against the parent voice:

This internalised oppression I have called the Pig Parent. It is the incorpo- ration of all the values which keep women subordinate – messages saying, for example, that she musn't outdo a man, she must be humble (i.e. not love herself), she must take care of others first, she must not be angry or bitchy . . . Women are oppressed in their Natural Child; they don't feel safe enough in the world to do whatever they feel like doing . . . they look to others to see if it's O.K. to do certain things rather than just trusting their guts and doing what feels good. When women nurture themselves, use their intelligence, trust their intuitions, and don't listen to their Pig Parent, they can act purely in behalf of what their Natural Child wants, which is their core – their center. We women can be truly powerful when we are in touch with this part of ourselves. Then we can know the truth of what feels right and what doesn't, what hurts and oppresses us, what causes us joy, fulfillment, or righteous anger.[9]

The terminology which Hogie Wyckoff uses here derives from a radical use of Transactional Analysis,[10] but can be applied in this context to the Gestalt methods for exploring parent/child conflicts.

When we are first finding the voice of our 'natural child' we often find anger, as Wendy did. Often we need to express some of the rage which we suppressed as children. But it is important to recognise this anger as part of a process. It would not be helpful for Wendy to assume that this was the last word on what she felt about her father. Nor would it be helpful for her to catch the first train home to tell her ageing father about her anger and dump on him her stormy feelings about how he behaved during her childhood. It is important not to get locked into childhood anger or to get stuck in the role of the angry child who is as bound up with her parents as the submissive child. The theory is that by exploring the roles of parent and child, and expressing some of our suppressed feelings from the past, we can actually clear ourselves of that past situation and *grow up*. The conflict between parent and child is defused, the personality can integrate and emerge as an adult. If we are truly autonomous from our parents we no longer need to expend a lot of rage on their behalf, but can use that energy to take clear and effective action in the present, living the lives we want. If we are autonomous, we can also allow ourselves to look at our parents' lives and actions with compassion. It can be surprising to learn that if we give full expression to our anger and resentment, we can begin to appreciate how much our parents were able to give us.

Working through the parent/child conflict to reach the 'adult' is, again, very important for women. We are not encouraged to develop into mature adults capable of being independent and acting in our own interests. We are encouraged to play a nurturing mother role, but not to become adults in our own right. As Hogie Wyckoff points out, women's groups are an excellent place for us to practise being 'adult' in a powerful way: we get support to use our skills and intelligence and have the opportunity to experience and respect the intelligence of other women.[11]

A powerful weapon used by many parents is guilt and, again, Gestalt techniques can be helpful to deal with this. As women we are particularly liable to carry guilt around with us much of our lives. The high standards of love, caring and service which we are expected to live up to as daughters, wives and mothers leave many of us feeling inadequate and guilty. One of the positive aspects of the Gestalt approach is a fairly dismissive attitude to guilt. Whereas Freudian psychology suggests that guilt is complicated, deeply instilled in us and inevitable, Gestalt therapy sees guilt much more simply: as projected resentment. As Perls put it, 'Whenever you feel guilty, find out what you resent and the guilt will vanish.'[12] Perls believed that unexpressed resentments are among the worst possible unfinished 'gestalts', and that expressing resentment is one of the most effective ways to make our lives more tolerable. Expressing resentment is more taboo for women than for men. Traditionally we are expected to love and serve ungrudgingly; the result often is that our resentment comes out in indirect ways, in 'cattiness' or withdrawal, which badly affect our lives and relationships. Letting out resentment directly can have quite a disruptive effect on our lives too when it is done without control, but using cushions is a safe way to become aware of what we actually feel, then to find ways of expressing it more directly.

A word of reservation about the cushion technique: when it does not work properly it can sometimes lapse into long and over-verbal dialogues with little release of feelings. It is important to watch for this and if necessary to encourage a person to repeat one simple phrase many times, or even make sounds rather than words, to help her connect with the feelings behind the words. She could be encouraged to combine the sounds with movements: cushions can be cuddled, strangled, trampled, thrown outside the door or whatever feels right to the woman concerned. Sometimes using a cushion at all can seem inappropriate or unnecessary if a person's emotions are ready to be expressed in a straightforward way. Maybe she just wants to cry for a while and it will not be helpful to put a cushion in front of her to talk to.

WORKING ON BLOCKS AND RESISTANCES

The process of learning to explore emotions is not easy and often the first material which comes up consists of the resistances which we use to stop ourselves feeling or expressing things. This happens in any therapy, but it sometimes seems especially depressing in a self-help situation where you can start feeling stuck and hopeless: 'We'll never get beyond this silence . . .', 'We'll never manage to break through into doing "proper therapy" . . .'

In fact, working on the blocks themselves is extremely valuable and Gestalt provides useful techniques for this. Some very basic principles are:

To stay with awareness of the body ('What is happening in your body now?')
To stay in the present ('What are you feeling now this minute?')
To realise that *everything* is material which can be used in the therapy process

As Fritz Perls says, even if you say you feel 'nothing', that nothingness has a shape 'which if you examine it still further has a very positive character like numbness, or coldness, or a gap'.[13]

Many of the examples we give in this book make therapy seem easy and flowing, but frequently it goes more like this:

June tells the group she is upset but is not sure whether she wants any help or attention from the group. She is clearly disturbed and the others do not feel they can ignore her and carry on with something else. There are long silences. Eventually June agrees to take some time to sort out what she is feeling, but does not know where to start. She doesn't talk much and the others find it hard to get any sense of what is upsetting her. More long silences . . .

The following Gestalt techniques are those we have found useful in a situation like this, to help June explore what is blocking her.

Body Awareness
The use of the so-called 'awareness continuum' is basis to Gestalt therapy. It operates through questions like:

'What are you experiencing in your body now?'
'I feel cold. I feel tense.'
'Where do you feel tense?'
'In the back of my neck, and my mouth feels dry.'
'Are you aware of what your eyes are doing?'
'Looking down so that I don't have to look at anyone.'
'Are you aware of how you are breathing?'

This is an effective way of guiding a person to the bedrock of her physical experiences, and away from explanations, fantasies or numbness. It is useful whether she seems to be talking too much in a way which may sound rational but which is disconnected from her feelings, or whether she is not talking at all. Body awareness is central, and almost all the techniques given below are aspects of it.

Using 'I' not 'It'
June makes remarks like:

'My hands are jittering nervously'
'I feel a compulsion to get up and walk out of the group'
'The atmosphere feels very explosive'

She would be encouraged to rephrase these remarks so she takes responsibility for what she is experiencing:

'Can you say "*I* am jittering nervously"?'
'Can you talk as if you were the compulsion: "*I*'ve got to leave the group"?'
'Can you say "*I* feel very explosive"?'

Rephrasing the remarks this way will help June to connect more directly with her feelings.

Exaggeration
June might be tapping her leg lightly with her finger. She would be asked to exaggerate this and it might develop into hitting her leg really hard as she gets in touch with some frustration she is feeling, expressed indirectly through the tapping.

Or, one member of the group notices that she keeps blinking her eyes and asks her to exaggerate this action. June frequently blinks and finally screws up her eyes altogether. 'What is it you don't want to see?' the group ask, and June realises that it is a painful situation which is upsetting her but which she has been avoiding recognising or sharing with the group.

This technique works equally well whether it is a purely physical action which is exaggerated, or whether it is a statement or attitude which the person is communicating to the group. For example, June, after a while, might say to the group 'I don't know why you're bothering trying to help me. I'm just hopeless, I can't get into anything . . .'

With this sentence she shakes her arms in a despairing shrug. She is encouraged to repeat the phrase and exaggerate the movement several times so that her whole body is involved in showing the group her attitude of hopelessness. This might put her in touch with a feeling of despair which she has been holding back and she might start to cry. Or a group member might ask her 'What situations do you feel hopeless in?', or 'Who makes you feel hopeless?', which might bring up more material to work with. Or a person in the group might observe that she really seems to enjoy being hopeless and might ask her 'What do you get out of being hopeless?' or 'What are you avoiding by being hopeless?' 'I avoid being angry', June perhaps replies, and this could lead into exploring anger which she has been keeping down under the 'hopelessness'.

Doing the Opposite

If June is sitting in a way which is tense and hunched up, she might be encouraged to exaggerate the tension to an extreme, or she might be encouraged to do the exact opposite:

'Try sitting the opposite way to how you are now.'
'That would be completely opened up . . . like this . . .'
'How do you feel in this new position?'
'Very vulnerable . . .'

The group might then ask June in which parts of her body she feels vulnerable, or what she feels vulnerable to or scared of, which might help her bring more of her feelings to awareness. Again this technique also works for exploring the opposite of a *phrase* or *attitude*: a person who claims to feel shy may be asked to play the part of being an exhibitionist; a person who claims to feel sure and determined (but doesn't sound it) may be asked to play the part of a very unsure and hesitant person. This helps her to get in touch with a part of herself she has been submerging, or with feelings she was covering up.

Making Dialogues

Another way in which June could explore any small body movements she is making would be for her to make a dialogue between two body parts. For example, perhaps she keeps putting her hand up to her brow. Another group member notices this, asks her if she is aware of it, and suggests that she transforms what is going on between the hand and the brow into a dialogue. It might go something like this:

June: Well, my hand is kind of saying 'Oh dear . . . Calm down . . .'
Tina: What is your brow saying?
June: My brow feels hot and bothered . . .
Tina: Can you speak *as if you were* the brow – '*I* feel hot and bothered . . .?'
June: I feel hot and bothered . . . I feel like I'm going to burst . . .
Tina: What does your hand say back? Can you keep the dialogue going a bit?

June: The hand says, 'Oh, don't burst, keep calm, calm down . . .' and the brow says, 'God, I feel really desperate, I can't stand it . . .'

Tina: Can you repeat that a few times – 'I feel really desperate . . .'

June: I feel really desperate . . . I feel really desperate . . . I feel DESPER-ATE . . .

At this point, June might start to tremble slightly and Tina might encourage her to let go into the trembling and see if any words came with it. This kind of dialogue might happen between one foot and the other (for example, if it is squashing the other down), between a tense stomach and a smiling face, between hunched shoulders and a pounding heart, and so on, depending on how June is expressing herself physically.

Even Nothing Has a Shape

As it becomes clear from these techniques, when you follow the Gestalt approach of dealing with awareness, *everything* is material to work with. June might say she feels 'numb' but if she were asked to speak as if she were the 'numbness' she might begin, 'I'm grey and closed in, I can't hear anything . . .', and already she is recognising and communicating a lot about how she experiences herself.

If she said 'I can't focus on anything that's happening in the group. I just keep staring at that matchbox on the floor', she could be encouraged to speak as the matchbox: 'I'm empty, I've been used up and thrown away'. Even a matchbox can throw light on what she is feeling.

If she said 'I can't say anything, I feel this pain inside me like a huge block and I don't want to open it up', she could be encouraged to act the pain. She might curl up into a tight ball and when the group ask her if the pain needs anything, she might say it needs to be cradled. (The group could rock her gently and gradually she might be able to uncurl.) What at first seemed to be a block or sticking point can actually lead to June being able to ask for something she needs and to receive loving support from the group. If June had said she couldn't express any feelings because of the group watching her, she might be encouraged to speak 'as the group': 'We're the group, and we're watching you, June, and we're feeling critical . . .' This might help June to own feelings which she is projecting onto the group, imagining they were being critical when in fact she was feeling critical of herself. Or she might be able to check out what people in the group were actually feeling. Whatever comes up in this way can be used. Even a refusal to follow a suggestion like the one above can be turned to good account.

June: I can't speak as the group. I can't pretend I'm the group. I'm not like other people in the group.

Tina: How are you not like the other people? Tell us what you're not.

June: I'm not superior and calm like you all are.
Tina: What else are you not?
June: I'm not confident . . . I'm not critical.
Tina: Can you say that again?
June: I'm not critical. I'm not critical.
Sarah: Does that feel right? Could you try saying the opposite?
June: I'm critical. I'm critical. (*Laughs*) Yes, I am, I'm really critical.
Sarah: You just criticised all of us.
June: Yes, and I criticise myself the whole time.
Tina: What do you criticise yourself for?

And so it could continue.

Stay with It

Often when a woman has expressed a difficult feeling she will rush on to talk about something else. It is good to stop her at this point, even if it means interrupting her, to ask her to 'stay with' the feeling. She may recognise that she is trying to avoid something. Perls believed that if you make a conscious effort to dismiss a feeling or 'sort it out' by a rational computer-like process, you complicate things and make them worse. If you try to avoid a feeling it doesn't go away but hangs around to prevent you from fully feeling anything else. You cannot overcome a feeling by resisting it, only by going deeper into it. So a commonly used Gestalt technique is to say, 'Can you stay with this feeling?', especially when a person has referred to a state of mind or body which is unpleasant and which they would like to dispel.

Often this involves staying with a feeling of frustration, of being blocked, of discouragement, or of confusion. As Perls put it: 'If you become aware each time that you are entering a state of confusion, this is the therapeutic thing. And again, nature takes over. If you understand this, and stay with confusion, *confusion will sort itself out by itself*.'[14] This is a reflection of Perls' confidence in the natural properties of our organisms and his wariness of the way we can use our 'rational' mind against ourselves. Most of the techniques given above are different ways of 'staying with' a present mood, movement or sensation in the body, exploring the various perceptions and fantasies which accompany it.

What we have found helpful in this method of focusing on body awareness and 'staying with it' is that it is immediate and simple. It does not take a lot of knowledge or expertise, only sensitivity, to be aware of this body language. As Perls describes it:

Everything a person wants to express is all there – not in words. What we say is mostly either lies or bullshit. But the voice is there, the gesture, the posture, the facial expression, the psychosomatic language. It's all there

... if you use your eyes and ears, then you see that everyone expresses himself in one way or another ... Gestalt therapy is being in touch with the obvious.[15]

SOME RESERVATIONS ABOUT GESTALT THERAPY

We have emphasised here certain aspects of Gestalt therapy which have seemed most relevant to women and to self-help therapy situations. There are other aspects, including very interesting work on dreams which we will treat fully in Chapter Six. But this school of therapy also has unhelpful aspects and limitations which must be mentioned.

Although Gestalt theory does have a vague critique of Western society, social factors are rarely included in the practice of Gestalt therapy. It is very helpful using cushions to own disowned parts of ourselves, to reclaim projections which we have put onto others, to realise that we are more powerful than we thought; but there is also a danger of seeing everything as projection, which could begin to make us feel that 'it's all in our heads', or 'it's all my problem'. Perls' motto 'I do my thing and you do your thing' is all very well, but if 'your thing' oppresses me then I will have to act to confront and change it. While conflicts usually *are* fogged with projection, there are also real issues of conflict of interest between people which Perls does not adequately recognise. For this reason it is useful to supplement a Gestalt approach with the understandings of someone like Wilhelm Reich who argued that after exploring our 'irrational' feelings and emotions from the past, which we bring into the present in an inappropriate way, we will be left with a clearer and stronger awareness of our *actual* situation and of who really is oppressing us so that we can then go out and act to change that situation. Recently developed radical and feminist therapy also recognise that the external world may give us good reason to feel bad, and it certainly is not 'all in our heads'. Perls offers no such positive link between therapy and social or political action, and yet our increased awareness, our new-found resentment or self-expression will not be easy to reconcile with the largely restrictive and hierarchical capitalist society in which we live.

Similarly, in dealing with childhood and our past, Perls points out ways in which we choose to hold onto the past to stop ourselves from having to take responsibility for being adult and living fully in the present. But we have often felt that he underestimates the power of conditioning and social pressures on us, past and present, to *make* us behave a certain way. It *is* helpful to focus on what is happening now, and to learn to take responsibility for ourselves in the present, but we have found that to do this we often need to spend some time thoroughly exploring our past. In doing this, we have found regression work and the ideas of Freud much more useful than Perls would suggest. There are times when delving into the past and reliving childhood situations seem a crucial part of our process of self-discovery and development. Each woman may need a different approach at different times, depending on her situation. As with all the therapy approaches we discuss, it's a question of taking from Gestalt what is helpful to us, making it our own, and developing it or combining it with other approaches to fit our sense of what we need.

Another difficulty we have with Gestalt therapy is its celebration of Fritz Perls. We have quoted Perls here, but sometimes the personality cult surrounding him and the 'showman' aspect of his work have made us feel unreceptive to his ideas. Predictably, he has little grasp of the particular situation of women. Here is one small but typical example. In one of his workshops he heavily criticised a woman who requested a light for her cigarette when she was carrying her own matches. He labelled her as someone who manipulates the environment for support and refused to work with her.[16] In a feminist group we would also confront a woman who behaves in this way, but with a compassion which comes from understanding that most of us have been raised to think it 'womanly' to depend on men for support in certain practical areas, and either undesirable or impossible for us to support ourselves. We did not choose our upbringing. Changing these patterns is an important struggle, but doesn't happen immediately.

Finally, Gestalt has very little to say about the group process. In our experience, where a group of people are doing therapy together the relationships between them will invariably come up at some point and affect what happens in the group: who feels safe to explore feelings, who is silent, and so on. Issues like warmth and hostility, competition, leadership, conflicts of interest, may need to be brought into the open and dealt with, and for help with this it is necessary to look away from Gestalt to one of the other therapy methods such as Encounter.

HOW TO FIND OUT MORE ABOUT GESTALT THERAPY

In many Western countries there are trained Gestalt therapists and institutions or centres which offer individual therapy or groups under the broad heading of Gestalt. In individual work, Gestalt does not focus intensively on the relationship with the therapist as some other therapies do. The workshop format, where a group of people come together for an intensive weekend of therapy, is typical for Gestalt and usually leads to a powerful opening up of emotions. The emphasis can vary as some therapists are more involved with the bodywork aspect of Gestalt, others more with dreams and symbolism, or with enabling a strong emotional release. Also, increasingly, therapists and group leaders include Gestalt as one of a battery of different techniques at their disposal, which they will choose between as the situation demands. In several countries it is possible to find feminist therapists working in Gestalt. For developing your own knowledge of Gestalt to use on a self-help basis we list at the end of this chapter some books which can be helpful. The techniques are suitable and accessible to being learned in this way.

EST

We want to mention briefly a form of therapy called 'est' (Erhardt Seminar Training) which has recently become popular. Est, with its emphasis on taking responsibility for your life and being fully present in the 'here and now', seems a direct descendant of Gestalt with an added dose of Zen and Scientology. Like Perls, the est trainers use the large workshop format: the initial 'training' consists of two weekend workshops attended by over 200 people. A workshop of this size creates an intense 'pressure-cooker' effect and dramatic changes can be made in people's lives. Other pressures – such as being shouted at by the (usually male) trainer, not smoking, eating or not going to the lavatory for long stretches of time – also undoubtedly wear down resistances and speed up the 'breakthroughs' which occur in the training. We have not experienced est ourselves. It seems that the techniques used are skilful and effective, but we doubt whether a therapy which involves being insulted and humiliated can lead to a genuine growth of confidence and self-esteem. We feel wary of any therapy which charges – as est does – exorbitant fees on the basis that if you want it badly enough you will find the money to pay for it. We also feel wary of any school of therapy which claims to be the only effective therapy there is. 'Big bang' therapy has a place, but our experience suggests very strongly that breakthroughs are valuable only if they are followed up and consolidated in a long-term way.

SOME EXERCISES BASED ON GESTALT

43 Talking to the Cushion

This is a simple structure to get used to the idea of talking to a cushion. You can do it on your own in your room, or in pairs, or in a group taking a turn of ten or fifteen minutes each round the circle. With a cushion in front of you, imagine putting on it a person or thing about which you feel unresolved. Now talk to it, allowing yourself to do something physical to the cushion if you feel like it: hug it or hit it, put it closer or further away. After a while, if you feel like changing sides to answer back, try that. Here are some ideas about who to try talking to, which Anne Kent Rush suggests:[17]

your mother	someone you are jealous of
your current mate	someone you feel afraid of

your boss	someone you hate
your father	someone you love but are afraid to tell
your sister	anyone you admire
your house	your femininity
	your sexuality

It can also be useful to try talking to your child, whether she is in your belly, has been aborted, an imaginary child you cannot decide whether to conceive, or a child you already have. In the case of the latter, it is good to let yourself really get into the part of your child and also to experiment with responding to her in ways you would normally censor: 'No!', 'Shut up!', 'I hate you!', are more safely released onto a cushion than left to explode in real life.

You can also put on the cushion, and have a dialogue with, any habit or addiction which gives you a problem, such as alcohol, food, drugs, or cigarettes: 'Drink, you attract me but you're no good for me', to which the drink might reply, 'You need me, I cheer you up when nothing else does', and so on. Or you can try personifying an issue such as money, sleeplessness, or old age which you have difficulty coming to terms with.

44 Dependence vs Independence

This exercise involves the whole group moving around. It will probably work best if you feel easy with one another and have done warming-up exercises to raise the energy level in the group.

Start by sitting for a few minutes with your eyes shut, breathe fully and think about the themes of dependence and independence in your life. Picture these two sides of yourself and decide whether you experience yourself primarily as dependent or independent.

Divide the room in half. The 'dependent' people go to one end of the room, the 'independent' people to the other end. Really let yourself go into the role: the dependent people might curl up on the floor under a blanket, suck thumbs, call for someone to look after them. The independent people might dance, jump or march up and down loudly telling everyone how strong they are. The people on the two sides of the room can try relating to one another, and people can change sides at any point when they feel they want to explore the opposite role. After five minutes you could suggest that everyone tries changing roles. Let this exercise run for about ten or fifteen minutes in all, so that people can explore the roles at leisure in movement, sound and feeling.

Afterwards share what you experienced, what you found easy or difficult, what patterns you became aware of which crop up in your daily life.

The idea of this exercise, as with much of the Gestalt work, is that by exploring and exaggerating opposites you can eventually arrive at a more integrated middle point: in this case, perhaps having a sense of your own strength while still allowing yourself to need others.

The same structure can be used to act out other contradictory roles, such as aggressive and passive, 'female' and 'male', happy and sad, failure and success. Or if you want to explore power relationships within your group, you could try exaggerating the roles of those who are most often the 'helpers' of others, and those who are 'helped' ('I'm strong and competent and don't admit my own problems', 'I don't have to take any responsibility'). In this way you might be helped to arrive at a balanced point of taking more equal roles in running the group, giving and receiving help from one another.

45 Parts of My Body I Like and Dislike

This is a good exercise for exploring feelings about your body. You can do it in turns around the group, taking up to ten minutes each.

Sit comfortably, shut your eyes and tune in to your body. Let your awareness move to a part of your body you like, and to a part which you dislike. Notice what it is you like and dislike in each case. Be aware of the history of each body part, of any memories it may be carrying. Allow plenty of time, then open your eyes.

Now speak aloud as the two body parts, starting with the dislike, for example: 'I'm Penny's hands. We're rough and scaly and clumsy. We have a scar here from being cut with a breadknife as a child. We're strong but very ugly . . .'

After the dislike, speak as the liked part, for example: 'I'm Penny's eyes. I see beautifully clearly. We're not very large, but we are alive and sparkling and sometimes we really make contact with other people . . .'

When each person has had a turn, take time for feedback and discussion of what has come up: 'I've noticed your eyes in the past', 'I was aware of avoiding choosing my genitals', 'I realised how much of my body I dislike'.

A variation of this, which can be helpful at the start of a session, is to speak as the most *tense* part, and then as the most *relaxed* part of the body. This helps people to share any tension or fear they are bringing to the group, as well as the positive relaxed energy they have to give, and may bring up material which could be worked on more fully in the group.

Another way of extending the exercise is to have each person say what that part of their body needs ('My eyes need to be touched', 'My hands need to hold something really strongly and tightly') and to see if you can give that to one another in the group.

You can also use this structure to give a voice to a part of your body which is or has been in pain, for example, speaking as your migraine, your cystitis or your womb. This can help to explore the source of a physical ailment and what messages it may be sending to the rest of your body.

46   Dialogue between Body Parts

This exercise helps you to be more aware of how different parts of your body dominate or conflict within the delicate balance of your whole organism. It takes at least ten minutes for each person to make the dialogue. You can do it in pairs or in turns round a group.

Choose which will be the two body parts in your dialogue. Some areas of your body may call your attention or you could choose a pair like: right hand and left hand; the top and bottom half of your body; your genitals and the rest of you; your eyes and your feet; your pregnant belly and the rest of you; the most tense part and the least tense part; your stomach and your brain.

Close your eyes and tune in to the chosen areas, noticing any sensations or memories.

Open your eyes and take a cushion for each part. Develop the dialogue moving from one cushion to the other as you change roles. Let each part start by describing itself: 'I'm Jane's stomach. I'm soft and plump. I feel squashed into these tight trousers'. It may help to touch the part of your body which is 'speaking'. Stay with your spontaneous feelings, don't worry about what you *think* your stomach would say, but let it to the talking. Now let it state what it feels about the other body part. Look directly at the cushion you are speaking to, and address it by name, 'Feet, you're beautiful to look at but I'm worried about where you might take me if I let myself follow you.'

Afterwards allow time for feedback about what you felt and noticed during the exercises.

47   Resentment and Appreciation

This exercise is useful for giving practice in speaking out your resentments and making demands for what you want. It also reveals the good feelings which often underly resentments, which cannot be expressed because of the resentments blocking the way.

Individually: One person can do this exercise alone, or you can do it in turns round the group.

Place a cushion in front of you. Imagine someone on it who is close to you: friend, lover or relative. Then, using their name, say, 'Joan, I resent . . .' and repeating this phrase tell this person all the things you resent in them. Try to really communicate with them so that you feel they are listening to what you say.

Once the resentments are finished, it is time to move on to the *demands* which Perls believes lie behind every resentment. Speaking directly to the person as before, bring out the demands you want to make of her, giving them as commands, not 'I wish you would . . .' but 'Go away! . . .', 'Do this! . . .', 'Take more notice of . . .'

When you have finished go back to the resentments and try to remember exactly what you resented in this person. Now replace the word 'resent' with 'appreciate' and repeat everything you said before, this time as 'Joan, I appreciate . . .' Then go on to tell the person what else you appreciate in them. Again, try to feel you are actually communicating with her.

Neither the resentments nor the demands have to be what you would normally consider 'rational' or 'reasonable'. For example, you might tell a small child 'Don't wake in the night!' or a husband 'Don't go out to work!' The aim is to uncover your own feelings and wants, and you can then decide how to act on them in practice.

Once the structure of the exercise is familiar, you can use it in a number of situations. For example, a woman might want to use it to explore what she resents and appreciates in herself, or in her job, or in the group.

In a pair: A variation of this exercise is useful for revealing games and loosening stuck patterns in the relationship of two people who are present who may be close friends, lovers or marriage partners.[18]

Sit comfortably facing each other on the floor, and take it in turns to say sentences starting with, 'I resent you for . . .'

After several minutes, move on to 'What I appreciate in you is . . .'

Continuing to alternate, move on to 'I spite you by . . .' then 'I am compliant by . . .'

Allow several minutes for each theme. Finally move on to 'I discover . . .'

Having cleared 'unfinished business' during the first part of the exercise, the partners sometimes feel that they are really seeing each other for the first time.

Gestalt theory stresses how in close relationships we often project our fantasies onto the other person and we need to learn to distinguish between our images and the flesh and blood person, recognising that we cannot transform her to fit our fantasies.

Separation or death: Another variation can be helpful when you have just separated from a lover, or if a parent or friend has died.

Sit with a cushion in front of you and imagine placing this person on it. Looking directly at the cushion and addressing the person by name, start with your resentments towards them, 'Father, I resent the fact you never talked to me . . .'

When these are finished, move on to appreciations, 'Father, I appreciate your sense of humour . . .'

When both resentments and appreciations are finished, try to say goodbye: 'Goodbye, father'. Repeat this several times and try to let yourself feel you are really letting go of the person. It can be helpful to say goodbye in turn to each of the good and bad qualities you have mentioned. *This exercise can be distressing* but also can lead to real acceptance of a difficult or important loss.

Resentments often keep us holding on to past relationships, and it can be hard to admit that we hold resentments against the dead, some of which seem very irrational: 'Father, I resent the fact you died and left me and mother alone.'

At the end of a group session: Gestalt groups often end with each person saying in turn who or what they have resented during the session:

'I resent the way you interrupted me . . .'
'I resent the fact that I didn't get any attention . . .'
followed by their appreciations:
'I appreciate the suggestions you made . . .'
'I appreciated your courage while you were working . . .'

This is one way of clearing up 'unfinished business' which can be destructive if it is left unsaid at the end of a session, though sometimes we have found that giving strong resentments at the end of a session when people have no space to deal with hurt feelings can be destructive too. Some reassurance should be given that the group will deal with this hurt the next time.

48 Action Replay
This exercise can help to resolve a difficult or painful incident from the past. It can be done individually, or a whole group can do it simultaneously while one person reads the instructions aloud. Allow several minutes pause at the gaps.

Sit comfortably and do some relaxing breathing to centre yourself . . . Go back in your memory to a recent or distant incident in your life which involved conflict. Replay it in your mind as it happened, recalling every detail of what took place and how you felt . . .

Now replay the incident again and imagine a new ending in which you change your response to the incident. If in the actual situation you kept silent, imagine yourself speaking. If you left, imagine yourself staying. Picture yourself behaving differently, imagine what the response of others in the situation would have been, and how you would have felt . . .

Now let yourself explore what other possible alternatives there were in this past situation . . .

Afterwards, share your experience of the exercise in pairs or in the group.

This exercise can be used for re-running a childhood situation (for example, imagining answering back to a parent instead of clamming up) or a recent conflict at work or painful episode in a relationship. It helps you to see that you did have an alternative and it can give you a sense of power in a situation where you felt helpless. If you chose a childhood situation it can help to look for patterns which you continue in your adult life, like holding anger back when you don't need to, or not asking for things because you're afraid of not getting them.

Another variation of this exercise is one which is also sometimes used as a theatre training game in 'emotional recall'. In this version you do not change the ending. One person simply sits, recalls a powerful, important or painful experience in her life, which may be an emotional blow or a racist attack, and recounts it to the rest of the group. She should tell the episode in the present tense as if it was happening now, and as the purpose of the exercise is to learn to reconnect with buried feelings it is crucial that the group help her to keep in touch with her emotions in the episode. They should watch out for a flat, dull tone of voice and help her to stay tuned by breathing fully; have her, repeat phrases or sounds which seem potent, and ask her how she feels at different points. This exercise is very simple but has seemed helpful: a woman who peed on the classroom floor at the age of nine finds that retelling the incident to a sympathetic audience clears away much of the shame attached to the incident; a woman who was raped two years previously retells the painful experience and finds that she need no longer blank the whole incident out as she is now more able to deal with what happened. You can also use this technique to re-experience and better understand a recent incident where an addiction such as food or alcohol took you over.

49 Talking Clothes[19]

Many feminists are looking at clothes in a new way, not as a disguise to make us conform to feminine stereotypes or look attractive to men, but as a vehicle for expressing our own moods and qualities. This exercise can help you realise what aspects of yourself your clothes express.

Shut your eyes and think of the article of clothing you are wearing which you feel most in tune with and comfortable in. Be aware of its qualities, shape and colour.

Now open your eyes and speak to a partner, or to the group, as if you were that item of clothing. 'I'm Sally's trousers. I'm workable and tough. Also a bit outrageous . . .' Take turns to do this and at the end share to what extent you are aware of those qualities as part of yourself.

A variation is to talk in turns round the group about the piece of clothing you thought most about putting on, or about the items you are wearing which you most and least like. In each case describe what the garment says about you.

NOTES

1   Frederick S. Perls, *Gestalt Therapy Verbatim*, Real People Press, Lafayette, 1969; Bantam Books, New York, 1971, p 1.
2   Miriam Polster in Violet Franks & Vasanti Burtle (eds), *Women in Therapy*, Brunner/Mazel, New York, 1974, p 261.
3   *Gestalt Therapy Verbatim*, p 17.
4   *Gestalt Therapy Verbatim*, p 4.
5   *Gestalt Therapy Verbatim*, p 3.
6   *Gestalt Therapy Verbatim*, p 6.
7   *Gestalt Therapy Verbatim*, p 6.
8   Miriam Polster in *Women in Therapy*, p 249.
9   Hogie Wyckoff in Claude Steiner (ed), *Readings in Radical Psychiatry*, Grove Press, New York, 1975, pp 90, 92.
10 We describe this method more fully in Chapter Eight.
11 *Readings in Radical Psychiatry*, p 91.
12 *Gestalt Therapy Verbatim*, p 51.
13 *Gestalt Therapy Verbatim*, p 14.
14 *Gestalt Therapy Verbatim*, pp 25–6.
15 *Gestalt Therapy Verbatim*, pp 57–8.
16 *Gestalt Therapy Verbatim*, pp 137–8.
17 Anne Kent Rush, *Getting Clear: Body Work for Women*, Random House, New York, and The Bookworks, Berkeley, 1973; Wildwood House, London, 1974, p 54. This book contains several other useful Gestalt exercises.
18 Joen Fagan & Irma Lee Shepherd (eds), *Gestalt Therapy Now*, Science & Behavior Books, Palo Alto, 1970; Penguin, Harmondsworth, 1972, p 173.
19 This exercise was devised by Marie Maguire and Lucy Goodison of the Red Therapy group for their 'Clothes and Self-Image' workshops at the Women's Therapy Centre, London.

FURTHER READING

Gestalt Therapy Verbatim (see above) gives gripping taped examples of Gestalt therapy at work and several lectures by Perls outlining Gestalt ideas.

Muriel Schiffman, *Gestalt Self Therapy*, Self Therapy Press, 340 Santa Monica Avenue, Menlo Park, CA 94025, USA, 1971. Offers a detailed practical description of how to start doing Gestalt self-help therapy at home alone.

Gestalt Therapy Now (see above) is an interesting collection of essays including some readable theory and illuminating case histories of patients treated by Gestalt therapists. Dr Laura Perls contributes a short but powerful interview.

John O. Stevens, *Awareness: exploring experimenting experiencing*, Real People Press, 1971; Bantam Books, New York, 1973. Contains dozens of Gestalt-based exercises from which to choose those relevant to your need or situation.

Chapter Four
Face to Face: Encountering Each Other

I walk into my friend's flat to visit her and find that her sitting-room is full of people I don't know: immediately I am aware of strong feelings that I have about people I've never met before. I take an instant dislike to one woman who is dominating the conversation and feel warm towards another who is listening intently. I have a fleeting image of myself sitting down next to the second woman, resting my head on her shoulder and then telling the first woman to shut up. Of course I don't do either of these things: the strength of my response to these strangers seems quite inappropriate and is only momentary. I push the feelings aside and try to concentrate on the verbal content of the conversation though probably my initial feelings will influence how I receive what people are saying and how I project myself.

In an encounter group the aim is to reverse this pattern: to use techniques to contact, hold on to, encourage and intensify the expression of the sorts of feelings and responses which in ordinary social interaction are denied. Through Encounter the feelings between members of a group are made explicit and public by using structures or exercises which involve direct verbal or physical confrontation. This contrasts with Gestalt where the focus is on inner conflict. Here is an example from a self-help group.

Jane has sat silently in the group for an hour. She says she wants to work and explains that Annie, another woman in the group, has asked her to take her turn on the baby-sitting rota and this has made her feel sulky. The group suggests that Annie and Jane sit opposite each other and replay the scene. Annie asks Jane to do her a favour and Jane stares back, pouting and unable to reply. Annie repeats the request but gets no direct response. The group decides to try to push Jane to help her to express what she is feeling. All the women pull Jane about saying, 'Come on Jane', 'Come and do what I want', until Jane screams and yells 'No' and jumps up and down in the fury of her denial.

Through physical and verbal means Jane is moved from holding in her anger to feeling, expressing and discharging it fully by shouting at all the women and leaping up and down.

WHAT IS ENCOUNTER?

The assumptions in Encounter are similar to the ground rules we outlined in Chapter One but there is more emphasis on the kind of direct confrontation experienced between Annie and Jane, rather than deflecting onto cushions. Encounter aims to make our emotional lives more intense and vivid, to bring feelings out into the open, which is valued as an experience in itself. Another assumption is that by expressing the anger (or sadness or hurt) we will clear ourselves of negative feelings.

Will Schutz,[1] one of the founders of Encounter, writing about the rules for an encounter group includes:

1   Pay attention to your body
2   Stay with the here and now
3   Express things physically rather than verbally
4   Speak for yourself
5   Speak directly to the person you are expressing feelings about
6   Don't generalise
7   Take responsibility for yourself and your choices.

We can see how all these rules apply in the example of Jane and Annie. Jane acts out her anger with the other women in the group physically pulling her about and ends up jumping up and down to express the full force of her 'No'. She doesn't talk to a cushion as she might in Gestalt: nor does she relate her feelings about being pushed around to early experiences in her family. She doesn't start talking in general terms about how she feels about 'people' pushing her around or how difficult it is for her in general to say 'no'.

An encounter group may often develop the initial confrontation by using other methods but the initial 'here-and-now' confrontation is specific to Encounter. For example, Jane might look at how her rejection of Annie relates to her feelings about her parents, but only after she has finished expressing her anger.

Encounter is based on a phenomenological theory of reality. We can explain this as a description of our perception of reality coming through a haze of filters which, in principle, could be identified and removed, to leave us with an undistorted reality. So, the personality is seen as being composed of layers laid down developmentally. At the bottom is a person's basic sense of self and her autonomy. To reach this layer through Encounter a woman will have to work from the top layer of superficial politeness and social exchange through subsequent layers of anxiety, anger, dependence, helplessness and aloneness. The actual construction of the layers will be somewhat different in different personalities but the process of unpeeling them in encounter groups is basically similar. As the layers are removed the woman is able to contact deeper levels of feeling. By ridding herself of these filters or layers she is increasingly able to be a free and responsible person.

The newer growth movement therapies, such as Gestalt and Encounter, developed alongside each other and were mutually cross-fertilising. Thus Encounter, starting in the late forties and early fifties, involved therapists or group leaders from many different schools of therapy including Psychoanalysis, Bioenergetics and Psychodrama, and elements of these different approaches are all present in Encounter. From the psychoanalytic group comes the emphasis on group dynamics and the idea that we can make use of the feelings between people in the group in the present as a representation of dynamics that occur for us in everyday life. From Psychodrama comes the idea that there is a healing process involved in acting out feelings rather than just talking about them. From Bioenergetics, Encounter drew its emphasis on the physical expression of feelings.

The direct predecessors of encounter groups were the 'T' groups (or training groups) developed in Boston where a group of people were simply left together with no structure or apparent purpose in being together other than to see what happened in the group. The variety and intensity of feeling and interaction which developed suggested that this process could usefully be refined and intensified.

Although Encounter has grown from other therapies it has its own particular approach and strengths and weaknesses. Its popularity is reflected in its rapid growth in the USA and, somewhat later, elsewhere.

WHEN SHOULD WE USE ENCOUNTER?

Encounter offers energetic and dramatic techniques for breaking down resistance and for dealing with feelings between members of the group. When the expression of feelings between people is heightened in this way it can help people to recognise and differentiate their feelings. This means that, if used carefully, it is a valuable technique:

1   When one person feels particularly numb, 'dead' or stuck.
2   When the group as a whole feels stuck and unable to work effectively. Other therapy techniques you may have been using, such as Gestalt or body-

work, may bring to the surface feelings between group members which they have no way of dealing with. Members may then begin to express their dissatisfaction indirectly by silence, arriving late or grumbling. Encounter can help by bringing these feelings back into the group.

3   When strong feelings between group members are already evident and need to be fully exposed and discharged.

If a clash between one or more members of the group erupts and is not dealt with immediately it can mean that the energy of the women involved will be distracted from whatever else is going on. Encounter can help. Here is an example.

I was leading a one-day women's group and was late. I hadn't planned to be late – nor had I planned to run an encounter group – but by the time I arrived the group was seething with anger sparked off by little disagreements over which room to use and whether or not smoking was allowed in the group. The feelings were so strong that I had to give up my plans for a gentle introductory exercise sharing our feelings about being in a women's group and work directly on the anger between two of the women. They were wrangling verbally, each one justifying herself, and to cut into this I suggested that they kneel down, place their elbows side by side and wrestle to see which of them could push the other's arm over onto the carpet. It soon emerged that one of the women could initiate aggression but could not put any force into the elbow wrestling contest. Underneath her apparently provocative behaviour she showed her fear of the group. She withdrew her threat to leave the group at lunch-time and we were able to continue.

In this situation it was not difficult to decide to use a physical struggle (a safe one) to focus the apparent anger between the two women. The confrontation had already been brought into the open but was being carried on at an apparently rational level which brought no emotional release for either of them. The direct physical contact allowed one woman to express her aggression without feeling she had to justify herself, and allowed the other to contact and express her fear which she too was covering with apparently reasonable arguments. Seeing her fear dispelled the other women's irritation at her threat to leave the group and they were able to ask her to stay with genuine warmth.

If you are going to use physical confrontation it is essential to make the ground rules clear. In this example both women were told to keep on their knees, to keep their elbows firmly on the ground, to clasp hands and only to push with their clasped hands to get the other woman over onto the carpet.

Sometimes a confrontation can be verbal rather than physical. This does *not* mean continuing the verbal wrangling or hurling accusations in the typical manner of a row between intimates:

'You never really: loved me anyway; bother to listen to what I say; want to go out with me.'
'You always: sneer at me when I'm talking; drop your clothes all over the house; forget to feed the cat.'

In an encounter confrontation we would take the essence of what the two people are expressing in the argument, get them to own what each is feeling, rather than projecting onto the other person, and then encourage them to express their feelings fully. So the 'You never' and the 'You always' statements might be condensed into, 'See me! Hear me!' and 'I'm angry with you!' The two people then put all their energy into shouting at each other. The aim is not to resolve the disagreement by rational or moralistic standards since the emotions involved are *preventing* the two people from listening or talking at those levels of discourse. Once they have expressed how they are feeling towards each other they will be far more open to dealing with any practical moral or rational issues that remain.

As well as being a useful technique to use in a group, we have found Encounter helpful in learning to quarrel more constructively. However, it isn't always so clearly appropriate to decide to involve a woman in direct confrontation in the group.

Kate tells the group she has been silent because she feels so ashamed. She cannot relate to anything the other women have been talking about because she feels wrapped up in her own misery. She says everything is wrong with her life. She is in despair. She cannot see any point in exposing her despair to the group. They can't help her. It seems that the feelings she *can* share are her responses to others in the group so they decide to risk asking her to sit opposite each woman in turn saying, 'I can't give you my attention this evening'. They emphasise that as she sits opposite each woman she should make eye contact with her. After she has been round the group Kate is on the verge of tears. She still feels very sad about herself but she does feel she has made contact with the women in her group and has gained something from their acceptance of her despair and negativity. They too feel relieved because they had been half aware of her resentment and withdrawal throughout the evening.

The aim of this exercise is to bring Kate's feelings into the open, to give her the release of expressing them to other group members and to show both Kate and the other women that her despair may be painful but that it cannot actually overwhelm and destroy the group, for this is a fear which women often have about their unexpressed strong feelings. In this group no one felt it would be appropriate to set up a two-way confrontation between Kate and another woman, who might have felt angry at Kate's behaviour. Somehow Kate appeared (rightly or wrongly) to be too fragile for this. If you do set up a confrontation, or you find one happening in your group, whenever possible make sure that both people are prepared to participate. When one woman spontaneously challenges another in the group you can intervene and ask if they are *both* prepared to participate. This takes courage in a self-help group where it is not any one person's responsibility to make interventions, but it is worth taking the risk to avoid someone being dragged into a conflict she feels she cannot cope with. When two people do confront each other it is important to make sure that both have time to say how they are feeling afterwards: otherwise one woman may be left with feelings aroused by the confrontation that she has to deal with alone. It seems crucial in any therapy group, but particularly when using Encounter, that group members stay in the group for whatever is the agreed duration of the session. No one should rush out in despair or leave in a fury without having a chance to deal with her own feelings, or those she has aroused, in the group.

Using Encounter with an Individual

Cathy is talking about how undermined she feels by the men she works with. She cries and snivels a little but does not seem to be able to go any further. She can't really cry or get angry. She wants to move and asks for suggestions. Amy suggests that the women in the group act the men who are oppressing Cathy. They could make a circle round Cathy and she could try to fight her way out. Some of the women in the group don't want to do it because they don't like the idea of being unkind to Cathy but she wants to try, and five women are prepared to do it with her. Cathy stands in the middle of the circle and the others link arms around her making provocative remarks, imitating the men she works with. Cathy shouts back and tries to force her way out of the circle, getting more and more angry until she hurls herself between two women's arms and escapes.

Through a physical enactment of Cathy's struggle, she is able to move out of self-pity into anger. The women who did not want to participate may feel differently about doing this sort of exercise now that they have seen it working. It is important that Cathy herself wants to work in this way. Of course this sort of pushing does not always succeed.[2]

Using Encounter with the Whole Group

Where a group as a whole seems to be stuck, or needs to find safe structures for airing hidden feelings, it can help to use exercises which increase contact or give permission to express feelings which are normally taboo. The simplest structure for increasing and intensifying group feelings is a 'milling' exercise where group members are asked to mill or walk around the room making eye contact with each person they meet (as described fully in exercise 50). Each woman will become more aware of how she feels about others in the group and after a few minutes the group can sit down in a circle and share their experiences, noticing who they could look at easily, who they found it more difficult to sustain eye contact with, whether they were surprised by any of their reactions and who, if anyone, they avoided.

In a new group this exercise can show how women have immediate and strong emotional reactions to each other, even when they hardly know the other group members. Sometimes they may project their own feelings onto others so that one woman may be convinced that another woman in the group despises her, when in fact she is the one who feels superior and is *projecting* her feelings onto another group member rather than admitting what she is feeling. In more experienced groups it can begin to reveal established patterns of relating and non-relating. Sometimes a group may be blocking a particular way of expressing themselves, such as having physical contact with each other, or may be outlawing the expression of certain sorts of feelings, such as jealousy. Here it may be useful to use a structure which specifically gives permission to do whatever is being implicitly tabooed in the group. For example, in a women's group where the women are blocked on expressing how they feel about each other, it may be helpful to pair up and do an exercise where they get to know each other with their hands (see exercise 15.) This can work on several different levels. It helps the women to be aware of difficulties in being physically close to each other, which may well be part of their fears of dealing with their feelings *about* each other. These fears can then be brought into the open. It may bring out feelings of closeness, intimacy and dependency which they have been afraid to express verbally. It may also introduce another way of knowing and relating in the group without involving words.

In a group which has been doing therapy together for some time (particularly where group members live or work together, as some of us did in our self-help group) members may have feelings about each other which they become increasingly afraid to express. These can be experienced as feelings which are taboo in the group because they might upset someone else, or because they might destroy the group. Alternatively, they are expressed in the group as hopes or fears about what someone else is feeling. For example, one person may feel that the others are angry with her for her dominating behaviour in the group. These feelings and projections need to be aired so that each person can learn what it is she is projecting onto others rather than dealing with herself. Sharing 'hidden agendas' (the hidden feelings we have about each other) can be frightening but can also be a real relief when it is done carefully. Here is an example of how it can be done.

The group sits in a circle. One member can tell another member of the group her 'hidden agenda' or secret feelings about that person. The woman receiving the 'hidden agenda' does not reply but takes in what is being said to her, allows herself to receive the comment, to note her response to it and to try to sift out how much of it she recognises as being true about her, and how much she thinks is a projection. This is quite different from what we normally do in conversation, or in an argument, when we feel we have to respond immediately. Each person has the space to be aware of how it feels both to give and to receive 'hidden agendas'. When it works well, everyone is able to recognise that she is not alone in having strong feelings which she sees as being socially unacceptable: that she can tell someone she feels jealous of them, that she loves them or that she hates their smile, and the world does not fall apart. It can feel far safer in a group to have these things out in the open rather than holding back for fear that someone will discover what an angry, weak or sexual person you are. It is vital to do this exercise at the beginning of the group session to leave plenty of time for people to work on the feelings which are exposed. It is likely that both opening up your feelings about others, and receiving their feelings, will stir up a new wave of emotions. For some, making negative feelings public may be the beginning of a release which they need to follow through. For others, particular statements may have touched on painful problem areas which need to be acknowledged or explored. Provided that everyone is clear that a 'hidden agenda' is as likely as not to be a projection on the part of its owner, and that plenty of time is left for working through the after-effects of this powerful exercise, it can be very helpful (see exercise 62).

'Hidden agendas' may help to look at particular feelings *individuals* have about one another, but there may also be a need to understand how the group *as a whole* is operating. In Red Therapy, when the group was still mixed, we felt that the group was stuck partly because it was dominated by certain key people. We needed to look at the group process particularly in relation to power and competition, inclusion and exclusion. We felt that we had to have an outside leader to take the responsibility away from the very people who had the power but were blocking the group's development as a whole. We also needed the reassurance of having a leader there who would hold us together if we criticised one another. She helped us to see some of the patterns by getting us to do an exercise in which we arranged ourselves around a central point according to our individual perceptions of who was most powerful, most loving, most unhappy and so on, in turn (see exercise **64**). Feeling yourself pushed nearer the centre or being pulled away from it, moving other people around and finally seeing the structure of the group laid out as a three-dimensional model, is a strong experience. Making the inner dynamics of the group public in this way opened up the possibility of change. One of the things that became clearer was the power relationships between the men and the women and the way in which these inhibited many of the women from being fully active in making suggestions in the group and helping others to work. This probably influenced our decision a few months later to continue meeting on a regular basis in separate men's and women's groups.

If you use a powerful exercise like this, again leave plenty of time for feedback and for individuals to work. It may be useful to encourage each person in the group to say briefly how she feels about her place in each model as it is arranged. Later on, individuals who need more time can then work. It is likely, for example, that a woman who has been placed on the outside of the 'loving' model will want to work on what makes it so hard for her to show love in the group.

WHAT ARE THE VIRTUES OF ENCOUNTER?

Encounter, like all the forms of therapy we are writing about, is based on the assumption that we live in a society which alienates us from our bodies and our feelings. While Freud saw this as inevitable, saw repression as basic to civilisation (as he understood it and defined it) growth movement theorists, and particularly those concerned with Encounter, have seen therapy as a way of encouraging people to contact their 'real' feelings and thus challenge some of the social values they have been brought up to believe in. Encounter has been seen as part of the 'counter culture'. For little girls, learning not to show feelings, and often not to feel them, takes a particular form. We are allowed to cry and to show warm feelings for others. As we played with our dolls we learned to care for others and to worry about what they were feeling. This was more important than knowing what we were feeling ourselves. We are encouraged to be sensitive to the feelings of others and to learn to behave accordingly. This has often been confused with the idea that as women we know more about and have more freedom to express our feelings. In fact, the numbers of women turning to therapy has been an acknowledgement that while we may be more attuned to and involved in the world of emotions, we need to learn to centre ourselves on our *own* feelings and to focus on those we find it hardest to express.

How useful is the encounter approach in helping us to do this? Encounter techniques, or an encounter group, can help a woman to recognise the strength of her own feelings and to open up dramatically the feelings towards others which we have found hardest to show. We have seen how Encounter can be used to give permission for feelings which, as women, we find difficult, such as anger, recognising our own power, and competition. It can also be used to give permission for our fear, dependency and loving feelings. The release of energy is a good experience in itself. A member of our self-help group went to an encounter group with her lover and said afterwards, 'It is really great to feel so much energy coming through you – even if it's anger or negative feelings. It's just really uplifting to see that people have so much power and energy in them, that I have so much power and energy in me.'

The difference between an *encounter* and a violent lover's brawl in the street is that in the encounter group the two people scream out their anger and hatred with the understanding that they are not trying to win a battle, but rather that they need to express the angry and hateful feelings and to understand and move on from them. They are assuming that behind the anger are loving and tender feelings too. In the street corner fight there is no acceptance of the notion that lovers may feel hate and anger for each other as well as love and compassion. Nor is pure anger expressed because people are always trying to score points which can later be used as evidence against the other person.

Like other oppressed groups, women have learned to express both their positive and negative feelings indirectly. If you don't have direct power you learn to manipulate: to get what you want from a situation by indirect methods. Instead of yelling at our lovers, we tend to turn our backs on them in bed saying we are tired. In doing this we may succeed in frustrating them, but we also frustrate ourselves. Encounter can help us to learn to express our feelings towards others more directly and can break through or *burst* some of our more manipulative and self-destructive patterns. It gives us practice in acting in the world in new and often exciting ways.

DIFFICULTIES IN USING ENCOUNTER IN A GROUP

Encounter, with its emphasis on taking defences by storm and pushing people into dramatic displays of emotion, can sometimes lead to a person's work becoming a kind of 'performance' with lots of sound and fury but little real meaning and no therapeutic value at all. Here is an example.

Julia is shouted at in a group and begins to tremble. The tremble develops into shaking and she lies down and begins to kick and shout. She seems to be contacting some early childhood feelings. She continues for about five minutes by the clock though to others in the group it seems to go on for much longer. People ask her questions and make suggestions but she continues to be oblivious. Each person is wondering what Julia is doing. 'I'm feeling detached', 'Maybe this is my block', 'I don't understand this sort of therapy but perhaps Josie does', 'I've already had a confrontation with Julia so I'm probably just resentful of her having time in the group'. Eventually Louise says, 'Julia, I'm really bored. I think you're just pretending'. Julia sits up as if she had just been drinking a cup of tea and agrees. The rest of the group is immensely relieved and Julia begins to talk about her inability to feel, in a way which sounds both painful and real.

It was difficult for each person in the group to be sure of her own judgement. Was Julia just performing or were they unable to be open to Julia's feelings? It is always worth checking out, as Louise did. If she had been wrong no harm would have been done and Julia could have gone on working. As it was, Louise helped Julia to move away from her faked therapy 'performance' into talking about issues in a way which was far less spectacular but more significant for her. Experienced encounter participants may particularly need challenging in this way. Some blocks can be broken by Encounter but others can be reinforced and another more indirect method may be far more effective.

Another thing that may go wrong in an encounter is almost the opposite to a performance: the situation may become too real. Here is an example of this.

Jackie and Sally are shouting at each other. Jackie thinks Sally is trying to lead the group. Sally feels that Jackie has been at the centre of the group for hours and should give space to other members of the group. The argument escalates until Sally is shouting, 'You're a hog. A group hog. Hogging all the time.'

Suddenly Bert, who lives with Jackie, shoves Sally.

Sally yells, 'Don't you dare hit me'.

Others in the group separate Bert and Sally. They feel that this kind of pushing and shoving is not part of the group contract and are angry with Bert. They tell Jackie she will have to give space to others in the group. Jackie lies down and a few minutes later walks quietly out of the group and does not return. Sally is left to deal with her guilt at having, as she sees it, driven Jackie out of the group.

Here Bert stepped over the line from structured physical contest into physical violence which scared the group. They then sided with Sally in order to reassert control but in doing so Jackie was effectively driven out of the group. If there had been a clear agreement about staying in the group Bert's explosion might have been stopped and the feeling behind it exposed and both Jackie and Sally would have learned from it. As it was, Jackie left feeling persecuted and Sally felt guilty. Bert felt confused. Situations like this make it clear how important it is that everyone in the group knows the rules, agrees to them and sticks to them.

At the end of a confrontation or an encounter group it is important to return to positive feelings. This doesn't mean falsifying but rather helping participants to recontact other parts of themselves. When two people have had an angry confrontation ask them to look at each other and see how they feel. Usually if they have effectively discharged a lot of anger they will feel much warmer towards one another. Encounter leaders often suggest hugging after a confrontation. We feel that this is fine if both people want to but have found that hugging can feel like another part of an encounter performance. Hug only by choice. There are other exercises which can be positive ways of ending an encounter and reaffirming the group's support for the person who has been working. For instance, when Cathy had managed to contact her anger and break out of the circle of women she may want to reaffirm that she does not have to be angry and tough all the time by asking for a group massage or pat or a cradle (see exercise 65).

CRITICISMS OF ENCOUNTER IDEAS

We do have criticisms and doubts about Encounter, as a technique for use in self-help therapy groups, as it is sometimes practised professionally, and at a theoretical level.

In itself, learning to feel and to express what we feel is insufficient to change the society we live in. Implicit in Encounter is the idea that expressing feelings is 'good' in and of itself. This can lead to the worst abuses of Encounter. There exists a stereotype of the rich middle class getting their weekend fix of 'real life' joys and sorrows at great expense in encounter weekends, led by comparatively rich and ego-tripping group leaders using strong emotions to control others. The participants return to lead their routine exploitative lives unchanged. This is possible as long as people fail to recognise that emotions belong in social and economic context. A personal and social history cannot be overturned by 'pure anger', but involves other real people who have to be related to differently; this in turn involves changes in the outside world. As women we know this already. We do need to learn to recognise and express our feelings. An encounter group may be able to help us to do this, but to use our new-found emotional knowledge effectively *outside* the group we have to create new supportive structures and fight old oppressive ones. A woman who discovers her anger at being chained to her small children, husband and house is not going to be able to use this knowledge effectively unless her anger is channelled into joining with others to get a collective childcare situation, finding a way of being economically independent and getting real emotional support inside and outside her family. Discovering her anger may help her to do this effectively as long as she doesn't see anger as an end in itself.

Some people have argued that the process of lifting off the lid can be positively counter-revolutionary by providing a safety valve. The extreme example of this are the Japanese workers who have been given effigies of their bosses to beat up at lunch time, presumably to defuse the anger they might otherwise use to organise an effective opposition to the real bosses. This could also be true for women using Encounter as a way of discharging emotion which would otherwise be directed at the real difficulties in their lives. It is important that we are aware of these limitations and abuses of Encounter. Then, when we use confrontation and other encounter forms in our groups, we can allow time for what we have learned to be made relevant, through discussion, to our everyday lives.

The second major difficulty we have found with Encounter is one which is intrinsic to the actual confrontation situations which Encounter encourages. Put at its simplest: Jill confronts Mary in a group and tells her she is ugly and stupid. How is Mary to cope with this? Is Jill merely projecting her feelings about herself onto Mary, or should Mary take Jill's statements as valid criticisms? At a rational level we can offer an explanation of what is going on. Jill has anxieties about her own physical attractiveness and puts a high value on intellectual facility so she has strong feelings about another woman whom she sees as being unattractive, and is impatient with what she sees as Mary's slowness. Jill is really talking about her own problems. If Mary is not worried about these things, she will be able to respond to Jill's statements without being upset. However, it may be that Jill touches off particular anxieties in Mary, in which case Mary is going to be upset and will need time to work in the group too.

The idea in Encounter is to express your projections. This works better with people you do not know as you are far more likely to make clear projections rather than confusing what you know about another person with what you are projecting onto her. You are less likely to feel hurt by judgements made by strangers than by people who are close to you. In practice these situations may be far more difficult to deal with, particularly in a self-help group.

Here is an example from our group of how confrontation between friends can go wrong.

Claire tells Susan that she hates the way she competes with her friends. Susan shouts back that it's easy for her to talk when she has a husband, a baby and a cosy home. Both believe what they are saying but are so aware of the other's judgement that they never really manage to release the anger. They and the rest of the group leave feeling uncomfortable and somehow the mud sticks for everyone.

The encounter was not liberating for Claire or Susan because neither had a sufficiently strong sense of herself to stay with her own feelings. They might have released their feelings and resolved their conflict if each had separately gone into the judgements and resentments and understood more fully the feelings about themselves which lay behind them. In Encounter, they lost themselves.

As women our socialisation leads us to tune into other people's emotions and to be insufficiently centred in our own process. We can often get carried away in an encounter situation into being far more preoccupied with the feelings flying around the group than with the things we need to deal with for ourselves. For many men Encounter may be useful because they tend to have more problems of emotional numbness and fewer problems with being over-receptive to other people's feelings. If we recognise that we are getting too caught up in other people's feelings we need to find ways of working which focus us on our *own* feelings and sensations.

However Encounter can help us avoid sitting on what is happening between members of a group – and for women this can be important as we tend to be peacemakers and mediators. So we do suggest using Encounter, but with caution.

Encounter with Caution

Using Encounter with caution means remembering that it is a potentially explosive approach to therapy. Encounter can be very painful in ways that are not always therapeutic: it can leave individuals raw and hurt, vulnerable and insecure. To ensure that this does not happen it is essential to remember:

1   Never force an encounter. Make sure that all participants are willing before allowing a confrontation to proceed.
2   Always allow plenty of time in the group session for people to recover after an encounter game, exercise or confrontation. This will allow anyone who has unfinished business or feels angry or hurt to deal with their feelings in the group.
3   Always balance Encounter with nourishing exercises: for example, the exercises we suggest under the heading of 'Positive Exercises' on p 106. There is a real temptation to let Encounter take over in a group and allow one painful experience to spark off another. In a led group the leader will ensure that towards the end of the group people will put the pieces back together again and concentrate on positive aspects of themselves. In a self-help group you will have to do this consciously for yourselves.

EXERCISES USING ENCOUNTER TECHNIQUES

We start with some exercises for raising the energy level and increasing awareness of feelings between group members. Use them to warm up a new group or to make explicit what is happening in an established group.

50   Milling

There are several variations on the basic milling exercise.

Have people walk around the room making eye contact and saying 'Yes' to each person they meet. After two or three minutes they change to saying 'No' when they meet someone.

For 'yes' and 'no' you can substitute, 'I love you', 'I hate you', 'I'm worse than you', 'I'm better than you', 'I'm scared of you' or any other pair of opposite phrases which will bring out relevant issues for the group. In a women's group where the topic of appearance and sexual competitiveness has been taboo it might be good to try 'I'm prettier than you', 'I'm uglier than you'.

Mill around the room with closed eyes and make contact with different people in turn, exploring their face with your hands and letting them do the same. Alternatively, explore hands.

Touching can help you to experience yourself and the other person in new ways. It also breaks down the barriers we often have about physical contact with others, apart from sexual contact.

Another variation of this exercise is to have one person guiding the rest of the group as they mill around. Instead of leaving it entirely to each individual's discretion suggestions are given to touch each other's face, shoulders, neck, hands, according to the group's tolerance for this kind of warm nonsexual physical contact.

51   Get Out of My Way

Have people walk round the room faster and faster without actually bumping into anyone else but as they meet or pass saying 'Get out of my way'.

Alternatively the group divides into those who feel pushy and those who don't. The pushy ones walk clockwise shouting 'Get out of my way' and the others walk anti-clockwise. Then change so that the passive ones are saying, 'Get out of my way'.

This exercise gives women permission to express their antagonistic and assertive sides to one another and to see how it feels. The speed raises the energy in the group.

52   Taking My Space

Divide the group into two halves. One half shares the whole of the room out between them so that each person has her own space. The other women walk around the room trying to get into a space, or whatever else they feel like. No words should be used. After five minutes change the groups around and let the others take the space. Come together at the end to share what has happened.

Women will react in different ways. Some may ask to share a space while others will sit on the edge feeling too scared to try; some will feel 'happy about sharing their space while others will not. See if you feel good about having your own space or do you feel guilty? Do you want to share it or do you feel you have to? Space and boundaries are difficult issues for many women.

53   Act into Your Emotions

Choose a person to lead the exercise. Have people stand with their legs apart and knees slightly bent. Be aware of your breathing and deepen it, saying 'No' as you breathe out. Take your breath right down into your belly. Begin to move around the room acting your anger using sounds but no words, letting your face and your whole body convey your anger. When you meet someone try to communicate your anger. You will probably find that you are no longer acting but really are angry. After two minutes (or longer) the leader asks the group to show their fear in the same way, breathing first, and then she moves the group on to expressing their grief and lastly to expressing their love.

People can feel and express their latent emotions and learn to distinguish between them. It raises the level of expressiveness in the group. It is surprising how, when you have got over the first hurdle of feeling silly, you can really 'act into' your emotions in this way.

54   'If You Really Knew Me . . .'

Choose a partner you don't know very well, or have least contact with in the group, and sit on the floor facing each other, holding hands. Each person has five minutes to say as many sentences as she wants, starting 'If you really knew me you would: fall in love with me, find me too aggressive, argue with me.' Let yourself imagine what it would be like to be in a closer relationship with your partner. Keep eye contact with one another and stay connected. After five minutes change roles. At the end take five minutes to give each other feedback.

The aim is to get to know one another better, and also to become aware how much you see in or project onto someone you don't know well or with whom you have little contact.

55   'I Don't Like You, Because . . .'

Each person goes out of the room in turn. The others in the group each say one thing they don't like about the person who is outside. Then they call her back into the room and she has to guess three things that have been said about her. Then move on to the next person.

It can be a relief to realise that the criticisms others have of you are no more powerful than the bad things you already think about yourself. Remember to allow space for people to work on what has come up for them in these exercises as *they can arouse painful feelings*.

There are many variations on these exercises that you can make up for yourselves.

These structures can be introduced when it is appropriate in the group to express and intensify feelings that you are trying to work on. They can be either physical or verbal. Invent your own or modify the following exercises to suit your needs.

56   Exclusion

These are useful when someone is feeling excluded or unable to fight for what she wants.

1   The group forms a circle and the person has to try to fight her way into the circle. This exaggerates her feelings of not being part of the group or not getting what she wants and may push her into her strength or anger. Sometimes she will give up in despair but this can also be useful (though painful) as it will help her to be aware of how she is stuck, which is a necessary preliminary to contacting her anger.

2   All the members of the group, except the person who is working, go out of the room and she has to call them back. They don't come in until they are really convinced she wants them back. This situation forces the woman to confront her pride and express her need for others. Women often do this in indirect ways and it is good to learn how it feels to risk being more direct.

57   Competition

The group sits in a circle and each woman takes her turn to sit in front of the others saying, 'I'm better than you because . . .','I'm worse than you because . . .'

This is useful when a group or individual needs to explore issues of competition which may include race, class or sexual comparisons.

Another version of this is for each woman to express her feeling without going into reasons, simply saying 'I am superior to you' or 'I am more stupid than you' or whatever. She should sit opposite each person in turn and remember to keep eye contact. The other person does not need to respond, just take in what she is saying.

This simple exercise can often have a powerful effect through exaggerating and can lead to new understanding as a basis for changing her 'superior' or 'stupid' feelings.

58   Ways I Compete

You may find it safer to start by becoming aware of your own competitive patterns individually. Take a pencil and paper and write down the ways you compete with others. Then share your list with a partner, in pairs, or in the group.

You may find it easier to do the list at home and bring it to the group.

It is not considered acceptable for a woman to express her anger in our society. With many pressures on us, and no outlet for our anger, we often end up turning this anger against ourselves. This frequently takes the form of depression or self-hatred. It is important for us to learn to accept our anger and to direct it outwards where it belongs. This area too is good to open up early in a self-help group.

59   'If I Got Angry I Would . . .'

Divide into pairs. Sit facing your partner and speak for four minutes with sentences beginning: 'If I got angry I would: hurt somebody; make all my friends hate me . . .', and so on. Then exchange roles. Afterwards give one another feedback on what came up. This is a good exercise for exploring the catastrophic fears which most of us have about the terrible things which might happen if we got angry. Making these fears explicit helps to show how exaggerated most of them are, and clears the way for us to experiment with expressing our anger.

60   'No, I'm Not Angry'

Divide into pairs and sit facing your partner, keeping eye contact. For five minutes your partner says to you, simply, 'You're angry with me.' Each time she says it, let yourself deny it, giving whatever excuses or rationalisations you usually use to stop yourself from expressing your anger:

'You're angry with me.'
'No, I'm not angry, I'm just a bit tired, that's all.'
'You're angry with me.'
'No, I'm not angry, I'm much too nice to get angry.'
'You're angry with me.'
'No, I am not angry, it really isn't that important.'

Then exchange roles and afterwards discuss what came up. This is a good exercise for exploring our defences against getting angry and can stir up strong feelings.

The next exercises are ways of exploring how the group as a whole is operating. You may like to start with a pairing exercise for exploring projections, just to make sure that everyone in the group has an experiential understanding of this concept, otherwise these exercises can seem destructive. They are particularly good to use either when working with a group which has a collective existence outside therapy or with a group which appears to be stuck in rigid patterns.

61   Exploring Projections
Often what blocks the relationships between people in a group is projection. This means that you are projecting onto other group members qualities and feelings they do not have. Sometimes you attribute your own feelings to them, sometimes you treat them as if they were your mother/boss/child/brother. You may experience strong positive or negative feelings towards them without understanding why. You may feel responsible for them or jealous of them without understanding why. Here is an exercise from *The Barefoot Psychoanalyst*[3] which can help to explore the projections which may be blocking developments in the group.

Divide into pairs with a person onto whom you feel you may be projecting something: perhaps someone who disturbs you, whom you idealise or whom you hold back from. Speak for five to ten minutes to your partner on the theme of 'You remind me of . . .' Your partner listens and when you have finished she gives you feedback on which qualities she actually feels she shares with that person. You can then exchange roles.

62   Hidden Agendas (see p 93 for a description of using this in a group)
Everyone sits in a circle. Each person who has something hidden to say to someone else in the group takes her turn to speak. The person who receives the 'hidden agenda' maintains eye contact but does not reply. People speak only when they feel moved to do so. Plenty of time should be left for people to share their feelings about agendas given and received.

This exercise can be frightening but is useful for airing feelings that are blocking a group. You must leave plenty of time for discussion of these feelings afterwards. Another way to do this is to have a ball which one person rolls to another as they give them the hidden agendas.

63   Stamps, Paranoias and Strokes

This is really a refined version of the previous exercise but we like it because it gives more control to the person receiving the hidden feelings, while at the same time clearing the air.

'Stamps' are resentful feelings that you have about another person in the group. When the group has decided to 'do stamps' people say to each other, 'I have a stamp for you. Do you want it?' She can refuse it if she doesn't feel strong enough to receive critical feedback. Women often hold back from honest criticism, justifying themselves by saying that they don't want to hurt the other person's feelings. 'Stamps' is a good way to take responsibility for your own feelings and to allow the other women in the group to take care of themselves. Once a person has agreed to accept a 'stamp', as in 'hidden agendas', she just takes in what is said and does not answer back or try to disagree or justify herself. This is because it is understood that a 'stamp' may say more about the feelings of the person giving it than about the person receiving it. It may be at least partly a projection and both people need time to think this through and see how they feel about it.

At the same time anyone who has 'paranoid fantasies' about another group member shares them. 'I have the paranoid fantasy that you feel superior to me.' Again no reply is given for the moment. Sometimes the fantasy may be very exaggerated but often there is a grain of truth in the paranoia. Later there will be time for feedback on the stamps and paranoias, but first it is important to share them.

After the resentments have been expressed, give each other 'strokes', or share good feelings. What often happens is that once a person has got rid of some of her resentments it frees up the more loving and appreciative feelings she has for others in the group. Leave plenty of time for feedback and to work on feelings which may have been brought up.

64   Centre of the Group

Find a centre point in the room and put a cushion on it. That cushion represents the centre of the group and you will be arranging yourselves around it to show your relationships with the group. For example: Who is the most mothering person in the group? She/they should stand at the centre and the other people arrange themselves around, the more mothering people near the centre, the least mothering people furthest away from the centre. You can move both yourself and other people until you find an arrangement of bodies which fits the collective consensus about where people stand. Next: Who is/are the most powerful people in the group?

Other possible questions:

Who is the most creative?
Who is the most loving?

Who is the most happy/unhappy?
Who is the most easy going?
Who is the most sexually attractive?

A word of warning: This exercise, especially if you include questions like the last one, can be very distressing. You can imagine how a woman feels who finds herself repeatedly placed on the outside of the group. The aims of therapy are not to brutalise one another into expressing feelings, so it is important to stop this exercise at the point where it has raised some questions and opened up some feelings without making anyone feel suicidal. It is also important that people get a chance to express what the exercise made them feel, so they do not have to take that feeling away and brood on it alone. One way of doing this would be to come back into sitting in a circle after the exercise and each say in turn the thing that made them happiest and the thing that upset them most, for example . . . 'I felt really happy that I was not one of the leading people, the leaders looked very isolated in the middle there . . .', 'What upset me most was when people didn't push me into the middle as one of the most loving people. I really try to be loving in the group, I don't know why I don't come across that way . . .'

You should allow enough time so that if one person wants to explore what the exercise made her feel, and sort out her relationship with the group, she has the chance to do so.

We have already suggested that it is good to end a group by helping people get back in touch with their positive feelings. Here are some exercises we have liked; invent your own too.

65   Rock-a-By Baby, or Cradling
Lie on your back with your eyes closed and your face up. Have the other members of the group line up on either side of you, gently lift you and rock you to and fro.

Simple as this exercise sounds, it is a very lovely and often emotionally powerful feeling for an adult to be rocked in this way. It is especially good for women since we tend to do a lot of rocking of others, rather than allowing ourselves to be taken care of.

66   Circular Chair
This exercise is fun and brings out the way in which everyone in the group depends on everyone else.

The group stands in a circle. One person bends her knees and the woman next to her balances herself on them and so on round the circle until everyone is sitting on one person's knees with somebody else on their own.

67 Group Hug

The name is self-explanatory. The group sits, stands or kneels in a circle and hugs each other. Sometimes people like to follow this by sitting in a circle holding hands and, if it feels right, letting a sound go round the circle.

68 Kneading Dough

One person lies down in the middle of the circle and the others all knead different parts of her body. This is a variation on a group massage and brings the whole group into close physical contact which can feel right after a difficult and emotional session.

NOTES

1 William Schutz, *Elements of Encounter*, Joy Press, California, 1973.
2 See Chapter Nine.
3 John Southgate & Rosemary Randall, *The Barefoot Psychoanalyst*, Association of Karen Horney Psychoanalytic Counsellors, London, 1978, p 199.

FURTHER READING

William Schutz, *Joy*, Grove Press, New York, 1967; Penguin, Harmondsworth, 1968. A good introduction to Encounter as it has lots of vivid examples. Allow for its being over optimistic and uncritical of Encounter.

Howard R. Lewis & Harold S. Streitfield, *Growth Games*, Harcourt Brace Jovanovitch, New York, 1970; Souvenir Press, London, 1972. Wide-ranging collection of exercises including most of the standard encounter exercises.

J. B. P. Schaffer & M. D. Galinsky, *Models of Group Therapy and Sensitivity Training*, Prentice Hall, New Jersey, 1974. Chapter on encounter groups gives an interesting historical and theoretical account of their assumptions and development.

Hogie Wyckoff, *Solving Women's Problems*, Grove Press, New York, 1977. Not a book about Encounter but useful to consult for a different approach to dealing with group interaction with an awareness of women's needs.

Chapter Five
Letting the Body Speak

Bodywork is more than just an aspect or kind of therapy. It is a crucial part of any therapy approach and is a key to the way we understand ourselves and our process of development. We *are* our bodies. Any changes that happen in the personality have their reflection on the physical level and need to be embodied in our muscles, posture and physical habits if they are to endure.

Most therapies include some work with the body, but there are also times when it is useful to *start from the body*, noticing its processes and using them to help open ourselves up. If a group seems caught in talk, rationalisations or arguments, bodywork can help to reconnect with physical reality. If the energy of the group seems low, body exercises can be exhilarating and energising, warming people up and helping unexpressed emotions to come to the surface. For someone who finds it hard to express herself verbally, bodywork can be an easier way in to therapy. For someone who is very articulate, and perhaps uses words as a defence, it bypasses that pattern and brings her down to the bedrock of her physical existence.

In this chapter we will discuss ways of working directly on our bodies through breathing, movement, massage or sexuality exercises, as well as discussing how the body is involved in *all* the changes we make in ourselves through therapy.

The women's liberation movement has long recognised the importance of physical health and of gaining understanding and control of our bodies. Very often we are brought up to be scared or disgusted by our body processes (peeing is 'dirty', belching is 'rude', sex can be 'immoral'). Very often we are ignorant of how these bodily processes work and are encouraged to believe that if we are ill the only person who can help us is a trained 'expert', usually a male doctor. By the time we are adults most of us have become alienated from our bodies and think in terms of a split between 'mind' and 'body'.

Recently women have been recognising that it is especially important for us to reclaim our bodies, to care for them better, treat them with the respect they deserve, and assert our natural beauty against the artificial feminine stereotypes of 'glamour' impressed on us daily by the media. We need to redefine our sexuality in our own terms and to recognise what is pleasurable and exciting in our body processes.

Many countries have seen the emergence of women's groups organised around 'self-help' health where, through self-examination, self-education and sharing experiences, we can learn to understand how our bodies work. Women have learned how to prevent, and in some cases how to cure, ailments through natural methods like diet, yoga, relaxation, massage and organic curatives. In most cases such groups have focused on purely biological understandings, and it seems unfortunate that this self-help health movement has been seen as separate from therapy and the 'growth movement'. In our experience, physical health is inseparable from emotional health: body ailments often reflect emotional tensions and the connections can be explored and illuminated in a therapy situation. This approach to the whole person was opened up in the West by Wilhelm Reich and though we would disagree with some of his theories, we have found his work invaluable for our understanding of the link between mind and body.

REICHIAN BODYWORK

Reich began his career as a pupil of Freud and owes a great deal to Freud's ideas, but he later broke radically with that tradition, criticising the slowness of Psychoanalysis in achieving change, its taboos on touch and disregard of body language. He introduced touch and bodywork into the therapy process and brought a socialist perspective to his work. He believed that the training and conditioning we receive as children becomes built into the the structures of our bodies. For example, a boy who is told not to cry eventually learns to tighten his lip muscles and tense his back to stop himself crying. That tension becomes a permanent part of his muscle pattern throughout life, giving him lines round the mouth and backache in later years. A girl who is not allowed to hit or use her arms aggressively may find her arms underdeveloped later in life. A child who has to carry too much responsibility too early in life may develop round shoulders. A child who is toilet trained too rigorously may develop tension around the buttocks, reflected perhaps in excess weight around that area or in constipation. These connections between physical tensions and emotional patterns are recognised in common expressions like 'He's got a stiff upper lip', 'She's carrying the world on her shoulders', 'He's spineless', 'She puts on a brave face', 'You are stiff-necked about this'.

Reich believed that once these emotional blocks have become rigidly fixed in our bodies as muscle blocks we need to work directly on the body, loosening muscle tension so that rigid patterns of behaviour can loosen too and we can release emotions inhibited since childhood. Incidentally many physical ailments (the aching back, constipation) could be dissolved at the same time. Reich believed that our vitality and the fullness of our emotional life depends on a rhythmic 'energy flow' through the body. This flow is hindered by blocks, tension and deadness in different parts of the body as a result of our conditioning, and our ability to feel and enjoy life fully is hindered accordingly. Reich described these blocks as an 'armouring' which we have developed to protect ourselves not only from painful experiences which may be inflicted on us by other people, but also from forbidden impulses which threaten to erupt from inside ourselves. He pointed out how much energy is wasted and expended simply keeping ourselves down, stopping ourselves crying, raging, dancing, or whatever it was that we were inhibited from doing as children. He believed there is a balance between input and output of energy from the body: when, because of our inhibitions, the *output* of energy is low, we restrict our *input* of energy accordingly, by breathing lightly or cutting ourselves off from people and situations. Reich's aim was to unblock tensions and to raise the level of energy flow through the body. His technique for doing this was to help a person to take more energy into the body (for example, by deep breathing) and to discharge more energy by expressing, for example, joy, grief or anger, and by allowing the 'orgasm reflex'. (This term describes involuntary convulsive waves passing through the body, which may happen while making love or at other times when the body is open enough to allow this release of energy.) Where this raised energy flow comes up against blocks ('I feel like shouting but I can't seem to make a noise', 'I seem to be holding all my feelings in my chest', 'My stomach is so tight I can't breathe fully') then he might do direct physical massage work on the tense area to loosen the block. He found that by applying firm but sensitive pressure to a tense muscle he could make it 'let go', often with a breakthrough of emotions and the recovery of buried childhood memories which were associated with, and causing, the tension. As these memories (of being told not to cry, of being scolded for wetting the bed, of a father's glare of rage) are re-experienced at a deeply emotional and physical level, with a release of whatever movement and sounds were held in at the time (kicking, shouting), the person is able to break the pattern of rigidity in her body. This raises her energy level, opening up self-expression, restoring the flow of feelings to the body and making it increasingly possible for her to change her behaviour in the present. Reich saw the ability to experience a full and feeling sexual orgasm as an important sign of the health of the organism, indicating that energy is moving freely through the body. He saw sex as a key outlet for the release and regulation of the high energy level of a healthy person.

From Reich's work his pupil and follower, Alexander Lowen, developed the technique and theory of Bioenergetics. While Reich followed psychoanalytic tradition in having his patients lie flat on their back during therapy sessions, Lowen started to work with his patients standing which encouraged 'grounding'. Lowen stressed the need to bring the legs to life and establish a firm connection with the ground, and to achieve this he developed the bioenergetic 'stress' positions which combine pressure on the body with deep breathing. These are now widely used and we discuss them more fully below. The Reichian use of touch has also been developed into bioenergetic massage. Lowen placed less emphasis than Reich on sexuality, seeing it as only one of many basic bodily drives including breathing, moving, feeling and self-expression.

Other developments from Reich's work are:

Rolfing: a vigorous and sometimes painful deep massage method which aims to unlock muscle tension without necessarily making links to the emotional life of the individual.

Postural Integration: another method of deep connective tissue massage which may involve Reichian, bioenergetic and Gestalt techniques to connect the physical work with your feelings and daily life.

How Reich Linked Therapy with Politics

Reich was very clear that there are connections between the kind of body-blocks we have been describing and the inhibiting or repressive factors at work in our society at large. These connections are complex, but here are some examples of the form they may take, according to our understanding: in a society where a disciplined and submissive work force is needed to work in factories, children will be taught not to question directives or answer back; in a society built around families composed of faithful husband-and-wife partnerships, adolescents will be taught to control sexual impulses outside this framework; in a society where men are expected to fight wars and work hard to support a family, little boys will learn not to cry, to act strong and to suppress their tender feelings; in a society where women are expected to devote much of their life to caring for a husband and children, little girls will be taught to enjoy serving others and to hold back assertive or aggressive emotions. This process of conditioning, by which children are taught to inhibit themselves in a way which prepares them to fit in and become acceptable members of society, is subtle and often happens unconsciously as parents, teachers and others in authority positions pass on their own norms of behaviour and teach by example. Reich himself was very explicit about the damage which a sexually frustrated teacher can do in stifling the healthy sexuality of children, or the damage which authoritarian parents can do in repressing children's natural curiosity. Because the adults themselves have rigid bodies and lack self-love, they cannot relate to their children in a gentle feeling way. Instead they treat children as objects, and thus teach them to deny and fear their own bodies in turn. He saw a positive identification with the body as the basis of self-respect. Cut off from his body and afraid of it, the average 'little man' is inevitably afraid of life:

... you did all this because you are incapable of feeling life in yourself, because you kill love in your child even before it is born; because you cannot tolerate any alive expression, any free, natural movement. Because you cannot tolerate it, you get scared and ask: 'What is Mr Jones, and what is Judge Smith going to say?'

You are cowardly in your thinking, Little Man, because real thinking is accompanied by bodily feelings, and you are afraid of your body.[1]

Those emotions of fear, emptiness and self-contempt, Reich saw as powerful factors contributing to national chauvinism and fascism: 'Your chauvinism derives from your bodily rigidity'.[2]. . . 'When you say "Jew" you make yourself feel superior. You have to do that because you really feel miserable. And you feel miserable because you are precisely that which you murder in the alleged Jew'.[3]

The 'Jew' symbolises what you have been taught to hate and repress in yourself. Self-contempt is projected outwards because when you feel so bad in yourself you need to imagine there is someone worse than you.

Only through a good relationship with the body can a person find their own power and the ability to take responsibility for their own life, rather than blindly following leaders; only through this can a person partake of 'the natural work-democratic relationships between working people'.[4] It becomes clear that Reich disagreed strongly with what passes for 'normal' behaviour in our society. He believed that most 'normal' people are unhappy, dissatisfied and fulfill only a tiny proportion of their full potential as human beings. He even created a satirical pseudo-medical term, 'homo normalis', which he used to highlight what is unnatural and almost pathological about the 'normal' person. It follows that a person with a healthy, unblocked body, in whom the energy flows freely and who is in touch with her own life and power, would be something of a misfit and would be at odds with contemporary society. The pressures of society will work against the process of re-awakening natural feeling and impulses to the body through therapy. As Reich's follower Alexander Lowen puts it:

Therapy is handicapped by the fact that the culture we live in is not oriented toward creative activity and pleasure . . . it is not geared to the values and rhythms of the living body but to those of machines and material productivity. We cannot escape the conclusion that the forces inhibiting self-expression and, therefore, decreasing our energetic functioning derive from this culture and are part of it. Every sensitive person knows that it takes considerable energy to protect oneself from becoming caught up in the frantic pace of modern living with its pressures and tensions, its violence and insecurities.[5]

Other writers on therapy have of course recognised how Western society is repressive and prevents the free expression of emotions and impulses, but they have drawn different conclusions. For example, some writers from the American growth movement suggest that if individuals become more open through therapy the world will somehow change too and become a more 'beautiful' place. Reich himself was under no illusions that this process would happen automatically. He felt we need to struggle consciously to make the world a better place. This struggle for him involved political activity against the economic system of capitalism, which determines so many of the social conditions under which we live. Unlike Freud, who suggested the existence of a fundamental 'death instinct' in human beings, Reich believed that we have a basic capacity and instinct to live our lives fully, freely and happily, without repression. He envisaged the possibility of a society with different laws, work structures, emotional relationships and attitudes to the body, 'When you will only shake your head at the time when one punished little children for touching their love organs; when human faces on the street will express freedom, animation and joy and no longer sadness and misery'.[6] In Germany in the 1930s he pioneered a unique form of political group for young people, called 'Sexpol', which combined a socialist perspective with work around the sexual problems of young people. He saw this therapeutic approach as an important part of any struggle for a freer society: 'No police force in the world would be powerful enough to suppress you if you had only a mite of self-respect in practical everyday living, if you knew, deep down, that without you life would not go on for even an hour.'[7] 'You would have overcome the tyrants long ago if you had been alive inside and healthy.'[8] Reich was critical of 'revolutionaries' who saw politics in narrow, purely economic terms. He believed they lost touch with the experience of most people by ignoring everyday issues, and he emphasised the importance of concerns about food, clothing, entertainments, leisure and education as well as emotional and sexual relationships, as part of any political understanding.

In this respect his ideas are close to those of the women's liberation movement, which highlights the specific practical, emotional and sexual pressures women face in daily life. Reich's theories can, therefore, be helpful to politically active women who often have difficulty, as Reich did, in convincing the more conventional left that the 'personal' is 'political', that oppression in an area like sexuality is as real and causes as much suffering as any other kind of oppression. In other ways he is less helpful, as he lacked an understanding of the situation of women in patriarchal society, and addressed his theories chiefly to the problems of the 'little man' in a man's world.

Reich's unique contribution lies in the way he linked therapy with social and political issues, not only in theory but in practice during his own life. It is ironic that several of his followers have run directly counter to his ideas and have almost completely depoliticised his therapy approach. Reich himself clearly saw his therapy work as revolutionary. He was persecuted for his views and activities not only by Hitler's regime but also in the USA, where he died in prison.

Some Reservations about Reich

We have discussed here only those ideas and techniques of Reich which we have found relevant and helpful; there are other aspects of his work which are not so helpful. For example, early in his career Reich made a widely acclaimed contribution to psychoanalytic thinking with his invention of 'character types' for classifying different kinds of neurotic personality (the 'oral' character, the 'masochistic' character and so on). We have never used them, although they have become part of the therapeutic vocabulary describing not so much character types as traits which we all have.

Another theory which we can only touch upon came much later in his career when Reich developed the idea of body energy into the concept of 'orgone' energy. He believed that orgone energy was active in all living matter and that its movement through the human body could be stimulated through the use of specially made 'orgone cushions', 'orgone boxes' and so on. This development of his work has provoked much controversy, although some Reichian therapists and self-help groups do use orgone cushions and find them helpful. We will come back to the difficult question of the nature of body energy later in this chapter.

Another aspect of Reich's work worth questioning is his emphasis on sexuality: 'People get into this or that frenzy, or remain stuck in this or that lamentation, because their minds and bodies have become rigid and because they can neither give love nor enjoy it. This, because their bodies, unlike that of other animals, cannot contract and expand in the love act.'[9] Freud too, from a very different standpoint, saw sexuality as a fundamental force in the make-up of human beings, and we think perhaps they both place an over-emphasis on sexuality precisely because of the intense sexual repression at the time when they were writing. The difficulty in discussing Reich's theories about sexuality lies in the way his ideas have been misrepresented and popularised in inaccurate ways. For example, he did not suggest that we should be obsessed with our sexuality. His idea was precisely that a dis-satisfied sexuality keeps our thoughts revolving around sex all the time, whereas a fulfilled sex life leaves our energy free for other things. Nor was his message 'Go out and fuck as much as you like'. As he himself protested, this attitude turns the 'loving embrace' into a 'pornographic act'.[10] Nor, when he recommends sexual release, is he referring to orgasmic potency in itself or simply 'making it' sexually, which can happen in an alienated way. For him the orgasm was distinct from an ejaculation or climax and was an involuntary response of the whole body, in rhythmic, convulsive movements. Similar movements may occur with the 'orgasm reflex' which can take place in the therapy situation when a person is breathing freely and surrenders to her body; but in this case there is no build-up, climax or discharge of sexual energy. Reich developed in his patients the ability to experience the orgasm reflex as a sign that the body could experience pleasure in a total way and as a basis for a full and feeling sexual orgasm.

Reich does perhaps over-emphasise sexuality, but at the time when he was working it was important to stress the healthiness and naturalness of sexual expression. He could not have foreseen ways in which sexual restrictions could be lifted without necessarily freeing people, ways in which the 'permissive society' could in some ways reduce sex to just another commodity released onto the market. It is hard to disagree with his concern that children and adolescents should be encouraged to have a positive attitude to sex and should have the freedom to explore sexually rather than being taught to hate their bodies by hearing that sex is immoral or dirty. It is hard to disagree with his emphasis on a full sexual experience between loving partners. We also feel that Reichian bodywork can help us to deepen our sexual responses in a way that no other therapy approach offers. *But*, we do feel that there are serious shortcomings in his thinking on sexuality, especially as far as women are concerned. He has little understanding of women's subjective experience of sex, or of the particular pressures on women around the issue of sexuality, or of the effects caused by women's relative lack of power in their interactions with men. He did not sufficiently appreciate how sexuality brings up different issues for women than for men. He did not question penetration of the vagina as the centrepiece of the sexual act. He did not sufficiently recognise woman's pleasure in the clitoris and other parts of her body, nor did his view of the 'naturalness' of sexuality include homosexual love. He believed that the natural outlet for our sexuality is through a series of genitally-oriented monogamous heterosexual relationships.

We find it best to take what is good and helpful in Reich's ideas – and there is so much – and to look elsewhere for more specific work on sexuality which is geared to and sensitive to the particular experience of women. Later in this chapter we discuss one such approach.

USING BIOENERGETIC BODYWORK IN A SELF-HELP SITUATION

Here is an example of Reichian ideas, as developed in Bioenergetics, being used in practice in a self-help group.

The group decides to do an exercise to raise their level of energy. They take up one of the bioenergetic 'stress' positions, lying on their backs and reaching towards the ceiling with their heels while continuing to breathe deeply into the abdomen. The idea is that the deep breathing increases the flow of energy to the body and combines with the stress position to stimulate and build up an energy 'charge'. This can be felt as a physical vibration of the legs and can extend to the whole body. The breathing both helps you contact feelings and the accumulating charge calls for a discharge. Whatever emotions are already present well up more strongly and you may be able to release them.

Sally is sitting out as this kind of work requires someone to direct and oversee. She encourages the others to keep breathing fully and to let out any sound they want to. A few give up when the exercise becomes painful. June continues and starts to make some loud 'aaaahhhh' sounds which carry a lot of urgency. After a while, Sally suggests that other people stop doing the exercise, to concentrate on helping June. She asks June if she would like to lie down and explore any movements her body wants to make.

'I feel I want to kick', says June.

The group puts a mattress under her body and cushions by her feet and arms. She starts to kick, slowly and hesitantly at first. 'Keep breathing fully. Let your body really go into the movement', the group encourages her. The movement gathers momentum until she is hammering violently and rhythmically on the cushions with both her feet and fists and her whole body is involved in the motion.

'Let yourself make a noise,' says Sally. June makes a few strangled sounds. Her jaw is tight so Sally gently loosens and massages it. 'Let your jaw relax. Now let the sound out.' June starts to release some loud fullthroated sounds in unison with the movement. The group encourages her to keep going until her body lets out the energy it was holding in.

One of the group asks, 'Is there a picture in your mind? Is this feeling familiar to you from any other situation?' (The deep feelings brought up by this kind of exercise are often linked with early childhood emotions. It is important to ask this question to help June make the connections between her body sensations and her history.)

June replies, 'I feel really small. I feel I'm lying somewhere, really small. And I feel angry, as if someone is trying to hold me down.' Sally suggests that June continue the kicking and try saying 'No! No!' at the same time.

She knows that often kicking goes with refusal, with pushing someone away, or with anger at not being satisfied, and she wants to help June locate what exactly it is expressing for her. This pattern releases more energy for June, and she yells 'No! No! No!' which then turns into 'Let go! Let go!' while she continues to kick. The group makes sure she is still protected by cushions from hurting herself on the floor, and encourages her to keep her eyes open so that she stays connected with the present reality. After a while June stops and says she had an image of someone, possibly her mother, holding down the lower half of her body.

Coming back into a sitting circle, June makes eye contact with other group members and talks about her experience. Ruth comments that her body curled like a baby during a nappy change and suggests that she might have been re-experiencing a memory of her mother holding her down rigidly at that time. June will probably need to explore these feelings again to get a clearer picture of the past situation, and details will emerge slowly. June talks to the group about her relationship with her mother and about that part of her body, describing tension aches in her lower back and a fear of being 'held down' by being underneath her partner while making love. She says that after the kicking she is now aware of more life and sensation in her pelvic area. When she feels she has had enough feedback from the group, she asks to curl up close to somebody to rest.

In this example a bioenergetic technique was used to raise body energy and to put pressure on muscle blocks until some of the childhood anger held by June in her muscle blocks burst out into expression. Here the group started with a 'stress' position, but they could equally have used deep breathing on its own, or bioenergetic massage applying pressure directly to tense muscles. Or the same experience might have been triggered by a physical experience, like someone in the group holding June down. These are all Reichian ways into exploring emotions which can trigger dramatic responses, as in June's case. The underlying principle is the same: to build up a charge of energy in the body, to notice where tensions or rigidities lie and to unblock them so that feelings can be released. This approach, which can be blunt and painful, needs to be used carefully. Here are some things to watch for:

1   Make sure a person is ready to open up in this way; there is no point in an intense experience she cannot cope with.
2   Give her protection, attention and reassurance. Make sure she keeps her eyes open as otherwise she may drift away and become overwhelmed by her emotions in a way that is scary for her. Make sure she does not hurt herself physically on furniture or walls. If her deep breathing leads to hyperventilation, or if she or other group members panic, bring her back gently from the experience through the methods described in Chapter Two, p 45.

3   Do not apply strong or painful pressure to another's body unless you know what you are doing. Bioenergetic massage requires training. A good guideline when using massage in this situation is to touch gently and take your lead from the person who is working, asking her where *she* would like to be touched and how. Throughout the process she should be in charge, doing only what feels right to her.

4   Spend time afterwards talking about what happened. There is a danger of going through strong non-verbal body experiences which seem to come from nowhere and are cut off from everything else, like going into another world. It is important to integrate these experiences into the world of talk and behaviour so that the body's messages can be used to change how we live from day to day. June needed to make the connection with her childhood experience (being held down by her mother) and her present patterns. Reliving a childhood memory may bring up feelings of helplessness or despair which are draining. June needs to re-contact her adult strength, to realise that though she was helpless as a baby she is not helpless now and can make changes in her life, for example, by telling her partner about her preference for being on top during love-making.

5   Follow up with other methods. Bioenergetics can bring up strong but undifferentiated feelings and you may need another technique, like Gestalt, to look in more detail at the issues involved and clarify what you have learned.

6   Don't expect to be 'cured' overnight. The body changes resulting from this work may be subtle: a tense ache may simply 'move on' like a ripple effect from one part of the body to another, which will then need attention in turn. It is possible to experience your body as *more* tense and constricted after doing Bioenergetics, rather than finding it freer and more alive immediately. Your awareness of tensions may have increased – which may be the first step towards loosening them.

Bearing these points in mind, a group cannot easily go wrong, and people quickly get used to the loud sounds and violent involuntary movements which Bioenergetics can trigger. We have often used Bioenergetics to start a session in order to raise energy and mobilise feelings. It is of course equally possible to do this work in pairs, with one person helping the other. It focuses on the individual, so will not help for exploring interaction between group members. In general we feel the main contribution of this work for women is that it can help us to contact *all* of our body, *all* it wants to do and *all* our feelings, including assertiveness and anger. It is a good approach for getting a sense of the volume of our power, physical and emotional.

Here is an example of using Reich's ideas to work in a more gentle and subtle way with the body. We have chosen to give an example of a man working. In response to the women's movement, some men are wanting to work on, and change, their sexist conditioning. We felt it useful to show how a therapy group can help with this process.

The group has decided Helen should act as leader for this evening as she has some experience of bodywork. After some warm-up exercises, Tom says he would like some time to explore negative feelings he has about his body, and tension in his arms. Helen suggests that he stands for a few minutes with feet apart and knees slightly bent to breathe and to focus his awareness and centre himself in his body. Then she asks him to start by talking about his body. He describes the lower half of his body as being 'weedy and thin' compared with the top half of his body which is strong, muscular and well-developed. The group gives him some feedback and one person says she had noticed while swimming with him that his skin changes colour at the waist; above his waist the skin is smooth and brown, while below the waist it is paler, mottled, and has a thin covering of hair. Tom finds this helpful and remarks that as a child he developed the top half of his body at the expense of the bottom half. He says he had a rough childhood and needed to 'act tough' and be able to fight to defend himself and impress other boys. He says that the top half of his body feels very tight at present and he would like to work on this. Helen suggests he takes his shirt off so the group can see what is happening in this part of his body. She stands facing him a few feet away and asks him to be aware of the sensations in the top half of his body and describe them to the group.

'Well, I feel like there's an iron bar across my shoulders, and when you came to stand facing me I felt muscles tightening in my arms, like I wanted to raise my fists to protect myself against you.'

Helen suggests he keeps eye contact with her and lets himself explore that involuntary movement, the clenching of the fists, the impulse to raise the arms. After a while he says: 'It's like you're the enemy. Like I'm saying "Keep away or I'll punch you".'

Standing there, Tom continues to explore closely the various muscle movements. There is silence in the group and everyone gives him full attention as he makes almost imperceptible movements, slowly clenching and unclenching one fist, a finger at a time, half-raising one arm. After some time Helen reminds him to keep breathing fully, and asks him what is happening to him.

'I was just feeling that this is how I relate to the world. Also it's how I relate to the woman I live with. I daren't let her close. When she tries to get close – emotionally – I feel aggressive and want to fight her off. I grew up fighting and I can't seem to behave any different now.'

Helen listens, waits for a while, then moves over to Tom and places her hand on the centre of his chest near the top: 'Are you aware that you are not really breathing out from there? It doesn't fall when you exhale. It's as if you're just holding your breath in there. What does that mean for you?'

Tom continues to breathe evenly for a while then says: 'It feels difficult to let the breath out from there. I feel scared of letting my chest collapse.'

'What message is your chest putting across to the world?'

Tom sticks his chest out a bit more, and says, 'Kind of . . . well . . . "I'm big and strong and tough so don't come near me . . . or I'll smash you".'

Helen steps back and asks Tom to experiment with letting his chest collapse more as he breathes out. She tells him not to push himself beyond what feels easy but to try it and let himself experience whatever feelings that brings up. There is silence again as the group watch the subtle body movements Tom is going through. His chest starts to collapse a little bit more as he exhales and a slight tremor starts in his body. Helen, who is moving round him, watching his back and his sides, asks what he is experiencing. He says his arms are feeling shaky and strange, as if they want to make a movement but he is not sure what. She encourages him to continue with the breathing and to explore what arm movements he might make. Eventually he says, 'I'd like to reach out. Reach out to someone. I never use my arms for reaching out, only for fighting and keeping people away. But when I go as if to reach out, something stops me.'

'What is stopping you?'

'I don't know . . . I get scared'.

Helen stands in front of him, a few feet away, and makes eye contact. Then she asks him if he can reach out to her with his arms. 'Only if it feels right. Don't force it. Keep eye contact and see what happens.'

Tom stands still for a long time. The muscles in his arms are moving under the skin, tensing and untensing. Eventually he very slowly raises his arms, holding his hands out towards Helen.

This way of working is very different from working with bioenergetic stress positions and pushing the body into energy release. What happens here may seem low-key or insignificant by comparison, but in fact an apparently simple act like Tom raising his arms can often be as important in the therapy process as a more dramatic release of emotion. What was crucial here was that through breathing and focusing awareness, Tom got closely in touch with his body and its patterns of movement. He became aware of tensions like puffing his chest out and clenching his fists. Then he was able to explore new movements which could express new patterns of behaviour: reaching out gently to people for what he needs instead of being locked in a fighting stance. This muscle pattern reflected clearly the pressures which society places on boys to act aggressively rather than tenderly, and this session was an approach towards helping Tom to change the patterns which this conditioning has imprinted in his body. Helen did not push him into making any movement he did not feel fully connected with. She might have taken it a step further and asked him if he could say a phrase like 'I want' to express his gesture verbally, and this in turn might have led him into releasing some tears. But the work would have been equally valid if he had not been able to raise his arms at all and the session had finished with him realising just how hard it is for him to hold his arms out towards another person.

When you work subtly with body awareness, a realisation like that is already a lot to have gained from a session. The understanding is that bringing patterns *to awareness* is an important part of the process of change because then a person need no longer blindly follow old unconscious patterns. The point was not that Tom should raise his arms, which he could do any time, but that he should really experience the body blocks which were stopping him from making that gesture in a feeling way, and from reaching out emotionally to those close to him.

It is sometimes difficult to know when it is best to work in this more delicate and gentle way, and when it is better to 'push' a person, for example, encouraging them to kick or make a noise even if they are initially resistant to doing so. Which approach is more suitable depends on the particular situation of the individual who is 'working'. Generally, if the person's level of resistance is high it may be more fruitful to explore her blocks and resistances rather than trying to 'break through' them, especially in a self-help group. If you are at a crisis point, you may feel that you need gentle and unpressured methods to help you contact your feelings. On the other hand you might be bored with yourself and want to do some really strong energy-raising body exercises to give yourself a shake-up. Any one individual probably needs a balance of both approaches during the therapy process. The approach used with Tom, emphasising awareness and focusing on the body as it is now rather than regressing to a childhood situation, is close to some of the Gestalt therapy practice. Fritz Perls (see Chapter Three) was strongly influenced by Reich, and therapists doing Reichian bodywork today often include among their techniques these Gestalt developments of Reich's ideas.

WORKING WITH A REICHIAN THERAPIST

A woman looking for a Reichian therapist often has a choice between these different approaches and should choose what feels most helpful for her. Reich, like Freud, worked with transference, exploring the strong feelings which patients projected onto him as the therapist. Many Reichian therapists today continue to work with transference in varying degrees and it is worth considering to what extent this relationship with the therapist may be helpful for you. Encouraging transference gives considerable power to the therapist and this can cause problems if the therapist's values are very different from your own. The specialised expertise in body techniques which this work involves can also be quite mystifying and can empower a therapist to make statements about your life which come, you might assume, from some superior knowledge of your body and its workings.

Another factor to consider is the nature of the social or political awareness which Reichian therapists bring to their work. This varies considerably: some neglect this aspect of Reich's work and use Bioenergetics as a neutral or even reactionary technique. Others share Reich's political understandings but lack, as he did, an understanding of women's issues. Working directly with the body can raise questions about male/female relationships quite sharply: for example, a woman might find it difficult to receive Reichian massage from a man without feeling sexually invaded or threatened. You cannot assume that a Reichian therapist will be sympathetic or understanding of this. Many therapists follow Reich in assuming that 'healthy' sex is heterosexual. There may also be a stress on the man being in charge in a sexual context and the woman being 'able to give in'. When choosing a therapist to work with it is important to find out where they stand on all these questions. In several countries you can find radical Reichian therapists, and there are also many women Reichian therapists who, though not feminists, are skilled, sensitive and sympathetic to the situation of women.

Even if you are primarily interested in using Bioenergetics in a self-help situation, we recommend attending some groups run by professionals in order to learn from watching them work. A more precise experience is needed than, for example, using Gestalt. You need to be familiar with the process so that you don't lose your nerve and get scared by what another group member is going through. Attending a professional group will teach you what to expect and will also increase your awareness of your own body and give you firsthand experience of what it is like to explore feelings in this way. It is never easy to help another through something you have not experienced yourself.

SOME EASTERN APPROACHES TO THE BODY

Reich's theories about body energy, developed from his work with patients as well as laboratory experiments with simple cells and even investigation of the energy forces involved in the weather, have much in common with various Eastern philosophies and disciplines which have developed out of a very different history. The body energy, or 'orgone' energy, which Reich describes, flows the length of the body in a healthy person along predetermined channels in a similar way to the energy patterns which are charted along meridians in the body by the 5000-year-old Chinese system of acupuncture. Recent experiments have shown a strong electromagnetic 'charge' between known acupuncture points and although there is still considerable doubt about the nature of this bodily energy charge (parallels with electricity are limited), increasingly it is becoming accepted in the West as a new dimension to our understanding of the way our bodies work.

Acupuncture can be seen as a physical approach for promoting and balancing energy flow by the insertion of needles at key points. Women have found it useful to deal with particular problems like migraine headache, tension, difficulty in ovulation. T'ai Chi Chu'an and Aikido are self-defence disciplines which emphasise the power of the body when its energy flows harmoniously and it acts as a unity from its base and centre; many women have preferred these to self-defence techniques relying on hardship, muscle power and brute force. They could be described as a kind of moving meditation: while bioenergetic bodywork emphasises emotional patterns and emotional release, these disciplines link the bodywork with a more spiritual development. Yoga, too, though often taught in the West as a way of keeping fit or 'body-building', is originally concerned with promoting the flow of energy and using physical exercise to open up spiritually.

Another interesting approach is the map of the chakras, which derives from India. This system locates centres of energy in different parts of the body, governing different areas of the body's activity. They are located at points where many acupuncture meridians cross and correspond with certain glands and parts of the nervous system. These energy centres, or chakras, are believed to radiate energy as well as receiving energy from the outer atmosphere for distribution through the body. Usually described as seven in number, the chakras range up the body from the base of the spine to the top of the head and again energy is believed to flow up and down the body between them. John Pierrakos, a follower of Reich who contributed to the development of Bioenergetics, has drawn parallels between different types of 'holding' in the personality and blockages in the chakras. Some critics find the chakra system too mystical or too literal to be acceptable, but it can provide a helpful way of looking at the relationship between the body and the personality and how we relate to the outside world. So here we give a very short description of one of the many versions of this chakra map.

The first or 'root' chakra is located at the base of the spine and is related to body activity in the areas of sex drive and 'grounding'. It is connected to the material and physical bases of our lives and our relationship with our material environment. The second chakra is located in the belly and is referred to as our 'centre'. It is seen as the source of our strength and physical power, our vitality, instinctual movement and sexuality in a wider sense. The third chakra, in the area of the diaphragm and the solar plexus, is seen as the seat of raw emotions, especially anger and fear, and of strong personal attachments. The fourth, or 'heart' chakra, is linked with wider and more compassionate feelings of love, while the fifth centre, in the throat, is linked with self-expression and creativity. The sixth chakra, on the brow, is connected with intellect and intuition, and the crown chakra at the very top and back of the head is the area linked with spiritual development. The centres are linked with the shades of the rainbow from red to violet. The system is more complex than we can describe here (for example, the solar plexus is also linked with understanding) and can be taken on many different levels (for example, as moving from animal characteristics through the human to the divine or from the physical aspects of our being to the universal).

When working with the chakra approach, the emphasis is usually on balancing the chakras to achieve a harmonious relationship between the various aspects of the personality (physical, sexual, emotional, intuitive, intellectual and spiritual) which the different chakras govern. In self-help, to get a picture of yourself in terms of the chakras, you might do a meditation sending your awareness through those parts of your body. Alternatively someone else might help you by noticing, through massage, which parts of your body feel warm and active or dead, or by giving you feedback about which aspects of your personality come across most strongly to her. The balancing work can be done by physical exercises, meditation, breathing patterns, emotional release, massage or practical changes in your life. For example, if a person is underdeveloped in her 'root' chakra, she might be helped by a leg and foot massage, by doing ten minutes vigorous stamping every day, by breathing and meditation which focuses on this part of her body, by some work exploring her feelings about sexuality, by altering her bedroom or moving home to where she will feel more able to put down roots. Though some clairvoyant people are apparently able to see the chakras, as vibrating whirlpools of coloured light or energy radiating from the body at different points, others use this map primarily as a symbolic way of getting an overall view of our lives and personalities.

BODY LANGUAGE

Becoming familiar with the symbolism which has been attached to different body parts can be very helpful when doing any kind of bodywork. Reich and other body therapists developed great skill in 'reading' the body and understanding how particular muscle tensions relate to holding in different parts of the personality. Though these connections vary in each individual, it is possible to make general points about this body language. The advantage of this in a self-help therapy situation is that you can bear in mind the most likely emotional connections and associations of the body tensions which a woman may be exploring. If she says she has stiff shoulders you can have some grasp of what this might mean for her personality: that she may have some feelings of being overburdened, or a tendency to be over-responsible. It is not possible to be dogmatic, but if you have a few alternatives in mind you can check out what fits for her and may be able to help her better. Some of the connections are based in common sense: for example, tension round the eyes may reflect tears that are held in or the desire not to see something; tension in the arms may be linked with wanting to hit or reach out to other people. Others are less obvious. For example, there is a common symbolism which connects the right side of the body with action, aggression and being 'in the world', while the left side is linked with passivity, sensitivity, emotion and the inner world. The lower half of the body has been linked with support, the top half with relating. The lower half of the body has also been linked with night and the unconscious, deep feelings and the irrational while the upper half corresponds to day-time and the conscious mind. Most symbolism is determined by culture: for example, the 'passive' left side is often described as 'feminine', which reflects only a cultural attitude in our society that women should be more receptive and less outgoing than men. But there are also elements in this body symbolism which reflect physiological facts about the body: for example, the heart *is* situated on the left-hand side of the body linking that side with the emotional life, the lower half of the body *is* more 'basic' than the top half. Clichés and proverbial sayings often reflect ancient wisdom about the body's workings which has been validated by modern medicine and body therapies: phrases like 'the bowels of compassion', 'you're a pain in the neck', 'he's venting his spleen', 'blind with rage', may have more basis in the body experience than we give them credit for. Other traditions yield interesting body symbolism: the Tibetan Chua'ka massage system makes a series of detailed links between, for example, the knees and 'fear of death', the throat and guilt, the eyebrows and anger. Astrology links each part of the body with a sign of the zodiac and the qualities it carries.

All these traditions may be useful sources to mine for ideas and may combine with your growing awareness of your own body, and intuition about others, so that you become fluent in perceiving and understanding the language the body speaks.

BODYWORK EXERCISES

Here are some exercises to use the kinds of bodywork we have described. We start with more vigorous, energy-raising exercises and some bioenergetic stress positions. Then we move on to exercises which work in a gentler way to explore body awareness and symbolism.

69   Walking Warm
This is a good warm-up exercise. You need plenty of clear space. Group members start to walk round the room in a circle. One person directs and

gradually tells the others to increase the speed of the walk until it is virtually a run. Then she gradually tells them to slow down until they are back to a slow walk, and then slower still until the walk is slow-motion then almost no-motion. She should encourage them to be aware of the muscles of their feet, the movements and the balancing involved in the simple act of walking. Then gradually she speeds them up again. This alternating can happen several times.

This exercise is good for bringing awareness down into the legs and feet, which we often neglect, but which are very important for our 'grounding', our connection with the earth and the basic support of our body and personality.

70 I Can Run

Again, you need plenty of space. One person should direct the others.

People should start to run in a circle round the room and keep going for several minutes. When they start to lag they should be encouraged to continue and to keep up speed. When they start to become really tired, they should be encouraged to continue and to start saying 'I can!' as they run. Keep them going. After a while they should be encouraged to add different phrases to 'I can', such as 'I *can* run', 'I *can* do a difficult job', 'I *can* love', 'I *can* ride a bicycle' or whatever statements they might like to make about what they can do in their lives.

This exercise warms people up and also increases your confidence in your own power and physical strength. Most people can keep running long after the point where they feel they have no more energy and must give up. It puts the body under some stress and may bring feelings to the surface.

71 Stamping

This exercise helps grounding and raises energy. It can also help people to let off or open out negative feelings which may be blocking the group and making it feel dead.

People simply stamp round the room, repeating a suitable phrase like 'Shut up!', 'No!' or 'Me! Me!' You may leave it open for people to improvise phrases, or you may decide on one phrase which feels right to the group. People should focus on letting their weight down into the stamp and feeling the ground under their feet as they shout.

You might like to experiment with stamping and shouting 'Me! Me!', then seeing how the feeling and movement change if you alter the phrase to 'I! I!'

72 Learning to Shout

This is a good exercise for getting in touch with the full volume and power of our voices, which as women we have often learned to inhibit. Having a tight throat blocks our self-expression in many ways, and in therapy can restrict a full release of feelings.

Stand in a circle, feet parallel and a shoulder's-width apart, knees slightly bent. Breathe evenly for a few minutes to relax. Now imagine you are breathing into your throat, and after five breaths start, on the exhale, to say 'No!', 'No!' Imagine the sound actually coming from the throat area. Repeat ten times, being aware of the muscles you are using, and of the quality of the sound.

Now start to breathe into your chest, be aware of your rib-cage expanding on the inhale, falling on the exhale. After five breaths, start to say 'No!' from your chest as you breathe out. Really imagine the word coming from there, and let the sound express the full force of your chest as it exhales. Again, say it about ten times, and be aware of the quality of the sound, which will be fuller and deeper than the sound from your throat.

Now start to breathe into your belly, it may help to put your hands there so that you can feel it expanding and contracting with the breath. After five breaths, see how 'No!' sounds if it really comes from down there and passes freely out through an open throat and relaxed jaw. It can be very full, deep and loud, and quite different from the sound which comes just from your throat.

If you feel shy about shouting, it can help to have one person directing so that you are all shouting at the same time, which makes it easier to let go. This is not a good exercise if you have sensitive neighbours!

73   Bioenergetic Grounding

These exercises involve placing some strain on body muscles to encourage them to 'give up' and relax the tension which is held in them. The focus is on the legs and on contact with the ground. The exercises will increase sensation in the legs, and may lead to 'letting down' or 'breaking down' into tears and sadness. In the long term this can be the way through to 'letting go' to deep pelvic sexual feelings, to establishing a more solid contact with reality (having your feet 'on the ground') and to finding your own strength to support yourself ('standing on your own feet').

These exercises are 'stress' positions and each person should decide carefully how far she feels ready to push herself in doing them. If you stay in the position for a long time, it can be painful and can trigger the release of strong emotions.

The Arch or Bow

Stand with your legs spread, toes turned inward, knees bent and back arched backwards. Feel the ground beneath your feet and let yourself breathe deeply into your abdomen. It helps to place your hands, as fists, against your lower back just below the waist. If this position is taken up correctly, the shoulders are directly above the feet and the line between them is a perfect arch. Ask a friend, or look in a mirror, to check that you don't lean too far back, stick your buttocks out, bend your neck, or break the arch in any other way. In this position the body is balanced and a flow of excitation can move through it. Because this position is charged with energy, after a period of breathing, the legs will begin to vibrate, usually as an involuntary tremor. It is good to allow this to happen and to let it become stronger the longer you hold the position. This exercise is also done by the Chinese under the name of the 'Taoist Arch', and can give a feeling of being integrated or connected.

Here is an exercise which is good to do after 'The Arch'.

With feet shoulder-width apart, knees bent and toes pointing slightly inward, bend forwards and touch the floor lightly with your fingertips. Continue to breathe fully into your abdomen. Again, after a while your legs will probably begin to vibrate. You can stop when this becomes painful, or push yourself to continue and see what feelings come up.

These exercises emphasise grounding because in Western culture there is a strong tendency to live 'in our heads'. To awaken energy at the centre of the body in the stomach, and at its base in the pelvis and legs, is a crucial part of making the body more balanced, whole and integrated. Lowen points out that grounding provides a safety valve for the discharge of excess excitation: 'Bioenergetically speaking, grounding serves the same function for the organism's energy system that it does for a high-tension electrical circuit.'[11] In a therapy situation where strong feelings are being aroused, grounding should ensure that a person does not split off, become anxious, or go into an unreal high of excitement followed by a slump into depression. It helps changes in the body and emotions to develop in a solid, connected way.

74   No No and Please Please

This exercise can bring up strong feelings of anger or pain. It is done in pairs.

Choose a partner. For 'No No', one of you lies with her pelvis, back and head flat on the floor, breathes deeply into her stomach and makes a bicycling movement in the air with her legs, repeating 'No! No! No!' on each kick. The other holds her feet and applies a firm pressure so that she has something to kick against. Make eye contact with each other and keep this movement going for about four minutes, then exchange roles.

For 'Please Please,' one of you balances on the balls of her feet with knees bent and back straight and her arms held out in front of her. She breathes deeply into her stomach and repeats 'Please, please, please' continuously. The other holds her hands (not supporting her). Make eye contact and keep the position and words going for about four minutes, then exchange roles.

Now share with your partner what you experienced. Did you want to bend your neck or look away to cut yourself off from the experience? Were you aware of stopping yourself? Did you kick furiously but find you couldn't let

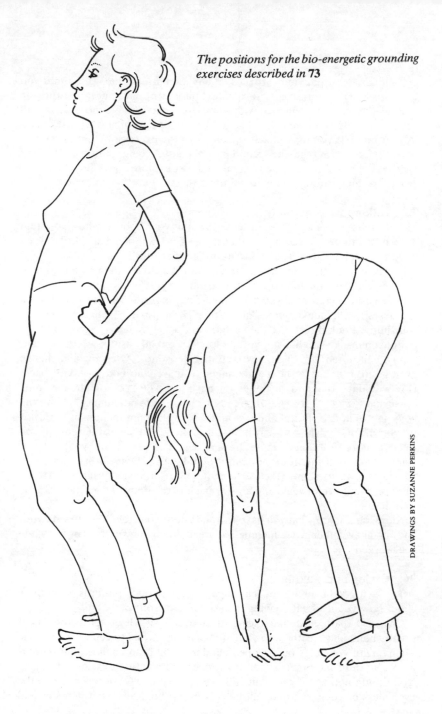

The positions for the bio-energetic grounding exercises described in **73**

DRAWINGS BY SUZANNE PERKINS

out a loud 'No!' from your throat? Did any memories come up of times you have felt like this in the past? It may feel phoney at first, but it is surprising how deep breathing, combined with some stress and suitable movements and words, can help you connect with a genuine emotion which is lying dormant in your body. If you let yourself surrender to the exercise the first part may bring up feelings of rage, the second part of painful vulnerability or loss. You may feel churned up and need some time to explore these further in the group, so think carefully how to continue the session after this exercise.

75   Talking to Your Body

This exercise brings to light your feelings about your body and how you treat it from day to day. It recognises that most of us experience a split between mind and body, and uses dialogue to bridge that split.

It is best to do this exercise in turns round the circle, taking ten or fifteen minutes each, with help and attention from the rest of the group.

Put a cushion in front of you and imagine putting your body on it, following the Gestalt technique described in Chapter Three. Imagine you are talking to your body. Look directly at the cushion and start by telling your body the things you dislike and like about it. Address it directly as if it were a person: 'Body, you're too fat', 'Your sexuality frightens me'. After a while, change over, go to sit on the cushion and imagine you are your body speaking back. How would it respond to the things you have told it? ('You don't let me enjoy my sexuality at all!', 'It's you who feeds me when I am not hungry'.) Have the body say what is beautiful about it and what valuable functions it performs for you. Then have the body say how you could live your life differently if you listened more to it. See if there are any demands your body would like to make ('Don't put me in those painful high heels!', 'Don't drink so much!', 'Do more yoga', 'Let me get close to another person sexually again'.) After a while, exchange roles again and answer back to the body and let the dialogue continue.

At the end, share what you have learned about your relationship with your body and have other group members share anything they noticed or felt while you worked.

76   Giving and Taking

This is a good exercise for learning, from your body patterns, something about how you deal with 'giving' and 'taking' in your daily life.

Choose a partner. Stand facing each other with legs apart and knees slightly bent, and breathe into your stomach for a while to centre yourselves. Then one of you holds out an open hand and you both imagine that there is an object in it; the other person is to reach out wanting to take the object. You should both keep your feet still. Move very slowly. In this exercise the awareness of your own body motions is everything. See what happens and notice how you handle the situation. If you are the person reaching, do you grab? Feel that you will never get it? Lose your balance reaching out for it? Pretend you don't want it? Give up if it's hard to reach? Which hand do you use? What do you do with the object when you get it? If you are the person holding out the object, do you withhold it? Tease? Give it easily then wish you'd kept it? Put your arm right out of reach? How do these body movements relate to your patterns of giving things or getting things you want in real life?

Try the sequence through a few times, always in slow motion, experimenting with different patterns that emerge. Then exchange roles so that the one who reached before, now holds the imaginary object. Do the sequence again several times, then give your partner feedback and discuss what you have learned about yourselves.

If nothing happens for you when you do this exercise, try a more vigorous one and come back to this one at a later stage.

77   Pushing and Yielding

This exercise is very similar to the one above about 'Giving and Taking'. Two people stand facing one another with feet apart and knees slightly bent. Keeping their feet still, they place their hands palm to palm and experiment with pushing against the other's hands. Allow at least five minutes and then stop to discuss what happened. Did you feel strongly that you wanted to 'win' and push the other person over? Did you give up? Were you scared of pushing? Did you play with one another? See how these patterns relate to your everyday behaviour.

These exercises sound very simple, but if they are done in a slow and aware way they can teach a lot. One thing which may come up for women in particular is realising how hard it is for us to assert ourselves or to go directly for something we want.

78   Picturing My Image

This exercise can make you aware of ways to let your body movements, image and appearance, reflect your inner potential rather than outer expectations of you.

Put a wide range of easy-to-use crayons in the middle of the room and give each person two large sheets of paper. On one you draw the way you feel you usually come across in the world, the image you usually present of yourself. Allow only three minutes for this. Use the colours which feel right but work quickly and spontaneously without worrying about an artistic effect. Turn the sheet over.

Now shut your eyes and remember a time when you felt you were very true to yourself, when you felt alive, or in tune, or able to express things you cannot usually express. Recall the situation in detail and remember what you were like, how you felt in your body. (*Pause*.)

Open your eyes and draw the person you were then. Again, work quickly but choose the colours you want. (*Three minutes for this*.) Choose a partner and decide who will go first.

Take your first picture and speak in the first person to describe the picture ('I'm stiff-looking, I haven't any feet', 'I'm mostly blue and brown') for three minutes. Turn the picture over.

Take your second picture and speak in the first person to describe this picture for three minutes ('I'm energetic and swirly', 'I'm completely orange'). Let yourself really own the qualities of this picture which may be those you don't usually recognise as your own. You could not have imagined and drawn the picture if those qualities were not present in you somewhere, though perhaps usually repressed or denied.

Now put both pictures side by side and take three minutes to tell your partner the ways in which you could express the qualities of your second picture more in your daily self-image, 'I could wear more colourful clothes', 'I could do some dancing classes, this one looks so fluid', 'I could share more of myself with other people – this one is so much bigger on the page, that one is all curled up'.

When you have finished, exchange roles.

The listener in this exercise simply listens and gives clear attention without comment. She should make sure that the speaker keeps talking in the first person as this helps her to identify with the qualities her pictures show. When you have both had a turn, take five minutes to give one another feedback. Do not give interpretations, but point out anything you noticed in your partner's drawings which she seemed to overlook.

In our experience such pictures can yield a wealth of information about how a woman feels about her body and the way she moves and presents it in her daily life.

79 Picturing Symbols for Your Body Parts

This exercise works best after some physical warm-up. You will need some pens, paper and crayons.

Have the group lie, eyes shut, flat on their backs on the floor, while one sits out to read the instructions slowly aloud.

Take a few moments to do some relaxing breathing and allow tensions and preoccupations to drain out of your body. (*Pause*.) Now send your awareness to your feet. Be aware of any sensations or emotions there . . . Be aware how you feel about your feet . . . Be aware what role or function your feet play for your body as a whole . . . (*pause*) Now see if you can find a symbol for your feet, it may be a colour, shape, object or animal which reflects how your feet are as part of your body (*pause*).

The person reading the instructions now repeats the last paragraph, instead of 'feet' substituting in turn calves, knees, pelvis, belly, chest, shoulders, arms, neck and head. When you have finished, ask people slowly to open their eyes and sit up. They should take pen, crayons and paper and jot down briefly what symbols came up. They might do a coloured drawing of the whole body made up of the symbols. Then people should get into pairs and take ten minutes each to share with their partner what they found:

'My feet are fishes, maybe because they feel watery and not stable enough, also it reminded me of the Pisces symbol . . .'
'My thighs are like heavy table legs carved in wood, very solid and supportive and unwieldy'
'My pelvis was like a bowl of fruit, a bit broad but full of goodies'
'I couldn't get anything for my neck, I think I'm very unaware about my neck'

What you found difficult is often interesting to explore.
When you have both spoken, give each other feedback.

80 Experiments to Experience Energy Charge in Your Hands

This is a very simple exercise which can help you to experience the body 'energy charge', which can be brought to a particular part of the body by focusing awareness on it or by putting it in a stress position.

Stand and hold your hand straight in front of you with your arm relaxed. Focus all your attention on your hand, and keep it there for about a minute, while you breathe easily. Soon you may start to experience your hand differently – you may sense a streaming into your hand, which may begin to feel charged and tingling. It may start to shake a little or vibrate, indicating that you have directed a stream of energy or excitation into your hand.

Now try the same experiment with both hands, holding them in front of you a shoulder width apart. When you have directed attention into both hands for about three minutes, bring them slowly together. When the palms are about three inches apart you may sense a charge between them as if it has substance and body.

81 The Steel Arm[12]

This exercise compares the power of muscle exertion with the power you can wield when you are centred and in tune with what the Japanese call the universal spirit or 'Ki'.

Stand facing someone of about your own size. Place your right arm on your partner's left shoulder, straighten it and tighten your muscles as hard as you can. Now your partner places both her hands on your elbow joint and, gradually increasing the pressure, she tries to make your arm bend. Resist bending with all your strength. Notice what this feels like.

133

Now relax your arm and put it back on your partner's shoulder. This time start by focusing your awareness in your belly and imagine all your strength is flowing from your legs and belly and out through your arm. Imagine your arm is a steel rod, hard and unbendable. Imagine it extends beyond your partner's shoulder in a long straight line to some point in the distance. When you have the feeling that your arm is unbendable, your partner can start trying to bend your arm in the same way. Concentrate and breathe calmly. Do not tense your muscles against her pull. You do not need to; your arm is a steel rod reaching effortlessly into the distance. Keep the image as your partner increases her pressure. Does it feel any different to meet her pressure this way?

Afterwards share what differences you noticed and exchange roles.

MASSAGE

Massage can be a wonderful medium for making contact with your own body or with another person. It can be used to re-educate into their body someone who is cut off from it. It can restore energy and circulation to neglected body parts. It can open a person to her emotions, to pleasure and sensuality, or can bring her a deep relaxation and peace. In a self-help session you might use brisk rubbing at the start to raise energy; apply pressure on tense muscles to help a person who is 'working' to express feelings, or relax each other by giving gentle stroking at the end of a session.

There are excellent books available outlining various massage methods and describing strokes and techniques to give a partner a pleasurable whole-body massage. So here we will not describe techniques but will outline the approach we have found most useful, which is known as intuitive massage. In Britain this approach has been introduced by Anne Parks who links massage with meditation, and works with sound, colour and healing.

Before you start make sure the room is warm enough and have ready sheets and the oil which you will need to use on all of your partner's body except her face. Remove as many clothes as feels comfortable, best of all is for both of you to be naked. Have ready a soft blanket to cover parts of your partner's body when you are not massaging them, if she gets cold. Before you start to massage your partner, take time sitting facing her or sitting at her head to relax and to centre yourself. You may like to do this through breathing, sending awareness through your body, concentrating on finding a quiet place inside yourself, or using one of the meditations which we give later in this book. One good meditation is to imagine breathing in calm white light through the top of your head and breathing it out down through your arms and hands – this helps to make your hands aware and sensitive before you start the massage. Then take some time to become aware how your partner needs to be touched. This does not require emotional involvement: it is a question of tuning in to her physical presence and body energy, not your feelings about her. When you start to massage, work slowly, stopping often with your hands resting on her body to feel contact with her and to be in touch with what her body is telling you. What is important is not mechanical contact but *feeling* contact. The action of the massage comes not from the head but from a deeper impulse. Don't try to 'fix' her body, looking for tension or 'things wrong' and setting yourself to pummel or push to 'make it right'. Instead let your hands be open to moving where you can feel her body wants to be touched. You will find that you become aware which parts of her body feel alive, where her skin is hot or cold, where it flinches from touch, where it is sluggish and is asking to be touched playfully or energetically, where it needs a gentle or reassuring contact. Keeping your eyes shut may make it easier to tune in to how her body is calling you. The ability to massage intuitively is in all of us and it is mainly a question of allowing your natural sensitivity to come through so that you can respond to your partner's body and her energy.

Do not touch any part of her body or do anything which does not feel completely comfortable to you both. The back is a good place to start if your partner is shy. Touch lightly on delicate places like the throat and the backs of the knees. To be sure you are relaxed, stop occasionally to centre yourself and check that your jaw is hanging loose, not clenched shut. Have your partner imagine she is breathing into the parts you are touching, so as to send her awareness there. Ask her often how the massage is feeling and what she would like done differently. You can experiment with using all the varied parts of your hands (thumbs, fingertips, heel of hand) and with making different movements (lines, circles, kneading, holding). It is good to start and end with long strokes. The most important thing is to have the feeling that you are allowing love and energy to pass into your partner's body through your hands. Applying heavy, even painful, pressure at certain points of the body obviously works under some massage systems, but in a self-help situation we have preferred to focus on giving pleasure to another's body, not pain. Painful pressure can feel like a punishment to the body, it can bruise, and it can sometimes merely shift tension from one part of the body to another. When drawing your hands off the extremities of your partner's body (head, arms and hands, feet), imagine you are cleaning and pulling negative energy out of her body. You may need to shake your hands occasionally to get rid of any charge they are picking up from your partner's skin. At the end, wash your hands and arms in cold water for the same reason. Leave your partner to lie for a while under a warm blanket. Then sit and share how it felt to you both.

Massage is very rewarding because almost everyone loves to be touched. Touch is one of the most basic and pleasurable forms of human contact, yet it is a very distorted and neglected medium in our culture, usually restricted to sexual relationships. If you give massage in a loving, slow and centered way, you can hardly fail to give your partner (and yourself) a good experience. Learning to give and receive pleasure is an important part of the process of re-owning our bodies and opening up the possibility of a fuller sexual experience. Massage also helps us to learn that we are not totally dependent on sexual relationships for the satisfaction of our basic need to be touched.

During a massage, people respond differently: you may send your partner into a calm state of deep relaxation, or the relaxation may open up some emotion in her and she might start to cry when different parts of her body are touched. In this case you may decide to move to a different part of her body and continue the massage, or you may decide to stay with exploring those feelings. Where several people are giving massage in the same room, it is not a good idea to encourage one person to do any loud shouting or crying as this discharge would be a shock to others who may be very relaxed and open during their own massage. It would be better for that person to leave the room, or to devote a later session to exploring the feelings which have come up. If you want to bring your partner back from her emotions, you can ask her to raise her knees, put her feet on the floor, open her eyes and talk to you about what she is experiencing.

Aura Massage

Body energy is said to radiate from the body in an 'aura' which extends several feet beyond our physical body. Some people describe seeing this aura, which can be of different colours, and recently Keirlian photography has registered flickering light emitted from the skin, changing in nature depending on whether the person photographed is calm, drunk, angry and so on. This phenomenon is reflected in popular expressions about 'personal vibrations': 'he gave off "bad vibes" ', 'I could really tune in to her "vibes" '. Some alternative medical approaches, for example, radionics, divide the total aura up into different layers connecting with different functions in the whole organism. Some people are able to feel the aura with their hands and to massage a person's 'energy' several inches or feet away from the body without touching the body at all. 'Aura massage' is not suitable for use in a self-help situation, but can be obtained professionally from psychic healers trained in this work. Some believe that this approach is one of the swiftest and most effective ways of bringing the body into balance and opening the full potential of the personality. It bypasses much work with the emotions and the conscious mind and deals directly with body energy. This may be very helpful for some, while others may feel the need to explore various areas of themselves (their emotions, their sexuality) more consciously before they would benefit fully from this approach. It seems important to be able to bring changes made through this work from the unconscious into the conscious level, so that developments in the personality can be reflected and consolidated through our relationships, and in our leisure, work and living situations.

Here are some structures to start exploring the possibilities of massage in a self-help situation. You should decide in each case which clothes you feel comfortable about removing.

82   Everybody Touch One
One person who feels needy goes into the middle and is touched by the whole group. She should ask for the kind of touching she wants, whether it is stroking, taps, light fingertip circles, or simply to be held.

83   Exchange Massage
Choose a partner and give each other a massage for an equal length of time, an hour, half an hour or even ten minutes each way, depending on how much time is available. At the end, share what it felt like for both giver and receiver. Ask for the kind of massage you want, unless you are doing this as a group and decide that you will all massage the same body part so that you can share in what way your experiences were similar and different.

84   Massage Yourself
The ability to massage yourself sensitively and lovingly is important as a means to nourish yourself and to get to know your body. If you are doing this at home, it is good to take a bath first. Create an atmosphere with lighting and sounds, use plenty of oil, and make it a special occasion. If you are in a group, it may help to have one person stand out to guide the others. Choose a body part which needs attention and, as you massage, be aware what that part of the body does for you every day. Afterwards note what you experienced, or share it with your partner or group.

A Caution
Even pleasurable activities like massage can sometimes be turned by us into a form of self-punishment: 'I let them touch me but it felt awful', 'I was terrified to take my clothes off but everyone else did', 'I didn't want to touch her but I was scared to say so'. If you don't want to touch or be touched, say so, rather than setting yourself high standards and forcing yourself to make contact in an alienated way. It is fine to sit out a massage, it is fine to explore your resistance to giving and receiving pleasure. The Berkeley Radical Psychiatry group sum up some of the ways we deny ourselves by talking in terms of the 'stroke economy'. (A 'stroke' is a nice contact, touch, compliment or hug.) The rules of this stroke economy, which deprives us of pleasure, are: 'don't ask for strokes you want; don't give strokes you have; don't

accept the strokes you get; don't reject the strokes you don't want; and don't stroke yourself'.[13] One of the ways of breaking this pattern is to be able to say 'no' to what we *don't* want, especially for women. In a mixed group it is important to be able to say 'no' to being touched by a man without feeling that you are being uptight, unliberated or unfriendly. Men sometimes try to exploit massage or dance in sexist ways. In any group, it is important to recognise that you may have good reasons for not wanting this kind of contact. A lifetime of self-denial does not vanish overnight and massage may not seem pleasurable at first, but upsetting and scary. It may make you cry. A self-massage may bring up massive feelings of anger. It is important at all times when doing massage that you be touched how and when you want to, and that any feelings which come up are accepted as fine and valid. Don't feel you ought to have loving or pleasurable feelings when you haven't. Don't make massage another tyranny!

DANCE

We have found dance a very good approach if you have a low level of energy, experience a poor relationship with your body or difficulty in self-expression – or simply if you enjoy dancing! Increasingly dance is being taught in new ways, with less emphasis on discipline, gymnastic ability or 'feminine grace', and more emphasis on contact between dancers, energy release, self-expression. This is based on the understanding that dance is not a restricted talent but a form of self-expression natural to the body. It is only a question of learning to free the natural dancer in all of us from the inhibitions and restrictions which have been imprinted on us by our upbringing and society. The process of freeing the natural dancer in us may take time and it can help to start with exercises which let you explore your defences and self-consciousness, or which start with a fairly restricted structure from which you can then branch out. If you feel especially self-conscious about dancing in front of friends you may find that attending a dance group run by a professional leader with people you don't know gives you confidence to start expressing yourself in this way.

Here are some exercises to try in a self-help group. Remember with all of these that you are dancing for yourself, not for anyone to look at you. Don't force yourself. Noticing what you find difficult can teach you a lot. There is no need to perform.

85   Dancing from the Ground Up
Stand for a few moments with your eyes shut and knees slightly bent to do some relaxing breathing, and imagine any tensions draining out through your legs and feet into the floor.

Take a record with several tracks of good strong dance music. On the first track, with your eyes shut, dance mainly just with your feet and ankles. On the second track, let your legs come into it, exploring the movements you can make just with the feet and legs. On the third track, allow your pelvis to become involved. On the following tracks allow the top half of your body, your arms and head to join in until you are dancing with your whole body.

This structure gives you a framework to get into dancing freely through gradual stages. It is also good for grounding, correcting a tendency to dance 'all up in the air' with the arms and chest while the lower half of the body is neglected.

If you want to dance with a partner, a good exercise is **111**. Here are some others:

86   Dancing Hands

This exercise can develop gradually into a whole group dancing freely with one another.

Stand in a circle with your hands in the centre, placed randomly on top of one another in a pile. Very slowly start to move your hands, exploring the other hands and eventually choosing one pair which interests you most. Trace the owner of these hands and, leaving the circle, let a dance develop between your two pairs of hands. You may want to start with very small movements, exploring the surface of the skin or touching fingertips. You may want to play with shaking hands, miming a boxing match, mirroring. Experiment with different moods and types of movement, and if it feels right develop it into a dance involving your whole bodies but still focusing on your hands. Later you may want to join up with another pair, and eventually with the whole group, in a dance centred around the way your hands touch and respond to one another.

87   Saying Yes and No with Your Body

Standing in a circle, make eye contact with someone opposite and say 'No' to her with your whole body. Notice how it feels, which parts of your body are tense. After a minute or two, change into saying 'Yes' to the same person with your whole body. Notice how this feels.

You can develop this into a dance: for one track of music move round the room experimenting with dancing 'No' to everyone you meet, then for the next track try dancing 'Yes'.

88   The Sphere

This exercise works best if you have already warmed-up and feel relaxed.

Choose some smooth and slow music. Tune in to it for a while with your eyes shut. Then spread your arms out wide and imagine your fingertips are touching an invisible sphere which encircles you at arm's length all around. This is your space. Keeping your eyes shut if you prefer, start to experiment with different ways of exploring the sphere, with your arms, legs, and so on. Let all the movements of your body reflect the shape of the sphere. Try out smooth, circling motions in as many different ways as you can find. When you feel ready, join up with a partner and let your spheres merge, then start to explore this larger sphere together. Again, focus on circular movements as you dance.

89   Being One Organism

This is a dance you can do together as a group. One person should sit out to read the instructions slowly.

Move in any way you like around the room, letting yourself touch other group members lightly as you pass them. Do this for several minutes.

Now, when you touch someone you stick to her. Keep moving around the room until you are all linked together in a chain of touch. You have become one organism. Keep exploring how you can move and how you are constricted as one of the limbs of this organism. Maintain touch and gradually see if you can let your breathing synchronise so the whole organism is breathing as one. Come to rest in a comfortable position, standing or lying on the floor. Continue breathing together and keep your sense of being one organism.

Now shut your eyes and imagine that a huge golden sun is shining down on you all, melting tensions and pains and filling you all with warmth and life.

Afterwards, share what you experienced. This exercise can bring up strong feelings about being part of the group, which may be claustrophobic, fear of being touched or a beautiful sense of belonging.

Here, in brief, are some other dance ideas you may like to develop.[14]

90   Resolution to a Situation

Standing, eyes shut, recall in detail a recent difficult situation in your life. Now take five minutes to dance out that situation *and a resolution to it*.

91   Dance Your Day

Standing, eyes shut, recall what your day has been like. Now take five minutes to dance your day, then share in the group what came up for you.

92   Tall and Small

Try dancing each of these, perhaps assigning half the group to each role and then exchanging after a few minutes. Do some curling up and stretching exercises first to help you get into the parts. Height is a difficult issue for many women. After dancing share how you felt and any connections you made with your life: 'Dancing tall I felt very superior', 'Being small felt more flexible and mischievous', 'I've always felt self-conscious about my height', 'I hated being small'.

93   Fear and Anger

The group lies down or walks, eyes closed, around the room while one person leads them on a guided fantasy[15] of being followed late at night down a dark street. You should notice any tensions in your bodies or movements you have an impulse to make (hunching so as to be unnoticed, sticking out the chest to look unafraid, running away) and then develop these movements into a fear dance, exaggerating, changing and exploring them.

After this, it is good to do some arm exercises (shaking and circling your arms on your shoulders) and some leg exercises (shaking them, kicking them to front back and side) and then to develop these arm and leg movements into an angry dance. Aggressive rock music may help you get into the mood.

Afterwards you can share what you found easy and difficult, what situations you were reminded of and how these themes of fear and anger have come up in your life.

SEXUALITY

Reich's work on sexuality, emphasising the importance for body balance of a full and regular sexual release, is only the background of a strong awareness in the women's liberation movement that we need to rediscover and redefine our sexuality. Moving from the Victorian attitude of 'Close your eyes and think of Jesus', women are asserting our right to a full and pleasurable sexuality on our own terms. To different women this means: making love when we want to instead of feeling it is a duty we owe to a partner; asserting our pleasure in the clitoris and in sexual practice not necessarily centred on penetration of the vagina; asserting our right to have sexual relationships with women; masturbating to give ourselves pleasure instead of being dependent on another; asserting our right to be celibate; organising to support rape victims and for better legal protection against rape and sexual harassment; campaigning for free and safer contraception and free and safer legal abortion so that no woman has to bear on unwanted child.

However, there are still many women, most of us probably, who have not yet reached our full potential for sexual pleasure and orgasm. The taboo on sexual pleasure as 'dirty' operates especially strongly in the case of little girls and young women, and many of us have also had some experience of being coerced or threatened sexually. These factors, combined with sexual tensions in the family during childhood, tend to make us associate sex with fear. Another complicating factor is the way in which sex has become a commodity in Western society. For women this can mean that making ourselves 'sexy' or a desirable 'object' for men can become an aim which has little to do with expressing anything about how we feel or our own needs. For the lack of other sources of power, a woman is encouraged to see her sexuality as a weapon. She can use it as a threat against other women or can exploit her ability to withdraw sexually from her partner. All these patterns contribute to our experiencing our sexuality in an alienated way. Undoing the effects of these social pressures, negative associations and conditioning can be a slow process. Almost all therapy which increases our awareness of ourselves and of our history, which releases emotional energy and unblocks body tension, will help open us to a fuller sexual experience. Gaining more sense of our real strength through the women's movement means that we have less need to use our sexuality as a weapon. But many women also find it helpful to work specifically on their sexuality and there are now available in several countries professional sexuality groups centred on the needs of women.

Most of these groups are outgrowths from the sexuality work developed in California on the basis of Masters and Johnson's recent research into the human sexual response. The approach is most clearly outlined in Lonnie Garfield Barbach's book *For Yourself*.[16] The method works very much in the present, teaching us to develop a better relationship with our bodies and to learn new patterns of behaviour. It usually includes a rigorous programme of daily exercises. This homework involves getting to know your body by touching it and looking at it in the mirror; physical exercises to awaken the pelvic area; making love to yourself as the basis of knowing what pleases you sexually; drawing and writing to explore your body image and sexual attitudes. Doing the homework is also a way of taking time to care for yourself and helps you to know yourself as a person who is worth something and deserving of sexual pleasure. Being better informed about the physical processes involved in sex, and more aware of how you like to be pleased, you are able to ask for what you want in a sexual relationship instead of exercising only the negative power of withdrawal. The group plays an important role in keeping you to the exercises and supporting the changes you may decide to make in your life.

One limitation of this method is that it does not deal specifically with the emotional dimension of any sexual problems, nor with issues arising from past or childhood experiences. But it has a very impressive success rate in helping pre-orgasmic women to become orgasmic and is an excellent approach for any woman who wants to take a closer look at her relationship with her sexuality. This work is clearly described in several books which are geared to self-help and include exercises. So here we give only a few exercises which may help you begin to look at your sexuality, either alone or with a group.

94   The Story of my Vagina

This exercise helps you to connect with the history of your sexuality.

Sit, close your eyes and imagine that you are your vagina. Include your clitoris and the whole of your genital area. Let your mind trace through the history of this part of your body – the beginnings of its awareness, the pleasant and unpleasant experiences it has been through, times when it has been in conflict and in harmony with the rest of your body. After several minutes, open your eyes. Now each take turns to tell the group or a partner the story of your vagina. Tell it in the first person as if you were the vagina: 'I am Pat's vagina. She used to touch me but felt guilty . . . It hurt me when she put a tampax in me for the first time . . . When she was a teenager I wanted to go with boys but she was scared to . . .'

Be aware when it is hard for you to speak honestly: embarrassment or sexual competitiveness may affect what you say. At the end, share what you got from the experience and give feedback on one another's histories.

This exercise also works at home alone, where you can speak out loud to yourself, or write the story down instead of speaking.

95   Moving in Water

All exercises which increase body relaxation and awareness will contribute to a fuller sexual experience, but we give this one here as it especially focuses on responding to another without becoming completely passive. Some of the relaxation exercises we have described encourage your body energy to be quite 'Yin' (passive). In this exercise 'Yin' is finely balanced with 'Yang' (active) energy.

Join a partner. One of you stands and for ten minutes the other moves her in any way she chooses. When you are being moved, you are relaxed but not floppy and you move as if you were in water or some thicker fluid: when she moves your hand to a position, you keep it there until she moves it again. She can lie you down, move you around, put you in poses, or experiment with moving your whole body through subtle pressure on one part – for example, a turn on the hand can move the whole body. She will probably put you in positions which are unfamiliar for your body and you will learn a lot about how your body works and moves, which parts are tense, and so on. This exercise is good for learning to trust another to touch and move you while staying consciously active and responsive yourself.

At the end of ten minutes, share with one another what the experience was like, then swap roles.

96   Awakening the Vagina

This is a very simple exercise which involves simply tightening and relaxing the vaginal muscles. If you are not sure which these are, practise stopping your urine in mid-flow, which uses almost the same muscles. The contraction and relaxation should be done slowly. You may find it helps to do it in time with your breathing, contracting the muscles as you exhale. The tone of these muscles is important during sex, pregnancy and childbirth, and the more they are exercised, the more feeling and awareness develops in them.

Another way of awakening the vagina is to lie down and imagine your breath coming into your stomach, and then being exhaled through your genital area. This, too, if done regularly, will increase the blood circulation and sensation in this area.

Some ways of starting to take time at home to learn about and care for your body are: regular long baths, paying particular attention to different parts of your body which you usually neglect; massaging cream into your whole body every night; standing naked in front of a mirror and being aware how you feel about different body parts; close examination and exploration of your genital area using a small mirror.

NOTES

1 Wilhelm Reich, *Listen, Little Man!*, first published in the USA, 1948; Penguin, Harmondsworth, 1975, p 60.
2 *Listen, Little Man!*, p 46.
3 *Listen, Little Man!*, p 33.
4 Wilhelm Reich, Preface to the third edition of *The Mass Psychology of Fascism*, first published in Germany, 1945; Farrar Straus & Giroux, New York, 1970; Penguin, Harmondsworth, 1975.
5 Alexander Lowen, *Bioenergetics*, Coventure, London, 1976; Penguin, Harmondsworth and New York, 1976, p 50.
6 *Listen, Little Man!*, p 105.
7 *Listen, Little Man!*, p 20.
8 *Listen, Little Man!*, pp 22–3.
9 *Listen, Little Man!*, p 50.
10 *Listen, Little Man!*, p 55.
11 *Bioenergetics*, p 176.
12 This exercise is adapted from Anne Kent Rush, *Getting Clear: Body Work for Women*, Random House, New York, and The Bookworks, Berkeley, 1973; Wildwood House, London, 1974, p 38.
13 Hogie Wyckoff in Claude Steiner (ed), *Readings in Radical Psychiatry*, Grove Press, New York, 1975, p 113.
14 These ideas were developed by Barbara Mound and Lucy Goodison of the Red Therapy group for their 'Womandance' workshops at the Women's Arts Alliance, London.
15 Guided fantasies, and how to improvise them, are explained fully in Chapter Six.
16 See 'Further Reading', this chapter.

FURTHER READING

Getting Clear (see above) is a beautiful book on bodywork for women and is invaluable for anyone interested in using the body as a starting point in self-help therapy.

Wilhelm Reich, *Character Analysis*, Orgone Institute Press, 1948; reprinted by Vision Press, Great Britain, 1969, 1978. Detailed account of Reich's early theories of personality and work with character armouring.

Wilhelm Reich, *The Sexual Revolution*, Vision Press, Great Britain, 1951; Farrar Straus & Giroux, New York, 1979. Contains Reich's ideas about sexuality, the family and young people. Reich was, and remains, the only person to link the physical and emotional with social and political issues. He writes with great breadth and has influenced and inspired us enormously.

Bioenergetics (see above) is a readable and practical description by Lowen of how his work developed from Reich's.

David Boadella (ed), *In the Wake of Reich*, Coventure, London, 1976. Interesting essays covering the many different offshoots from Reich's work.

Stanley Keleman, *Your Body Speaks Its Mind*, Simon & Schuster, New York, 1975. Presents a clear vision of the human being as one organism in which our muscle habits *are* our personality.

Ken Dychtwald, *Bodymind*, Pantheon Books, New York, 1977; Wildwood House, London, 1978. Lists the many issues, messages and symbols which may arise when working with each part of the body.

Jack Schwarz, *Voluntary Controls: Exercises for Creative Meditation and for Activating the Potential of the Chakras*, Dutton, New York, 1978. Describes the chakras and shows ways of working with this approach to the body.

George Downing, *The Massage Book*, Random House, New York, and The Bookworks, Berkeley, 1972; Penguin, Harmondsworth, 1974. A practical manual describing clearly and sensitively, stroke by stroke, how to give a whole-body massage.

Robert Delong Miller, *Psychic Massage*, Harper & Row, New York, 1975. An inspiring and practical book on this little recognised approach.

Lonnie Garfield Barbach, *For Yourself: The Fulfillment of Female Sexuality*, Signet, NAL, New York, 1975. Outlines a highly successful approach to sexuality work.

Jack Lee Rosenberg, *Total Orgasm*, Random House, New York, and The Bookworks, Berkeley, 1973. Contains many exercises to do alone or with a partner, designed to open up the whole body to sexual experience.

Boston Women's Health Book Collective, *Our Bodies Ourselves*, Simon & Schuster, New York, 1971, 1973; Revised British edition, Angela Phillips and Jill Rakusen (eds), Penguin, Harmondsworth, 1978. The most useful and comprehensive book on health, written by and for women.

Mike Samuels and Hal Bennett, *The Well Body Book*, Random House, New York, and The Bookworks, Berkeley, 1973; Wildwood House, London, 1974. How to take control of your physical health and practise preventative medicine with the minimum of professional intervention.

Chapter Six
Buried Treasure:
Dreams, Fantasies and Meditations

To some extent all therapy is concerned with making the unconscious conscious – whether it is childhood memories, repressed emotions or unnoticed body sensations which we are bringing to light – but in this chapter we will focus on what our unconscious mind tells us through the language of dream, symbol and fantasy. The aim of this approach is not only to increase our self-awareness, but also to help us recognise and use our intuition or inner wisdom, and to reach a deeper sense of who we are beneath the conscious level of personality with which we normally identify. It helps us to realise that our unconscious contains not only deeply repressed fears and problems but also a world of creative pictures and symbols, a rich perceptive power and much strength which we do not usually tap. This can be an exciting process which emphasises what is positive inside us; it can be especially helpful for women. Because our role in this society often excludes us from the public world of achievement and action, many women are in touch with this inner world of intuition, dream and fantasy but have not yet found ways of using it to enrich and change their lives. We will describe three different starting-points for this approach: dreams, symbols and guided fantasies and meditation.

DREAMS

Freud described dreams as the royal road to the unconscious. Because they reflect our imagination and creativity, they can be a very exciting means to explore some parts of ourselves of which we are not aware in our daily lives.

Every therapy approach to dream is indebted to the work of Sigmund Freud and also to Carl Gustav Jung who developed and modified Freud's ideas. But for practical use we have found the dreamwork method of Fritz

Perls most helpful. So, we will briefly review Freud's and Jung's theories on dreams then give a more detailed description of Perls' method showing how it can be used in a self-help group, with a friend, or alone.

Freud's Dream Theories

Freud shocked Europe early this century by suggesting that the unconscious mind is a storehouse of many things which we do not admit into our waking mind: not only repressed memories, but censored desires, primitive or infantile impulses, thoughts which in normal life we would judge 'shameful'. He understood dreams as largely the product of this unconscious mind. He believed that the buried impulses or desires disturb our sleep and the function of the dream is to help us rest by resolving these disturbing stimuli. Often the dream reflects the fulfilment of a wish which had been unsatisfied. He gives the example of a small boy who dreams of eating a basket of cherries which he had not been allowed to eat the day before; in this case the unsatisfied wish was recent, but in many cases it can be an unsatisfied urge or desire from the distant past which is acted out in this way in a dream. Behind this 'wish-fulfilment', and behind the shape of the dream as it appears to us, Freud believed there often lay a disguised message or meaning which he called the 'latent dream-thought'. This hidden message had to be tracked down by a process of detective work, deciphering and looking behind the superficial elements and events of the dream. To find this meaning, Freud used a method called 'free-association': he would break the dream down into its different elements and ask the patient to let her mind roam freely and say what associations each item brings up, what recent events it might be connected with, what meaning is suggested. This process might lead a long way away from the apparent contents of the dream. Together with the free-association technique, Freud based his dream interpretation on the theory that certain elements in dreams have a common symbolism for many people; for example, that a house would usually represent the human body, king and queen represent parents, water stands for birth, and travelling often symbolises dying. Many of the common symbols he refers to are sexual, for example umbrellas, poles, trees, knives, guns, pencils and other implements in dreams are thought to represent the male penis, while caves, bottles, boxes, rooms, cupboards and other containers are thought to stand for the female vagina and womb.

Here is a very brief example which Freud gives of his techniques at work, interpreting the dream of one of his patients:

A young woman who had already been married for a number of years dreamt as follows: *She was at the theatre with her husband, and one side of the stalls was quite empty. Her husband told her that Elise L. and her fiancé also wanted to come, but could only get bad seats, three for a florin and a half, and of course they could not take those. She replied that in her opinion they did not lose much by that.*[1]

The associations which the woman patient makes to the different elements in the dream include recent news that Elise L., a friend of her own age, had become engaged; a recent theatre outing where she herself had unnecessarily booked seats too early and had to pay more; and to the mention of the one florin and a half she connected that her sister-in-law had wasted 150 florins by rushing off in a hurry and spending it all on a piece of jewellery. When asked for any associations to the number 'three' in the dream, she said only that the engaged girl, Elise L., was only three months younger than herself who had been married for ten years. Freud points out in these associations the theme of 'too early' and 'too great a hurry' which was not apparent in the dream itself at all; combining this with his understanding of going to the theatre as symbolising marriage, and the number three as commonly representing a man, he uncovers the woman's hidden dream-thought for which the dream was a highly-distorted substitute:

It was really *foolish* of me to be in such a hurry to marry! Elise's example shows me that I too could have found a husband later on.' (The over-haste is represented by her own conduct in buying the tickets and that of her sister-in-law in buying the jewellery. Going to the theatre is substituted for getting married.)[2]

Freud interprets the dream to the woman as expressing disparagement of her own husband and regret at having married so early.

In this case the latent dream-thought which is painstakingly tracked down deals with an event in the patient's adult life (getting married), but often the meaning of the dream is traced back many years to thoughts which are very deeply repressed and taboo, for example, sexual desire for a parent or the urge to kill a parent or sibling which had been experienced in childhood.

In recent years a heated controversy has raged about the value of Freud's work for women. There is much to be said about the shortcomings of his understanding of women's experience; but feminist interest in his theories continues.[3] Here we will touch only on some limitations of his dream method.

Although the patient participates in the interpretation process by offering her 'associations', there is a danger that the analyst's own values and prejudices may affect the interpretation she or he makes as to what the 'real meaning' of the dream is. Traditional Freudian thinking is strongly male-oriented and this can lead to a woman's dreams being interpreted in a distorted way. We also question whether the patient gets a chance to *feel* the emotional content of the dream fully, and how much use she can make of any interpretation which is handed to her. Freud himself remarked how difficult his patients found it to relate to the interpretations he made of their dreams. For example, the woman who dreamt about the theatre tickets had not been aware of having disparaging thoughts about her husband and didn't understand why she should be having them. Accurate interpretation, and assimilation of that information, depends on the continuing relationship between patient and analyst. In a self-help situation this doesn't exist, and group members have neither the training nor the experience to do interpretative dream work. It seems best to avoid trying to use Freud's technique or to act like home-grown psychoanalysts 'interpreting' one another's dreams. We find it more helpful to offer loving support and techniques which allow a woman to connect *directly and emotionally* to her dream and discover what it means for herself. Perhaps this meaning cannot in any case be reduced to a disguised thought which can be spelled out in words. More often a dream may seem to be speaking to us in a different language, revealing conflicts, shapes, tones, feelings or buried parts of our personalities.

We would also question Freud's theory that certain symbols regularly and almost 'naturally' stand for certain elements, an example being boxes and other hollow receptacles which, he claimed, represent women's sexuality. As it has been popularised, this approach can degenerate into trying to interpret dreams mechanically from an index of symbols, and it does not allow for change. What if a woman developing a more positive sense of her sexuality dreams about it using a strong outgoing symbol like a goat? We would see the symbolism we use in dreams as being determined by the society and situation we live in, varying from one individual to another and changing as we change.

Jung's Dream Theories

Jung made a useful criticism of Freud in this area. He emphasised that you cannot reduce symbols to a set formula, that it is important to find out why one symbol is used rather than another and to explore the quality and texture of a symbol rather than just looking for the meaning behind it. You might dream of your father as a lorry or a flight of stairs, and in each case the specific image has been chosen by your unconscious to convey different qualities. Rather than seeing a symbol as a disguise for something else, Jung believed it should be recognised as having a power in its own right. He believed that 'dream symbols are the essential message carriers from the instinctive to the rational parts of the human mind'[4] and that such symbolic ideas by their very nature 'cannot be formulated in a way that is satisfactory to intellect and logic'.[5] While Freud believed that the process of dreaming started with a thought which was then disguised and distorted by a number of symbols to make a dream, Jung believed that picture and symbol are the natural language of the unconscious and that a dream symbol expresses a psychic fact which can only partially be described in verbal and rational terms. Accordingly, he laid less emphasis than Freud on the interpretation of a dream, and felt that the *experiencing* of a dream was an important therapeutic process in itself. Some of his patients at the end of their treatment with him experienced a very strong dream, with a mandala or other harmonious symbol, which Jung accepted as a psychic landmark in their lives whose meaning did not need to be spelled out. Jung often worked with a series of dreams rather than a single dream and stopped using Freud's method of free-association which could lead away from the dream itself. He preferred to focus on the qualities and mood of the actual symbols and events of the dream, all of which he felt were important: he believed that dreams are a self-representation of the unconscious mind of the dreamer and that each element or symbol in the dream portrays a mood, emotion, or part of the dreamer's personality. The 'I' in the dream usually represents the conscious ego of the dreamer, while other figures in the dream stand for her less known, unconscious qualities. Jung gives an example of a patient who had a very high opinion of himself and an irritating air of moral superiority; this patient dreamt about a drunken tramp rolling in a ditch. Jung suggested that the tramp represents a part of his personality not expressed in his daily life and repressed under his mask of moral superiority.[6] The dream is bringing the image of the tramp to light to balance the one-sided picture of himself which the man generally communicates and is thus trying to restore psychological equilibrium:

> This is what I call the complementary (or compensatory) role of dreams in our psychic make-up. It explains why people who have unrealistic ideas or too high an opinion of themselves, or who make grandiose plans out of proportion to their real capacities, have dreams of flying or falling. The dream compensates for the deficiencies of their personalities, and at the same time it warns them of the dangers in their present course.[7]

Here is a short example of the Jungian approach at work, from the case history of a man who is given the name 'Henry'.

> . . . Henry had another dream in which he was once again confronted with the disturbing problem of the irrational: *Alone in my room. A lot of disgusting black beetles crawl out of a hole and spread out over my drawing table. I try to drive them back into their hole by means of some sort of magic. I am successful in this except for four or five beetles, which leave my table again and spread out into the whole room. I give up the idea of following them further; they are no longer so disgusting to me. I set fire to the hiding*

place. A tall column of flame rises up. I fear my room might catch fire, but this fear is unfounded. [8]

In the interpretation of this dream by Henry himself and his Jungian analyst, the beetles are seen as his 'dark qualities' which have been awakened by the analysis and have come to the surface. Black is described as the colour of depression and death and Henry being alone in his room is seen as a situation which could lead to states of introversion and gloom. In the dream there is a fear that these dark qualities represented by the beetles may overflow Henry's professional work (symbolised by the drawing table). The analyst sees Henry's attempt to destroy the beetles' breeding ground by fire as a positive action, because fire can, symbolically, lead to transformation and rebirth, as in the ancient myth of the phoenix. The impression is given that the fire is a symbol of Henry's inner power to transform these 'dark qualities' and give them a new life in a different form. Jung is clear that tendencies or qualities which might under some circumstances be beneficial can become dark and demonic when they are repressed.

Jung's work *also* has limitations. While Freud perhaps overestimates the role played by repressed sexuality in dreams, Jung probably underestimates the sexual element. There is too little reference in his work to the body and physical sensations or symptoms. His lack of understanding about the situation of women is discussed later in this chapter. Perhaps the most helpful aspect of his dream work is his respect for the unconscious: he sees it not just as a repository of everything objectionable, infantile and animal in us, but as a treasure house abundantly creative in producing symbols and teaching us through this symbolic language about our lives. He shows that it has a natural tendency to balance and heal us and that its treasures, when brought into consciousness, can strengthen the personality and give psychic energy for an individual to grow and mature.

Perls' Dream Theories

The ideas of Fritz Perls, founder of the Gestalt school of therapy, have been outlined in Chapter Three. Here we deal only with the method he developed for exploring dreams. His basic idea is to bring a dream to life by having the dreamer tell the dream in the present tense as if it were happening now and then identify with, and speak as, each element in the dream. His theory has some similarity to Jung's in that he sees the characters and items in a dream as repressed parts of the dreamer's personality: parts which have been buried or denied by day and which emerge in dreams to compensate. Through Perls' method you act out these repressed parts in order to re-own aspects of your personality which you have alienated, and thus you can come to a fuller and stronger sense of yourself as a whole personality. He saw the main function of dreams as being to resolve unfinished situations and to fill holes in your personality. In the example above, Perls' approach would be to ask the morally superior man to speak as the tramp, to describe himself and explore this role ('I am a tramp. I'm drunk, I'm lying here not caring about anything . . .'). In this way the man might come to terms with a part of his character which he was denying under his superior image. Similarly Henry would be asked to explore *being* the black beetles in his dream, Freud's woman patient would speak *as* the empty theatre, *as* the friend who had put off marrying. Perls was dismissive of Freud's method of interpreting dreams which he felt could be just an intellectual game; he claimed that while Freudian analysis cuts up and analyses a dream, Gestalt therapy brings a dream to life. In fact, if the woman had explored her theatre dream using Perls' method, she might have reached similar realisations as with Freud's method, but her experience as she reached those realisations would have been more physical and emotional as she re-experienced the conflicts and moods of the dream in the present. Perls' is a vivid method for bringing disconnected or discredited parts of ourselves into consciousness. For a self-help group it is especially helpful as it emphasises direct experience and allows the dreamer to do most of the work exploring the symbols in her dream herself, with other group members helping her to use the techniques. The whole dream becomes accessible and by the end of a session she has usually learnt what issues the dream is dealing with and what it can teach her about the way she lives her life.

The idea that every character or object in our dreams is actually a part of our personality may seem difficult at first. Here is an example where an apparently obscure and alien object can come to be seen as part of the dreamer's character and experience:

Rose describes a dream in which she is standing under burning sunshine on a railway station platform. The group asks her to 'be' the platform, to speak as if she were the platform. Rose looks surprised and sceptical as if she has nothing in common with a station platform and does not know how to talk as one. Finally she shuts her eyes and begins 'I'm cold and hard and people walk all over me'. This connects so strongly to her present experience of herself that she bursts into tears and the session carries on from there.

These dream elements often seem negative or frightening: for example, a horrible insect crawling on us, a plane bombing us, a wall cutting us off from others, a giant wheel about to crush us. Usually they reflect the way we have projected our own qualities outside us and so experience them as alien, destructive forces beyond our control. In this way our own power turns against us. By acting the insect we might contact a 'naughty girl' in us who has gone sour through being repressed; by acting the wheel we could re-own strength and energy which we had pictured as a force separate from us. Perls believed that each time we identify with some part of a dream, turning an 'it' into an 'I', we reclaim energy and increase in vitality.

Sometimes it is hard to accept that everything in a dream is part of us, not just because it is scary to recognise ourselves, but because the dream very clearly concerns a parent, friend, or recognizable actual situation from every-day life. Here's an example:

Penny has recently moved house and feels insecure in her relationship with Craig. Things are going well for him, badly for her. She dreams that they are on a rocky seashore, that he is running ahead, leaping nimbly from rock to rock, while she is left behind, stumbling, trying to catch up, scared of falling into the sea. Surely, she says, this dream is about a real present situation, about Craig and how things actually are in her life, rather than about different disowned parts of her personality?

This dream obviously does reflect a real situation and an actual tension in her relationship with Craig. Dreams can often be very useful in this way, bringing to our attention things we have unconsciously noticed but failed to register in our waking life: for example, a dream about teeth may be a way of reminding yourself that you need to go to the dentist, a dream that a friend is drowning may mean that you have picked up, but not consciously registered, signs that she really is in some trouble. Ann Faraday, in her book *Dream Power*,[9] gives many examples of using dreams in this way. But if we are using dreams in therapy, we are interested in learning what they can tell us about *ourselves* and it is clear that Perls' method would still work with Penny's dream. Though the dream reflects an actual situation, the aspects of the situation she has singled out and the symbols she has used, also reflect an inner landscape of her own. She might have dreamt of Craig as rejecting, as distant, or as angry; but in fact the themes she recreated are those of confidence, stumbling and fear, which are probably themes important or unresolved in her own life and personality. Craig may in reality be a confident person, but the fact that Penny picks up on this quality, registers it and recreates it in her dream suggests that it is also a quality which resonates in her, which corresponds to something present but not fully resolved in her own personality. Otherwise that quality would not be sufficiently internalised in her mind to be recreated by her in the dream. By acting out the confident Craig, the sharp spiky rocks, the deep wild sea, Penny might well contact confidence and strengths in herself which are buried, which are not being fully expressed in the weak fumbling role she finds herself playing at present.

USING PERLS' METHOD IN A SELF-HELP SITUATION

Here is an example of a woman using Perls' method in a self-help group:

Diana retells, in the present tense, a dream where she is in a house which has been broken into; there is broken glass, an atmosphere of fear and 'bad magic'. Outside in the dusk a monstrous white goat ('the Devil') looms menacingly, larger than the house. She is frightened. To her relief, a person arrives to cure the 'bad magic', an androgynous figure from Mars, supple and radiant in white and silver. As this figure moves into the next room of the house, the giant leg of the goat bursts in the outside door. Diana shuts the door and runs in terror after the 'person from Mars'.

When Diana has finished retelling the dream, she will play the roles of the goat, the house and the space person in turn. The group suggest that she lies down and starts by speaking as the goat. She shuts her eyes, breathes evenly for a while to tune in to this character, and then starts to describe herself as the goat 'I'm huge and white and terrifying . . .' The group ask her how the goat feels about Diana and the house: 'I feel shut out. I want to break that house open . . .' Next Diana speaks as the androgynous person from Mars: 'I'm supple and silver and beautiful . . .' but after a few sentences she dries up. The group notice a funny expression on her face and ask her what is stopping her.

'It doesn't feel like me at all. This person is so radiant and alive, I feel such a mess . . .' Diana starts to sob.

'Diana, it's your dream, it *is* you. See if you can carry on.'

Through her tears Diana carries on describing herself as the spaceperson and gradually manages to own that radiance. Then she says how the spaceperson feels about the goat, Diana and the house. Next she speaks as Diana, then as the house. 'I'm all shut up, but I'm scared someone's going to break in . . .' One group member notices that she has clenched her fist, and comments on this, 'What are your hands doing?' Diana replies 'I'm tight and frightened, I want the goat to go away'. The group encourage her to exaggerate the fists, and she tenses her whole body into a ball. They encourage her to repeat the one phrase 'Go away! Go away!' several times. Then they suggest she put her body into the opposite position; she stretches, out, expands, lies relaxed on the floor. The group suggests she tries to develop a dialogue between the goat and Diana in the dream. She sits on one cushion to speak as the goat, and changes to another to speak as Diana. The dialogue starts quite antagonistically ('I'm scared', 'I'm going to overwhelm you'), but the two characters become more reconciled towards the end, as the goat agrees to be gentler and Diana realises she can leave the house to speak to the goat out in the night air.

When Diana feels she has finished the group asks her what the dream means to her. She says she feels that the goat represents her sexuality, and the spaceperson her spirituality, both parts of her personality which she has repressed and been scared of. 'I like to be in control: like being in the house, it's brightly lit and cosy but I'm always scared of what is shut out.' She talks about how she has been opening up recently to these different sides of herself – through grounding exercises and meditation – and sees this as a positive process which she wants to continue.

Using this method effectively requires some skill. In an unconfident or inexperienced self-help group, you may draw a complete blank, getting stuck on simply retelling the dream or on an unrewarding dialogue between dream characters. So it seems helpful to summarise the techniques in clear steps to follow:

1   The dreamer recounts the dream from the start in the present tense: 'I *am* in the house', 'There *is* a leg coming in through the door'. The group makes sure she does not lapse into the past tense. If the dream becomes long and confusing, stop. In any one small section of a dream, there is usually enough material for a whole session. So short dreams are best, and with a long dream choose one episode to work on. The group may ask the dreamer which episode has the most power or attraction for her, or notice as she recounts the dream which part affects her most; this may be reflected by her becoming excited, or hesitating, by a gesture or a change in voice.

2   When she has decided which episode to focus on, the dreamer speaks as the main elements of the dream whether these are characters ('Speak as the spaceperson', 'Speak as Craig') or animals ('Speak as the goat') or objects ('Speak as the house', 'Speak as the broken glass'). Remember they may be elements which seem hostile to the dreamer, and it is often useful to act out elements which are not actually embodied or which are noticeably *absent* from the dream (the 'bad magic', the person who broke the windows). If you dream of a guitar without strings, it is clear that the strings are somewhere in the dream but are missing; the basis of the guitar is there, but where music and sensitivity should be, there's a hole. Here are some guidelines about which elements will be most helpful to act out:

Ask the dreamer what is most powerful for her
Notice which elements play the most energetic or powerful role in the dream
Notice as she tells the dream which parts affect her, making her change her voice, expression or posture
Notice what is conspicuously absent from the dream

In each case, she should describe herself ('I am the house. I am small . . .')

155

and then say how she feels about the other characters and elements in the dream ('I am protecting Diana; I am afraid of that goat bursting in . . .').

3   Develop a dialogue. For example, Diana developed a dialogue between the goat and the 'I' in her dream. She might equally have explored a dialogue between the goat and the house, or between the spaceperson and the 'bad magic'. Look for any conflict or potential conflict between elements in the dream and develop a dialogue to explore it. When doing this, it will help to have the dreamer sit on a different cushion for each character and swop between them, using the Gestalt method described in Chapter Three. The group should watch that the dreamer continues to breathe fully, and should ask her to repeat any phrases which seem to carry a lot of significance or energy for her, as Diana repeated the phrase 'Go away!' A significant phrase may initially come out strongly, or may come out surprisingly softly: for example, Diana speaking as the goat at first introduces herself in a whisper, 'I'm huge and terrifying . . .' The group encourage her to repeat this phrase until the emotional charge connected with it is expressed appropriately in a huge voice.

With experience it becomes easier to sense when is the right time for the dreamer to switch roles between the characters in the dialogue. To develop your skill, you may find it helpful to read *Gestalt Therapy Verbatim*[10] which gives many full-length examples of Perls' dream work. It is important to stay in touch with the present, with the dreamer's sensations and feelings as she works. Notice her gestures, tone of voice and facial expression which all give strong clues about what is happening for her. In our example above, group members were quick to pick up on a movement of Diana's hand while she acted the house, and a change of expression when she acted the spaceperson. In this process it helps to avoid the question 'why?' ('Why are you clenching your fist?') which can lead to explanations and interpretations; instead use 'how?' questions which will keep the dreamer in touch with her immediate experience ('How are you feeling now?', 'What is your hand doing?', 'Who are you hitting with that fist?'). If she makes a gesture, it is often helpful to ask her to exaggerate it, to give it a word, to explore what the opposite of it would be.

4   There are several ways in which a therapy session can develop from exploring a dream. For example, Penny's dream might lead her to put Craig on a cushion to explore in some depth the current problems in her relationship with him. You could do the same with any friend, parent or child who appears in your dream: it is possible to use the dream as a springboard for working out any difficulties in a relationship or resolving an unfinished situation. Similarly, you could go on to explore any issue the dream has brought up, for example, Diana might work on her sexuality or her fear.

Another good technique is to relate issues from the dream directly to the group. For example, after Diana has told the goat in her dream 'Go away! You frighten me!' She might be encouraged to go round the group saying this same phrase to each person in turn, then to experiment going round again saying the opposite. In this way she could connect the theme of the dream with how she relates to people in real life. How does it feel to tell people to go away? What does she experience when she says the opposite? A woman who dreams that a man gives her permission to cross a field might be encouraged to go round 'giving permission' to group members to behave in certain ways ('I give you permission, May, to be angry as you have this evening'), then to go round refusing them permission. In this way she could explore in the group the theme of 'permission' which the dream shows is a tense, unresolved area for her.

5   Feedback. Here it is important, as usual, to stick to what you *noticed* and *felt* during the session rather than trying to interpret another's experience. Two points which Perls thinks are helpful to look for in summing up the dream are: what is the 'existential message' in the dream? ('You're too high up' in a falling dream); what is being avoided? ('leaving the house' in Diana's dream).

We think it is helpful also to ask yourself: 'What does this dream tell me about the way I live my life?' and 'What kind of changes might I want to make in my life?'[11] In learning from our dreams it is important to understand *why* we have disconnected ourselves from those parts of our personality which we project outside us into alien or frightening characters. Perls can sometimes sound quite blaming, as if we decide to deny and impoverish ourselves for no good reason, but it is possible to see this more positively as the way we have learned to survive in the world. Jobs, social norms and power relations in society often require us to deny parts of ourselves so that we fit in. Even if we reclaim those parts of ourselves during therapy, it will not necessarily be easy to express them freely in our daily lives, but being aware of them is enough to give us a stronger sense of ourselves and to release in us the energy to move towards situations where we can express ourselves more fully. In our example, Diana had cut off her powerful sexuality which could get her into trouble (because it's 'unfeminine' and could lead to 'sleeping around') as well as from a spirituality not widely recognised in Western society outside the confines of the Christian church (because it's 'mystical nonsense' or 'like witches' black magic'). At the end of the session she might talk about changes she could make in her job, relationships or social life, or political changes she could work towards, to enable her to express these re-owned parts more fully.

I Don't Remember my Dreams

If you are interested in working with dreams but have difficulty remembering yours, it may help to take the following steps. When you go to bed, allow yourself a period of relaxation – for example, looking at a candle – for a few minutes immediately before going to sleep. Concentrate on remembering your dreams. You might even like to suggest to yourself a topic you would like to dream about and as you drop off remind yourself, 'I will remember my dreams'. When you wake up, don't open your eyes until you have looked for any dream memories that have lingered. Instead of fretting about what has slipped away, grasp *any* remnant which you can recall, get into the feeling of it and let it lead you back into the rest of the dream. Some people remember dreams better when they wake up naturally rather than with an alarm clock. Keep pen and paper or a 'dreambook' by your bed to write in as soon as you open your eyes. Work out a way of recording your dreams. It may be with a few key words or a drawing which helps you to catch the dream on paper quickly. You can refer to the book to refresh your memory when you work on the dream in therapy. Everybody dreams several times each night, so if you don't remember yours it may be there is some material in them you are avoiding or not ready to face. Below we describe an exercise to explore what process may be going on with these 'missing dreams' as well as some other preliminary exercises which may make it easier to start using the Gestalt dream method.

97   Dream Warm-up in Pairs

Sit comfortably in pairs on the floor, facing each other with paper and pencils to hand. Shut your eyes and take several minutes to recall a recent or important dream. Recall the characters, events, moods and feelings of the dream. Open your eyes and note down, in word or picture form, some of the dream's main points. Now you have ten minutes each to share something of the dream with your partner. In your time, start by retelling the dream in the present tense. Then pick two interesting characters or objects from the dream. Speak as each of them in turn, using the first person and describing yourself, what you're like, how you feel about the other elements in the dream. Your partner simply listens and makes sure you keep to the present tense and the first person. At the end of ten minutes, exchange roles.

Coming back together as a group, you can share what came up for each of you and may find that one woman is interested enough in her dream to explore it at greater length in the group.

98   Talking to Your Dreams

This Gestalt exercise helps to find out what your dreams as a whole represent for you. It is a short exercise which you can do in pairs or in turn sitting in a circle.

Place a cushion in front of you on the floor. Imagine this cushion stands for your dreams. Addressing the cushion, talk to your dreams: 'Dreams, I find you exciting and I want to remember your better . . .', 'Dreams, you scare me . . .', 'You're unpleasant, go away . . .' and so on.

After several minutes, swop places and sit on the cushion representing your dreams. Take a little while to get the feel of 'being' your dreams, then start talking as if you were the dreams talking back to yourself: 'I have a lot to tell you, but you won't listen to me . . .', 'I'm very elusive, I slip away from you when you wake up . . .', 'I'm strong and colourful and much more spontaneous and creative than the other parts of you . . .'

By playing the role of your dreams in this way you often find that the dreams emerge as symbolising your inner self, the hidden part you don't often show or act out in the world. If you don't remember your dreams, just talk to the missing dreams: 'Dreams, I wish I knew what you're like. What happens to you? I feel cheated by the way you just disappear . . .', and answer as the dreams in the same way: 'I frustrate you by going blank. I'm too weird, you couldn't cope with me, you just don't know what goes on in the night when you're not conscious . . .'.

Afterwards share what you learnt.

99   Exploring the Dream Setting

This is another exercise to get used to the dream techniques.[12] You need pencil and paper handy, and can do the first part together as a group.

Sit comfortably with your eyes shut and do some relaxing breathing. Now go inside yourself and tune into a recent, powerful or important dream. Focus on the background of the dream, the setting (for example, a large house, a theatrical performance, a mining camp, the countryside). If the dream had several settings, focus on the one which seems to hold most interest or power for you. When you are ready, open your eyes and note down the main qualities or characteristics of this setting.

Now take it in turns, round the group or in pairs, to spend three minutes describing the dream setting. You are to use phrases which start with the phrase: 'Life is . . .'

'Life is a big house. It's crowded – sorry, *life* is crowded, too many people around, makes me feel confused . . .'
'Life is a theatrical performance. I'm meant to perform and I don't know my part. Life is having to perform . . .'
'Life is a mining camp. Life is grim and grey with machines everywhere . . .'
'Life is a spacious countryside. Life is green. Life is things growing.'

It is surprising how much can emerge from this simple exercise about a person's situation, her attitude to life and how she currently experiences the world. The dream setting appears as a condensed reflection of her existence. Afterwards share what you learnt and give each other feedback. Remember to avoid 'interpreting' each other's experience from an intellectual viewpoint. Stick to your own feelings and impressions of what happened.

FANTASIES AND SYMBOLS

Guided Fantasies

A 'guided fantasy' is like a waking dream. Instead of exploring a symbol or situation from a dream, you are encouraged to relax and let yourself *imagine* a certain symbol or situation which you can then explore. You can learn what symbols mean for you in a more deliberate way. A common exercise is to imagine walking through a meadow and then to describe how you experience this meadow: how long the grass is, whether it is hard or easy to walk on, whether it slopes, whether the sun is shining. The theory is that the qualities and moods conjured up in the fantasy give information about our lives, feelings and personalities. The weather in the fantasy might reflect your general state of well-being: close-clipped grass might reflect inhibitions in self-expression or over-intellectualisation; if you are cut off from your inner life you may find it hard to imagine any grass at all.

Techniques for using symbols in this way have developed in the wake of Jung's work. They are perhaps most clearly brought together in the writings of Roberto Assagioli, founder of the 'Psychosynthesis' approach to therapy, but they are also occasionally used in Gestalt, Psychodrama and other methods. Assagioli's theory is that when you are offered a symbol or situation to imagine – whether it is a meadow or a journey – you project meaningful material into it and attribute to it qualities you have yourself, often ones of which you are unaware. This process of projection is not conscious. When we imagine a meadow, its size, contours and colour will be shaped by unconscious forces. We may be surprised by the bleakness of the meadow we have pictured, or by its richness, or by the fact that we have imagined a frightening animal in it. The fantasy brings to the fore issues of which we are unaware. The process is not very different from that described in connection with dreams, and here again the experience of re-owning our own qualities makes us stronger. Even nasty or frightening images are revealed as buried treasure with their own message of power, energy or anger to bring into our lives. Guided fantasies offer certain practical advantages: you are not dependent on remembering a dream and a whole group can be led through the same guided fantasy together and can discuss it as a common experience. A fantasy can be useful to start a group session, giving everyone a chance to participate and raising issues which one woman may go on to explore in depth later in the session. It can also be useful if a person or group feels stuck, offering a chance to look at things in a new way and get a new, symbolic, angle on them. Of course this kind of exercise can be used just as effectively in pairs or individually. Here is one woman's description of being led through a guided fantasy.

> We all lay down with our eyes shut and one woman took us on a magical journey across the countryside, with streams, forests and mountains. It was so hypnotic that at one point I fell asleep for a few minutes. Afterwards we sat up and shared what had been most important for us. Two things stuck in my mind: at one point we were asked to visualise coming to a wall and getting over it. The wall I imagined was high and I thought I would never get over, but somehow managed to vault it lightly and effortlessly. We were told afterwards that the wall could be taken to represent obstacles in our life, and as I was bogged down in a very difficult situation at the time, I experienced a sense of exhilaration and confidence that I had the means to get over my problem. I somehow contacted in the fantasy a strong, sure-footed part of myself which I was not aware of in my conscious life at the time. The other part which struck me was at the end when we were led up to a house and in it found a wise person of whom we could ask any question we needed answering. I was amazed by the answer I received – to realise I had the answer to this question inside me all the time – and the idea of a wise person inside I could consult just by opening up to my unconscious mind.

This example shows how a fantasy can enable a woman to recognise and re-own strengths of which she is not fully conscious. The natural setting used here is typical of these fantasies, and it is sometimes claimed that certain symbols will relate to a particular part of the personality: for example, that a mountain will symbolise your aspirations; the depth of a stream you visualise will represent the strength of your emotional or sexual energy; for a man a rose bush may symbolise his sexual development, and so on. We have found it best not to be too literal in interpreting these symbols but to let each person discover what particular symbols mean for her. There is no attempt to spell out the 'meaning' of the visualisation in full. It can be helpful to clarify what you have learnt about yourself, but the value of this kind of exercise, as with dream work, lies in *experiencing* it and not in interpretations.

The psychosynthesis writings offer many guided fantasies similar to this one, including some which follow a process like the cycle of wheat (from the seed right through to the bread giving energy to human beings) or imagining the gradual growth and flowering of a bush from a seed. This last is thought to be especially helpful for symbolising and fostering your own psychic process of growth and development. Some are more explosive, like visualising meeting a lion or the eruption of a volcano. The psychosynthesis techniques also include leading people through part of a mythic story like the legend of the Holy Grail. The episodes of the story are taken to symbolise certain themes like ascent, contemplation and co-operation. As women we might prefer to use a myth like that of Demeter and Persephone: this story could yield themes like loss, search, concealment, reconciliation and could help us to focus on what these themes mean in our daily lives. Paintings can be used to stimulate the imagination in a similar way. You may find that you are most stimulated by a certain kind of symbol: mythological symbols, abstract symbols (triangle, star, mandala), animal symbols, human symbols (witch, heart, dancer) or technological symbols (bridge, spaceship). In the exercise section below we describe how to create the atmosphere and situation in which these fantasies work most fruitfully, and we provide several structures which you could adapt to a variety of themes, improvising fantasies based on different myths or symbols which best fit your needs at any time. You can also improvise how you follow up a fantasy, acting out the symbols as in dream work (speaking *as* the stream, *as* the lion), doing movement and dance or linking the themes to how you relate to one another in the group.

Using Symbols for Healing

Guided fantasies and symbols can be used not only to learn about ourselves, but also to heal ourselves. Here are two examples:

> One woman leads the group through a guided fantasy where they imagine walking through a garden. Afterwards Brenda tells the group that the garden she imagined was dry and infertile with hardly a blade of grass. She is encouraged to return to the fantasy and it is suggested that she look under every stone in the garden until she finds a living plant and then that she imagine bringing water to the plant to help it to grow.

> Lorna has asked Hazel to help her explore a nightmare in which she falls into the sea at night and drowns. Towards the end of the session she suddenly gets an image of a big, warm sun shining down on her. Hazel encourages her to bask in this sun for a while, and to remember this image. Lorna starts to use it regularly at times when she feels overwhelmed by events, weak, collapsed, or unable to sleep. She finds that this strong positive image from her unconscious helps her keep a sense of her own health and strength.

What happens in this fantasy and symbol work is that, unlike with dreams, the unconscious is *actively* stimulated and invoked. While you are imagining a journey or summoning up the image of the sun to give you strength in a difficult situation, you are actively using your powers of visualisation. As women it can be particularly helpful for us to take responsibility like this for making our unconscious resources available in the healing process.

Making Your Own Symbols

There is another approach where, instead of being offered a symbol to visualise and project onto, you think up your own symbol to represent a part of your body, personality or experience. For example, you might think of a symbol for your sexuality, for your head, or for your interpersonal relationships. Here is one woman's account of exploring symbols this way in a mixed self-help group.

Our group began by working on a theme important for all the members: the split between the things we wanted to do and the things we felt we ought to do. The session began by one person leading a guided fantasy. We lay on the floor and after thinking about these two aspects of our lives, these two sides of ourselves, we were asked to find symbols for them. The symbols which came into my mind were an orchard and a millwheel. We were asked to imagine speaking to each of these symbols in turn, and imagine them speaking to us or to each other. After this we shared our experience. We decided I would explore my feelings about this split in my life with the help of the group.

Firstly I was given two cushions, one to be the orchard, and the other to be the millwheel, and chose to begin by sitting on the orchard cushion and being the orchard. I described what it was like in the orchard: calm, secure, unforced, the sense of natural growth and warmth. Then I moved over to being the millwheel and described the sense of being pushed on to action all the time, a never-ending task, the noise, the sense of being worn away and the mechanical nature of the experience. After I had explored my feelings through these symbols I began to feel my fear of being like a millwheel. I began to say No, I wouldn't be like the millwheel. I was encouraged to repeat 'No, I won't' more loudly. At this point I was clenching my fist so it was suggested that I expressed this anger by hitting a cushion as I was shouting 'No'. At first I was thinking specifically of all the various tasks in my adult life which I ought to be doing, all the things other people expected of me. After a while my voice became more and more childish and when someone asked who I was speaking to now, I realised I was speaking to my father. I talked with the group about my feelings about my father, how I felt he had always demanded too much in terms of affection from me, that he had made me feel, as a young girl, that I was too important to him, that he didn't want me to have my own life, and that I had to get away. I was encouraged by the group to see if I could get further into these feelings about my father, and some of the men in the group began to take the role of my father. I began to feel a mixture of fear and disgust very strongly. I started shaking and trying to hide. Eventually I felt able to stop hiding and confront my father to tell him no. I felt that I had never done this in real life: I had never openly said 'You want too much, I can't be what you want'. I felt a strong sense of relief at having done so, and I stopped working at this point.

This experience brought up a lot of feelings which I have continued to explore and work through. I think the most obvious benefit is that I feel more able to withstand the pressure of other people's expectations and wishes and feel a greater sense of control over my own life. As far as my relationship with my father is concerned, I feel less uneasy when I am with him and less afraid of building a warmer relationship with him.

This example shows how symbols work can lead into exploring an issue in more emotional terms using different techniques like Gestalt and role-playing. The advantage of thinking up your own symbols is that they have a particular power for you and you can often find a personal way of using them to help you: for example, this woman could use the orchard regularly as a calming image. Allowing images to come up for you like this often shows a new way of looking at things. You can follow the process through by checking the image against reality as this woman explored the particular qualities of the millwheel which connected to her 'driven' quality.

Using Symbols to Explore a Resistance

When a person needs to express some feelings but finds it hard to do this, it is often unhelpful to push her and may be more fruitful to explore what is blocking her. You can use symbols for this. Here is an example:

In a mixed group, Sandy is upset but has tried unsuccessfully to discover what is bothering her or to release any of the tension and emotion she experiences. She is withdrawn and hostile to the group. She says she feels stuck and resistant and has flashes of being made of tubular steel. The group encourage her to explore this image. She describes it as feeling hollow and shiny, like a sculpture which people walk past when they are shopping and don't really notice. She describes herself as elegant steel tubes in a beautiful structure: 'This is Art!' she says, laughing.

'Good!' Peter replies, 'I've had a good look, and I want more action now!'

'Fine Art', Sandy continues, 'done by people with high minds. People like you can't appreciate me! It'll probably get dented and graffiti-ed in the end, though.'

'What do you feel, tubes of steel?' Cathy asks.

:It's quite nice being a huge shiny bit of Art.'

'I think it's a real drag,' says Peter. And so the session continues.

Running through this session's level of joking, a process is going on in which Sandy expresses, through the tubular steel symbol, being unnoticed, cut off from others, unappreciated, and compensating by feeling that she is 'too good' to be appreciated by other people. At the same time she also expresses some aspects of her personality she likes, feeling large, shiny and artistic (Sandy's creative work is an important part of her life). The symbol also allows other group members to share with Sandy some of their frustration at her withdrawal from them and her steel-like resistance to expressing what she feels in more emotional terms. A way to develop the session might have been to ask Sandy to find, and explore, a symbol which represents the opposite of the tubular steel.

Free Drawing

This is another way to work with symbols and fantasies. When we draw a picture we often project as much of ourselves into it as we do into the symbols of a dream or the landscape of a guided fantasy, imagining atmosphere and features which reflect our mood and qualities. For example, if we draw a bush we may show it in full flower or in a wintry, withdrawn state; we may show it close to other plants or standing very much alone, with deep roots or about to topple over, and all these qualities can be explored as reflections of our personality or present life situation. Below, with the exercises, we describe how to lead into this spontaneous drawing, which has nothing to do with being 'able to draw'. It can be applied to any theme and you can easily improvise your own exercise to fit what an individual or group needs. Here's an example from a newly formed group.

The group decides to draw pictures on the theme of 'How I am with other people'. Afterwards each woman talks to the group about her picture. Ruth has drawn groups of people separated from one another and talks about her distress at the loss of several close friends who have moved away. Kath has drawn swirling warm colours with a black bit round the edge. She talks about the black bit as a barrier which shuts out the warmth other people try to give her. She explores this by following the Gestalt technique of talking in the first person *as the barrier*, describing what function this barrier serves. Lynn has drawn red circles and tentacles. She just had an abortion and says she feels all womb and ovaries at the moment. The group suggests that she speaks as her womb and when that doesn't work they ask if she would like to explore being in the womb, being the baby. She curls up and everyone holds and surrounds her. Gradually she grows and stretches until she is standing up tall and says she is glad to see the world again.

In this case drawing served to increase self-awareness, to open up and share issues in the lives of the women present, and to provide the impetus for one woman to start to deal with a recent painful experience.

Using a Fantasy to Confront Reality

There is another way of using fantasies or projections which is less symbolic and more closely connected to daily reality. These are a kind of imaginative evocation of an everyday situation which you will be in, or have nearly been in, or fear being in.

One use of this method is when you are aware of a difficult situation ahead in your life: you would be encouraged to imagine it with all your worst fears realised, recognising what you are afraid of and releasing some of the emotions this brings up for you. By summoning up your worst fears, you will be prepared for them and will probably see that they are irrational. When you have to some extent cleared the difficult feelings you have projected into this future event, you would be encouraged to visualise it again but this time to imagine yourself capable of dealing with it and sailing through the occasion. For example, a woman who is anxious about speaking at a big trade union meeting would first imagine all her worst fears being fulfilled, then by visualising herself going through the event successfully she would be helped to get in touch with the part of herself which is calm, confident and perfectly able to cope with a taxing situation.

This approach can also be helpful to examine an important decision you have made in your life. You visualise walking along the same road but taking a different turning, re-making the decision and deciding the other way. By visualising how your life would be now if you had decided differently you gain a sense of what this decision meant to you.

It can also be helpful to visualise a desired situation. This method has been used successfully with women who have a compulsive eating problem; they are led in their imagination into a situation where they have lost weight and are mixing socially with other people. They often experience severe anxiety in this imagined situation and contact unconscious fears which are actually stopping them from getting thinner ('I shall be too weak and powerless', 'I shall be too sexually exciting and this will be dangerous').[13] In this way it is possible to uncover feelings which are actually preventing you from reaching a desired goal.

Another use of this technique is to clarify what changes you might want to make in any one area of your life. For example, in a session where several women have expressed dissatisfaction with their housing situation, one person might lead the group through a fantasy in which everyone imagines approaching, and then going on a room by room tour of, your 'ideal home', noticing who and what you find in the home. Then you could repeat the process visualising your present home, noticing how it is different from the ideal. This will help you to crystallise what is unsatisfactory in your present living situation and in what direction you might like to change it. The method can also be used to help you make a decision or choice between one path of action and another. Here's an example.

Kate asks Denise to give her a 'therapy session' as she feels she needs some urgent help with a problem. She starts by describing difficulties she has been having recently in her two-year-old sexual relationship with Sandra. She cannot decide whether she should go on with the relationship. It has been going badly for both of them but there is still a strong and loving connection. She feels she needs help to sort out her feelings.

She agrees to do a fantasy. Denise starts by asking her to sit comfortably, close her eyes, and do some relaxing breathing. Then she asks Kate to imagine that she has separated from Sandra and it is a year later. She asks her to re-create the situation in detail.

She is sitting at home alone. How does she feel? What is her life like? What are her relationships like? What is she still missing from the relationship with Sandra and in what ways has her life opened out since they parted? Denise allows plenty of time and asks Kate to describe, speaking in the present tense, how she feels in this imagined situation. Then, when she seems to have explored this enough, Denise asks her to change and to imagine now what her life will be like in a year's time if she stays with Sandra. Where is she living? How is she feeling? How are things between her and Sandra? Kate describes fully again how she imagines this situation and then opens her eyes for some feedback from Denise.

Kate feels she has discovered some important things: one is that to her Sandra seems to represent youth, energy and fun and without Sandra she imagines her life as dull and grey. At the same time, she finds it easier to imagine a workable living situation if she is not in the relationship with Sandra. Denise gives her some feedback based on things she noticed during this session: 'You looked very scared and tired when you imagined being without Sandra . . .' and so on. The idea is not that Kate will 'make a decision' at this point, but she does feel clearer about what the issues are, many of which she had not consciously recognised before.

In this example, projecting a decision into the future helps Kate become clearer about the issues involved in that decision. The same technique can be used for working on any decision ('Shall I have a baby or not?', 'Shall I change my job?', 'Shall I move into this living situation or that one?'). The idea is that we often know a lot more unconsciously about what these decisions mean than we do consciously; by opening up to a visualisation of what effect a decision will have on our life, we can tap some of this inner knowledge. In this way we also become aware of irrational factors which are unconsciously affecting our decisions and actions ('If I'm not with Sandra I'll be totally dull', 'If I'm not fat I'll be too vulnerable'). This unconscious material may need to be worked on before a problem is resolved. Sometimes so much anxiety gets focused on making a decision that it becomes impossible to make it. If you allow yourself to feel the feelings involved, very often the decision will make itself. To give yourself space to do this, you could agree with your group not to make a decision for a certain period of time after working on it in the session.

Later in this chapter we give several helpful exercises using imaginative evocation, and describe how to create an atmosphere and time the instructions for greatest effectiveness. Within this framework you can improvise any number of exercises relevant for you.

SOME PROS AND CONS OF FANTASY WORK

There are several arguments which could be voiced against the kind of dream and fantasy work described in this chapter. Critics argue that much of our striving in life is pure fantasy, chasing after illusions, and what we really need is to come to terms with *reality*. Too often we want to become an ideal, a fantasy, instead of accepting who we are. We would use these arguments as a strong argument *for* and not against doing this work. It is true that we live with fantasies all the time and most of these are fantasies created by the male-dominated society in which we live. We have not created them, they do not fit us but make us deny ourselves and feel powerless or passive. For example: 'I can't survive without my husband', 'If I dyed my hair I'd look like Racquel Welch', 'A perfect mother thinks only of her children', 'I dreamt Paul Newman kissed me, it was wonderful'. These common fantasies project power and desirable qualities onto people and symbols outside ourselves: the husband, Racquel Welch, the 'perfect mother', Paul Newman. Television programmes and advertisements encourage us to do this. We give a lot of our own power away. We feel inadequate and it becomes hard to discover our own qualities and what we actually want for ourselves. The way to clear this kind of binding fantasy is not to ignore it, but to expose it and explore it. In this way we can take more control over it and re-own power we have projected outside ourselves. Then we can use fantasy work to contact qualities and symbols inside us which express our own truth and power and strengthen us to act in the world. We have shown ways of using symbols not to avoid reality, but to learn about how we relate to the world, to change our self-image, to strengthen us and to heal wounds and patterns from the past which keep us stuck. We can open up the private world of dream and fantasy to share it and use it in positive, creative ways. We can move from a situation where dreams frighten us, fantasies dominate our waking lives and anxieties cut us off from the world, to a situation where we have more of our own inner power available to live our lives creatively in the present.

There are both practical advantages and dangers about doing this work in a self-help situation. It may be less threatening for those new to therapy as it does not directly confront people's defences in the same way as strong emotional release or interpersonal Encounter. So it can be an 'easy way in', but with this goes the danger that it can be used to avoid difficult feelings or tensions which really do need to be worked out between people in a group. Another danger is that if a person is too sophisticated or self-conscious about the techniques, she will not use her imagination freely and spontaneously as in a dream, but will intervene with her conscious mind to create symbols which reflect the image of herself she wants to put across to the world. She may contrive to create an 'interesting', 'dramatic' or 'attractive' picture, a lush meadow or a romantic tree. She may censor her visualisation or be dishonest about the first thing that came into her mind. This is more likely if there has been no physical warm-up to get her out of her 'head'. This does not invalidate the work, but it is important that the group is ready to point out any tendency to inhibit, gloss over or 'doctor' a fantasy, which often reflects a tendency to do the same thing about life in general: 'Your landscape sounds very pretty-pretty. It reminds me of the way you always tell the group that things are going fine for you even when there are problems in your life.' 'Your picture looks very neat and controlled, as if you worked it out beforehand rather than putting your energy into it.'

Symbols work comes more easily to some people than others. Sometimes a woman finds it hard to get into a fantasy at all, and is disturbed by the whole idea of it. It is then worth exploring what she fears, what she is avoiding, what she believes might happen if she did it.

A final danger is that you become too absorbed in the workings of your unconscious mind and lose a sense of proportion in the way you relate it to your daily life. It is worth remembering that dreams and fantasies, as well as being grand and meaningful, can sometimes be trivial or plain silly. As Jung remarks, the unconscious 'contains all aspects of human nature – light and dark, beautiful and ugly, good and evil, profound and silly.'[15] It is important not to get lost in exploring your world of dreams, and to remember that the goal of this work is not a mystic experience, but the practical use of increased creativity and a greater ability to use your energy in the here-and-now of your life. Here are some useful exercises, mainly based on Psychosynthesis, which can be done in pairs, or alone, as well as in a group.

100 Guided Fantasy through an Imaginary Landscape
This exercise gives examples of several of the symbols most commonly used by Psychosynthesis and other therapy approaches. It is quite long and is a

good introduction to exploring the landscape of your inner world. There are steps you need to take to prepare for a fantasy if you want it to be successful.

Do some physical exercise first as this will make you more responsive and your imagination will be less likely to function in a disconnected way cut off from your body (we list several warm-ups in Chapters Two and Five). Guided fantasies work most deeply when you are in an almost trance-like state similar to hypnosis, so you will need to prepare the atmosphere: darkening the room, lighting candles, holding hands together or humming can help to prepare you for the experience and make you receptive to messages from your unconscious mind.

You will need to choose one person to sit out and read the instructions. She should ask people to lie on their backs on the floor, eyes shut, legs uncrossed, arms by their sides, and lead them through some relaxing breathing before starting on the fantasy. When she starts to read the instructions, she should do so sensitively and remain responsive to the mood of the group. She will need to allow long pauses between instructions. It takes *much longer than you would think* for a person to visualise a meadow or a mountain.

At the end of the fantasy she should allow people plenty of time to 're-enter' the group, and it is worth giving feedback on the reading – was it too fast or too loud? – so that you can develop your skills in guiding fantasies.

Here are the instructions.

Shut your eyes and imagine you are in a meadow. If you find it hard to visualise, think of a meadow you know. Be aware what it is like (the size, the grass, the weather, the smell, the time of day, what there is in the meadow . . .).

You find a road and you start to walk along it. What is the road like? (Let yourself be aware if it is smooth or difficult underfoot, bending or straight or forked; do you walk quickly or slowly?)

You come to a stream. What is it like? How do you cross it?

You walk further. Be aware what the weather is like now, how the ground feels under your feet, what the landscape is like around you.

You find an obstacle in your path. What is it . . .?

How do you feel facing it? How do you get across it or around it?

Now you come to a hill and you start to climb it. What is this like?

At the top of the hill you find a building. What kind of building is it? You walk towards it.

Outside the building you find a chalice and a spear. What are they like? What size are they, what condition are they in, and how do you feel when you see them? What do you do with them?

Now you go into the building. How do you get in? (Do you knock, wait, is it opened for you . . .?) Be aware what the building is like inside. In this building there is a wise woman waiting for you. Be aware what this wise woman looks like . . .

Now you have the chance to ask this wise woman one question the answer to which is important to you. Be aware what you want to ask: very often it may be the very first thing which comes into your head . . . Now ask, and hear the answer she gives you.

Now leave the building, and retrace your steps, down the hill, and back to a place on the road or in the countryside where you feel comfortable.

When you feel ready, open your eyes.

At the end of the exercise, share with one another what you experienced. Which was the strongest part of the visualisation? It can be helpful to notice which parts you found hard to imagine or blanked out on. What did you get out of it? It is not necessary to analyse the experience, which will be different for each person. Various meanings are often attached to the symbols: for example, the road can stand for the 'path of life', hard or easy, simple or confused. The chalice can symbolise love, and the spear, power or will. So how you visualised or reacted to these items may reflect the way you relate to these characteristics in your own personality. However, if the suggested interpretations do not fit for you, ignore them and stick to your own intuition. The wise person is a healing or strengthening image representing your own inner wisdom.

Once you are familiar with the principle of guiding a fantasy – suggesting scenes or events and asking people to fill them out in detail imagining colours, shapes, smells, light, sound, qualities and feelings – you will be able to improvise your own exercises. Guiding a fantasy can be a very satisfying way of sharing your imagination and creativity with other women.

You could spend a whole exercise just exploring a stream or looking at how you deal with obstacles. Here are some other possibilities:

Ask people to think of a symbol for their mind and a symbol for their body and then lead them on a journey to the wise person to ask how to bring these two together.

Describe a deep forest. Have people imagine they are an animal, noticing how it moves and how it deals with adversaries. (This can lead on to free movement exploring the motions and behaviour of your chosen animal. Afterwards people could describe what the animal expresses or compensates for in their personality.)

Have people imagine they are hidden in the dark outside a cave waiting for a person or thing to emerge from it. They could then explore that apparition in a number of ways.

171

Someone who is depressed could think of a symbol for her depression and then explore it.

Lead a journey through a garden, exploring different moods: wild or cultivated, lush or maze-like. People might take this journey to represent the creative process or the development of a relationship, or may simply choose to be nourished by the images of a garden.

Lead the group on an exploration through an old house in the cellar of which people find an old book with many pictures. Have them imagine some of the pictures. This is an open-ended format which can bring a wide range of unconscious issues into the open.

101   The Journey back to Your Conception

This is a long meditation to help you get an overall view of your whole life. It can also help put you in touch with the 'essence' or quality of your life energy which is often buried under layers of personality and conditioning.

Follow carefully the preparatory steps described at the start of the previous exercise (**100**). After some relaxing breathing, the instructions are:

Send your awareness slowly through your body, noticing what you find. Start at your feet . . . ankles . . . calves . . . knees . . . thighs . . . up to your pelvis and your genital area . . . Continue up your spine, through your stomach . . . diaphragm . . . chest . . . back . . . arms and hands . . . Now let it move on up from your shoulders, through your neck, up through the centre of your head to the top of your head . . . Now send your awareness up out of the top of your head to a point about six inches above the top of your head. Now imagine you are looking from there down onto yourself, as you lie on the floor.

Now look down onto what has happened to you today, what you have done, see yourself doing it. Run through it, picture it in front of your closed eyes. (*pause*) Now run through what happened yesterday.

Now look back over the last week, see your life over the last week.

Now let yourself look back over the last six months. What have they been like for you? Picture yourself, the circumstances of your life, your work, your leisure, how you have been feeling?

Now look back over the last year. (*Repeat the same questions as above.*)

Now look back over the last five years. (*Repeat the same questions again.*)

Now let yourself travel back to your teens. Picture yourself then. How do you live? What do you do? Who is around you? How do you feel inside?

Now you are eight years old. (*Repeat the same questions as above.*)

Now travel back to look at the first five years of your life. (*Repeat the same questions again.*)

Now travel back to the time of your birth. Re-live that event, imagine it happening in front of your eyes. What is it like?

Now you are in the womb. What is this experience like for you during the nine months you are in your mother's womb? Can you find any impressions, sensations, pictures?

Now let your consciousness travel back to the start of the pregnancy, to the moment of your conception. What is this moment like? Now ask yourself if there is a word or picture, a symbol which comes up for you which summons up your essence at the moment when you were just that first spark of energy or life. Take the first picture or thought which comes into your head, it will probably be right. A symbol or quality of your essence at that first moment of conception.

Now follow that essence through your nine months in the womb. What was that like? How did your essence come through it? Now through your birth, how was your essence expressed or hindered through the experience of your birth?

Now watch that essence as it moves through the first eight years of your life. Follow those years through again from the point of view of how they affected your essence. How did it survive? Or thrive? Did it express itself or was it suppressed by its surroundings? How much of it came through in your life?

Now follow through to adolescence. (*Repeat the same questions as above*.)

Now trace your life through from adolescence to the present day. (*Repeat the same questions again*.)

Now let your awareness come back to this room and again see yourself lying here, today. How much are you in touch with that essence, your essence, as you lie here now? If it is covered, how is it covered? How much of it is here with you now and expressed in your life as it is at present?

Now let your awareness come right back into your body. Be conscious of any sensations in your body. Be aware of your breathing. Gradually, when you feel ready, open your eyes, sit up and come back to a circle. Share what the exercise has been like for you and what you have learnt.

This exercise is a good one for rediscovering memories of your childhood which you thought you had completely forgotten. It seems fairly clearly proven that we carry the memory of birth and pregnancy recorded in our body like every other experience of our lifetime. Occasionally, in therapy, people re-live these experiences very vividly and if most of us have no recollection it is because the memory is buried or repressed. Finding a symbol for the essence, and then following that essence back through the years of your life, can be a very good way of getting an overall picture of how your original or natural energy, your instinctive qualities, may have been suppressed and distorted by pressures from your family and from society as a whole. The symbol that comes to mind for your essence might be 'fire', and the picture which emerges of your childhood is of your parents consistently hemming in and containing that fire until there is very little left of it in your present life. You may treat the idea of the 'essence' as reflecting an understanding of our most early and basic development of consciousness, or you may choose to see it more as an allegory or metaphor, a way of separating out the quality which we intuitively feel is more true to ourselves, more reflective of our own native tendencies as opposed to character traits which we have learnt to adopt to fit in with the world. It can be difficult, but helpful and strengthening, for a woman to get a sense of who *she* is in herself, separate and independent from relationships, demanding children and the many definitions and 'oughts' which are laid on her by others.

102   Higher Than the Mountains, Deeper Than the Sea

This is a long and dramatic guided fantasy. It can help you to explore your spiritual side as well as the depths of your subconscious and to relate what you learn to practical changes in your life.

Follow carefully the preparatory steps described at the start of exercise **100** to create a suitable atmosphere before one person starts to read the instructions:

You are going on a journey. Imagine yourself getting ready. What are you taking with you? You set off first to go to the bottom of the sea-bed. How do you get to the sea? How do you enter the depths of the ocean?

You are in the depths of the sea. Water is all around you. You are exploring. How do you feel? What do you find there? What happens?

Now, when you are ready, you are going to come to the surface. Is there anything you want to bring up with you? Gradually you come to the surface and you find yourself on dry land. What is it like back in the daylight?

Now you see a mountain and you walk towards it. You are going to climb it. Be aware how high it is, how easy to climb. Do you still have anything with you from the sea-bed? Now you are starting to climb. Let yourself feel your feet on the ground, let yourself experience every part of the ascent, stage by stage.

Now you have reached the top of the mountain. You are standing at the top. Above you there is only light and sun. Now you will leave your physical body behind and travel upwards into the air. You may like to imagine yourself rising up as a bird, a cloud, a ray of light, or as pure energy. You merge and blend with the light that fills the sky . . . Be aware of the quality of your movements, the quality of your light or energy, how it feels to be one with the light of the sky.

What you are experiencing is the quality of your pure energy, of your essence. Ask yourself now, what is the aim or purpose of this essence in your lifetime, how could it best express itself, what has it to give to humanity?

Now look down on your life and imagine how it would be if you fully expressed and realised this energy of yours, your essence, in your daily life. Picture how your life would be if the quality of your energy was there in everything you did. You may need to imagine changes in your life-style, your work, your relationships.

You are still blended with the sky, but gradually you start to come down towards the top of the mountain . . . There you find your physical body again. When you feel ready enter it, go back into your body and start walking back down the mountain.

You are walking back now towards your home. You get to the foot of the mountain . . . What is the countryside like? What is the light like? Be aware of changes you want to make in your life when you return, ways it is within your power to change your life so that the essence you contacted can shine through in your life more.

You have reached your home. Be aware what you have brought back with you from your explorations under the sea, on the mountain, and above the mountain. What have you learnt?

When you feel ready, open your eyes and return to the room. It may help to put your hands on your belly or on your face to help yourself come back gradually. Look at a detail in the room before you sit up and try to take in the whole room.

When you feel ready, write down or share what you have learnt so that it is easier to remember and put it into practice in your everyday life.

The shape of this guided fantasy is quite common, tracing a descent followed by an ascent. The descent into the depths of the sea (it could have been a cave) can represent an exploration of the unknown and maybe threatening parts of the unconscious, and images which come up often represent deep and difficult feelings associated with your past, your parents, or other repressed material. The ascent is aimed at bringing out positive and constructive feelings, to evoke images which will foster positive energy; the height and difficulty of the mountain climb can reflect the nature of your aspirations, or of your process of self-development through therapy. Rising from the top of the mountain is an exploration into your spiritual side. You may find difficulty with this idea, and with the concept of the 'essence' which comes up in this exercise. Even if you do not accept the idea of any kind of spirituality, you may still find it helpful to think about, and get in touch with, the natural quality of body energy which vitalises you. Given what has been written about the nature of body energy, it is not hard to believe that each person has a quality of energy or vibration which is as unique as a fingerprint, as well as being more in tune with the energy of others, of plant and animal life, and of the natural world, than other parts of the personality. This is the kind of idea suggested by the 'essence' which blends with the light of the sky. The last part of the exercise, where you return back down from the mountain is very important: the spiritual world is not cut off from daily reality, but is a source of strength and direction for it.

103   Free Drawing Your Tree

This is a simple and effective exercise for beginning to explore your personality through creative drawing.

For any free drawing exercise to be effective, you need to have large sheets of paper and a full range of easy-to-use coloured crayons so people can express themselves without hesitation in exactly the shade that feels right. Set a time limit of *three minutes* for any drawing so that people will work quickly and intuitively. It is important to follow your first impulses rather than taking time to 'correct' anything or trying to produce an 'artistic' finished product.

Here are the instructions for this exercise:

Take one sheet of paper and on it *draw your tree*.

After three minutes, put the pictures together in the middle and each person takes ten minutes to present her tree to the others. To help her connect with what she has drawn, she speaks in the first person as if she were the tree, describing every aspect of herself in detail: 'I'm large and solid, but I don't seem to have any roots. My trunk is beautiful, strong and smooth, but my branches are a bit spindly and my leaves aren't very full . . .' and so on.

Here are some questions which she can be encouraged to answer in her description of her tree:

Does it stand alone or close to other plant life?
Does it have leaves, flowers or fruit?
Are there any severed branches?
Are there animals or birds around?
How strong or deep are the roots?
What is the weather like around it?
Does the energy move smoothly through the tree or does it block, say, at the top of the trunk?
What is the general message or impression which the tree gives?

She should be reminded to keep talking in the first person, speaking as if she were the tree – 'I've got a funny black animal lurking in my branches . . .' When she has finished, the others can give her feedback about any additional features they noticed in the tree. All these qualities in the tree can be related to qualities in the personality: for example, grounding, self-expression, relationships with others, disowned parts of the character, energy patterns in the body, general attitudes to life. When the tree is drawn swiftly and unselfconsciously it is surprising how faithful a mirror it can be of its drawer: a narrow constriction at the top of the trunk reflecting tension in her neck, an amputated lower branch reflecting the early death of a parent, a creature burrowing at the root reflecting negative feelings about sexuality. However, these connections vary with each person and the drawer should make her own links. Avoid 'interpreting' one another's trees and instead ask questions or just comment on what you notice: 'Can you tell us about this bird's nest?', 'I notice that all your fruit is at the top, nothing lower down . . .'

This exercise could lead into one woman exploring in greater detail a theme which came up for her (she might discuss her loneliness or ask for a neck massage). Or she might take more time to look at her picture, perhaps giving a voice to the fruit, the roots, the constriction in the trunk.

Following carefully the instructions we gave at the start of this exercise, you could apply this structure to any theme, improvising to fit your needs. For example, you could draw:

Myself and my child(ren)
My sexual relationship
The first five years of my life
Myself as a woman alone[15]

For the following themes, we suggest you sit for one minute with your eyes shut before drawing, to recall or tune in to what you want to capture on paper:

My essence (this works best if you have done exercise **101** or **102** above: it may come out as a colour, a symbol like a flower, or a geometric shape)
A symbol or situation which stands out from a dream
Where I come from, Where I am going in my life, *and* What is stopping me from getting where I'm going (three pictures, one after the other).

If you do more than one picture, be sure to turn over the first one before you start drawing the next. When you have finished a drawing, it can help to write quickly on the back any words which come up for you in connection with it. If you do not have time to present your pictures in turn round the group, take ten minutes each to share in pairs, then put all the drawings in the middle of the circle to see the range of different responses and hear what was most important for each woman.

104 Fantasy on Monogamy

This exercise, which will take at least an hour, helps explore what monogamy means for women. The women's liberation movement has raised for many women the question of whether they want to follow the traditional social pattern of living in a monogamous partnership with one person. Feminists have explored alternatives which might give women more freedom, space and opportunity for self-expression. This fantasy opens up issues around this area of our experience.[16]

With all imaginative evocations such as this, people should sit or lie comfortably with their eyes shut and do several minutes of relaxing breathing before starting the fantasy. One person should sit out to read the instructions, allowing *several minutes* to pass at each pause:

Imagine that you are in a monogamous relationship. Take time and choose carefully: it may be a real relationship you are in, or a past one, or an imaginary relationship. Settle on a choice which feels right and then stick to it during the exercise. Let yourself get a feel of what this relationship is like.

Now imagine that you are with your monogamous partner in a social situation. Be aware what the situation is like: colours, smells, atmosphere, who is there . . . Now picture your partner who is there with you. How aware are you of your partner in that situation? How aware are you of the other people there? Do you spend your time with your partner or separately? What do you like and dislike about the situation?

Now it's time to leave and you go home together. How does this leaving happen? How do you feel as you go off alone with your partner?

Follow the journey home, how it feels . . . You get home. How do you feel as together you get ready for bed? Now you are in bed together. What do you do? Read a book? Go straight to sleep? Make love? Let yourself follow the experience through in your imagination. What is it like? How do you feel? What are your last thoughts as you fall asleep?

It's morning, you wake up and your partner is still asleep next to you. You turn and look at her or him. What do you see? How do you feel about your partner? You are going to wake up and see this person in this way every day for years . . . How does this make you feel?

Now let yourself slowly come back to the group and open your eyes.

After this guided fantasy you can, in pairs or in the group, describe fully in the present tense what happened in your fantasy. You should also share what you have learnt, what was important for you in the issues raised which may be around security, safety, dependability, boredom or frustration.

This kind of fantasy can be followed by one person 'working' in depth, or by relating the issues in the fantasy to your present lives. Once the structure is familiar (allow people to relax; offer them a situation and encourage them to

fill out the details in their imagination; share the experience) you can improvise your own on a variety of themes. The monogamy fantasy could be
followed by similar ones looking at the alternative possibilities of multiple
relationships or celibacy.

Here are some other topics.

105   Dependency, Guilt, Competition

This exercise helps make you aware of your patterns around any one of these
issues.[17] Remember to allow several minutes at the pauses:

Sit or lie comfortably with your eyes shut and do some relaxing breathing.

Now recall a recent or important time when you felt dependent (or substitute 'guilty' or 'competitive'). Remember the situation in detail: Who was
there? What did others say or do? How did you feel?

Now recall a situation where you did *not* feel dependent (or 'guilty' or
'competitive'). You might have expected yourself to feel that way, but you
did not. Again picture the situation fully: the setting, the events, the feelings
you had.

When you are ready, open your eyes and share what you experienced.

Working alone, you can use the same structure to imagine the results of a
decision you are trying to make. Sit comfortably with eyes shut, then take
several minutes to imagine your life in a year if you decide one way, then if
you decide the other way (see pp 66-7).

106   Yourself as a Mother

The ideology and the myths of motherhood are often experienced as contradictory: on the one hand a series of 'oughts' which few women feel able to
live up to; on the other hand being a 'mother' is a socially acknowledged role
bringing certain sorts of privilege and acceptance which a childless woman is
denied. This exercise helps explore your feelings on this issue, whether you
are actually a mother or not.[18]

Find a relaxed position, close your eyes and let yourself breathe deeply.

Now think of someone you know who represents a more conventional view
of the world (and what women should do with their lives) than you hold
yourself. Is it a woman or man? Friend, relative, or boss? Choose anyone
who is more conventional than you.

Now give yourself time to picture this person clearly: appearance, hair,
clothes, facial expression.

When you can imagine this person clearly, let yourself switch roles so that
you become that person looking at yourself. *You have children.* What does
the person think of you as a mother, as a woman? What have you failed at or

succeeded in? What does this person like about you? How would they think differently of you if you didn't have children?

Now imagine you are this person looking at yourself and *you don't have children*. How does this person see you as a woman? What have you succeeded in and what have you failed in, according to this person's point of view? How does this person see your femininity? How would their sense of you alter if you did have children?

When you are ready open your eyes.

Now describe, in pairs or in the group, who the person was, how this person sees you, and how you feel about that.

MEDITATION

The guided fantasies we have described can work like a kind of meditation, but there are many other forms. What we feel can be gained from meditation, which is not always easy to gain from the therapy approaches we discuss, is a sense of finding our 'centre'. Therapy can be a disruptive process: it can open up difficult emotions, question our patterns of behaviour, expose roles we play with other people, reconnect us with childhood memories, reveal whole new areas of our personality. Sometimes we get thrown off balance, for old patterns of behaviour are changing and it is not yet clear what the new ones will be. In this process it can be very important to be able to contact an inner calm and awareness, a sense of ourself which underlies all the games, behaviour patterns, defences and conflicts with which we usually identify. Finding your centre through meditation gives you the strength to make other changes in yourself. It can be especially helpful for women, whether they are doing therapy or not, to find this sense of self which is independent of other people and not just determined by, or reacting to, the many demands, pressures and expectations which are laid on us in our relationships and in society as a whole.

The kind of meditation we have found useful is really just a quiet way of spending time with yourself. It can work through meditating on a colour, or it can be a structure for becoming more aware of body sensations, or for looking at your present life situation. It can often help us to find in ourselves the answers to practical questions in our lives, as well as giving a glimpse of peace and the deeper sense of identity we describe above. It is not just a mental exercise where the mind works on the mind and ends up going round in circles. It does not work if you are trying to 'achieve' a certain state of mind which you think is 'spiritual' or 'enlightened'. We experience it primarily as a clearing process where you let go of the usual constant chatter inside your head (the worrying, rehearsing, judging, repeating things which go on inside us most of the time). When you do this, and relax, it becomes possible to open up in a whole-body way to experiences, qualities or insights which are normally crowded out by the mind's activity. There *is* a kind of concentration involved, but it is very different from the concentration required to park a car or solve a mathematical problem. It is like letting your mind become a clear pool of water, or a ray of light which rests on one object or idea and holds its attention there in a single-pointed, steady way. The body is comfortable and relaxed and at one with your total experience. This state is hard to achieve at first: in the beginning you can find yourself sitting eyes closed and cross-legged on the floor with a thousand thoughts about work, friends, shopping, milling through your brain. After what seems an eternity, you open your eyes and find only four minutes have passed. But if you persist, it becomes easier. Daily concerns ebb and you may start to feel a few moments of peace smoothing out your forehead. Sit with a straight back, and you may find it useful to place your feet on the floor to ground you. Some women have found it helpful to cover the head with a shawl to bring your consciousness more inward, and to focus on a 'seed thought': a word or phrase to come back to every time your mind wanders, like 'I am a wave of peace', 'Birth, death, rebirth', or 'I am the centre'.[19] It also helps a lot to start with some regular easy breathing to relax your body. You might try meditating to a favourite piece of calming music; this eases anxiety about time because you know you will stop meditating when the music ends. Below we list some simple meditations which are useful for people just starting to meditate. These can be used individually at home or for starting a self-help session where they provide a way for people to recover from a scattered day, to tune in to themselves and to ask inside what they need from the group.

Meditation can be misused: it can be used as a way of 'cutting-off' from other people or from emotions, for denying real problems and difficulties ('I'm spiritual, superior, and above all these petty concerns and feelings'). This danger should be watched for. Meditation should not be used as a way of kidding yourself that everything's O.K. when it's not, but rather as a way of gaining the space and strength to deal in a clear way with whatever you need to face. We have found it valuable for its emphasis on what is healthy in the psyche, and as a way to go inside and spend time with ourselves. It is another way of contacting inner resources which can then be used in our daily lives.

107   Basic Meditation for Relaxing and Finding Your Centre
This is a good meditation for clearing preoccupations and allowing yourself to become more centred and more fully present in the 'now'.

If you are alone, you can just read the instructions with suitable pauses while you do the meditation. If you are in a pair or a group, it works best for one person to read the instructions aloud to lead the others through the meditation. The reading should be slow and sensitive, with long pauses:

Be sitting comfortably on a cushion or on the floor. Let your hands rest relaxed, palms upwards. Close your eyes and go inside yourself.

Be aware of your breath coming in and out of your body.

Be aware of your weight resting on your base: let yourself feel your contact with the ground, your buttocks and legs against the cushion or on the floor. Let your spine be straight, your head as if floating slightly forwards and upwards from the crown of your head.

Now let yourself become aware of what is stopping you from being fully present in the here and now, what is distracting you. It may be aches or tensions in your body, unresolved feelings or emotions, anxieties, thoughts or concerns. Let yourself be aware of all the things that are preoccupying you on these different levels: sensations, feelings and thoughts.

As you breathe in, let yourself deal with them, and as you breathe out imagine that you are letting go of them. Take them one at a time. You can do this slowly: one anxiety might take several breaths to resolve. Breathe it in, see how you can deal with it or sort it out, and then let go of it as you exhale. (Allow a particularly long pause after this instruction as this process can take several minutes.)

Now see if you can recall a time in your life when you felt very centred: that is, when you felt very much *yourself*, very true to yourself. Recall the situation as fully as you can: where you were, what happened, how you felt, how you acted.

Let yourself bring that feeling back into your body at this moment. If there is an image, a colour or a word which sums up that centred feeling for you, then use it to help you connect with it and bring it into yourself now. It may help to place your hands at the centre of your body, on your belly.

Imagine yourself moving through different situations in your life and keeping that awareness of your centre. Picture some difficult situations, those which would normally throw you off balance, and imagine yourself remaining calm, and true to who you are, in those situations.

Now gradually bring your awareness back to the present. Be aware of your breath. When you feel ready, open your eyes and focus for a while on your hands or an object on the floor before returning your eyes to the room.

This meditation can be helpful to do regularly at the beginning of the day. Imagine the day ahead and picture yourself moving through the different events and situations in it while remaining completely centred. Picturing this helps you contact the resources you have inside you to go through the day this way in reality.

108   A Body Meditation

This is a good exercise for giving some attention to a part of your body which needs it. Remember to allow several minutes for each instruction:

Be sitting comfortably and go inside yourself. Take several moments to be aware of your breath . . . of your weight on the floor . . . of sensations in your body.

Now let your awareness go to a part of your body which attracts you or which is calling your attention. Take the first part which comes to mind. Put your hands there and imagine you are breathing into that part of the body. Now explore:

The physical sensations you can feel there
Any emotions connected with that part of your body (always trust the first thing that comes to mind, without censoring)
Any memories you may find there
Any colour it brings up for you
Any sound it suggests to you
Any symbol, picture or image you find for that body part
Any song or words which come up

Now ask yourself. What does this body part need? What is it saying? What can it teach you?

How can you give it what it needs? (You may find a healing image for this part of your body or you may decide you need to wear different clothes or change an activity in your life.)

When you feel ready, gradually open your eyes, come back to the room, and share your experiences.

This exercise involves various helpful processes: using your intuition, becoming more aware of your own body, and taking time to give your body positive, caring attention. This kind of exercise, like self-massage and some of the body exercises listed in Chapter Five, are good for helping us to realise how we can nourish ourselves and can develop a more positive image of our own bodies.

You may be sceptical about the idea of using a 'healing image'. It may help you to think that if you send a healing image or awareness to a particular part of your body, you are allowing more blood to circulate there, more energy is available, and all this can have a positive physical effect.

109   A Colour Meditation
This is an exercise to experiment with using colour in your therapy process. Allow plenty of time between each instruction:

Be sitting comfortably. Let your breathing be relaxed and take a few moments to let your mind empty.

Now find your colour. Sticking to colours from the rainbow range, and avoiding browns and blacks, choose the colour which feels most right for you at this moment. Don't think about it, take the very first colour which comes into your head as this will usually be the right one. Be aware of the quality of your chosen colour, of any associations it has for you.

Tune in to the colour and let yourself harmonise with it. Now absorb it into your body, imagine you are hungry for it as for food, and let it fill every part of your body.

Now radiate the colour. Imagine you are letting it expand a few inches beyond your body all around you. It may help to do this if you imagine you are breathing it out from all over your body as you exhale. Now release the colour further – let it spread and fill the room you are in.

Now see if you can generate enough of the colour to fill, in slow gradual stages, the house, the street, the town or countryside.

Now, following the same stages, gradually bring the colour back, to the house, the room, to you. Let it get more solid and condensed. Lastly, bring it right back into yourself, into your skin, your muscles and blood, your bones.

Now return again to the empty state you were in at the beginning, just observing the colour. Notice how you feel different from the way you felt at the start.

It is increasingly becoming recognised that colours can have a very powerful effect on us, stimulating, calming or restoring us. There are various systems for understanding the effects of different colours, for example Assagioli believes that 'Certain shades of blue are usually considered as having a soothing, harmonising effect; light green is refreshing; red and bright yellow are usually stimulating, while pink suggests serenity and happiness'.[20] However, it is best to find your own personal connections to different colours; you will learn which colour you need to be in contact with at the moment.

At the end of the exercise, share what you experienced. Does the colour symbolise something you need to give yourself in your life? You may find that you have been unconsciously choosing to wear this colour recently. Some people take this work a step further: for example, choosing a number of objects in the colour and spending time looking at them and meditating on them.

110   Meditation on Joy

This exercise is for contacting and nourishing the joyfulness that is inside you. Therapy can be painful and sometimes our political activity feels like an uphill struggle. We need to keep in touch with our own positive energy, which is a powerful source of strength and renewal. You can do this through meditation alone or in a group. Allow about two minutes' space between each of the instructions.

Have pencil and paper beside you. Sit comfortably and let yourself feel your weight on the floor. As you breathe out, imagine that you are breathing out tensions from your body.

Now start to focus on joy. Let your mind wander back to recall situations and times when you felt joy. Picture yourself as you were then, as you are when you feel joyful. Be aware of the words which come to your mind when you picture that state of joy: they may be the names of places or people, or descriptions of feelings or qualities . . . As words come up for you, open your eyes to write them down in your piece of paper. Close your eyes again to see if more words come to you.

Now, with your eyes still closed, imagine that you take these words and place them in a bowl on the top of your head. You may like to choose just one or two of the words to focus on. Imagine that the sun is shining down on them. Let yourself bask in the sun as it shines down on those words on the top of your head.

When you feel ready, and with your eyes still closed, let yourself stand up. Keep the feeling of the sun shining onto those joyful words on the top of your head, and if it feels right let your body start to move in whatever way it wants.

(The person reading the instructions may want to put some suitable music on at this point to help the others explore this quality in movement or dance.)

This meditation could work just as well with any other positive quality or mood which you feel you need to foster: love, strength or calmness.

JUNG AND PSYCHOSYNTHESIS

Someone wanting to go to individual therapy or professional groups using symbol and fantasy work would look for therapists trained in the Psychosynthesis school of therapy, or in the work of Jung.

Psychosynthesis is based on the work of the Italian psychotherapist Roberto Assagioli who believed that our need for meaning, for higher values, and for a spiritual life is as real and urgent as our biological and social needs. It is an approach which embraces many techniques (emotional release, therapy through free drawing, writing, clay modelling, music, colour, movement and meditation) but it differs from other approaches in stating clearly that every human being has an essence or spiritual self which lies behind the personality and the conscious ego. Assagioli suggested that what we call the 'personality' is, in fact, a bundle of different roles which we play at various times and in various situations. He called these different roles 'sub-personalities' and believed that by becoming identified with, or stuck in, these roles we lose touch with a deeper sense of identity and restrict our possibilities of living life fully and harmoniously. The example is given of a man who is authoritarian at work and a lamb in his private life, two sub-personalities out of harmony

185

with one another. In psychosynthesis work, sub-personalities, when they are recognised, are often given a nickname ('the tartar', 'the lamb', 'the mother', 'the clown', 'the workhorse'). The idea is that by becoming aware of them, we are less bound by them. Here is one woman's experience of working on sub-personalities at a psychosynthesis group.

We were encouraged to think of the main image of ourselves we put over in daily life, and then to put our bodies into a position which reflected that role. My image was 'the orator' – a role I use a lot in my political activity – and the position I got into was like a statue, standing strong and rigid with my mouth and hands open. Then we had to get into a position which reflected the opposite of that (mine was 'the hippie' lying flat on the floor, a collapse I get into every so often). Then we were encouraged to move slowly between the two positions. Feeling the transition was very powerful for me, being aware of the muscles I used and the movement between the two absolutes, and realising that I have a place which is between the two opposite roles.

Later we did a guided fantasy of walking over a field towards a cottage where we could hear three of our sub-personalities making a noise inside. Mine were 'the orator', 'the mother' and 'the frightened thin one'. Then we imagined them coming out. We were to imagine talking to them and choosing one in particular who needed some attention. I chose 'the orator' who was tense, desperate and busy. She said she couldn't take a walk till she had achieved something. When we were asked what this sub-personality needs, I realised that she needs to take things a lot easier. Then we had to go back to the field after saying goodbye to them, and we had to see how we felt about them.

I think I am more self-aware now when I find myself getting into this 'orator' role, and I don't feel so stuck in it. I can see more that it is *part* of me rather than '*me*'.

Psychosynthesis suggests that when we learn to recognise our sub-personalities and harmonise them, we can increasingly bring them under our conscious direction. Instead of being stuck in one or two roles, we can move fluidly between different ways of being appropriate to different occasions. Assagioli believed that behind these sub-personalities, and behind the conscious self which experiences itself as a separate individual, we have a 'Higher' or 'Transpersonal Self' which exists on a spiritual or universal level and experiences a sense of freedom, expansion and communication. He saw this 'Higher Self' as a source of energy and harmony for curing emotional problems, and felt that our aim in life is to discover and express this true essence or Self as fully as possible. This Higher Self, he believed, draws its power from a higher unconscious part of ourselves which he calls the 'Superconscious'. While the 'lower' unconscious contains baser and primitive impulses, this 'Superconscious' is thought to contain 'altruistic love and will, humanitarian action, artistic and scientific inspiration, philosophic and spiritual insight, and the drive for purpose and meaning'.[21] We repress the 'sublime' as well as the 'lower' unconscious, and Assagioli stated that this higher unconscious needs to be integrated and actualised through therapy.

Psychosynthesis is one of the few therapy approaches which recognises the spiritual dimension of our existence and can, therefore, offer some useful methods and ideas for women who want to explore this as part of their therapy process. But, aspects of psychosynthesis theory present difficulties for women. Assagioli is very clear that the aim of realising the spiritual Self is not to withdraw into a mystical realm but to act more effectively and creatively in the daily world, and individual responsibility (not blaming others) is strongly stressed. Yet he had little idea what difficulties may hinder this process of self-realisation in our society, especially for women. His picture of self-realisation for women seems to be the role of mother and little else. We also find unhelpful the way in which Assagioli divided up the unconscious into 'higher' and 'lower' sections; this seems to go with a playing down of sexuality and the belief that much sexual energy should be 'sublimated' onto a 'higher' level. This kind of hierarchical view and divisions into 'higher' and 'lower' seem like another version of the traditional Christian split into 'soul' and 'body', and could prevent us from recognising and accepting ourselves as whole people with a strong positive sense of our bodies and sexuality. Some other spiritual approaches, for example Tantric Yoga, seem to integrate sexuality with spirituality far more successfully. The unconscious can be seen as one integrated and harmonious source of energy, and not divided up into pieces.

There are many other aspects of the psychosynthesis work which we do not have space to discuss; we will mention only a few practical approaches which we have found useful in a self-help situation. One of these is the emphasis on the 'positive'. When you come across difficult emotions, or parts of yourself you don't like, you are encouraged to 'turn the shit into manure'. You ask, 'What do these parts of me need?', or 'What can I learn from this difficult feeling?'. The idea is that everything negative is a distorted positive. For example, perhaps you are competitive because you have a sense of how your own life could be fuller than it is; by seeing things in this way you learn to use difficulties positively. Of course, there is a danger in this in that you may avoid exploring thoroughly your negative feelings. In our experience you sometimes have to go right into them before you get out of them. A solid sense of self and a positive self-expression would only seem to develop along-side a very thorough clearing of difficulties and blocks in the body and the emotions. This may mean spending some time exploring 'unpleasant' aspects of your present relationships and past history. There is a danger in trying to develop a very positive and spiritual awareness without a firm grounding of the personality.

Psychosynthesis also offers useful work on symbols; much of the guided fantasy work we describe above draws on this approach. Assagioli saw symbols as '. . . accumulators, in the electrical sense, as containers and preservers of a dynamic psychological charge or voltage'.[22] This 'charge' or psychological energy could be transformed by the symbol, or channelled by it, or integrated by it. Assagioli did not believe that symbols need to be 'decoded'; simply experiencing them can be a form of catharsis or healing process. He believed that symbols are especially powerful for transforming the unconscious which does not operate with the language of logic but with pictures and images. His approach is useful, but we would question many of the actual symbols he suggested to work with: for example, his list under the heading of 'Modern Human Symbols' includes explorer, television technician, electronics engineer, but not a single female figure with which women could positively identify – and why did he always use the symbol of the 'wise old man' and not the 'wise old woman'?

Many of the ideas expressed by Assagioli are indebted to the work of Jung who also laid a strong emphasis on the reality of the spiritual world, stating that the inner world of the psyche is as real as the physical world, and has its own laws. To Jung the unconscious is like a huge sea above which the individual ego rises like a small island. He believed not only in a 'personal unconscious' made up of individual memories and subliminal perceptions, but also a deeper 'collective unconscious' containing instincts, memories, intuitions and perceptions derived from the whole history of the human race. Jung said that many symbols in our dreams and fantasies derive from this collective unconscious; he saw this as explaining the similarity in the dreams and mythology of people from completely different cultures and periods of history. In this way dreams enrich our consciousness by re-connecting it with the forgotten language of instincts and memories from the remote experiences of humankind. These symbols from the collective unconscious Jung called 'archetypes', and he picked out the principal archetypes affecting human behaviour: the 'persona' (our social mask or role), the 'shadow' (the dark, unpleasant part of us), the 'anima' and 'animus' (representing respectively the female and male principles which co-exist in every woman and man), the 'wise old man', the 'earth mother', and the 'self'. In Jungian therapy these archetypal symbols are used as entry-points to explore and work through subconscious elements in ourselves (for example, the 'shadow' might be used as a way in to exploring things which we dislike or fear in ourselves). They can also be used as healing and transforming agents: for example, a woman who did not receive enough love from her mother and lacked any concept of good mothering might contact inside herself the archetypal symbol of the 'earth mother' and use this part of her to nourish herself, to fill the gap in her experience and transform her sense of herself as a woman. This could be compared to the way the 'goddess' has been used as a healing and transforming image in some feminist circles during recent years. Women have wanted to rediscover symbols which validate the more active aspects of our identity, and of these the 'goddess' has seemed to assert most effectively the legitimacy and beauty of female power.

Jung believed that the deepest and most difficult to reach of the archetypes was the 'self'. This might be symbolically expressed in dreams in different ways: as the sun, a child, an egg, jewel, flower, chalice or geometric symbol. This 'self' lies behind the ego centre of the personality, and is seen as a kind of deep individual spiritual identity which consists in '. . . the awareness on the one hand of our unique natures, and on the other of our intimate relationship with all life, not only human, but animal and plant, and even that of inorganic matter and the cosmos itself. It brings a feeling of "oneness", and or reconciliation with life . . .'[23] This 'self' is the core or centre around which patients of Jungian therapists often re-shape their personality as they develop through therapy.

There are many elements of Jung's work which we have not space to describe here (for example, his division of people into 'extrovert' and 'introvert' character types); we have touched only on the aspects of his theory most relevant in this context. There are aspects of his work too which we have found unhelpful: for example, his female archetypes tend to be stereotyped 'emotional', 'caring', 'intuitive' figures while the male archetypes tend towards the 'strong' and 'rational'. If he saw the archetypes as the product of social factors and conditioning, reflecting the experience of human beings over the last few thousand years of history, this might be understandable. But he goes further and attributes the archetypes with an independent life of their own, seeing them as having 'their own initiative and their own specific energy' which enables them to interfere in situations and 'create myths, religions, and philosophies that influence and characterise whole nations and epochs of history'.[24] This view, that the symbols create us rather than that we create the symbols, leads to some topsy-turvy thinking. It denies the material forces at work in society and in history, and can be deeply reactionary by suggesting that we can never develop beyond certain previously existing archetypes of feeling and behaviour. Even feminists who follow Jung have tended to perpetuate his vision of a mystical and static 'other world' which determines our behaviour. For example, Esther Harding describes the 'feminine principle' positively, but still sees it as a static force. Woman is controlled by the 'crude untamed feminine being within her',[25] who is inevitably changeable, emotional, moon-like and womb-like. We have found it possible to question this rather limiting view of history and human behaviour, while still finding much that is helpful in Jungian ideas.

It is interesting to notice how different therapy approaches are often not so much conflicting in ideas as offering a different view on the same phenomena. For example, Jung's 'shadow' might be explored in Gestalt therapy as a 'bad girl' voice or a sinister creature in a dream, while the 'anima' and 'animus' might be acted out through the Gestalt technique with cushions as the internalised image or voice of your mother and your father. There are also certain similarities between Jung's 'archetypes' and Assagioli's 'sub-personalities' as characters on our interior landscape.

Jung and Assagioli have both worked within the traditional structure of Psychoanalysis, a series of one-to-one sessions between therapist and patient. Today most Jungian and psychosynthesis therapists still work within this format of individual therapy. But some therapists trained in these schools also offer professionally run groups and workshops where you can learn the techniques to take them back into your life and maybe share them with other members of a self-help group. In a client's (or a group's) work with a psychosynthesis therapist (guide) she is actually taught the techniques the therapist is using, the idea being that the client becomes her own therapist and that gradually her need for a guide disappears. This should help to avoid the problems of mystification and dependency inherent in most therapy/client relationships.

There are women therapists who find themselves able to adapt and combine the ideas of Jung and Assagioli with a feminist perspective. Chapter Eleven will help you when finding the therapist who best combines the elements you are seeking.

ASTROLOGY

An area which is proving of growing interest to feminists is astrology. Some of us have found that even if you do not 'believe' in astrology, it offers a set of rich symbols representing different forces at work in the individual experience (control, friendship, expansiveness, communication, earthiness, fieriness, regeneration and so on). It can be helpful to picture your life in these terms, like taking a fresh look at yourself, becoming aware of strengths and weaknesses, seeing areas to emphasise or change and finding out possible new directions. To us, this discipline has not seemed fatalistic but rather like looking at a map on which you can choose your route. If you are interested in having your chart read, it is best to go to a feminist astrologer who will reinterpret some of the more stereotyped symbols (for example, why are all the inward signs described as 'feminine'?). Whoever you go to, it is worth reading on the subject first so that you are not passively receiving an interpretation of yourself from an 'expert'. It can also be good to think first about which signs or qualities you relate to and maybe write them down or do a picture of them. In this way you can actively participate in your chart-reading and use astrology as another tool to increase your self-awareness and take control over your own life.

WOMEN'S SPIRITUALITY

Spirituality is becoming increasingly recognised in the women's movement as one of the areas where women are traditionally strong and where we need to reclaim and re-assert our experience. To this end, feminists in different countries are exploring not only dreams, symbols and astrology, but also the Tarot, the I-Ching, pre-patriarchal forms of religion, extra-sensory perception and psychic healing. In each of these areas, women are sifting out male-oriented ideas and prejudices and creating their own feminist perspective. Unfortunately there has often seemed to be a conflict between these 'spiritual' interests and the political activity in which many women are involved:

> To 'political' women, 'spiritual' means institutions and philosophies which have immobilised practical changes and have channeled women's energies into serving others to their own detriment. To 'spiritual' women, 'political' means institutions and philosophies which deny the unity of people and have channeled women's creativity into destroying and fighting each other. But each stream is trying to examine deeply the human experience – on the material and on the non-material levels. Women are revolutionizing their consciousness in both directions and challenging the patriarchal ideas and institutions of religion and government by holding to their own women's experience of life.[26]

For us, many of the 'spiritual' disciplines seem to be other ways of tuning in to the hidden powers of the unconscious, which no one as yet fully understands. During the therapy process, we work with the emotions and our relationships to other people. 'Spiritual' approaches can be useful in balancing out this emphasis on the emotions, reminding us that we are also part of nature and offering us a wider perspective on our lives.

NOTES

1   Sigmund Freud, *Introductory Lectures on Psychoanalysis*, Allen & Unwin, London, 1922; Pelican Freud Library, Vol 1, Penguin, Harmondsworth, 1978, p 153.
2   *Introductory Lectures*, pp 154–5.
3   Relevant writings on this topic are listed at the end of Chapter Eight.
4   Carl G. Jung (ed), *Man and His Symbols*, reprinted by Aldus Books, London, 1964; Doubleday, New York, 1969, p 52. (The page numbers refer to the Aldus edition.)

5   *Man and His Symbols*, p 91.
6   *Man and His Symbols*, p 62.
7   *Man and His Symbols*, p 50.
8   *Man and His Symbols*, p 295.
9   Ann Faraday, *Dream Power*, Coward McCann, New York, 1972; Penguin, London, 1978.
10 See 'Further Reading', this chapter.
11 This is based on techniques used by Marie Maguire and Lucy Goodison of the Red Therapy group in their Dream workshops at the Women's Therapy Centre, London.
12 We have based it on Frederick S. Perls, *Gestalt Therapy Verbatim*, Real People Press, Lafayette, 1969; Bantam Books, New York, 1971, pp 288–9.
13 See Susie Orbach, *Fat Is a Feminist Issue*, Hamlyn, London, 1979; Berkley Publishing, New York, 1979, for this and similar guided fantasies.
14 *Man and His Symbols*, p 103.
15 Used by Tricia Bickerton and Barbara Mound of the Red Therapy group for their 'Women Alone' workshops at the Women's Therapy Centre, London.
16 It was devised by Jo Ryan and Sheila Ernst of the Red Therapy group for their 'Feminism and Monogamy' workshops at the Women's Therapy Centre, London.
17 This format for working on themes relevant for women was devised by Luise Eichenbaum and Susie Orbach of the Women's Therapy Centre, London.
18 It was devised by Jo Ryan and Sheila Ernst of the Red Therapy group for their 'Mothers and Children' workshops at the Women's Therapy Centre, London.
19 This passage is indebted to *Country Women* (issue on spirituality), Country Women, Box 51, Albion, CA 95410, USA, April, 1974, pp 29–30.
20 Roberto Assagioli, *Psychosynthesis*, Turnstone Books, London, 1975; Penguin, New York, 1976, p 285.
21 From *Synthesis*, Issue 3/4, Synthesis Press, 830 Woodside, Redwood City, CA, USA.
22 *Psychosynthesis*, pp 177–8.
23 Frieda Fordham, *An Introduction to Jung's Psychology*, Penguin, London, 1953, p 63.
24 *Man and His Symbols*, p 79.
25 M. Esther Harding, *Woman's Mysteries, Ancient and Modern*, Harper & Row, New York, 1976; Rider/Hutchinson, London, 1971, 1977, p 35.
26 *Country Women*, p 1.

FURTHER READING

Introductory Lectures on Psychoanalysis (see above). Freud describes his theory and method on dreams to which all other dream methods are indebted.

Man and His Symbols (see above). A readable illustrated account of Jung's work with dreams and symbols.

Gestalt Therapy Verbatim (see above). Contains long and instructive taped examples of Perls' work on dreams.

Ann Faraday, *The Dream Game*, Harper & Row, New York, 1976; Penguin, London, 1978. A good handbook if you are starting to explore dreams on your own.

Psychosynthesis (see above). A variable collection of writings which includes descriptions of Psychosynthesis theory and guided fantasy work.

Ram Dass, *Journey of Awakening: a Meditator's Guidebook*, Bantam Books, New York, 1978. A readable book to help you start meditating.

Quest, PO Box 8843, Washington DC 20003, USA, *Women and Spirituality*, Vol 1, No 4, 1975. An excellent collection of articles exploring different feminist approaches to spirituality.

Bhagwan Shree Rajneesh, *The Ultimate Alchemy*, Rajneesh Foundation, India, 1976. The Bhagwan, who has many followers in Europe and the USA, writes inspiringly and offers a good introduction to a more 'spiritual' perspective on life but *beware* his views on women.

Liz Greene, *Relating: an Astrological Guide to Living with Others on a Small Planet*, Coventure, London, 1977. Intelligent humanistic astrology.

Mary Anderson, *Colour Healing*, The Aquarian Press, Wellingborough, 1979. A very good short introduction to this interesting area.

Nor Hall, *The Moon and the Virgin: Reflections on the Archetypal Feminine*, Harper & Row, New York, 1980; The Women's Press, London, 1980. The author, a Jungian feminist therapist, explores feminine archetypes and frees them from the limited social context in which they have been trapped.

Chapter Seven
All the World's a Stage:
Psychodrama

WHAT IS PSYCHODRAMA?

Psychodrama is a way of acting out our feelings in a structured situation. Re-enacting a real or fantasy situation, using movement and dialogue, can help us to explore and resolve a current problem (especially when it involves other people) to replay a childhood scene or to practise a new role.

It is a good method for exploring complex problems since it is possible to set up a scene involving several characters and/or places if necessary. It is often used in regression work to re-enact an unresolved childhood experience and is also helpful when current relationships are blocked and tangled or when someone is trying to choose between confusing alternatives.

People often shy away from Psychodrama because they think they can't *act*, but far from being a performance, Psychodrama involves acting from your own feelings. J. L. Moreno, the Viennese psychiatrist who pioneered Psychodrama early this century, was one of the first therapists to recognise the value of a technique which helped people express their feelings directly, rather than merely talking about them.

Psychodrama is not the simplest approach for a self-help group to use but it can be very illuminating. Once you have understood the roles and techniques, it can offer insight and release, even when the group is relatively inexperienced. It also has the advantage that many people can be involved at one time.

There are various role names and technique descriptions used in Psychodrama which will be referred to in the following pages. These are:

Protagonist: Central figure, an actor, in the drama.
Auxiliaries: Supporting figures in the drama, also actors.
Director: Someone chosen by the group who will take responsibility for what happens.
Audience: Other members of the group who watch the psychodrama and

from whom *doubles* will be selected. Their attention is an essential part of the psychodrama.

Double: She will place herself next to, and in the same position as, the person for whom she is *doubling*, and will say or do things which she feels may express the 'inner self' of the person she is *doubling*. The protagonist or auxiliary she is doubling for can choose to accept or reject this information, which is intended to help her, rather than to tell her what to feel.

Soliloquy: The protagonist's attempt to verbalise aloud her thoughts and feelings, to warm herself up and set the scene for all involved.

Role reversal: Two actors in the psychodrama change parts. Often one is the protagonist who can then (a) show how she perceives the other actor; (b) experience the psychodrama from a new viewpoint.

HOW DOES PSYCHODRAMA WORK? THE THEORY BEHIND THE ACTION

Unlike Freud, his contemporary, Moreno made no attempt to construct a theory of psychological development based on his clinical experience of Psychodrama but he did make some basic assumptions about human nature. He believed that people are born with the capacity to feel freely and, through this, to take full responsibility for their own lives. However, he recognised that society limits our capacities to respond fully and suggested that what he termed the 'cultural conserve', by which he meant the social and political expressions of moral standards in society, often works as a pressure towards conformity. People will often, therefore, respond to situations in stereotyped ways, automatically using responses which they have learned are socially acceptable. Psychodrama can prepare people for free action, teach us to respond in the here-and-now in an alive and *relevant* way, rather than being tied to limiting and even inappropriate responses. A woman whose car breaks down may respond in a stereotyped way by assuming that a man will know how to fix it and allow him to take over. Had she been able to respond freely to the situation she might have acknowledged that her own knowledge about the car was sufficient. Years of giving way to male opinion on mechanical matters leads her to give a stereotyped but inappropriate response.

Moreno used the terms 'spontaneous' and 'creative' in a particular technical way. These terms are not easy to define but our sense of what he meant by 'spontaneity' is the capacity of a person to respond in an immediate way, appropriate to the situation. For example, a woman is at a market looking at fruit and trying to decide what to buy. A second woman offers her a grape, saying 'They're really good. Taste one'. Without thinking, the first woman refuses. This is not a spontaneous response but is a stock response, perhaps learned as a child when being told not to take anything from strangers. This stock response has blotted out her capacity to recognise the woman's genuine friendliness.

The idea of 'creativity' is closely linked with spontaneity. It refers to the ways in which our feelings and behaviour are unique. To behave 'creatively' means to act according to inner processes, rather than to external notions of how we should behave. We could see the offering of those grapes as 'creative' behaviour. When people do relate 'creatively' and 'spontaneously' then there is the possibility of what Moreno called 'tele' between them, that is, real communication. When people relate in a stereotyped way, not treating each other as individuals, there is no 'tele', no real interaction and sharing, no giving and receiving in a direct and simple way.

When our 'spontaneity' is curbed and we are acting and responding in stereotypical ways, we will often feel confused, blocked or angry. We are not actually expressing any of our emotions. We are responding in conventionalised ways which are not related to our inner experience. Through Psychodrama we are helped to act from the inside, to act 'creatively' and 'spontaneously', to act from an emotional level. Where emotions were previously blocked, they are now released, often with an intensity which relates to the former level of pent-up emotion. This release Moreno termed 'catharsis', which in turn can lead to 'insight', the last step of a psychodrama. Real 'insight', according to Moreno, can be achieved only after emotional release and clarification. Otherwise it is merely an intellectual insight which cannot change a person's feelings.

PSYCHODRAMA: SOME ILLUSTRATIONS

Using Psychodrama to Explore a Current Problem

This is how Alice used Psychodrama to clarify her relationships in a situation which involved other people and where she felt angry and helpless.

We began as we often do by going around the group and saying how we were feeling. Alice was tense and upset about how badly she was getting along with the people in her house. If she didn't find a way to release her pent-up feelings she was in danger of starting a fight over some trivial matter and making it doubly difficult to live comfortably there. She wanted some insight into what was going on between herself and her housemates and to explore possible changes in the way she was relating to them.

   Alice is in her late twenties. She has a young son who lives with her and also in the house live Karen, Karen's daughter and Lisa, a third woman. During the summer Karen had moved her boyfriend, Julian, into the house.

Alice hadn't felt able to protest but didn't feel happy about Julian living there. This feeling had grown worse since Karen had told her that she and Julian were expecting a baby.

Alice describes how she feels in the house now.

'I can hardly go into the kitchen – which is where we usually meet – without girding myself in case Julian is there. I feel as if there's a smouldering tension between us, with every word I speak, every move I make.'

Mary offers to take the part of director in working on a psychodrama with Alice. Even in a self-help group there is usually a director for a particular psychodrama as the process of setting up the drama and keeping it going is quite complex.

Alice, the protagonist, gives her soliloquy, describing the kitchen and how people sit in it. The women help her to set up appropriate props and Alice is asked by Mary to choose people to play Karen and Julian, the auxiliaries.

Alice chooses Cathy and Susan and when Mary asks why she has chosen them – to let them know how they should act or, rather, which parts of themselves they should draw on – Alice says, 'Cathy is Julian because there's a similar tension between Cathy and me. We're polite but underneath we're often angry or hurt and it's always me who shouts and Cathy who goes silent. Susan is Karen because she is very quiet, feminine and beautiful. I feel an intuitive warmth between us but it's difficult to talk things through.'

Mary checks with Cathy and Susan that they are willing to be these auxiliaries then seats them at the table where they sit, eating and chatting. We will now refer to them by the names of the people they are acting.

Alice walks into the 'kitchen'. Karen and Julian look up from their breakfast; they say good morning to each other politely. Alice puts the kettle on, begins to make toast and then asks Julian to move, 'Can I get the marmalade from behind you.'

'Sure.'

To bring out what is happening for Alice and Julian underneath this rather banal conversation, Mary asks them to *reverse roles*. This means that Alice will play Julian and vice versa, and will help to show what Alice thinks that Julian is 'really' feeling. Alice sits in Julian's chair and says, 'I can't even have my breakfast in peace in this house with Karen. Alice makes me feel it's a crime to be sitting between her and the marmalade and now Karen's offering her tea and she'll probably sit down and have breakfast with us. I hope she'll go back to her room.'

Mary asks them to change back to their own roles. Alice finishes preparing her breakfast and Julian and Karen get up and leave. Alice looks angry. She now asks Lisa, the other woman in the house, to come in. She chooses Chris to play Lisa, saying that it has something to do with Chris's not being so soft and feminine as Karen, and the slightly jerky quality of her movements. She explains that Lisa always supports her complaints against Karen and Julian.

Lisa comes into the kitchen and Alice says, 'It's so awful living here with Karen and Julian. I felt like an intruder when I came to get my breakfast. I couldn't sit down and eat with them.'

Lisa agrees. 'They're so much a couple they just seem to take the place over as if we were the lodgers. Never mind.' Lisa puts her arm around Alice but Alice moves away from her.

'I don't feel comfortable grumbling with you about them. I'd be embarrassed if they came back into the room.'

Mary (the director) signals to Karen and Julian to re-enter the kitchen. She has picked up on what Alice is saying and wants to reproduce this situation in all its conflicting emotions. Karen and Julian sit down at the table again. Alice stands between the table and Lisa. She looks from one to another and says in a cold angry voice, 'I don't want to take sides. I don't want to line up with you, Lisa, against them. I don't want to be identified with you as older and straighter and sensible.' She looks at the other two, 'But you just put me down. You make me feel like an asexual old woman. I hate you – I hate your trendy clothes – all you care about is your image and each other.'

Now Alice is shouting and clenching her fists. Karen and Julian shrink back in silence; they are holding hands. 'Can't you hear me, you two love birds! – I'm here, I'm here.'

Mary gives Alice a cushion and suggests that she goes on shouting at Karen and Julian while beating the cushion. This will help Alice to release some of her anger. She shouts and beats the pillow until she is exhausted and falls on top of it. After a few moments she looks up and sees Karen and Julian still silent and withdrawn from her – she looks at Karen, then at Lisa – puts her hand out tentatively and then pulls back and bursts into tears.

Through her tears she asks, 'What's wrong with me? I seem to be doing it all wrong. I want to be closer to all of you in the house but all I do is drive you away.' She cries some more. By expressing her anger fully and directly, Alice has experienced a cathartic release of her blocked emotions and is able to feel her good emotions for Lisa, Karen and Julian.

Mary asks Alice what she would like from the group. Alice wants to know what Lisa, Karen and Julian felt like when she expressed her anger so directly. Julian says that he felt very scared by Alice's anger, both when she was coldly hostile and when she shouted. He found her so self-righteous and unapproachable that all he could do was withdraw. He felt defined as a naughty child and since Alice obviously wasn't going to listen to his 'excuses' he wanted to avoid her.

Alice asked him if he felt angry with her.

'Of course, but I'm not going to get involved in a confrontation with you.'

'What about you Karen?'

'Well, I was scared by your anger and bitterness. I felt safest to stay with Julian, or I'd have been between you two and I'd have got the worst of it'.

'And Lisa?'

'I felt let down by you when you wouldn't be on my side. I thought when you were standing by the table between me and them that you were going to be the mediator and end up getting on well with everybody, leaving me to get angry for you. So I was relieved when your anger came out.'

Alice says she feels much calmer now, less consumed by her anger and understands that Karen and Julian are not 'all powerful'. She thinks she will be able to deal with her relationships in the house more easily. She hopes to relate to Julian as a person, which may make him less tense when she is around. She also sees that she does not have to 'line up' either with Lisa or with Karen and Julian, but that she can maintain her own position.

Alice chose Cathy, Susan and Chris to play the members of her household because she felt they had some characteristics in common with Julian, Lisa and Karen. In the Psychodrama they exaggerated these characteristics and learned something about their responses to others and the responses they evoke in others. For instance, Julian learns about dealing with aggression by blocking it. Susan/Karen uses her passivity and Chris/Lisa is trapped into acting out other people's aggression and being seen as the bad person.

Alice has used the psychodrama to enable her to act more positively in her present reality. To do this she needed to unravel the indirect ways in which she had been expressing her feelings, and release the tension. This kind of experience is particularly important for women since we often feel we have very little control over our work or home environment, and resort to indirect means of trying to get what we need.

Using Psychodrama to Explore Future Projections

Psychodrama does not have to be bound by reality, but can look at people's projections and fantasies of what might be. Here is an example.

Jane is an Australian who has been living in London for two years. She is about to return to Australia for a holiday and is worried about how she is going to deal with her relationship with Roger. When she left Australia Roger and his family assumed they would marry on her return. Jane explains she has already stayed in England a year longer than she had intended and has really changed her ideas on how she wants to live. She now has other goals besides making a good marriage or having a financially successful career. She does not know how she is going to explain herself to Roger and his family.

Julia suggests that they set up a psychodrama so that Jane can explore her feelings and reactions to returning home. Julia offers to direct so that, as in Alice's psychodrama, one person will take responsibility for what is to follow.

Jane imagines out loud the scene where she meets Roger again. She describes a suburban bungalow with large windows looking out on to a luxuriant garden. This description will help Jane to contact her feelings and will begin to create an imaginary situation for the rest of the group. All Roger's family are there. Roger's mother will be in the kitchen cooking dinner. Jane picks Angela to play the mother and tells her, 'You're the dominant person in the family. You put all your energy and intelligence, which is considerable, into your home, encouraging your husband and children to be successful. You talk more than anyone else and you have a sort of conviction that your opinions and world view are right.'

Janet is chosen to play Roger's father, an amenable man, successful in his business but at home concerned to placate his wife and children. He is genuinely fond of Jane and she doesn't want to hurt his feelings. Jane hesitates before choosing Mary to play Roger's sister, Alison. She says that no one in the group really reminds her of Alison. At this point Julia, who is directing, needs to find out why it is hard for Jane to pick someone for Alison's role. Julia thinks it may have something to do with whatever special feelings Jane has about Alison so she asks Jane to tell her something about their relationship. (This will also prove useful information for the person who plays Alison.)

Jane describes their friendship. 'Alison admires me but wants to please her parents so she is on my side but is also threatened by me. In fact, she's very like me.' Jane laughs. 'Perhaps that's what's so difficult about choosing someone to play the role.' She looks around the group and decides that Jo might be right for the part, then she picks Sally to play Roger.

Jane arranges them in the sitting-room. Father is in an armchair doing a crossword puzzle, Alison is making phone calls and Roger is adjusting the stereo. Julia explains to the auxiliaries that they can feel free to improvise within their given roles and they may find Jane has intuitively picked them for appropriate parts they can play from their own feelings. If they want to check something out with Jane they can do so without destroying the flow of the drama and, similarly, if they do say something that sounds wrong Jane can easily correct them. This seems to work well and does not remove people from their feelings.

At this point Roger's mother says she isn't sure how she is supposed to be. Julia reminds her that she is the dominating member of the family and suggests she try to follow her own emotions. Often a group member needs just this sort of encouragement to get the confidence to act according to their own feelings. Jane explains that all members of the family (with the possible exception of Alison) assume she is coming back to take up her life as Roger's girlfriend, soon to be his wife. They are prepared to treat her absence as 'difficult' but 'interesting'. There is no awareness that things may have changed significantly for Jane. This situation will be familiar to many women whose families will somehow assume that whatever the woman herself has been doing will be secondary to their joint plans.

The scene is set.

The other group members have moved to one side of the room and they will be the audience. Their attention is most important and if they feel they want to add to what the protagonist or any of the auxiliaries are expressing, they can participate by doubling.

Julia suggests that Jane starts by walking up the driveway to the house and, using 'the soliloquy technique, to describe aloud how she is feeling.

'I'm not looking forward to this meeting. I'm afraid that I won't be able to be myself. I don't know if I can tell Roger that I don't want to marry him, especially with his family around. His mother will be angry with me. How could anyone reject her son? I don't want to hurt his father, he's a nice man and I know he's fond of me. I feel I'll get trapped into being the old amenable Jane and if I do stand up for myself, I'll really be on my own. Even Alison won't support me with her mother there.'

Jane reaches the front door, pauses and rings the bell. Roger jumps up saying, 'That must be Jane', and hurries to the door, opens it and hugs Jane. Jane avoids kissing Roger on the mouth but he does not appear to notice. He ushers her into the sitting-room. Jane hugs each member of the family. Roger's father pulls up a chair near him, his mother offers food and Roger hovers around her. Roger's father takes over, asking Jane how she is. Jane responds easily, talking about her flight. Then Roger joins in and asks Jane what her plans are. Jane visibly tenses and tries to avoid the question. 'I'm going to rest and spend time on the beach.' Lana decides to double for Jane and comes to stand beside her. She copies Jane's posture and gestures to help her get the feel of the part even more closely. The director, Julia, explains to Jane that she can use anything that Lana says as her double but that if it doesn't sound right she can ignore it.

Doubling for Jane, Lana says, 'I've only just got back and I can't tell you what I'm really thinking – I don't want to be rude and hurt your feelings.' Jane nods and tries to turn the conversation to a more neutral topic. Mother comes in offering more food and saying how nice it would be if she and Roger began to look at houses. Jane refuses the food aggressively and Lana, still doubling for her, says, 'Oh God, this is just what I feared. I don't know how to be myself in this situation. Anything honest I say will just sound rude.'

Jane nods at her double and says, 'I don't know how to be myself in this situation.' It seems that Lana's doubling has helped Jane to express more clearly what she is feeling.

Father asks Jane about her work and life in London. Alison also seems interested and begins to ask her more detailed questions. Mother puts her arm around Roger's shoulders and says, 'Well, this is all most interesting, a little fling before you young people settle down.'

Roger again asks Jane what her plans are and Jane becomes silent, her eyes on his mother's face. This is a cue to Julia that Jane may be feeling something strongly about mother but is not sure what it is or how to express it. She suggests that Jane and mother reverse roles. When Jane plays mother it will make it clearer how Jane is perceiving mother and what is making it so difficult for Jane to be herself.

Jane takes up mother's position behind Roger's chair. As mother she says, 'I don't really think you're good enough for my son but he wants you so I'll have to accept you if you can fit into the model I have of a suitable wife. I'm not interested in what you were doing in England. Let's put that behind us and get on with the serious business of marriage in Australia.'

Julia suggests that Jane and mother change back to their own roles. The situation is clarified for everyone, particularly for Jane, who can now respond more directly.

Roger asks Jane a specific question. Is she going to try and get her old job back? Jane blurts out. 'You and your mother, neither of you seem interested in me. At least Alison and your father want to know what I've been doing, but you don't care. I've changed. I don't want to live in a suburb or go back to my old job. In fact I'm going back to England to finish my course.'

Roger looks horrified and angry. 'But Jane . . .'

His mother interrupts, 'Jane, you must be tired after your journey. I'm sure you'll feel differently about this in a few days.'

Roger is not to be put off. 'No – I really want to have this out now.'

Roger and Jane argue heatedly and Jane insists, 'You're got to see me as I am. I haven't come back to settle down and marry you.'

Jane sighs, looks relieved and says she has gone far enough. Julia asks Jane what the experience was like for her. Jane says that at first she was nervous and didn't know who she was but as she pressed to be recognised for herself, she lost her fear and guilt and became more convinced that by letting Roger and his family know how she felt was the best thing to do. It was also important for her to be able to feel angry at the way Roger and his mother denied her reality. Roger and mother both confirmed this. They had been taken aback when Jane had asserted herself and shown she wasn't the person they imagined her to be. Jane felt that moving from her sense of depersonalisation to being able to reassert her identity would enable her to recognise those feelings and deal with them better in the future.

PSYCHODRAMA IN A SELF-HELP GROUP

If you want to use Psychodrama in your group it may be helpful if some group members try to see an experienced director at work. The exercises which follow this section will help you to approach Psychodrama in a more confident way but it is a technique which can be used with great variation of skill, much of which comes only with time, experience and confidence. Its great advantage is that several or all the members of a group have a chance to contribute their insights to a situation and to learn something about themselves. Psychodrama can also effectively take into account the social and economic background of a situation. For example, a woman who has a successful career could vividly recreate the scene where she visits her working-class parents in the tiny house she was brought up in. Psychodrama is often easier when group members know each other well as then the situations and auxilary roles are familiar to the group. But you must also be aware of the possibility of stereotyping in a familiar group, and avoid that when you can.

A psychodrama usually arises from:

A current situation, like Alice's problems with her housemates
A future situation, like Jane's fear of returning to Roger
The reactivation of a past situation which remains painful or unresolved

Setting up a Psychodrama

Strong feelings have been aroused in a woman, set off by a childhood memory of family mealtimes. She decides with her group to use Psychodrama to recreate such a meal, hoping to illuminate her relationships with family members and to give her insight into links between her family and her current problems with food.

Choose a director, or have a woman volunteer, though the protagonist should feel comfortable with the choice and may even like to make the choice herself.

The director recreates the scene, asking the protagonist to describe physical surroundings in detail, using the present tense. Remembering how your brother tipped his chair from the table or how the plastic tablecloth had traces of the last meal on it can make the scene come alive.

As the protagonist mentions other characters the director will ask her to choose members of the groups to take their parts, to be her auxilaries. The protagonist helps them by describing the characters or sometimes by reversing roles (protagonist becoming auxiliary briefly, and vice versa).

The auxiliaries play out of their own feelings. If the protagonist feels they have gone wrong she can stop them and tell them why and how.

The director can ask the protagonist to brief the auxiliaries directly and the auxiliaries will also draw on the protagonist's opening soliloquy. Auxiliaries and protagonists should speak as directly as possible.

When the protagonist appears to have released some feelings and to have reached a new equilibrium, to have gained the insight she was seeking, the director has the responsibility to close the drama, checking with the protagonist that she is ready for this, and then with the group members who may like to deal with feelings the drama has raised for them. If it is a childhood scene the protagonist should verbalise any connections she is able to make between her childhood feelings and her current experience. This should take place after the psychodrama is over.

Common Problems in Psychodrama

Sometimes the psychodrama appears to be stuck. No one is speaking. If the dialogue has been between two people, it may be that there is some feeling between them that they cannot quite reach or express. To help them the director can:

(a) *Encourage members of the group to double for the two actors.* The doubles may be able to express some of the hidden feelings, as Lana did when she doubled for Jane, and expressed how Jane felt about Roger's mother. The dialogue can then continue freely.

(b) *Reverse roles.* Each actor can then express what she senses the other person to be feeling, rightly or wrongly. These fears may be blocking the dialogue. When Alice and Julian seemed stuck in polite conversation they reversed roles and Alice is able to express the resentment she fears Julian must feel at her presence.

(c) *Call in another character or change to another scene.* Sometimes a particular character feels at a loss. Roger's mother felt like this at the start of the psychodrama and needed the director to remind her that she was the dominant member of the family and that she should play the part from her own feelings. The director may need to ask the actor what she is feeling herself; often the feelings will be appropriate to the part she is playing.

But what if an actor is playing her role according to her feelings and it just does not fit the part as perceived by the protagonist? It is better to bring these feelings out into the open rather than hoping that they will go away. It doesn't destroy the flow of a psychodrama to pause and discuss how an actor is interpreting her role. It may be that she has had insufficient briefing or can be helped by role reversal or doubling to get into the swing of the part. Similarly, if you do not know how to end a psychodrama but feel that it should stop, take a break and check out with the actors and the audience how they perceive what has happened. Anyone can suggest that catharsis seems to have taken place in a psychodrama, and therefore the action should close. It is open to the protagonist or others to dispute the suggestion.

Perhaps the most common problem when Psychodrama is suggested is the fear of some or all of the group that it won't work because they can't act. We have already explained that Psychodrama does not need acting skills in the conventional sense, but this will not necessarily stop group members from feeling anxious. It is important to let a group have the opportunity to 'warm up' to a psychodrama. Use one of the 'warm ups' suggested in the exercise section or take an exercise from one of the other chapters which looks to you as if it will be relaxing and enjoyable. Physical exercises are often good warm ups for Psychodrama as after them people are less self-conscious.

PSYCHODRAMA PRACTISED PROFESSIONALLY

In most countries Psychodrama is offered as part of a humanistic psychotherapy programme. You can learn a lot through working with a good director as it takes great skill to elicit the most sensitive emotional response from the actors. The role of the director does have some contradictions. In theory she will have a warm interaction with group members while taking responsibility for what happens. She will share her feelings with the group and may tell a group member if she feels sympathetic or angry. However, even in a self-help group where the role of director is rotated, the director's involvement is different from that of other group members. She is looking at what is happening and while she must rely on her subjective responses to what is happening (how would *I* feel in that situation) part of her is working out what she is learning from the situation to intervene where necessary to develop the action. This split means that the director will not share the same level of emotional involvement and release as the other group members.

The attitudes of the professional psychodrama leader are important. Psychodrama does not have a theory which leads to a specific interpretation of a woman's behaviour in any given situation, but the assumption of how people *should* behave can have an implicit influence on how we respond in the group. While a technique like Psychodrama can be used to increase our power and self-determination, it has no built-in understanding of women's emotional stresses and conflicts. This means that it may expose a strong emotion – such as a woman's fear of change – without having an adequate understanding of the other side of the dilemma; namely the strength of the woman's need to change.

In a led group, the psychodrama actor may also have strong feelings projected on to her, rather like the transference process in psychoanalysis which we discuss in Chapter Eight. This can occur in most led groups, not just in psychodrama groups, and can usually be used and dealt with in the group situation. It does not help to ignore such feelings as otherwise they may emerge in indirect and confusing ways.

SOME LIMITATIONS OF PSYCHODRAMA THEORY

Unfortunately Moreno did not follow through his criticism of society to recognise that changes in society are needed to enable us to lead emotionally richer lives. He saw a well adapted or 'normal' person as one who is spontaneous and creative and can live out many roles in life. A woman who can be a daughter, mother, lover, creator and worker would be seen as well adapted. A woman who related to all situations as mother, and had not developed other aspects or capacities, would have been seen by Moreno as pathological or maladaptive. This fails to recognise that we live in a society where it is adaptive *not to feel* and *normal* for a woman to restrict her life. Moreno did not acknowledge the social and economic pressures which may reinforce a woman's mothering response, in the family and outside it. Moreno sidestepped the issue of the kinds of changes we would have to bring about in society for his definition of normal to be appropriate. If we take Moreno's work seriously it will lead to a questioning of the way in which society does restrict our personal lives, rather than seeing individuals as self-determining with unlimited possibilities for change.

Psychodrama has particular potential – despite Moreno's limited view – to help us find strength and insight to work to change society. The possibility for acting out social situations can be applied to political understandings which may lead, in turn, to broader political analysis and activity. We may discover, as Alice did, that as women we can feel stronger in a situation when we understand what is happening and can express our emotions, especially anger, directly. We might also use Psychodrama to explore sex-role stereotyping since in the drama we can play stereotyped and non-stereotyped roles, learning to distinguish between the ones which feel good for us and practising unfamiliar roles which we may come to prefer.

The following sequence of exercises, 111—116, is a systematic introduction to Psychodrama which has been used to teach Psychodrama to members of self-help groups or others wanting to use Psychodrama in their work situations. Each exercise teaches a different technique.

We start with a light exercise as a warm-up and then move on to some which are more emotionally intense.

111   Mirroring

Mirroring gets the group moving and feeling together and also encourages close observation of another person, which is an important part of role play and doubling in Psychodrama. The other function of starting a group with an active exercise like this is that it allows group members to fool around or play, gives them implicit permission to act in ways they don't usually feel comfortable with in everyday life. It's fun to do this exercise to music, especially something which changes mood and tempo which may suggest different movements to the group. The group divides into pairs and each pair decides who is A and who is B.

A starts by looking at herself in the mirror, and B is her reflection. Stand facing your partner and bring your hands together so they almost touch. A begins to move as she wants and B mirrors her movements. Be aware of the movements you choose: how you feel leading or being led, how you feel seeing yourself portrayed by someone else. Do you feel self-conscious when you see your mirror image? Do you lose yourself in the pleasure of movement and become oblivious to your partner? Does your mirror image influence your moves?

After about three minutes change roles so that B is leading and A is mirroring. Notice how you feel in this new role. Are you more comfortable in one rather than the other? After another three minutes change again and then continue to change and see if you can reach a point where no one is leading or following, but you are moving together. This may not be as easy as it sounds; notice what happens for you.

Later come back into the group and share your experience. How did you feel moving? What sorts of movements did you find pleasurable/easy/difficult/fun? How did you feel leading and mirroring? Were you comfortable moving together? Did any particular feelings come up for you? Did you notice anything in particular about your partner's movements: heaviness, bubbly energy, anger?

If you are doing this exercise as part of a learning sequence to familiarise yourself with psychodrama techniques, then it seems valuable to give a detailed report to develop your powers of observation. If the exercise is being used as a warm-up to relax group members and increase the energy level in the group then keep the feedback brief. Try sharing only the most striking parts of the mirroring.

112 Introducing Ourselves

This exercise involves paying close attention and observing your partner carefully as a preparation for role play. It is a good exercise for a new group but can also have interesting results in a group where members know each other well.

Each group member should think of someone outside the group who knows her well and whom she would trust to do a good job of introducing her. Take a minute to picture this person clearly; how does she/he walk, dress, talk or laugh? You are going to become this outside person. Try to see how much you can be like the person you have chosen in posture, intonation and gestures. Now, in turns around the circle, act the 'outside person' introducing her (him)self to the group and then allow the 'outside person' to introduce you to the group.

This exercise is a good opportunity to use your powers of observation and to select words, incidents and gestures which project the emotions you want to communicate to the group. At the same time, the process of selecting a person to introduce you, choosing how you want to be presented to the group, may arouse strong emotions which could lead into individual work.

You may decide to give feedback after this exercise, either in pairs or as a whole group, depending on whether you want to use it as role play practice or to generate a psychodrama in the group.

113 Being with Children

Take a partner. This is a role playing exercise and you will take it in turns to be an adult and a child. Decide who will play which part first. The child should decide what age she's going to be and what she wants to be doing. She should start being how she wants to be and ask the adult to participate when she wants.

The adults' role is divided into two parts. In the first part be *with* the child and notice how you feel, what you do, what you want to do.

Then you decide that you want to do something different, something which involves your intervening in what the child is doing. Try to enforce this – the child may protest – just let yourself go and see how you deal with this situation.

When both partners have played both roles come back into the circle and share your experience keeping to the form

'As a child I felt . . .'
'As an adult I felt . . .'

114 Male/Female Roles

Another role playing exercise, this one is for exploring our sexual stereotypes. To be able to escape from them, we need to know what they mean to us.

Take a partner. One of you will play the man and one the woman. Take five minutes to act these roles using movement, gesture and words. Then change roles. After ten minutes stop and take five more minutes to talk about what happened for both of you. Ask yourselves whether you noticed any differences in the way you moved, looked, the words you used, how you saw the other person.

115 Couples

'Couples' involves role playing but here doubling is also specifically built into the exercise. (We have found it useful to practise doubling to get the feel of how to tune into the person you are doubling for and what sorts of interventions it is possible to make as a double. Of course when a psychodrama is in progress the doubling will often happen spontaneously as a member of the audience sees one of the characters doing something she identifies with and feels she could make it more explicit. Frequently practice at doubling will give group members more courage to intervene in this way. We have found that in the early stages of a self-help group women will often not intervene by doubling or making suggestions in case they are 'wrong', so we need to practise these interventions.)

Divide the group into smaller groups of four. Where this is impossible, smaller groups can do the exercise leaving out one or both doubles. Now describe a familiar situation in which two people interact with each other. For example, a couple who have been married for ten years having breakfast together; a mother trying to put her small child to bed; a policeman trying to move someone off a pavement at a demonstration. Choose a situation you are sure will be almost a 'stereotype' for the group members so that there will be very little possibility of anyone being unable to work out what to do in any of the parts.

Decide which members of each small group are going to play the two parts and have the other pair act as their 'doubles'.

The role players enact the scene and the doubles place themselves beside or just behind them, following their gestures and entering into the dialogue whenever they feel they can help the scene along by saying something the role player has left unsaid.

In the 'married couple' scene the husband might come into the kitchen, sit down at the table, look at his wife, sigh and pick up his newspaper. His double might say, 'Quick, I'd better put this paper between me and her before she brings up some problem.' The wife, meantime, is chewing her toast and her double might say, 'It's impossible to get through to him – he's emotionally impenetrable. I'll just bite into this toast instead.'

We can add to this exercise by asking the two characters and their doubles to change parts. This introduces the technique of role reversal, used earlier in the chapter. By playing the wife, the husband gains some insight both into her feelings and the effect his behaviour has on someone else.

Doing an exercise like this can show group members that even if they think they 'can't act' they can play a role in Psychodrama where it is open for them to act out their own feelings in a given situation which can be varied to suit the group. For instance, in a workshop on monogamy and non-monogamy we might ask participants to role-play a triangular relationship with doubles to see if it gives any fresh insights.

116   Setting the Scene

This exercise illustrates one of the methods the director may use to begin a psychodrama by using the inanimate objects in a situation to create atmosphere or to recreate the physical environment of your childhood. It is also a warm-up which can be used effectively at the beginning of a group to get participants to act the part of neutral 'objects'. Choose one person in the group to read the exercise aloud, with long pauses. Everyone sits or lies in a relaxed position and closes their eyes.

Picture yourself in a place you know well. Let yourself choose a place that is special for you in some way. (*Pause*) Look around and notice where things are, their shapes, sizes and colours, the smells and the sounds. What can you smell? Where are the noises coming from? (*Pause*, and after every sentence.) When you have a clear picture of the place look around again and pick on an object. Take your time and decide which object you want to select. Now I'm going to ask you, one by one, to become that object, to speak in the first person and describe yourself, then to describe where you are and how the person who has chosen you feels about you and the place you are in.

Each person can then take her turn to act as the object. Whether you do this in the whole group, smaller groups or pairs will probably depend on how much time you want to spend on the exercise. (For a fuller description of how to prepare a fantasy exercise, see exercise **100**.)

Many of the exercises suggested in other chapters for warming up a group may lead into a psychodrama. However, there are some exercises which are more likely to guide a group in this direction. We give three examples here of warm-ups we have particularly enjoyed using.

117 Empty Chair
A good exercise for stimulating a psychodrama but the group will probably need to have done a simple introductory exercise first, involving some movement.

Have one woman lead the exercise. Everyone sits in a semi-circle and in front of the group is an empty chair. Ask them to visualise someone sitting in the chair – someone they need to talk to (it may be themselves). Ask them to come up when they're ready and say a few words to the person in the chair. If it is appropriate you can ask them to reverse roles and sit in the chair, but keep it brief and make sure everyone has a turn. (The use of the chair here is similar to the use of the cushion, as described in Chapter Three.) This gives the group a chance to see what problems and issues are concerning other group members and will often lead to one person wanting to develop her dialogue further.

118 Picture Frame
In this exercise visualising a scene can lead a group member into a psychodrama.

Have one woman direct the exercise. Prepare the group for a fantasy as described in exercise **100**. She sets up a picture frame (real or imaginary) on the wall and asks group members to visualise a scene in which they are a part.

The scene can be anywhere, past, present or future, real or imaginary. It might be a painful or violent scene you have experienced. Picture the physical details clearly. You must be in the scene. Allow the group about two minutes to form their pictures and then have each one in turn briefly describe the scene. Ask what has just happened and what is about to happen. Other members of the group can ask questions too. If any of the scenes seem to contain a lot of emotional energy the person herself or another member of the group may suggest developing it into a psychodrama.

119 The Magic Shop

This is a fantasy which raises questions about what a person really wants from life, what the significant choices are for her and how ready she feels to make them. It can be valuable as an exercise in its own right, though often the issues raised can usefully be developed further.

Choose one person to lead the exercise. (It does involve more responsibility than just reading a fantasy aloud.) The leader asks everyone to sit or lie down comfortably, dims the lights and has them close their eyes. Then she slowly reads these instructions, *with long pauses* at the end of every sentence.

Imagine that you are walking along a small path in a forest. Picture the trees. Look around you. Is it dark or light? Can you hear any noises in the forest? What else can you see? Suddenly you walk around a corner in the path and see a small wooden house. You are curious and decide to go inside. The walls are lined with shelves and on each shelf are jars of different shapes and sizes. It is a shop. A strange shop. A magic shop. I am the proprietor of this shop. Welcome. This is a most unusual shop for each of these jars contains values or qualities, which you may want, such as happiness, love, strength, consistency, patience. We use a barter system, so if you want to purchase anything from these jars you will have to find something to give me in return.

When a group member feels ready she can come to the proprietor of the magic shop and ask to purchase whatever she wants. The proprietor will ask her what she wants to give in return. She is now faced with a dilemma. She will either accept or reject the bargain. Does she want the new quality enough to be prepared to give up some old part of herself? In the process of making these choices she will learn something about herself and her needs.

FURTHER READING

Howard A. Blatner, *Acting In*, Springer, New York, 1973. Useful introduction but don't read it to inspire you to try Psychodrama because it won't. It is helpful if you are already excited by the idea and want to read up on practical details.

Ira A. Greenberg (ed), *Psychodrama: Theory and Therapy*, Behavioral Publications, New York, 1974; Souvenir Press, London, 1975. Articles and extracts from writers on Psychodrama including some of Moreno's confusing theory. Good to browse through and get a flavour of the historical and intellectual climate in which Psychodrama originated. Also has accounts of Psychodrama in practice which are more inspiring than those in Blatner's book. Not useful as a practical guide.

Joel Badaines, 'Interview on Psychodrama', *Self and Society*, Vol 3, No 10, October, 1975. Clear account of what happens in Psychodrama, giving a good sense of how Psychodrama works.

Joel Badaines, 'Psychodrama: Concepts, Principles and Issues', *Drama Therapy*, Vol 1, No 2, Autumn, 1977. Clear summary of psychodrama theory which amplifies what has been said in this chapter.

Chapter Eight
Roots in Childhood: Regression

WHAT DOES REGRESSION WORK MEAN?

We often recognise past patterns and influences in present relationships. A woman storms out of a pub leaving behind a bemused friend. Later she realises she got so angry because her companion's manner reminded her of her cold and authoritarian father. Another woman nags at her daughter about her untidiness, to no effect. She hates herself for nagging but can't stop doing it. She remembers that this was how she was treated by her own mother. We don't want to go on treating men as if they were our fathers: nor do we want to repeat our mothers' mistakes. We can *escape* our childhood, rather than return to it, through using 'regression' in therapy.

People often question the use of digging up the past. Why dwell on old experience when there is so much to deal with in the present? When memories of childhood are pleasant and happy we don't want to disturb them. If they are painful we resist the suggestion that we should relive them. Some of us feel we have made a clean break with the past, rejecting our class background or the values and lifestyle of our parents. Others of us feel that we are still involved in complicated conflicts with our parents. In both cases we may want to avoid exploring early experiences. We may need some convincing about the value or necessity of re-experiencing our past and exploring those defences and blocks against intense pleasure and pain whose roots go back to early childhood.

The term 'regression' suggests going back into childhood: literally becoming a child again. This is not what is meant by regression work in therapy. In daily life we can sometimes regress in unproductive ways that are out of our control. The woman rushing out of the pub is behaving as if she were a child responding to her powerful father. Leaving her past experience buried means that she has little power over it and it can erupt in ways that are unproductive. In therapy we re-experience childhood emotions in a safe situation where we can slowly learn how to come to terms with our early fears, losses, love and hate, and this will free us from automatically using old blocks and defences which may twist and destroy our relationships in the present. Regression in therapy is aimed at enabling us to experience fully the feelings we blocked off as infants or children because we feared their effect, but this time the outcome is different and enables us to change as adults.

Often in our group we found that while exploring present feelings we were reminded of childhood situations. These were the times when we found regression work useful, though it can be difficult and disturbing. It is probably not the best technique to start with in a self-help group but we found that as we gained in experience we felt confident enough to use the methods described here.

Julie comes to her self-help group feeling lonely. The women greet her warmly but she stays cold and aloof. Alice tells Julie that she felt frozen out by Julie's response to her warm hug. Julie seems unable to reply, though she knows that she is desperate for some contact. She sits curled up tight like a small child, hugging herself for warmth and protection. Alice says that she really cares about Julie and is hurt by her coldness. Julie begins to cry: she weeps for a long time and will not let anyone touch her. As her sobs finally quieten down the other women help her to regain contact with the group and hug her. She explains that she felt like a helpless baby. She needed love and comfort but was convinced that none would be forthcoming. The group would be bound to find her neediness repulsive and overwhelming. Alice's remark released her sadness which she had been keeping at bay by maintaining her distance from the group.

Julie's adult behaviour was not getting her what she wanted or needed. It seemed that her loneliness triggered off childhood feelings of frustrated need which she had found intolerable and had defended against by withdrawal. Through re-experiencing this, within the supportive atmosphere of the group, she was able to let go some of her old defences; to experience her sadness at being alone and to get comfort from the other women, in the present. Julie was beginning to unlearn her old childhood response to loneliness – withdrawal – and to see that she could ask for and receive loving attention.

Since childhood feelings emerge in most forms of therapy it is not surprising to find that there are almost as many theories as there are therapies about how a child develops psychologically and how this is best explored in therapy. Underlying these are some common assumptions which we will try to summarise before looking at the different therapies and theories. How we perceive the world, other people and ourselves is shaped by our early childhood experiences. As infants we are totally dependent on our caretakers, whether they are parents or childminders. Our experience in infancy is of extremes:

love and hate, life and death. At the simplest level, when a baby experiences her mother's absence and needs to be fed or touched or comforted, she has no way of knowing that her mother will return so she experiences strong feelings of fear and anxiety. At other times she will experience intense feelings of love and satisfaction. When the negative feelings become too dangerous, conflictual or painful we develop defensive structures or blocks which stop us from being overwhelmed by feelings we could not deal with at that age, which can also severely restrict or damage our capacity to feel and to relate to others. As we grow up, our defences may be strongly reinforced and in the end may become counter-productive. It is often at a point when a woman experiences her defences and blocks as having a destructive effect on her life that she will be most open to therapy. We do not give up our defences easily because we have learned to live with them and often get what Freud called 'secondary gains' from them. We may also be afraid to re-experience the pain which the defences are blocking so that unless we are really pushed by our experiences of pain and frustration, we are unlikely to want to begin this process. When we do begin we will need to reassure ourselves constantly that we are in a space where it is safe to let go some of our protective armour.

PSYCHOANALYTIC THERAPY

The psychoanalytic therapies are not directly applicable in a self-help therapy group but are an essential starting point since they do contain ideas and practices which are basic to all forms of therapy. In a self-help group we don't interpret each other's behaviour, nor do we aim to reproduce the relationship between psychoanalyst and 'patient'. Nevertheless, understandings which originate in Psychoanalysis form our assumptions, such as the existence of hidden or unconscious feelings, the value of uncovering them and our recognition of the dynamics within a group.

It is the psychoanalytic writers who have developed detailed theories and descriptions of what happens in a child's inner psychic life, based on their findings in Psychoanalysis, and their observations of infants and children. Other theories provide less detailed outlines of a child's development.

Some women seeking professional therapy will be interested in this way of working. It seems particularly important to understand something of the theory and practice of Psychoanalysis since many women may find that they need to consult public mental health facilities, such as out-patient psychiatric departments or child guidance clinics, where the psychotherapists and social workers often have a psychoanalytic training or orientation. It can be very helpful to understand how they work since they often fail to explain themselves which can leave a prospective client feeling mystified and helpless.

Freud, the founder of Psychoanalysis, recognised that the aspects of people's behaviour and experience which they found most distressing and irrational had a meaning in terms of their life history.[1] He realised that people could re-experience past unmet needs and unexpressed emotions in the present, through the feelings which emerged in their relationship with him, as their psychoanalyst. This he termed the *transference* relationship because feelings originally aroused by significant others, for example, parents, were *transferred* to the psychoanalyst. However, in the transference relationship the outcome would be different. People could learn that feeling love and need would not necessarily be associated with abandonment and fear: that feeling anger would not always lead to rejection or withdrawal of love and approval.

In orthodox Freudian Psychoanalysis the patient (we use the term deliberately, since we feel it is significant that psychoanalysts still talk about patients) is asked to allow her thoughts to flow freely and to share them with her analyst, however disconnected or irrational these thoughts may appear to be. This process is known as 'free association'. To encourage free association and to develop the transference relationship the patient is given as little information about the analyst as possible so that she can develop her own picture of who the analyst is for her. To help her do this she lies on a couch and the analyst will often sit behind her. In psychoanalytic therapy (a variation of Psychoanalysis) the process is basically the same except the patient attends less frequently than the strictly orthodox five sessions a week (which are the norm for a full-blown psychoanalysis) and usually she sits in a chair, facing the analyst.

At its best, Psychoanalysis or the slightly less intensive psychoanalytic therapy, offers the possibility of slowly exploring unconscious feelings within the transference relationship in detail which does justice to the complexity of the person's experience and allows for a basic restructuring of aspects of the personality. Far from being cerebral it *can* be a highly intense and emotional experience. Interpretations are offered but the patient will, in theory, accept them only if they feel right. The process may appear slow and undramatic since it does not involve literally regressing to early infancy or childhood, lying kicking and screaming on the floor, but the release and relief can be great and can lead to basic changes in the way a woman relates to herself and others.

Some Criticisms of Psychoanalytic Theory

We have many criticisms of the theoretical basis of orthodox Psychoanalysis (and psychoanalytic therapy) and of the structure of the therapy situation. Freud's account of the psychological development of girls allowed him to see the problems of his women patients in terms of their failure to adjust to their role as women in patriarchal society. Followed strictly, his theories fail to recognise the real experience of girls' growing up and lead to a therapy aimed at adjustment rather than change. We need to look briefly at Freud's account of how girls develop their sense of themselves as girls (gender identity) to understand how Freudians see women.

Having recognised the existence of an unconscious emotional life, Freud emphasised that sexuality, far from arising only in puberty, is a crucial – though repressed – part of every person's infancy and early childhood. The central experience is the point at which a boy or a girl recognises themself as such and identifies with the parent of their own sex. He saw the boy's and girl's attachment to their mother as being similar. However, in order to enter society and identify with his father, the little boy, who unconsciously sexually desires his mother, has to give up or defer his desires to his father's superior powers. He internalises his experience of his father's power and this becomes what Freud termed his 'superego', or powerful conscience. This process is what is known as the oedipal complex.

Having established an account of the way in which boys learn to repress their infantile sexuality and channel it into socially acceptable forms, Freud tried to modify this to include girls. He emphasised a crucial difference between boys and girls: that while boys can still maintain their relationship with their first love object, their mother (though deferring sexually to father), girls have to detach themselves from mother and focus their love and need to be loved onto father, in preparation for future heterosexuality.

Freud recognised this process was determined by existing power relationships within the family and society, but did not question them. A girl, unconsciously recognising her mother's lack of power and, through identification with her mother, her own lack of power, finds that to compensate (or gain access to power indirectly) she must win her father's love (and of course this means winning other men's love later on). So, she must separate herself from mother, with whom she is supposedly angry. This is partly because she is in rivalry with mother for father's love and partly because mother's lack of power has put her, like mother, in a powerless position.

This account does contain a recognition of how girls are socialised within patriarchal society[2] but because Freud did not have any critical perspective on patriarchy he failed to recognise the extent of the pain and damage which this causes girls and women, and assumed that the goal for a woman is to adjust herself to the prescribed female role. He did not see Psychoanalysis as giving woman 'permission' or insight or support to make demands for ourselves but, rather, as teaching us to adjust to subjugating those demands.

Some women analysts, of whom the best known is Karen Horney, criticised Freud's account of female development. She argued that his conception of 'penis envy' was *symbolic* of women envying male *power* in a male-dominated society. If society were not male dominated then quite different unconscious formations would occur.[3] This argument has since been further developed to suggest that only a fundamental change in the sexual division of labour, with women ceasing to be the primary child rearers, can lead to a basic restructuring of men's and women's unconscious processes.[4]

We would accept the description of the oedipal triangle (the term used to describe the unconscious rivalry between father/son, mother/daughter, and the resolution of this conflict through identification with the parent of the same sex and repression of the overtly sexual aspects of the desire for the parent of the opposite sex) as a useful model for describing a stage of child development in our society. We would question the Freudian emphasis on this stage as crucial. We would also raise the question of changing child rearing practices as a move towards altering women's psychology.[5]

Criticisms of the Structure of Psychoanalytic Therapy

The theoretical basis for the psychoanalytic approach to women can lead to oppressive interpretation of a woman's feelings and the structure of psychoanalytic practice reinforces this. Psychoanalysis makes it clear that one person is the analyst, the healthy person, and the other is the patient, the sick person. This is further reinforced by the élitism and conservatism of the training which can remove the psychoanalyst from the daily realities of all but upper-class patients' lives. The transference relationship inevitably means that the patient will feel like a child in relation to the analyst/authority figure. Yet it is this re-experiencing and working through of childhood fears and fantasies in relation to the analyst which is central to the therapeutic effects of Psychoanalysis and which can be so helpful. The difficulty arises for women when Psychoanalysis fails to recognise the contradictory demands placed on us: namely, the demands to be both childlike *and* simultaneously nurturers of men and children. Where the psychoanalyst does not recognise this contradiction there is a danger of its being reinforced in the transference relationship, instead of the therapy being used to expose the contradiction and to enable women to receive nurturance for themselves.

Interpretation is the main form of verbal communication from the analyst to the patient and this can be misused to assert the analyst's power as the person who *knows best*.

If a patient rejects the interpretation this may be seen as resistance on her part. A patient's perceptions and feelings may constantly be invalidated which may accurately reproduce her everyday experience as a woman, reinforcing her familiar role as an inferior. Psychoanalysis can also be a very long drawn-out process which may become too cerebral. While we may recognise intellectualisation as a defence, it is one which Psychoanalysis cannot always overcome and sometimes even encourages.

Feminist Psychoanalytic Therapy

In feminist psychoanalytic therapy the processes of free association and developing and interpreting the transference relationship are similar to orthodox therapy. There are, however, important differences both in the theory (and therefore in the content of the interpretations) and in the understanding of the power relationship between the two women involved in the therapy. The aim is to counteract the dangerous power imbalance that can be so misused in orthodox psychoanalytic therapy, while developing what is valuable in this approach within a feminist perspective.[6] A woman therapist is not interchangeable with a feminist therapist. Some of the psychoanalytic writings which are most deprecating and defeatist about women were written by women psychoanalysts who, like other professional women, have become male identified as they achieve success in a male-dominated profession.[7]

Feminist interpretations will inevitably be different because they are based on a political critique of women's role in this society and an understanding of the effects this has on women's emotional development. The client and therapist have *shared* these effects. Thus a woman's fear of her anger, or fear of experiencing her vulnerability as insatiable, would be understood within the context of the woman's socialisation by a mother who knew that anger was not an acceptable feminine trait, and who herself felt that she had no one to care for her emotional needs. Feminist psychoanalytic therapy draws from the Object Relations psychoanalytic theory.[8] In this theory human relationships are seen determining a child's development and point to the breakdown of a genuinely personal relationship between the mother (as primary caretaker) and infant as the root cause of adults being unable to form close relationships. This is a real break with Freud and later Freudians, whose account of a child's development was couched in terms of a child learning to repress his/her instincts. Providing an alternative to an instinct-based theory means that we can do away with ideas of little boys and little girls having basically different instincts: similarly, we do not have to attribute mother's role in child-rearing to instinct. The theory allows for the possibility that a child's development is determined not by natural or instinctual forces, but by social relationships. While Object Relations theorists have not seen the significance of the links between women's wider social role and our psychology, their theory provides the basis for a feminist development in which these implications are fully drawn out and the possible significance of fundamentally changing our child rearing practice can be explored.

A feminist approach to therapy avoids the traditional framework of 'What has gone wrong with this person's development?' Jean Baker Miller characterises it clearly: 'So-called symptoms [may be] seen in a new light – no longer merely as defences, manoeuvres, or other such tactics, but as struggles to preserve or express some deeply needed aspects of personal integrity in a milieu that will not allow for their direct expression.'[9] This makes for a far more loving view of therapy than we find in the earlier psychoanalytic writers.

Feminist therapists should have a commitment to recognising and dealing with the power relationship between therapist and client. This involves recognising the contradictory nature of the relationship. The therapist is professionalising her role as nurturer: she is being paid, among other things, to be a 'good mother'. For the client who is asking an 'expert' for help, there may be feelings that she is the inferior woman and the therapist is the whole and healthy woman. In feminist psychoanalytic therapy the therapist would not share her problems with the client because she is trying to provide a clear space for her client to look at herself. Otherwise the client might repeat the old pattern of subsuming her own needs to express her concern for others: in this case, the therapist. Instead the therapist would try consciously to demystify the therapy process, somewhat in the same way as we are trying to do in this book. She should be ensuring that the client understands what is happening in her therapy. This does not appear to impair the transference relationship, but gives the client a double level experience. She can allow herself the feelings of the frustrated and fearful child in therapy at the same time knowing that her feelings about her therapist are projections from childhood. At times the therapy relationship will feel like an experience of re-mothering. The clients may often find the process painful but will understand the point of it. If women have control of their therapy in this way then they will be more likely to benefit from regression work and less likely to have harmful patterns further reinforced.

TRANSACTIONAL ANALYSIS: SCRIPT THEORY

Another model for the child's psychological development which derives from psychoanalysis is Transactional Analysis, usually known as T.A. In T.A. the assumption is also that the way a person experiences the world in the present will reflect the way she learned to see it in her original group, that is, the family. The way we behave in the present may be more comprehensible if we can decode the messages or orders (in T.A. terminology, 'the script') we carry with us from our past. The goal is to help us see how we live these scripts, how we maintain them and, when our scripts keep us from leading satisfactory lives, how we can substitute alternative ways of being.

For example, a child may make decisions when she is small and powerless which allow her to deal with her parents. She may realise that her parents can't cope with her anger and as she needs their love she foregoes expressing that anger and instead casts herself into the role of victim, needing help and love. This kind of defensive measure is seen in T.A. as a 'decision' and the significance of the word is that this decision *can* be re-made differently.

In one self-help group a woman allowed herself to be criticised until it reached the point where the group was divided between those who wanted her to leave and those who felt she was being scapegoated. Through asking her about her past the group realised that she had been reproducing her 'victim script' both inside and outside the group. She began to see that being the victim was not helping her to get anything from the group or from her other relationships. What might have been survival strategy in her childhood was now being used in a situation where other alternatives were possible. The group began to work with her to point out how she fell into the victim role, to help her express the feelings that accompanied that role, and then to find different ways to act with other people.

T.A. sees people as having three ego states or sub-systems of the personality:

Child: in which we react on the basis of strong – often pre-logical – thinking or feeling
Parent: in which we are judgmental and evaluative
Adult: in which we objectively appraise the world

The aim in T.A. therapy is to recognise which ego state you are acting from and to achieve a harmonious balance between all these. T.A. involves a clear mixture of thought and feeling. It does not aim literally to regress people back to childhood but it does help to clarify whether we are acting from our rational 'adult' or moralising 'parent' or spontaneous 'child' states. Confusing these roles can lead to an untenable situation, such as in this example.

When Jane had her first baby she made what she saw as a reasoned adult decision to give up work. She then became very depressed and frustrated. Later she realised that in fact she had based her decision on the injunction she had internalised from her mother; you cannot be a good mother and go out to work. When she realised this she was able to reassess her feelings and make a genuinely adult choice based on knowing that, for her, work outside the home was essential.

T.A. operates within the context of *conscious* feelings and choices, far more than any of the other forms of therapy discussed in this book, but does recognise that insight alone is not enough to enable us to change. We also need support to risk changing ourselves. In T.A. this is schematised as the three P's: *Permission*, *Protection* and *Potency*. When the group or therapist see the change a woman wants to make, and feel they can support it, they give her *Permission* to change. This means supporting her to go against her old internalised messages. A woman may feel she does not want to have children. After the group has explored the issue with her fully, and all feel that she really does want to go against the message that she should have a child to prove she is a 'real' woman, several women in the group tell her they feel fine about her not having children. They are in effect giving her the group's permission to go against the prescription that she should have children.

The next stage is to provide *Protection*. This means that the group will be available to reassure her when she gets frightened and feels unsafe about breaking away from her old assumptions and feelings. When she goes to visit her mother and tells her she has decided not to have children she feels shaky afterwards. She comes to the group and knows she will have the space to explore her fears, to share how scary it is to confront her mother and how vulnerable it makes her feel to incur her mother's disapproval and anger. The group is not just a place where she can get reassurance, but is also a place where she can look at the things which make it hard for her to change, to act according to her own desires.

The group or therapist also needs to be there in a powerful way when the struggle gets really hard. When she tells her husband that she does not want to have a child and he threatens to leave her, the group must be available to listen to her insecurities and anger and also be able to stand firm in their support of her fight to refute her 'script'. This is what is referred to in T.A. as *Potency*.

You may feel that all this is familiar and we can see that permission, protection and potency are essential elements in all forms of therapy. What T.A. does is to make them explicit, give them names, and this can be useful and clarifying (particularly for a self-help group) in thinking about what you are doing to help a group member to work consistently on herself. We found in our group that we were often better at helping someone to work on how she was feeling one week, than at helping her to follow through change in any explicit way. These ideas might have helped us when we were an inexperienced group.

T.A. is usually practised in groups with trained leaders but can be used individually too. If you are interested in professional T.A. you can find groups through an Institute of Transactional Analysis which exists in many countries. T.A. has also been used extensively in the Radical Therapy movement in the United States and in the Women's Self-Help Therapy Network in Holland.

There are three aspects of T.A. which have led to its adoption as an acceptable form of therapy by radicals and particularly by women.

1   The theory allows for the social, economic and political influences on emotional development to be incorporated easily into the therapy. A simple example is that of the woman we have already looked at who was internalising not just her mother's and her husband's desires for her to have children, but also society's definition of a 'real' woman as someone who has children.

2   The language of T.A. has been deliberately created to make the therapy process as explicit as possible to anyone who learns it. *Permission, Protection*

and *Potency* are terms which clarify the role of the group and therapist rather than making it into some kind of secret or indefinable process.
3 T.A., operating as it does on a more conscious level, appeals to people who feel that more traditional forms of therapy encourage an elevation of the therapist, over-dependency, and a picture of clients at the mercy of uncontrollable unconscious forces which only an expert can hope to unravel. We feel it is this last aspect of T.A. which is the least satisfactory since we have found that much of the most important work done in therapy does involve first making unconscious feelings conscious. It is only then that we can make decisions which are based on real knowledge rather than rationalisations. This is the work the other regression therapies deal with.

In T.A. the first step is often to make an analysis of a person's script, working out what course her life is taking and which aspects of it she may want to change. The new client will work out with the therapist or the group what crucial decisions she took as a child to enable her to cope with the world and which of these she needs to alter. She will discover what mythical character or heroine she is trying to emulate and how she is playing games to advance her script. She will also try to identify the 'pay-off' she gets from the games which gives her the incentive to go on playing them.

This analysis provides the direction for the second stage of the therapy. The person will then make a contract with the group or therapist to change particular aspects of herself. In T.A. a person always makes an explicit commitment as to what she wants to change. Her contract must be specific enough to be clear to her and to others. It must be possible to monitor the contract; that is, for someone else to be able to challenge her as to whether she is really working towards fulfilling it. An acceptable contract for a woman who discovers that part of her script is 'I'm not important' would be to learn to take herself seriously and get others to do so too.

Having made her contract, she will then work in the group to discover what ego states, that is, Parent, Child or Adult, she is operating from, what games she is playing and how she can use her ego states more appropriately and substitute alternative behaviour for her games. She will be learning to get her satisfaction through more direct ways of relating to others.

Using T.A. in a Self-Help Group
There are some aspects of T.A. which we feel would be appropriate for a self-help therapy group as part of their work on childhood issues.

Making a script analysis may be a good way to look at your childhood if your group has not done this in any detail yet, especially if you feel nervous about moving into uncharted territory and are daunted by what you have read about regressing to early infancy. (In the exercise section of this chapter we give a detailed account of how to make a script.)

This is how the script analysis worked out for one woman in a self-help group.

Claire found that the theme which consistently came up for her was, 'I've got to be twice as good as anyone else.' She didn't like the picture of herself which emerged and tried hard to think of situations which contradicted this, but looking at the messages from her parents, her body image and the figures she identified with confirmed this picture of herself. Her parents both said to her, in different ways, 'You have to be very special because you are our only surviving child.' (Her brother had died at an early age.) The mythical character she identified with was a female version of Superman and her body seemed to reinforce this by being large and solid. So, as an adult, she felt she had to make super-human efforts to be both a successful full-time worker, competent housewife, hostess and mother, and to be politically active outside her work. As a result she felt constantly harassed, rushing from one thing to the next and feeling she never did anything as well as she might. The idea of having time for herself seemed an undreamed-of luxury and she often missed the group because of another meeting, or to catch up on her housework. She realised from her script analysis that she needed to make a contract with the group to give up her role as superwoman. To do this she would have to work out practical strategies, such as changing the division of labour in her family and sharing the housework and childcare more equally with her husband. A first step towards taking more time for herself was making a full commitment to the therapy group one evening each week. She would also work in the group on her relationship with her parents and her feelings about the death of her brother.

Claire's script was a particularly clear one but if yours are less clear you may find that further experience in your group helps you to identify key issues quickly when you try to make a script analysis again.[11]

T.A. can also help in a group to clarify an apparently confusing situation by separating out the different 'ego states' or voices which a person is using. Here is an example:

Susan was feeling guilty, angry and confused at work. She felt very tense with John, one of her co-workers, and found it impossible to relax and concentrate on her work as a printer. Her mind was filled with thoughts like, 'I know he thinks I'm not working hard enough,'; 'I hate the way he glares silently at me'; 'I feel very angry with him'; 'He's better at the job than I am'; 'I'm having the morning off to work at the community festival if I want to'; 'It's better to work at a leisurely pace and allow time for discussion between workers'.

She simply didn't know if she was being reasonable, or what she should or shouldn't do, nor why she felt so tense with John. To clarify her own mixed messages the group suggested that she make each cushion into a part of herself: 'critical parent', 'nurturing parent', 'adult', 'free child' and 'adapted child'. Here the Gestalt cushion technique is being modified by naming the cushions according to T.A. terminology. It seemed to other members of the group that messages she might have internalised as a child were still with her and that unresolved conflicts from her childhood were being re-evoked in the present.

Susan sat on each cushion in turn and expressed its viewpoint.

'Critical parent' said, 'You ought to work extra hard because you are a girl.'

'Nurturing parent' said, 'You need to take good care of yourself. You need time to talk to your fellow workers to get support from them.'

'Adult' said, 'Just be sensible and work out what tasks have to be done and whether there is time available for you to have the morning off.'

'Adapted child' said, 'I must be good and make sure that everyone knows what a hard working person I am.'

'Free child' said, 'I want to have some fun, even if I am a responsible print-worker, so I'm going to the festival to enjoy myself.'

Susan could then see she was stuck with conflicting messages from her parent, adult and child parts. She could use this knowledge of how her childhood messages were confusing her to guide her in working more deeply on the emotional meaning of these messages through Psychodrama, for example, or with the use of Gestalt techniques. On a more conscious level she was able to discuss how she might deal with her work situation in a clear way.

While writing this section we found that an awareness of T.A. concepts was helpful in therapy groups even when we were not using the technique as a whole. We used it to ask questions such as how does what is being said fit in with this person's script, or what was her parents' message about expressing anger. You may find this helpful in your own self-help group.

REICH AND LAING

Reich was struck by the physical effects of repressed emotions on the child. While not providing a detailed model for how this repression takes place, Reich suggested that as a child developed she was forced by the family (acting as an agent for an authoritarian society) to repress emotions, and that these repressions were incorporated into her character armour, or rigid muscular framework. Through breathing and other forms of bodywork, he enabled his patients to re-contact early childhood emotions and thus alter or release their armouring. For a detailed discussion of Reich's theories and methods, see Chapter Five.

Reich, and R. D. Laing in his earlier work, emphasised the repressive nature of the family and its function in society, as does a feminist analysis.[12] This did not lead Reich into 'family therapy' but rather into working on young people's sexual development so that as freer sexual beings they would be able to struggle against the family and capitalist society. Laing concentrated on the effects of the family on a child's development, seeing the child's personality as an expression of the family dynamics; in particular, he saw the people he worked with who had been labelled 'psychotic' as in some sense carrying their family's problems. Thus his task was to unravel the whole family dynamic. Laing's ideas have been very influential in the growing awareness of the relationship between the personal and the political. While there are no specific techniques which can be applied to a self-help group, Laing's ideas are illuminating when we begin to think of our childhood and family dynamics. Laing and Esterson showed us how we had to see a person's development being influenced by her role in the family, as well as particular relationships between individuals.[13]

In Britain Laing's ideas, and those of his co-workers, were used and developed in two therapeutic communities: the Philadelphia Association and the Arbours Association. Both now run houses for people who want and need to live in a therapeutic community either for a brief crisis period or for longer. They also offer individual therapy and train therapists. Feminists are and have been involved and trained in both of these organisations and, while neither could be called feminist, there is an awareness of issues raised by feminists.

PRIMAL THERAPY

We have seen how in psychoanalytic therapy and T.A., childhood emotions and experiences can be talked about and, in Psychoanalysis, re-experienced through the transference relationship. With Reich, and using bioenergetic techniques, we can move into a different arena of therapy where the aim is to enable the person through a physical approach literally, though temporarily, to regress to early childhood. (For an example of this, see Chapter Five, p 116.) Primal therapy develops this approach by allowing the person, in therapy, to regress to what Arthur Janov, founder of primal therapy, termed the 'primal scene'.

The theory is that a child is born with needs which cause her a great deal of pain if unsatisfied by the parents. The frustration and pain of her unmet needs may be so great that the child cannot tolerate the experience and finds ways of shutting out the pain by shutting out her needs from her consciousness. Janov explains the process like this: 'This separation of oneself from one's needs and feelings is an instinctive manoeuvre in order to shut off excessive pain. We call it the *split* . . . because of their pain, the needs have been suppressed in the consciousness . . . the individual . . . must pursue the satisfaction of his needs *symbolically*.'[14] A woman who, as a child, suppressed her need to be held by her mother may later pursue the satisfaction of this need *symbolically* by striving for an ever bigger and more luxurious home. The home symbolises, or is substituted for, her real childhood needs.

According to Janov, the child continues to split off her needs until at some point the cumulative pain becomes so great that an event (not necessarily in itself worse or more traumatic than preceding events) shifts the balance. The child, feeling that there is no hope of being loved for herself, splits off completely from her feelings and begins to act as her parents want. The split-off feelings do not disappear but develop into the adult's neurotic behaviour. This childhood point of intolerable pain and consequent hopelessness is the 'primal scene' and it is to this scene that the adult must return in therapy to re-experience those emotions and reconnect with them so that she can become 'real' again. Janov uses 'real' here to mean expressing and experiencing feelings directly rather than symbolically.

Using Primal Therapy with a Therapist

Primal therapy is a very powerful technique. Its drama, initial impact and speed, and the way it has been publicised by Janov, may give the illusion that it is only through doing Primal therapy that a person can change radically or be cured. If things have gone wrong in our development way back at birth or in early childhood, then regressing back to those stages and reliving them differently would seem to make sense. Janov writes in a way which is easily accessible to ordinary readers. The situations he describes are identifiable with and probably evoke or trigger off primal feelings which may lead people to seek Primal therapy. His account of early childhood development is far simpler than any of the psychoanalytic accounts. This is appealing, as is his more positive conception of the child as being basically healthy, which contrasts with the Freudian view of the child carrying destructive forces which need containment by an inner defence system.

The method Janov pioneered in his Primal Institute is designed to encourage a rapid breakthrough of a person's defensive structure. He begins Primal therapy with a three-week intensive period during which the person stays in a hotel room, leaves it only to go to therapy, and is deprived of all the usual ways of maintaining repression such as drink, drugs, alcohol and television. During this period an individual therapist is available to the person almost all the time. This is followed by a year or more of individual and group therapy at the Institute. The person has been placed in a physically and emotionally defenceless position aimed at lowering her resistances. The therapist gets her to talk directly to her parents, rather than talking about them, so that she recontacts early experiences and returns to the situation in which she first began to cut off from her feelings. Instead of 'cutting off', this time she will scream out her pain: the 'primal scream'.

Some primal therapists who have broken away from Janov have developed slightly different ways of working. Unfortunately it is difficult to know which of these therapists are reliable except by reputation and your own assessment. In general the primal therapists who have broken with Janov seem to agree with our own criticisms of him,[15] particularly of his early writings where he states that Primal therapy will lead to cure and will do so quickly. In his later work Janov does modify his claims for Primal therapy in the light of his experience and recognises that there is no simple cure and that people do not stop 'primalling'.

Some Criticisms of Primal Therapy

While Janov recognises that the way children are born and brought up in Western societies is repressive, he does not realise that it is in the nature of this society to demand repression. Nor is his own critique very far reaching: he still sees homosexuality as a form of neurotic behaviour even though he understands the mechanisms of repression and self-hatred involved in hatred of homosexuality. He does not appear to understand the contradictions between the demands of life in a patriarchal society and being a person who is very open to her feelings. Perhaps as women, whose role it is to be the emotional carriers in a society where emotions have second-class status, we are more easily aware of the ways in which there is constant contradiction between being emotionally open and dealing with the daily demands of our lives. This lack of awareness is reflected at a more theoretical level in the therapy itself in its failure to offer bridges between the past and the present. Other forms of regression work offer this bridge through the relationship between therapist and client or through giving positive attention to making links between the childhood experience and ways the person may change in the present.

This is not say that Primal therapy is useless or impossible but rather that its founder's grandiose claims to cure people are based on the notion that individuals can be healthy in a sick society: we do not talk about therapy as a cure because we see its role differently. Therapy may make us more receptive to feeling pleasure and pain and may encourage us to find ways to struggle for better lives and a better society. But only broader social change can provide the conditions for a healthy life.

The Primal Institute reflects Janov's lack of social and political awareness. Therapy there is very expensive and therefore likely to be given by and experienced by people with access to money. Primal therapists who have broken with Janov have made Primal therapy more widely accessible, but in refusing to recognise any of these therapists Janov himself replicates the élitist attitudes of the various official psychoanalytical institutes.

With an intense approach such as Primal therapy, where the client is likely to be particularly vulnerable, it is vital to be able to trust the therapist and the structure in which she works. You need to be confident that as well as breaking down your defences you will be able to reintegrate. If you are seeking Primal therapy with a therapist, find a structure where these needs are recognised and where it is understood that you will want to stop 'primalling' and integrate the experience into your daily life.

Using Primal Therapy in a Self-Help Group

A self-help group can use Primal therapy techniques if you feel that as a group you can provide the necessary continuing support. It is particularly important when doing primal work to have a room which is physically safe, where there are cushions which can be used to stop the woman who is working from hurting herself and where, if she screams, she will not disturb anyone. Often while 'primalling' a woman will scream, retch, find her body moving involuntarily or will lie moaning. The group's role in this is to support her, to allow her to go through what she needs to experience and to make sure she does not hurt herself and is not interrupted.

We found in our group that the cool, more analytic approaches to looking at childhood did not really acknowledge or allow for the intensity, rich chaos and terror of our early emotional experiences. Sometimes childhood issues would emerge in a surprising way and a woman would regress without this being planned by her or by the group. Here is an example.

Nan was telling the group how she had forced herself to climb up and down a high mountain to prove to the men she was with that she could do it, while many of them had felt quite easy about taking the cable car down, not having the same need to prove themselves. Sophie took exception to this. She couldn't see why Nan had to exhaust and hurt herself in this way. She persisted in her criticism of Nan until Jane, feeling that there must be something behind Sophie's persistence, asked her how she was feeling. Sophie said she was terrified of her own attempts to injure herself. She showed the group the scars where she had tried to cut her arms with a razor blade. Sophie was looking so frightened that Jane, in an attempt to help her back into contact with the group, suggested that she look around the group. Sophie looked scared, glanced briefly up at Jane and said, 'You look just like my father. Your eyes are just like his. I don't want to see him.'

Sophie was encouraged to keep eye contact with Jane and to say what was happening for her. She became more and more terrified until she could hardly bear to look at Jane. The group suggested that she lie on some cushions and Jane stand over her so that Jane's menacing qualities and Sophie's defencelessness were exaggerated.

'He's going to hurt me, to beat me.' Sophie tried to shield her eyes and her body from Jane/father and other members of the group encouraged her to stay with her fear. Sophie was shaking all over. The group asked Sophie what she wanted to say to her father. At first she covered her eyes and ears saying, 'Nothing. I want to do something to myself to make it all go away.'

The group persisted, trying to prevent Sophie from returning to her old pattern of self injury by encouraging her to deal directly with her father. They asked her what she would like to do with her hands. It seemed that slowly, with the group's support, Sophie was beginning to gain strength. She wanted to hit out. Jane/father held up a cushion and Sophie began to hit it, screaming at her father to go away and not to hurt her. As she hit the cushion her rage grew and her fear lessened. She continued for several minutes until, exhausted, she lay back on the cushions.

The other group members took some time to share how they had felt while Sophie was working. One woman had not understood what was happening. Another felt very close to Sophie and was helped to see how she, too, had found her father menacing even though he had never been physically violent towards her. Another woman found that she had cut off emotionally from what was happening, perhaps because she was scared.

Sophie was still feeling very shaky. She said she had thought she was going mad. Connecting her self-destructiveness and her fear of her father was a great relief. She could now see ways to deal with her fear other than trying to avoid it by producing an alternative form of pain. She was worried lest she slip back into her terror and arranged with two other women in the group to phone them during the week. The group arranged that Sophie should have some time during their next meeting to report back. Jane, who had done some regression work before, suggested to Sophie that she try to have as gentle a week as possible, as often after work like this, people feel especially vulnerable and in contact with childhood feelings.

If you are using primal regression in a group you will want to go through the following stages. The process is likely to take at least an hour, so make sure you have enough time.

1   Set up the situation

In the example we have given it happened spontaneously. Sometimes a group member may say she wants to work on a particular early incident, or the group may split into pairs and help each other to contact early experiences. This can be done deliberately by having the woman who is working lie down, breathing deeply and allowing emotions to come up freely. You can suggest to her that she thinks back to her childhood and focuses on an incident. It may be appropriate to get her to 'talk to' her mother or father.

2   Make sure that the woman working is physically safe and in a position which encourages and intensifies her feelings
For Sophie, lying down made her seem small and her father large, so her defencelessness was exaggerated. If someone is feeling very shut off it may help to ask her to curl up or, if she is feeling precarious, you might want her to stand on a chair or stool, making sure that there are cushions or mattresses around her so that she will not hurt herself if she falls off.

3   Encourage her to stay with her frightening feelings and express them physically and verbally
For Sophie this meant not running away from her terror of her father. This part of the primal is central because when Sophie originally experienced her fear of her father's frequent physical violence towards her, as a small child she couldn't cope with it and it was at this point that she cut off from what the primal therapists would term her 'real feelings' and developed 'neurotic ' behaviour. In Sophie this took the form of attacking herself so that she could at least control the attack, while she had no control over her father. By experiencing the terror, and not cutting off from it, she is introduced to a new possibility: that she can survive her fear and fight back.

4   Encourage her to respond to her pain directly instead of introducing defensive measures which are ultimately harmful for her
So Sophie hits back at her father. The most basic pattern is when the person who is primalling experiences the loss of her mother and cries out for her instead of retreating into a passive denial of her pain and need.

5   Help her return safely to the present and to talk in the group about what has happened
This will ensure that she does not push the experience aside as too powerful for her to cope with.

6   Make sure that other group members have a chance to share their own often powerful reactions and to give feedback

We found that we did primal work occasionally in our group, and over a period of years each person had experience of some Primal-type therapy.

REBIRTHING

Other theorists, whom we can see as historically developing from Primal therapy, have pushed their ideas of the 'crucial' experience further back, even to birth as the initial traumatic experience. They centre their therapy around rebirthing. Others see the intrauterine development as being a key determinant in the child's development and might work on implantation as vitally important.

The approach we have found most useful is to see rebirthing and Primal therapy as parts of an exploration of early childhood which each individual will make at her own pace and according to her own inner needs. Birth will have been an important experience for every individual, but its significance will be different for different women: nor will it be the one key to a woman's therapy.

A Birth Primal

Another kind of primal experience which may happen in a self-help group is a 'birth primal'. This is an extension of the sort of experience we have already described and is not something to push yourself, or anyone else into before you feel it is appropriate. The goal is similar to that of other regression work: namely, to re-experience the event without having to cut off from its pain and thus to begin to give up the defences you have established against the pain.

> Joan was talking about her mother. As she talked she began to feel increasingly claustrophobic. She described how she felt as if her mother was sitting on her head and she could not get away. The group asked Joan if she would like to intensify the feeling to see what it was about. Joan said she felt ready to try provided they would agree to stop if she felt she couldn't cope. She lay on the ground and some of the women held a cushion against her head while others encouraged her to push. She pushed and struggled with her head for several minutes and finally managed to escape. It seemed to the other women in the group that Joan might have experienced a 'birth primal'. She herself was not sure what had happened except that her struggle seemed like a matter of life and death and afterwards she felt very fresh and open. She told the group that her mother had had a very long labour and at one point it was feared that Joan would not survive.

As with other primal work we should not make the mistake of thinking that one primal or rebirthing is going to be a cure: this is the kind of claim which sometimes appears to be made for primal or rebirthing experiences. For Joan, her work was important and she felt a new strength and also a new vulnerability which she needed to work on further to consolidate.

There are other ways of working on childhood experience using Bioenergetics and Psychodrama, both of which are discussed fully in Chapters Five and Seven. As women we have special needs to establish our own identities. Part of actively developing an identity must mean knowing our own past. Therapy can be an important part of this process if we ensure that our past is interpreted with an active understanding of what it means to be born a woman in a male-defined and dominated society. Reclaiming our past becomes part of our present strength.

EXERCISES FOR REGRESSION WORK

One way of ensuring that everybody in your group makes a start at exploring their childhood is to devote an evening to making a 'script analysis'. This may also be a safe way in for women who feel nervous about getting lost in their childhood feelings. Here we give a detailed account of how a self-help group structured such an evening.

120   Script Analysis
A long group meeting was devoted to this method, which is described fully on p 224. Women paired up and did twenty minutes co-counselling each way on the subject of 'significant events and experiences in my childhood'. The rest of the first hour was taken up with ten minutes feedback for each woman, in the same pair, saying what patterns she had heard in her partner's account of her life.

The group then took ten minutes for each woman to think about what had happened so far and to write down any themes which she could find in her own life. She included:

The injunctions and attributions she had been given by her parents
The script she had decided to follow
The ways in which her body reflected her script
The mythical hero or heroine with whom she identified in her script

The group reformed and the women paired up with different partners to share what they had written down about their scripts and to try to reduce what they had learned to a message. (The message might be 'stay on the losing side where you're safe' or 'don't give an inch or they'll take a mile'.)

The rest of the time was used to share what each woman had learned with the whole group. Time was divided equally between group members and each woman shared her script as she chose.

Remember that your script message is not fixed over time. You can break out of your script. You can also find some aspects more significant than others at different times in your life.

This preparatory script analysis can be developed and understood more fully by using some of the exercises listed below. They will help you to explore relationships with parents, messages which your body carries from childhood and emotionally important childhood events. We suggest you choose the exercises you feel most comfortable with. They can of course be done without using the script analysis. For more exercises taking you back to childhood see exercises 73 and 74, to encourage a primal approach, and exercise 101 which guides you in fantasy back to your conception.

121   Speaking to Your Parents

Imagine putting each parent in turn on a cushion, then speak to them for a few minutes. Try to tell them how you feel about them, and in particular, try saying the things which you have never managed to tell them in real life. In each case, follow this by sitting on the cushion and imagining you are that parent talking back to yourself.

122   Getting a Group Member to Act a Parent

To follow this, you can try asking another member of the group to sit on the cushion and 'act that parent'. To do this she needs some basic guidance about how that parent comes across, and some key phrases or messages which that parent communicated to you. ('Don't be so stupid!', 'I would love you more if you were more like your brother', 'Please make less noise, I am tired', or whatever). You can then sit facing the 'parent', see how the messages make you feel and explore any responses you may want to make.

123   Parent Teachers' Association

This is an energetic exercise and can be enjoyable to do. Each member of the group imagines she is her parent of the opposite sex. Stand up, explore body posture and movements which are typical of that parent. Then imagine you are at the meeting of a Parent Teachers' Association attended by your parents. Move around the room, make eye contact with the other parents, and talk to them in the way that parent might have done about yourself. ('Difficult child, I can't understand her', 'She's too big for her boots'). It can be fun to see how different people's parents get on with one another. This exercise helps you to 'get a feel' for that parent. After a while you can exchange and act the other parent. At the end, stand for a few moments to let yourself feel in your body the ways in which you are like that parent – the ways you move and talk like them, the ways you have internalised their attitudes yourself.

124   My Childhood Clothing

This exercise makes you aware of how you were dressed as a child, and may show you how patterns set then still affect you.

Choose a partner and decide who will speak first. There are four stages, and you should allow five minutes for each stage. Your partner simply listens and gives her attention. When you have finished, exchange roles.

Stage 1 Recall the period until you were five years old. Can you recall any items of clothing from that time? Describe your favourite garment and your least favourite garment. How did your parents feel about you in those garments? How did your siblings or friends feel about you? How did you feel in them?

Stage 2 Repeat, recalling some time in the period between five and ten years old.

Stage 3 Repeat, recalling your teenage years.

Stage 4 Share any of the ways in which you think those childhood experiences might affect the way you dress now ('I still love anything in red corduroy', 'I tend to dress boyishly in baggy clothing the way my mother dressed me', 'I feel I have to try extra hard to look attractive because they made me feel so ugly').

125 Seed Sentences

This is a good exercise to use in a group where people don't know each other as it involves introducing yourself and relating childhood feelings. Choose someone to give the instructions.

Sit in a circle. Breathe into your stomach for a minute and turn your attention inwards. Then think of some things that your parents used to say to you when you were a child. Things like, 'Keep your mouth shut while you eat', 'Little girls don't sit like that', 'Make an effort'. Try to fix on a few sentences that were particularly characteristic of your childhood. (*Pause*). When you've chosen your statements stand up and go round the room introducing yourself to each person you meet saying, 'I'm Jane – little girls should be seen and not heard', or whatever sentences you have fixed on. You can say the same sentence to each person or you can vary it. Notice how you feel saying the sentences and associating them with your name.

After about three minutes people can sit down again in a circle and share experiences. You may find that saying these sentences brings back a lot of feelings – your fear of being too noisy or your shame and anger at being told that you shouldn't sit with your legs wide apart. Your memories may be quite vivid. Or you may find you are suddenly aware of how these statements affect you now. 'I always wear jeans so that I can sit how I want to and it gives me a lift to know that I am being defiant and getting away with it.' See what use you can make of the feelings the exercise brings up.

126 Acting In

This is another exercise which is good to use in a new group as a way of introducing yourselves. It also brings up feelings about people who were important to you in your childhood. One person should read aloud, slowly.

Sit in a circle and direct your attention inwards. Close your eyes if this helps. Think of someone who knew you very well as a child – a parent, a friend, a relative, a teacher. Choose someone who you feel will be able to give you a good introduction to the group, someone who'll say some things you'd like the group to know about you (these don't have to be nice things). When you've chosen, try to remember how she/he was and become that person. Walk the right way – try to talk as she/he talked and try to think the same way too. Take a minute or two to walk round the room and feel your way into the part. Then come back into the circle. Each character will introduce her/himself to the group and then introduce you. For example, 'I'm Nanny and I live with the Jones family. I look after Fran while her mother goes out to work. I'm devoted to the family – I'm like a second mother. This is Fran – she's eight years old' and so on.

As with other introductory exercises this may be used at very different levels. Some women may stick to fairly superficial accounts while others may raise deep issues in their early relationships.

127 Melting Mirror

This is a guided fantasy which helps to make you aware of the feelings you carry around with you from your childhood.
  Choose someone to lead the fantasy. Read slowly.

Lie down, close your eyes and breathe deeply. Turn your attention inwards. Think of a time when you were less than eleven years old. Now become that age. Where did you live? Take a walk around the house. In one room is a full-length mirror. Walk up to it and look into it. What are you wearing? How do you look? Feel your hair and your skin. How do they feel? What do you like doing? Who are your friends? Do you have brothers and sisters? What are they like? What are your parents like, your mother, your father? What's it like to live with them? What do they like about you? What do they dislike about you? Do you have any secrets? What makes you angry? What makes you hurt? What would you like to change in your life?
  Now, as you stand in front of the mirror, someone else enters the room. It is the adult you. Stay as the little you and look at your big self walking over towards you until she is standing beside you in front of the mirror. What do you think of this person? Have a conversation and make contact with each

other in any way you want. Is there anything special you want to say to one another? Now's your chance.

As you're both looking in the mirror an amazing thing happens. The two of you begin to melt and fuse into one person. Watch that happen and then, when you are ready, bring that person back here into the room.

Share what has happened for you either in the large group, or if it's too big (say, over six), split into two groups.

128 From Defiance to Choice

Our experience suggests that when you are exploring your relationship with your parents, you often go through a phase of defiance and denial – a phase where you need to say 'No!' loud and clear to a lot of their messages to you in order to create your own space and get a sense of *who you are* as distinct from them and from how they wanted you to be. After this phase in therapy, it is possible to move on to a state where you are not so locked in defiance, where you have exorcised much of your anger and can have a much easier 'take it or leave it' attitude towards your parents, sympathising with them and understanding who they are, while keeping a clear sense of your own identity. The following exercise is good for exploring this later stage of the process.

Each person takes a pen and paper and writes down a list of the parental messages they received as children, not just the spoken messages ('Shut up!', 'Work harder at school!') but the unspoken ones ('Don't be sexual', 'Don't assert yourself!'). Then choose a partner and have her read the list through to you. After each instruction reply 'No!', and see how it feels. Then you read the list through to her, prefacing each instruction with 'I won't': 'I won't shut up!', 'I won't work harder!' Now try reading it through again, this time prefacing each message with 'I could': 'I could shut up', 'I could be lazy'. This phrasing helps us to own the responsibility and control we have over our own lives and it introduces an element of choice which is absent when we are simply reacting in defiance of our parents.

NOTES

1 We concentrate here on Freud and the neo-Freudians. Jung's theories are discussed in Chapter Six.

2 For a clear and fuller account of Freud's ideas, and another perspective on the oedipus complex, see: Juliet Mitchell, *Psychoanalysis and Feminism*, Penguin, Harmondsworth, 1975; Pantheon, New York, 1975.

3 For selections from the writings of Karen Horney and other important psychoanalysts on the subject of women see: Jean Baker Miller (ed), *Psychoanalysis and Women*, Penguin, Harmondsworth, 1973; Brunner/Mazel, New York, 1973; also Jean Strouse (ed), *Women and Analysis*, Dell, New York, 1974.

4   See Dorothy Dinnerstein, *The Mermaid and the Minotaur*, Harper & Row, New York, 1976; published in the UK as *The Rocking of the Cradle and the Ruling of the World*, Souvenir Press, London, 1978. Fascinating exploration of the relationship between childcare arrangements and the present structure of society.

5   This way of understanding Freud's theories and the emphasis on the object relations school in Psychoanalysis, from a feminist perspective, is discussed fully in Nancy Chodorow, *The Reproduction of Mothering*, University of California Press, Berkeley and Los Angeles, London, 1979.

6   This section is based on many discussions with Luise Eichenbaum and Susie Orbach, and on discussions in the Women's Therapy Centre study group and the Socialism and Therapy study group in London. Accounts of this approach to therapy can be found in interviews with Luise Eichenbaum and Susie Orbach in *Spare Rib*, May, 1977, published by Spare Ribs Ltd, London, *Humpty Dumpty*, No 8, published by Humpty Dumpty, London, 1976.

7   A good example of this is Helene Deutsch who wrote two of the most orthodox psychoanalytic texts on women and who allocates to women an extremely limited and unsatisfying role in life – her own life can hardly have conformed to the pattern she prescribes.

8   *See Note 5 above*. For those interested in pursuing this theoretical tendency the most accessible approach is through the writings of Harry Guntrip, *Personality Structure and Human Interaction*, The International Psycho-Analytical Library, Hogarth Press, London; International Universities Press, New York, 1961; *Schizoid Phenomena, Object Relations and the Self*, The International Psychoanalytical Library, Hogarth Press, London; International Universities Press, New York, 1968. Be warned that these books are *not* intended for the general reader.

9   *Psychoanalysis and Women*, p 381.

10 See: Claude Steiner, *Scripts People Live By*, Grove Press, New York, 1974; Hogie Wyckoff, *Solving Women's Problems*, Grove Press, New York, 1977. Radical texts presenting the theory and practice of Transactional Analysis as used in the Radical Psychiatry groups in the USA. Not designed for self-help groups but you will find lots of ideas, structures and exercises you can use.

11 Detailed instructions for making a script analysis are given in Exercise **120**.

12 See the earliest writings from the women's liberation movement, for example, Robin Morgan (ed), *Sisterhood Is Powerful*, Random House, New York, 1970; Michelene Wandor (ed), *The Body Politic: Women's Liberation in Britain 1969–72*, reprinted by Stage One, London, 1978. Also Wilhelm Reich, *The Sexual Revolution*, reprinted by Farrar Straus & Giroux, New York, 1979; and R. D. Laing, *The Divided Self*, Penguin, Harmondsworth, 1965. Reprinted by Pantheon, New York, 1969.

13 See R. D. Laing and A. Esterson, *Sanity, Madness and the Family*, Penguin, Harmondsworth, 1970.

14 Arthur Janov, *The Primal Scream*, Dell, New York, 1970; Sphere, London, 1973, p 23. In spite of all our reservations this book gives a very vivid picture of what it is like to do Primal therapy.

15 See: 'The Primal Issue', *Self and Society*, Vol 5, No 6, June, 1977, published by Self and Society, 62 Southwark Bridge Road, London, SE1, UK.

FURTHER READING

All the books mentioned in the notes to this chapter can be recommended. A good way to begin to feel the value of regression in therapy is to start from a child's experience. Try, Virginia Axline, *Dibs: in Search of Self*, reprinted by Penguin, Harmondsworth, 1971; Ballantine, New York, 1976. A moving account of therapy with a child which enables you to enter a child's emotional world.

Hannah Green, *I Never Promised You a Rose Garden*, Holt Rheinhart & Winston, New York, 1964; Pan, London, 1972. A novel about a young woman's experience of therapy which gives a clear picture of the process, the nature of the therapy relationship when transference is used; the outcome is not idealised.

For the beginnings of a feminist account of girls' psychological development see three books which re-examine the relationship between mothers and daughters: Signe Hammer, *Daughters and Mothers, Mothers and Daughters,* New American Library, New York, 1976; Hutchinson, London, 1976; Nancy Friday, *My Mother/My Self,* Delacorte Press, New York, 1977; Fontana, London, 1979. While the conclusions drawn in this book are *not* feminist, the material nancy Friday presents us with is very relevant to the development of a feminist perspective on the significance of the mother-daughter relationship. Judith Arcana, *Our Mothers' Daughters,* Shameless Hussy Press, Berkeley, 1979; The Women's Press, London, 1981. This is a deeply feminist and woman-centred book on the relationship between mothers and daughters based on interviews.

NOTE TO SECOND EDITION

In clarification: some of our criticisms of Primal therapy in this chapter, for example, about the tendency to place insufficient emphasis on re-integration, refer not to the work of the Primal Institute in Los Angeles but to other types of therapy available in the United States and elsewhere using the same name. It is important to ensure that the professional therapy you undertake offers continuing structures to assimilate the primal experience and a commitment to reintegrating that experience into daily life, as is done at the Primal Institute.

Chapter Nine
Self-Help Isn't Easy:
Keeping a Group Going

Whatever techniques you may be learning and exploring – whether Gestalt, Bioenergetics or Psychodrama – the experience of being in a self-help group will, in itself, raise issues and problems for you.

This chapter is divided into two sections: *What will my self-help group be like?* gives examples of how leaderless therapy sessions work in practice, while *Common problems* deals with the most common stumbling-blocks you may have to face.

WHAT WILL MY SELF-HELP GROUP BE LIKE?

A group may take several months to get going and may last for years. It will be different at every stage of its life and its atmosphere and dynamic will also be affected by the experience and number of people involved. Here we give three examples of very different groups to show how difficult or complicated running a self-help session can be. The process can be very exciting, is rarely smooth and is often slow and fragmented. The first example is of a group where fear and inexperience make it hard for people to express any feelings at all.

Rose, Betty and Sandra are in a newly formed women's group. The group's fourth member has not turned up this evening. They feel daunted by their low numbers. They are not confident as a group and in Betty's flat they are worried about disturbing the neighbours. They start with coffee, and chat until the evening is nearly gone, then wonder if it is worth doing any therapy at all. Each waits for the other to take a lead in starting the session. It is easy for this to happen when you have no agreed structure. Eventually they decide to focus on Rose who is feeling upset at her lack of a social life.

She keeps going out hoping to meet people but is always disappointed. Being a lesbian makes it especially hard for her to feel at ease in heterosexual social situations and to meet people she might get close to. She shrugs her shoulders – it can't be helped. Long silence. Nobody has ever opened up into crying or showing emotion in the group so far, and they are all nervous. Rose is clenching her hands. Long silence. Betty, who has a little therapy experience in Gestalt, finally ventures on a Gestalt approach starting from Rose's hands:

Betty: What are your hands doing?
Rose: They're clenched.
Betty: Can you describe it a bit more?
Rose: Well, my right hand is kind of holding on to my left hand. Rather tight.
Betty: With that movement, what is your right hand saying to your left hand?
Rose: Saying? I don't know . . . It's kind of keeping control over my left hand.
Betty: Can you speak as that right hand: 'I'm keeping control . . .'
Rose: Well, I'll try it: 'I'm keeping control of you. Pull yourself together. Don't go floppy . . .' Oh, I don't know . . .

At this point Rose unclasps her hands and shakes them out: 'I can't really identify with this hand thing.' She sighs and there is a long pause. Betty feels that her tentative approach has been rejected – perhaps it was a mistake.

When the silence gets embarrassing, she asks Rose what the sigh was about. Rose says it was her annoyance and frustration with herself for being so scared to go out. Betty asks if she could imagine putting herself on a cushion and talking to herself to show that annoyance. Rose snorts dubiously. Betty gets a cushion and puts it in front of Rose. She feels nervous and clumsy: is she pushing Rose too much? No one in the group has, so far, talked to a cushion, though they have read about it as a technique. She feels embarrassed at having more therapy experience than the others, and worries whether she is acting too much like a leader. She feels responsible for the group and wants to make it work. Sandra, who has said nothing so far, is both relieved and resentful that Betty is making all the suggestions. She has had some ideas of her own but is nervous to share them in case they are not 'as good as' Betty's. She is scared of the whole therapy idea and this makes her feel numb and lifeless. Rose herself is shifting uncomfortably in her armchair (neither of the others have suggested that she move onto the floor). She feels embarrassed, that she is being put on the spot and asked to do something which nobody else has

241

done. She does not feel that the others, as heterosexuals, can fully appreciate the social difficulties she faces through being a lesbian. She has felt too shy to discuss this issue. She resents Betty's helpful manner. She doesn't like the suggestions but is not sure if the suggestions are bad or she is just feeling unresponsive. This situation shows how unspoken issues between people in the group (Betty's greater confidence, Rose's lesbianism) slow down the progress of therapy.

All three stare silently at the cushion for several minutes. Finally Rose says, 'I might as well try it', and starts, rather hesitantly, to talk to the cushion as if it were herself. Looking at it, she expresses some of her annoyance towards herself: 'You're really pathetic the way you're scared to go out', 'You've just got to pull yourself together and stop being so floppy', 'You should act really confident and strong and then people will *want* to get to know you'.

The others encourage her to keep going in expressing this annoyance. Suddenly she laughs and stops. Sandra asks her what she laughed about and Rose says, 'I realised I was sounding just like my mother. She was always telling us to be tough, she was a very tough woman herself, she had to be, she brought us all up single-handed. So I think I get that from her.'

'What kind of things did she say to you?'

'Oh, you know, she didn't talk mucn. But her general message was – be tough, don't moan, pull yourself together, belt up'.

Sandra and Betty do not know how to go on. Should Rose talk about her mother some more? But Rose is feeling very satisfied about making this connection and does not want to spend any more time on it. Her main concern is with her present problem around going out. 'I think I'd like to answer myself back a bit', she says. After some hesitation she moves to sit on the cushion and looks back to the chair, speaking as her nervous, shy part, 'It isn't so shameful to feel scared. It *is* difficult meeting people. Putting on that act of confidence doesn't work. It's a pretence and it's such an effort I always collapse afterwards. Don't be so hard on me . . .' In this way Rose contacts a more gentle, self-accepting voice in herself. She reassures herself and when she changes seats again and switches back to the scolding role, the hard mother voice softens in response.

The session doesn't last much longer. It is tentative throughout and there is no spectacular breakthrough or release of feelings – no shouting, screaming or crying. But Rose has taken a real risk by working this way in the group and has learnt a lot about herself. Later she tells the group that she goes out feeling calmer, without a façade of acting stronger than she really feels. This works: being relaxed and more true to herself helps her to deal better with meeting people, and she comes home without the angry disappointment and self-blame she had felt before.

This was a small group session which focused on one woman. The next example gives some impression of the early days of a larger group, where one person's work can ramble and trigger off feelings in another, time can over-run and more issues come up than can be dealt with in the time available.

A mixed group starts with Robert saying he feels dreadful, he thinks he shouldn't be at the session and wants to go home. The group persuades him to stay to find out what is distressing him. Sarah says, 'If you can't get help from a therapy group when you're feeling dreadful, then what's the point?' So he sits and breathes evenly and starts by talking about his children, whom he is afraid of losing in a divorce case. One of the group, Lisa, gets upset about the painfulness of his situation and begins to cry but feels there is no room for her to receive any attention so she leaves. Steve goes to fetch her back and the group tells her that she will have some time later on. She sits crying quietly. Robert connects how he feels about his son with how he felt when he was sent away to school as a boy. He lies down and talks about the memory of acting as a 'big boy' by not crying as he left on the train. Robert's talking sparks off some feelings in George, who begins to scream and shake. Two people move off to one corner of the room to help him. This reflects the flexibility of a larger group, but it would be important to make sure enough people were left to help Robert. Robert moves on to a memory of his headmaster lecturing the boys about mastur-bation. He tells the group he is claustrophobic. The situation is confusing at this point, and group members do not know which memory to follow. They try holding Robert down so that he can explore the feeling of claus-trophobia, but he gets too terrified and after a few minutes he asks to be allowed up. Sarah tries to pressure him to talk more about his feelings when he was shut up in a little room at school, but he says he can't see the point and doesn't know where it's leading. Is he avoiding an important issue? Sarah doesn't know whether to push with the suggestion. But Robert is in charge of his own therapy process and feels that the significant link is his relationship with his own father, a methodist minister who gave a lot to his parishioners but had never been close to his own son. Robert describes his childhood feelings about being distant from his father. Then he stops. He has taken a long time, and has pursued various issues in an episodic and unfocused way – no 'big bang' – but he feels the process has been helpful. He was not able, as he had hoped at the start, to solve his present problem and reach a decision about how to deal with the divorce case. But he felt a release through making the connection with his own childhood and realising that a lot of the intense pain he felt about being separated from his children derived from his own childhood experience of distance and separation. By discharging this distress from his past, he felt freed to act in a more adult and appropriate way in the present. He had previously, without realising it, been acting in the present with the same numbness and helplessness as the little boy leaving on the train. He also felt a great relief from having exposed his fear of claustrophobia. This had previously been a shameful secrect hidden from other people.

It is now late, but the group asks Lisa what was upsetting her. She says that Robert's sadness had made *her* feel sad, she'd felt depressed for a long time but doing anything about it seemed hopeless. There was always someone more upset than her. Group members say that they want her to have some time, but it is getting late. There is a long period of false starts with several people, who have decided that 'really' she is angry, trying to provoke her into anger. (There is a danger in assuming you know what another is feeling.)

Two group members have to leave to catch the last bus home. One person is almost asleep. It seems that Lisa needs a long testing period before she will express her feelings in the group. She needs to make sure that there really is time and space for her. It emerges that in her family her deaf brother, who was difficult and demanding, got most of their parents' attention and there was little space left for Lisa's needs. It is as if she needs to make sure that the group is not like her family. Eventually she lies on the bed and as people ask her to express feelings and sensations which come to her, she has a memory of a time when she was a child of about nine. Speaking as that child, she describes a huge tantrum her brother had. She had gone to her room and lay crying on her bed while her parents tended him. Then her mother came in saying, 'Not you too, this is too much', but then realised that Lisa was deeply upset and sat down to comfort her. 'A lovely experience, but so rare', Lisa recalls.

During feedback afterwards, it emerges that Lisa still sees her brother as having all the problems, having nothing, while she feels guilty that she has everything. In adult life she has continued to feel that there is always someone more upset and deserving of help than her and has repeated this pattern in the group: leaving in tears, not daring to use her time. The group point out that her brother was actually given things that she hasn't had. It has felt like an enormous release for Lisa to be sharing some of that pain and need which she has tended to squash down. It was clearly a big risk for her and she feels quite fragile afterwards. People in the group knew that she was breaking new ground, that what she experienced was serious and real although, again, it was not spectacular or dramatic.

The next example shows how fluidly and economically an experienced group can function, although the group is not 'perfect' and people do not always resolve problems neatly.

Six out of eight members are present in a women's group which has been running, with various changes in membership, for over three years. Group members are to a large extent able to ask for what they need and take responsibility for one another. At the start Rosemary and Terry ask for some time, and as Pauline seems tense and anxious the others offer her time too. Lindsay says she feels weird about the group. It is decided collectively to divide the time between Rosemary, Pauline, Terry and Lindsay. Lindsay is to start as she expressed doubts about being in the session at all. She says she feels she doesn't belong and is close to no one there. Slowly making eye contact round the circle, she realises that it is, in fact, Brenda she feels most tense about. 'I feel angry at you for sleeping with Brian when I was having a relationship with him. You didn't think about me.' She repeats her resentment and Brenda eventually replies that it is true she had not thought about Lindsay. Their dialogue is intense but they do not shout. Lindsay complains that Brenda has had no time to see her for ages. On the group's suggestion, she turns this into a demand, 'I want to see more of you, Brenda', and she and Brenda agree to meet socially soon. Eventually the air has cleared and they hug. Their experience of therapy shows up in their level of honesty about actions and emotions which aren't easily acceptable, and the fact that they don't immediately leap into primal feelings of sexual jealousy but are able to deal with this problem on the level of present reality, discriminating how much they feel in this particular incident where neither is very involved with the man. They are able to realise that a more important question is needing things from each other, and the group recognises this rather than accusing them of avoiding the 'real issue' as a non-feminist group might have done.

Now there is an interruption. Rosemary forgot to explain that she has to leave early this evening. At this Hannah suddenly explodes, 'That makes me so angry! My life's really difficult, I have so little free time with the children, yet I take the trouble to be here!'

Rosemary replies, 'I'm tired of hearing how hard your life is. How much more you suffer than anyone else. If you don't like your life, then change it!'

'I am!' Hannah shouts back. 'You just don't notice anything outside your own life!'

There is a long silence while Hannah and Rosemary look at one another, shaking with emotion. These two women once lived together very closely but then their friendship broke up and Hannah had been forced to find somewhere else to live. They have worked several times in the group on the anger and competition between them. This unplanned confrontation was messy and has disconcerted the group. Rosemary states clearly that she does not want to work further on this conflict as she feels it will get nowhere. Should they push her? No one feels sure about moving on when so much bad feeling hangs in the air. The very closeness of the women present leads to conflicts which the group cannot always contain or resolve; many long-standing groups have skeletons in the cupboard.

Pauline is next. She wants to explore not knowing who she is, 'I have been so many different people in my life, it's confusing.' Brenda suggests a psychodrama technique. Pauline could use the women in the group to stand for those different parts of herself and explore the relationship between them. She chooses women who fit the roles and arranges them round the room: rebellious art-student, hippie, serious political worker, sensual lover, the new role of 'wife'. She describes how she feels about each character and her confusion between them. Then she switches to a Gestalt approach: she focuses on the art-student and, acting both roles, develops a dialogue between herself and a lecturer who used to put her down. The lecturer's criticisms are strong and powerful. In spite of the encouragement of other group members, the art student wilts under his contempt. Pauline's time is up and she stops. This example showed the flexibility of a skilled group, switching from Psychodrama to Gestalt when it became more appropriate; but also shows how dialogues don't always work out comfortably with integration or victory to the underdog. However, during feedback, the others do not tell her that her work was 'politically incorrect' or that she 'did it wrong'. They comment that she has a lot of energy to put herself down and regret that the work couldn't end differently. They give her some validation about her creativity which she seemed unable to give herself. Pauline says that being recently married and having little time or space on her own has raised these questions of identity and self-worth more keenly. The others suggest that since her home is not large enough to have her own room, she could make one corner of the bedroom clearly hers, with objects and pictures she likes and a place to sit when she meditates.

Now it is Rosemary's turn. She has some experience of professional Primal therapy and this is reflected in the way she approaches her problem. She describes her situation at work, where people have been isolating her because she dresses differently and has different ideas from them. She lies on her back and starts to cry with deep racking sobs. Her heavy crying is interspersed with moans and phrases: 'It hurts', 'Don't treat me like that!', 'No!' After about ten minutes her crying slowly subsides. Her body is now very relaxed and she sits up. The group have used their experience to stay silent throughout, respecting her ability to direct her own work and simply giving her their supportive attention. But they know that primal work can leave you feeling very vulnerable and, during feedback, Terry comments that Rosemary seems quite collapsed and suggests that she make some positive or assertive statements about herself. After a long pause Rosemary starts, 'I'm different from them and that's OK', 'I like dressing scruffy', 'My sex life is different and that's OK'. After a pause she adds, 'I'm a nice person. I have a lot of love to give'. She is encouraged to repeat the last phrase, making eye contact round the room. Each woman meets her eyes, letting her know she believes it. Whatever their internal conflicts, Rosemary knows that the whole group is staunchly behind her in her struggles with the world.

Now it is Terry's turn. The session has moved swiftly and economically. The experience of the group shows up in that four women are able to explore a problem each within a meeting of two hours. Terry says she would like to do a guided fantasy. Hannah comments, 'You told me you were splitting up with Roger. I have the feeling you may be using the guided fantasy to avoid looking at that.' In a long-standing group, people use their intuition and may intervene more strongly in one another's work, knowing that each has the confidence to remain in charge of her own time. They even learn to make interpretations in a non-oppressive way ('I have the feeling that you're . . .', 'My fantasy is that you're . . .'). In this case Terry agrees and tries to use cushions to develop a dialogue with Roger. But she falls silent after saying she feels tingling all over. Rosemary encourages her to describe the tingling, but Terry says it has gone and she feels as if a fog has come over her. Pauline encourages her to speak as the fog, but she soon stops, 'I've lost it'. And so it continues. Terry is bombarded with different suggestions and follows a number of blind alleys without reaching any insight or release until her time is over. Her example shows that sometimes the more therapy you do the harder it gets as you work through superficial problems to face nitty-gritty issues of resistance or self-hatred in yourself which are very difficult to tackle. During feedback several people acknowledge they made too many suggestions, a danger in a group of experienced people. Terry thinks she might have worked more profitably with the guided fantasy after all, and Lindsay does not withhold honest feedback, 'I get very frustrated when you blank out like that'.

Rosemary has by now left and those who remain share how they are feeling and have a long close hug together on the floor.

COMMON PROBLEMS

Each group has its own individual dynamic but is likely, at various times, to confront problems and difficulties common to almost all self-help groups.

When a Group Is Too Small
A large group of about six to twelve people can sometimes generate an almost magical atmosphere, where the focus of attention from a lot of people can give an individual the energy and sense of credibility to express feelings

which might not come out in another situation. If your group is smaller than this, you may feel disappointed: the energy in the room may feel low, and you may feel you have too much responsibility to carry the group and make suggestions. A small intimate group may seem too personal, and you may also regret that there are not enough people for you to explore how you relate to groups, which may be an important issue for you.

However, there are also advantages in a small group. It is easier to get to know one another and to build up trust. Some women find the attention of a large group scary and feel freer to explore their problems with smaller numbers. Therapy *does* work with two or three people, or one alone. It does not depend on numbers.

A small group may feel demoralised when it is the remains of a larger group which has dwindled through people dropping out. This is a common pattern in the history of a self-help group. The best way to tackle it is:

1   Raise it in the group instead of bravely pretending it isn't happening. Recognise feelings of demoralisation and express them. They can be good material for the therapy process and sitting on them may block other feelings from being expressed.

2   Discuss *why* people have left. Often it is because they have become scared when they realised what the therapy process would involve. Perhaps they do not feel ready to use it, or have realised they need a different form of therapy (a led group or an individual therapist). Recognising these reasons can help the remaining group members to feel less undermined.

3   You may feel that people have left because of real shortcomings in the group which remaining members feel too. Common stumbling-blocks are the amorphousness of the group, or its lack of experience. It is worth discussing these shortcomings and taking steps to remedy them. In Chapter Two, we list many useful structures.

Here is an exercise to clarify what you feel are the advantages and disadvantages for you in having a small group.

129   Big Group, Small Group

Face each other in pairs in the usual co-counselling format. Decide who will take her turn first. She has three minutes to speak in sentences starting: 'If the group was bigger I could . . .', and 'In a small group I can . . .'

Her partner keeps eye contact and gives attention. After three minutes, exchange roles. When you have both had a turn, share feedback about what came up, either in pairs or in the group as a whole. If you are a group of three, you could do this exercise taking turns in a triangle.

Who Makes Suggestions?

When a woman is exploring her feelings, she needs sensitive suggestions to guide her through the process. In the absence of a leader, there may be a vacuum in a self-help group because people are too nervous or inexperienced to make suggestions, or group members may offer conflicting suggestions. Usually one or two women will feel particularly in tune with her and able to help her. We have found it best for other group members to respect their approach and offer suggestions which harmonise with it. For example, if a woman is lying on a mattress doing deep breathing, it might be jarring and confusing to suggest that she sits up and talks to a cushion, but comments like 'Keep breathing' or 'I notice your hands are shakihg' might be very helpful. If you are very emotionally involved with the woman who is working (whether identifying with her or feeling upset or angered by her) your feelings may not allow you to be sensitive to her and it is often best not to offer suggestions.

If a suggestion is refused it is often hard to tell whether the suggestion is inappropriate or the person working is resistant to it. Learn to be explicit about the process of making and taking suggestions:

'I won't take that suggestion, because I want to continue this dialogue'
'I feel stranded, I'm not getting enough help'
'That idea sounds too frightening'
'I'm confused now about which direction to take'.

You may find you need to set aside some time to discuss various approaches and techniques and make mutual criticisms of how you tackle making suggestions.

It is always important to bring to light any dynamics in the group around this issue. For example, two women may often offer competing suggestions. In this case explore the sources of their competition in the group. Another common situation is where one woman is considered less skilled or sensitive, so her suggestions are often overlooked or ignored. Here it is worth finding out how this woman feels about her suggestions being rejected and looking for a way to change this pattern. Maybe she needs others to keep completely silent for a while to give her some space. It is important to recognise that receiving and acting on a suggestion is as supportive as giving one. By taking a woman's suggestion you help her to realise that she can make a worthwhile contribution to the group.

When a Few People Dominate the Group

It is common for one or two people to emerge recurrently as the 'guide' for others, making suggestions while the rest of the group sits silent. This dominance may be the result of confidence and conditioning derived from race, class or sex (for example, in a mixed group it is usually a man who takes this role). It may also happen where one person has more therapy experience than other group members. She may feel ambivalent about having this greater confidence or experience, but may still effectively run the group, leaving little space for others to contribute and perhaps making them feel that their suggestions would anyway not be good enough.

A common pattern is that this person holds sway over the group until the other group members gain some solidarity and confidence and one or more of them finally confronts this 'leader'. The confrontation may take the form of a moral tirade ('You're behaving like a dictator! We don't believe in hierarchies!') or of a bitter personal attack ('I don't trust you!', 'You never look at your own problems!', 'You think you're better than us!', 'You don't want to change!'). Or it may be expressed more directly and honestly, ('I feel jealous of your superior knowledge', 'I don't like the way you control this group, I want more power in the group myself'). Either way, the confrontation is usually effective if the group stands strongly together. It may emerge that the leader really does want to lead (one man in our mixed group wanted us to start paying him) and when it becomes clear that the group do not want this, the person will leave. But if the person is committed to self-help therapy between equals, then she or he will remain in the group, probably feeling demoralised and trying to keep silent as much as possible. This does not necessarily solve the problem. Others in the group may not have the confidence to make suggestions themselves, especially with the 'leader' sitting watching them. Long embarrassed silences may result in the 'leader' attempting a come-back: 'You don't like what I suggest, but you don't have anything as good to offer yourselves . . .', 'You see – when I don't talk, no one does . . .'

Clearly the 'leader' falling silent solves nothing and can be very repressive. It is important to tackle this problem seriously, if possible before it reaches a crisis point. Asserting moral principles ('We *should* all be equal') will not help the real difficulties of a group where the practical skills and assurance it needs to survive are not distributed equally. We suggest the following approaches.

1   Recognise feelings brought up by this situation. Some group members may feel relieved that someone is carrying the responsibility for the group. They might discover the reasons for their own fear of speaking up. Another group member may feel competitive with the 'leader', or may be projecting onto the 'leader' feelings about her dominating father or mother which carry a lot of emotional charge. The 'leader' may feel resentful with others for not taking more responsibility. Or she may feel that unless she does twice as much work as everyone else, she has nothing to offer the group. To work on these issues with a therapy approach of exploring feelings does not deny the present problem, but can clear the air and actually make it easier to work it out. Understanding the *roots* of this kind of pattern in the group helps in working out how to change the pattern.

2   If the inequality derives from the 'leader' having greater knowledge, it is

important to recognise this and arrange for this knowledge to be shared. Don't deny that knowledge or pretend to be equal in skill and experience when you are not. Instead have the 'leader' explain what therapy she has done before, what books she has read, what ideas she bases her suggestions on. Then others in the group can gain access to the same knowledge and are not mystified by it. It may even help to arrange one evening for the 'leader' to share explicitly what she knows with the group. In addition, it is worth arranging for other group members to go to some professional groups so they can develop their own skill and confidence by learning new techniques from an outside source. There is a lot to be learned too by comparing professional groups with your own self-help group and understanding the differences in ideology and approach. If the cost of these groups is a problem, pool money to sponsor one group member to attend such a group with the agreement that she will afterwards teach the rest what she has learned.

3   If you have a problem with imbalance of power in the group, it is even more important to use the equalising structures we describe in 'Starting a self-help group': speaking in turn round the circle, rotating leadership, meeting in pairs outside the group, and so on.

You may feel disillusioned that your group has created leadership patterns and unequal relationships in spite of a commitment to avoid them. Because of our conditioning it is not surprising that we tend to re-create the modes of relating prevalent in our society. You will probably never succeed in eradicating differences of skill or creating an island of complete equality. Don't aim too high, but rather see your leaderless therapy group as an excellent situation for exploring and starting to change those social and childhood factors which make it difficult to work collectively. This process can be very helpful for people involved in any kind of group situation, for example, an office team, parent-teacher association, communal living or collective political work. It can also be seen as an important part of the therapeutic process to regain control over our process of growth and development by learning to play a fuller part in running our own therapy group, realising that *each of us has the ability to heal ourselves and to help others*.

Running the group with ideas and suggestions is not the only way of dominating a group, though it is perhaps the most obvious. There are many different ways in which some people may acquire more power than others. One may dominate by criticism. One may unwittingly collect a powerful role as the unspoken 'Big Mummy' of the group through sessions being held at her home. One may dominate by sitting dead and withdrawn, casting a pall of depression and despair over everyone. One may build power by being the 'nicest' person. One may dominate by creating a morality about what kind of feelings we should have and what kind of people we should be. If a few

251

women within the group are closer friends than the others, they very often form a powerful clique. In our group, those of us who were also living together often had more support and confidence during sessions, and at different points of time formed a hierarchy within the group. With all these different patterns of unequal relationships bring them out into the open, not to take moral stands against them, but to discover how and why they are happening, and how to change them. Encounter provides useful techniques for this.

It is not uncommon for one woman to dominate a group by 'suffering most'. She may put out an endless monologue of complaint about how terrible her life is, making other group members feel they don't deserve time to work on their own problems. Or she may seem to have 'more feelings' than anyone else, brimming over every session into dramatic outbreaks of emotion which overwhelm other group members. If these patterns continue, the woman involved has clearly got 'stuck' in ways of behaving which are probably not making her feel better or helping her to change the objective situation which may be distressing her. In addition to discussing the situation openly, and adopting structures which will help (for example, sharing session time equally between all group members), the group needs to tackle the problem of how the woman might be helped to get 'unstuck' and how the others can point it out without being unkind.

Here are some exercises to explore power relations.

130   O'Grady Says

This is a children's game which can be illuminating for adults to explore their relations to authority. It can also be quite good for warming up. Clear the floor so that you can move around. Take it in turns to stand at the front and give movement instructions to the others. For example: 'O'Grady says jump up and down', 'O'Grady says pull a horrible face'.

Take equal turns of about three minutes each to play this leader role then sit in a circle and share how you experienced the game. Were you happy to take instructions from some women but not from others? Were you more comfortable being told what to do or telling? Were you unable to take the little power the exercise gave you as leader? Did you expect people to ignore your instructions? Did you feel furious at having to take any instruction from anybody even within this game framework? Recognising each person's patterns of dealing with authority may help you understand why certain relationships have developed in the group.

131   Master and Slave

We have not renamed this exercise 'Mistress and Slave' because it seems to us to be concerned with exploring a particular type of power relation which we have learnt as part of patriarchal culture.

Divide into pairs and spread out in the room so that each pair has as much space as possible. Decide which person in your pair will play master first, and which will play slave. Take five minutes to explore the roles in whatever way you like. The master may give physical or verbal instructions or exaggerate any aspects of the role. The slave responds as she chooses, also allowing herself to exaggerate the role. When the time is up, exchange roles.

Afterwards, discuss with your partner what the experience was like. As slave, did you submit or rebel? As master, how did you respond if your authority was questioned? Were you unable to assert any authority at all?

It may seem strange to use an exercise to explore precisely those power relations which we are trying to get away from, but in our society we have all internalised those relations at different times in our lives and it is important to recognise what is there inside us before we try to change. It often happens that we avoid precisely those areas we feel most tense or unresolved about. A refusal to play a master in any form or to play a submissive slave in any form often covers a fear that we might actually find those roles attractive and compelling. These are precisely the kind of contradictions which a leaderless therapy group can help us to work through and resolve.

You could also co-counsel on 'Times when I have been in or under authority', and fruitfully use the structure of exercise **44** (Dependence vs Independence) to explore the contrasting roles of 'helper' and 'helped' within the group. This may help to reveal what some people get from playing a large part in 'helping' others, and what others get from being relatively 'helpless' in the group.

When One Person Gets 'Stuck'
It frequently happens in a group that a woman gets 'stuck', whether in silence, in complaint or in expressing one feeling without being able to move on.

1   Getting stuck in silence

Ruth comes to her newly formed self-help therapy group in an obviously depressed mood. The other women in the group ask her what she is feeling and whether she would like some time but she barely answers their questions, saying only that she feels very remote. The session proceeds with several other women taking time to look at some problems. Ruth says nothing until feedback time at the end, when she states, 'I suppose I do want to say something but I can't think what to say. I can't open my mouth in case I let the cold wind in.'

'What would it do to you?' one woman asks.

'Hurt', Ruth replies. Further questions, ideas, offers of cups of tea or a lift home are all refused and Ruth tells the group she feels she needs to work something out for herself. The other group members go home a bit sad and worried about Ruth not trusting or opening up.

It is important to remember, especially in a self-help group, that each woman is in control of her own therapy process. If Ruth wants help from the group, it is *up to her* to express her willingness to work. The group are right to express their concern, and pass on. It is doubtful that pushing her or shouting at her (as is common in some groups) would have helped. It is a good guideline for the group to assume that each woman 'knows best' about what she needs. People are very different, and Ruth may take longer than others to learn to trust the group, or she may be confronting powerful resistances in herself which she does not yet feel able to challenge. She may be at a stopping-place and needs to absorb what she has learnt so far in the group.

We have found it realistic to *honour our resistances*. If we try to batter them down we often merely develop other defences to replace them. We developed them for survival, to deal with pressures we have met during our lives. Gradually, through therapy, we can learn what they do and don't do for us and, as we feel stronger, we will be able to let go of them at our own speed rather than in a pressured way.

So, in the case of Ruth, the most useful approach for other group members to take might be to help Ruth to *explore* her resistances through the Gestalt techniques we describe in Chapter Three. For example, she might:

Exaggerate the way she holds her mouth closed, and the feelings that go with that holding, repeating the phrase, 'I won't open my mouth in case it hurts', 'I *won't* show my feelings' or 'I don't trust anyone to help me'
Become more aware of that resistance, noticing between therapy sessions in which situations her mouth tightens particularly
Discover the function of that resistance, answering questions like 'What do your resistances stop you from doing or feeling?', 'What is your fantasy of what would happen if you were without them?', 'What do you fear might happen if you worked in the group?'

These would all be ways for Ruth to respect her resistances and to gain a deeper understanding of how and why she is stuck. Fritz Perls suggests that, instead of wishing to be in a different state, the best way to get out of being stuck is to go further into it. He tells one woman, 'I suggest that you use the words, "I'm stuck", about a hundred times a day. Talk to your husband about how you're stuck, and talk to your friends, until you fully understand how you're stuck.'[1] His idea is that once you really feel your 'stuckness', you will be willing to do something about it and move on.

2 *Getting stuck in one feeling*

Elaine separated from her lover a couple of months ago and has explored her pain about this several times in the group. This evening she has again put her ex-lover on the cushion and talks of her loneliness, her sense of betrayal, the grimness of her life while tears of self-pity run down her cheeks. The other group members make suggestions which might help her to move on, for example, asking if she feels anything positive about the separation, asking her what sensations she has in her body, asking her if she would like to lie down to enable her to cry more fully. But Elaine does not accept these suggestions and complains that the group cannot help her to feel any better. The other group members feel guilty about Elaine's suffering so they struggle on making suggestions which she does not take. They begin to feel increasingly frustrated and resentful and finally Hannah explodes, 'Elaine, you're impossible! You're manipulating the whole group and nobody else is going to get any time! You're messing around without getting anywhere! I think you're really angry and you're covering it up!'

At this, Elaine's crying redoubles, she crumples even further and seems inconsolable. The session continues fruitlessly and ends with Elaine feeling no better and the other group members feeling a lot worse.

Here Elaine was stuck in self-pity and the group did not in any way help her to break that pattern. To avoid this situation, some signs to watch for are:

If the woman who is working refuses to take any suggestions
If she continues endlessly with the same feeling
If what she is doing seems unreal
If you find yourself feeling bored or unsympathetic

Trust your own impressions. If you start feeling restless, bring the issue into the open and find out how other group members are feeling. This does not mean blaming Elaine, as Hannah did, but simply owning your own feelings and sharing what you experience. Here are some examples:

'Can I check this out? I'm feeling impatient. I feel you're stuck, Elaine, and it's not worth going on. What do others feel?'

In this situation Elaine might agree to stop and come back to her problem at a later point. She might even be helped to explore her stuckness as we described above. Being perpetually unhappy can bring certain rewards (sympathy, attention, guilt from others) and if a person realises she is playing this kind of self-defeating game she may be able to see its disadvantages and let go of it.

Another intervention might go, 'Elaine, I'm feeling bored by the way you're going on and on. Does anyone else feel the same or is it just me?'

Though this remark seems unkind, its honesty might help Elaine. It might provoke in her some anger which underlines her self-pity. Very often when one emotion is expressed endlessly, it is a cover for another feeling which underlies it. If Elaine were encouraged to stay with her anger, she might find she has some rage towards her ex-lover which she had never previously expressed and letting it out might help her to regain a sense of her energy and vitality instead of feeling like a helpless victim.

In different situations useful interventions might be:

'I am feeling uncomfortable with all these silences. What is going on? What are others feeling?'

'I have the feeling that you don't really want to work on this now. Is this true?'

'I wonder what would happen if you explored being happier. Does that seem at all scary?'

'I can't cope with you being so unhappy all the time. I find myself wishing you'd stop crying.'

'Can I check this out? Your anger seems unreal to me. I wonder if there is anything else going on for you, maybe some sadness . . .?'

'The experience of being raped which you described sounds so terrible, I don't know how to respond appropriately. I can't think of any suggestions to help you deal with it. Is that why others are silent too?'

'I'm frustrated by what's happening. I've realised that I'm sitting on a lot of anger myself. If you don't think you're going to get unstuck about expressing your anger, I'd like some time to express mine.'

Notice that all these interventions break open or 'bust' a pattern of stuckness in the group, but do it lovingly. There is no blame, judgment or emotional charge laid on the woman who is stuck. It is far easier to withdraw into a resentful silence and 'freeze' the woman out, or make sniping criticisms, but far more helpful to take the risk of exposing yourself and make a statement about your own feelings. It may even emerge that the difficulty lies in you rather than in her.

3   Others in the group make it hard for someone to work

If you are one of the other group members it is important to be aware that you may not be giving the woman the help she needs to work fruitfully. A number of factors may be colouring your response to her:

Your own unresolved feelings may be interfering. You may find that your desire to push her, or your frustration at the way she blocks her anger, arises precisely because you block your own anger so much. Maybe it is you who really needs to get angry and not her. Maybe you find her crying 'unreal' because you dare not allow it to stir up unexpressed tears of your own. If you do not allow yourself to cry easily, it is unlikely that you will be able to allow another to do so. Maybe you are bored because your fear caused you to cut off from her.

You are out of your depth. The woman may be dealing with a very painful experience, such as rape, which you have not experienced. Or she may be going through an emotional crisis more intense than any you have known. You may simply lack the understanding and the vocabulary to help her through. It is hard to help a person go over territory which you have not crossed yourself. There are sometimes issues which are too difficult for a self-help group to cope with.

You may be feeling hostile towards her. Perhaps you are feeling resentful because of something which happened last week, perhaps you are reluctant to give her your attention because you feel she gets enough attention already. Perhaps you feel competitive with her, and in your heart of hearts do not want to help her.

You may be feeling more involved in another dynamic in the group. You may be preoccupied with a conflict between two other women, concerned with your own problems, or wondering whether you are accepted in the group.

If any of these processes are going on, you will probably not be able to give the woman who is working your clear attention, nor gain an accurate perception of what she is experiencing, and it is unlikely that you will be able to give her helpful suggestions. You may even be sending out a lot of unspoken hostile messages which make it hard for her to feel safe enough to express her feelings. If more than one person in the group is doing this, it may be an even more powerful influence blocking a woman from working. Together group members can unwittingly create an atmosphere of approval for the expression of emotion – or not.

In all these situations, it is important to express your own discomfort, resentments, fears or preoccupations. This might superficially appear unkind, but it is far more unkind to allow the woman who is working to flail on in a vacuum, feeling that her being stuck is her own fault. If these issues are brought into the open, she can understand why she is stuck and has a choice whether to struggle on or to work on something different (her relationship with other group members) or to leave her problems to explore in a safer situation.

This raises the whole question of what we mean by being 'helpful' to another person. It emerges that the best way to help another is to be yourself. As women, many of us have been brought up to sacrifice our own feelings and needs to others. We have been taught to be more aware of others than of ourselves, and to help and give to others unselfishly. In a therapy group this may lead us to feel that the right thing to do is to deny our own feelings in the interests of 'helping' another, as the group members tried to do with Elaine. But this approach assumes that the person we are helping is herself 'helpless', that she is a passive victim needing someone to rescue her and make her feel better. We keep her stuck in that helpless role and do not give her a chance to find her own strength. The two roles of 'rescuer' and 'victim'[2] are very easy for women to slip into playing. It can become a collusive game whereby the 'rescuer' denies and avoids her own feelings by helping another in a motherly way, thus enforcing the passivity of the 'victim' who denies her own power and is stuck in self-pity. The result, as in our original example with Elaine, is often mutual resentment and then 'rescuer' or 'victim' can become 'persecutor' of the other as Hannah did of Elaine. This 'vicious triangle' can be an illuminating model for understanding unequal relationships.

Feminist therapy will aim to help each woman to take responsibility for her own life, to find her power to act and move. Playing victim and rescuer does not help this process; responding honestly to another does. We make contact by staying with what we are, not by 'trying' or playing the helpful roles we were brought up to play. If you are true to yourself, you open the possibility for another to respond honestly in turn and contact her own sources of power. You will be more real for her and will not lay things on her. This is why it is better to intervene when someone is stuck and clearly state your own feelings.

4 Hidden 'stuckness' which happens over time

Over the long term a woman may be stuck in patterns which are hard to spot. If she perpetually explores one problem or dwells on one emotion to the exclusion of others, without any appearance of release or clearing, it may be that there are certain feelings or topics which she is avoiding. For example, one woman might explore her childhood repeatedly while never once admitting any difficulties or conflicts about her relationship with her husband. Another woman might spend several sessions reiterating her anger at her boss while refusing to look at her family upbringing ('I don't feel anything about my parents any more. That's all over'). This kind of denial often covers unexpressed feelings. When someone is stuck, it is a good rule to look for what is being *avoided*.

There may be a woman who seldom asks for the group's attention to explore a problem or feeling, always for an apparently good reason. It may be that she has difficulties in the area of receiving attention or trusting the group.

Below we list some exercises to explore these issues of receiving attention, trust and avoidance.

132 Blind Walk

This exercise can highlight the feelings you have about trusting another to look after you.

Divide into pairs. One of you is blindfolded and the other leads her on a blind walk around the room. After ten minutes, exchange roles.

Afterwards, share what you experienced, in pairs and in the group.

133 Exercise for Uncovering Avoidances

Each person has a pen and paper and takes five minutes to write a list of the emotions and topics she avoids touching on in the group. Write down everything which comes to mind, without judging. Then share your list with a partner or with the group. You may not feel ready to work on those topics, but if you are aware of avoiding them, you at least have a choice to change that pattern. And if you are stuck, you may gain some illumination about how this has happened.

134 Exploring Difficulties in Trusting

Divide into pairs, choosing a person from whom you are aware of withholding yourself. Speak to her for five minutes, taking responsibility for your mistrust by using the phrase 'I won't . . .': 'I won't trust you because you look strong and superior . . .' 'I won't trust you because I think you look down on me . . .' At the end of this time, your partner can give you feedback about how accurate your projections actually are in her case, 'I do feel strong . . . but that doesn't mean I look down on you . . .' 'I thought you were very brave in the group the other evening . . .' and so on.

Exchange the roles and repeat the exercise.

135 Receiving Attention

A woman who finds it difficult to receive attention can explore this by moving round the circle, telling each person in turn 'I don't want your attention'. The group members give her eye contact and sit silent. Then she goes round again, this time asking each person 'Please give me your attention'. She can say whether she wants a response this time.

Afterwards she can talk about how it felt, what resistance she was aware of in herself, and what situations it reminded her of.

Getting 'Stuck' as a Group

Sometimes not just one person but a whole group becomes 'stuck'. The symptoms of this may be getting locked in long silences, or a recurring woodenness in the atmosphere of the group. It may feel tense or unreal. You may be at one another's throats all the time without being able to resolve anything. You may feel bored about coming to the group, knowing that there won't be anything new.

People may be missing sessions. The group may even be functioning fairly well but you are aware that there are certain areas or feelings which are never touched on.

In these situations the group may be operating with certain unspoken agreements which are restricting and deadening the group. These group collusions may be to avoid certain feelings, for example:

'Act strong and never express weakness': This can be undermining in the long term as it denies the contradictory nature of our experience.

'Be supportive to each other and don't talk straight': As many women in consciousness-raising groups have found, a group which is only positive ends up making you feel vulnerable as it seems so unreal.

'Stay in the past and don't look too closely at the present': People work repeatedly about how much they wanted their mummies when they were two, while present issues between group members are ignored.

'The more you freak out the better it is': Group members get a lot of approval for making a noise, shouting, crying, or hitting cushions. People learn to put on good 'performances' in the group without always being fully connected to what they are doing. The important areas of talking, experiencing resistances and making connections with everyday life are omitted.

'Take every possible risk and show your determination to change at all costs': Group members mask their fear of therapy and apply themselves to it with the same ambition and self-denial that drives them in the rest of their lives.

'Avoid politically incorrect emotions': Group members may tackle many areas of their experience but regard some areas as taboo: for example, sexism, racism, jealousy, competitiveness, possessiveness, difficulties in collective sharing. As a result people may find it hard to raise in the group the conflicts which are troubling them most, and also become increasingly alienated and withdrawn from the group.

There may also be collusions to avoid dealing with particular problematic dynamics within the group. For example, one person getting consistently scapegoated, or the taking of sides between two people who are in conflict, or the existence of glaring hierarchies in the group. People may be feeling hurt or resentful about these patterns and because this is not brought into the open other feelings get blocked too.

Sometimes the collusion is necessary to keep the group intact (rather like a person needing her defences). Even so, it is better to recognise that this is happening and clear the air. You can undertake to challenge it when the group feels ready.

If you feel you may have difficulty locating collusions yourselves, try asking in a professional group leader to run a session with you. You can pool the money to pay for this if necessary. An outside leader can be very helpful in opening up locked patterns in the group (for example of power or competition) which you may be avoiding. Choose a leader you know and trust so that you do not have to spend a lot of time challenging her methods instead of getting the help you need. Alternatively, you might decide to make a conscious effort to bring new people into the group. They will have a fresh eye to see what is 'stuck' about the group, and will probably challenge old and entrenched patterns, provided you encourage them to do so and don't let them collude with you or take a role of being 'the group problem'. An 'intensive' can also help to shift stuck patterns (see p 50).

If you decide to tackle the collusions yourselves as a group, here are some exercises which may help:

136   How I Stand in Relation to the Group
This exercise was useful to us when several people were arriving late, and others seemed reluctant to put energy into the sessions.

Place a cushion in the middle of the room and imagine putting 'the group' on it. Everyone moves to one side of the room. Now have each person in turn stand as near or far from the cushion as feels right for her, and have her talk to the cushion, telling 'the group' how she feels about it, what she likes and doesn't like in it, what difficulties she has about putting energy into the group. Afterwards give feedback on what came up. You may find you have the material for a full discussion and may be able to make decisions about changes in the group's structure or activity so that it better meets people's needs.

137   Divide the Group then Rejoin
When you are feeling stuck as a group it can help to break into pairs for, say, ten minutes, to talk about the problem and release your individual feelings about what is happening in the group. It is important to follow this by coming back into the whole group to share these feelings. After dividing up in this way, the problem often seems clearer and more easy to resolve.

If you are a mixed group, you will probably find it very helpful to divide into a women's group and a men's group to discuss the problem, then rejoin as a whole group to discuss any fresh illuminations which came up.

138 Group Sculptures

This exercise is good for looking at the dynamic of the whole group.

Clear a space in the room. Take it in turns to do a 'sculpture' of the group using the group members. For example, one version might show two close friends who are central to the group standing in the middle arm in arm; a woman who is challenging their power could be facing them with an arm outstretched; a woman who is ambivalent about belonging to the group or who never asks for attention might stand slightly apart with her head half turned away, and so on. When one person has finished making the sculpture (including herself in it), stand in silence for a while, letting yourself feel what it is like in the position you have been placed in, what feels right and wrong about it. Then you can talk about it and people may want to make adjustments: 'I feel I should be standing a bit closer to Gaye, but looking towards Penny . . .'

Then have a couple more people take a turn at doing their version of the group sculpture.

A variation is to do a 'moving' sculpture, with people doing characteristic or repeated movements in relation to each other or to the group. Another variation is to do a sculpture of the relationship between only two or three group members who have said that they want to work things out between them.

This exercise can be upsetting, and people may misunderstand the positions they are put in, so it is important to leave enough time afterwards for everyone to discuss what came up and share what they felt: 'I was annoyed that people kept putting me in fighting positions', 'I was upset to be put on the outside'.

One or two women may even need time and help from the group to express their reactions and assimilate what they have learnt.

139 What We avoid

This exercise can help you to locate areas of avoidance in the group. Give each person in the group pen and paper and have each person write a list of the feelings, topics or issues which are consistently avoided in the group. Then share your lists and talk about about them.

Another approach to 'stuckness' is through direct confrontation, physical or verbal. The advantages and disadvantages of this approach are discussed in Chapter Four, on Encounter.

Doing Therapy with Close Friends
This can bring up various problems:

1 A woman may clam up. She may fear that if she expresses her most vulnerable or angry feelings, her friends will never forget it and may not like her any more. She may find it particularly hard to express her feelings towards those friends. She might find the direct confrontation techniques of Encounter terrifying. As a result she may become increasingly tense, withdrawn and defensive in the therapy group.

In this situation, the group needs to recognise her feelings and she needs to be encouraged to explore her fears rather than force herself to take part in exercises or confrontation which she finds very threatening. If the situation does not get easier over time, she may decide it would be more fruitful for her to do therapy in another group where she has less at stake.

2 A woman may express strong irrational feelings towards a friend and this damages their relationship. She may become very angry or contemptuous of a friend and express strong criticisms or insults towards her in the group. Afterwards she may realise that those feelings were fuelled by a childhood memory or by disgust or anger at herself. She regrets having directed these hurtful and inappropriate sentiments at her friend but it is too late to withdraw them. The incident may leave a barrier, or scar their relationship.

It is easy to project onto a close friend strong feelings which have little to do with her. For this reason, when a woman is experiencing what seem difficult or irrational feelings towards a friend, it may be better in the first instance for her to explore those feelings separately if she doesn't feel confident about dealing with them in the group. In a co-counselling situation, or with a group of strangers, she can work out how much of what she feels is projection and how much is really connected with her friend. Afterwards she can talk to the friend, sharing what she learned about herself and their relationship, and bringing up in a loving and centred way any resentments or criticisms which she feels sure are appropriate.

3 People open up too abruptly and then shut off. Sometimes when people who know one another well do therapy together, releases of emotion are swift and explosive and they may very quickly open up a level of total honesty and intense communication which they are not ready to sustain in their everyday living. A woman may be embarrassed to see at work the same friend in whose arms she wept for hours the night before. The split between the world of her feelings and her daily coping personality may be too great and she may feel threatened. The result may be a strong counter-reaction: she may withdraw from her feelings, her friends, therapy, or all three.

To avoid this, steer away from a big bang approach and start gradually, perhaps using Co-counselling most often at first, allowing time for people to integrate the changes they make into their daily lives and relationships.

4   People believe therapy can do magic. Sometimes friends think that therapy can work as a panacea for their relationships. Our group has been invited several times to visit communes who hoped that therapy would help them to iron out interpersonal difficulties. It is tempting to hope that if you express loudly and often enough feelings of, say, resentment or jealousy, and understand their origin, then those feelings will somehow go away. Our experience suggests that therapy serves to clarify, not remove, conflicts of interest and differences of personality which may be causing trouble in relationships. It can unravel misunderstandings and demystify projections, but it cannot make people like one another who don't.

Having said this about the difficulty of doing therapy with close friends, we should say that it is what we did – and we survived. The links between friends sometimes hold a therapy group together when it might otherwise falter or die, and can provide a context for supporting and validating the changes therapy helps you make in your everyday life. As many close relationships seem to fall apart through difficult feelings *not being* expressed as through difficult feelings *being* expressed, in however an imperfect way. Where close friends do manage to stay together through the therapy process, they can develop a very full trust and acceptance of one another and their relationship is strengthened and enriched. Here is how one woman in our group described it.

A bunch of women meeting together in each other's rooms, or in impersonal centres. Exposing our worst fears, hating our best friends; self-denial, self-denigration. Discovering our collective and individual power and strengths. Hours of screaming, crying, talking, laughing – anger, pain, jealousy, love, hate, joy, fear. Understanding the political context of our personal experiences. Hierarchies breaking down. Trust building up. Sharing skills. Unfeminist desires battled with. Feminist support inside and outside the group. A safe place. A scary place. A very important part of my life.[3]

Other People's Feelings Stir You Up
You are especially likely to be affected by the feelings expressed by close friends, but anyone exploring a problem in a group may touch a raw nerve in you and turn calm into storm clouds in a few minutes. We have said that nobody can make you feel what you do not feel already. However, it is helpful to recognise that there will be times when you aren't ready to have

your feelings stirred up in a particular way and in this case you need to know how to protect yourself from being too affected. Here's an example.

Sue has just been exploring feelings of fear. She is now lying curled up in a blanket. Nora starts to express some angry and violent feelings she has towards her brother. Sue is very open after working, and feels the peace and resolution she had reached being disturbed in a way that is jarring and out of tune with what she needs. She briefly interrupts Nora to explain she doesn't feel ready to be churned up again, and leaves the room.

Another step Sue might have taken would be to ask a group member to put her arms round her as a form of reassurance or protection. Some people perceive emotional energy as a visible phenomenon which can be released by one person into a room, and can then be physically picked up by someone else who is open or vulnerable to it. It is said that if you are in a weak or low-energy state yourself, you are more likely to pick up energy from others. If another woman is expressing feelings which you don't feel ready to deal with, then don't put yourself in the firing line. Certainly don't offer to be the person she has an encounter confrontation with, and don't volunteer to act in her psychodrama. If you are feeling strong you may be able to protect yourself in an active way. Here is an example.

Barry is working in a mixed group. Tina, who has a sexual relationship with him, feels herself drawn in to what he is doing. She feels alternately anger at him, pity for him and anxiety about what the rest of the group will think of him. She realises she is losing touch with herself. She closes her eyes and does a meditation which involves imagining a cone of golden light around her, separating her from Barry and from the rest of the group. She imagines this light is protecting her from picking up emotional vibrations from Barry. She lets herself be aware of who she is, what she is feeling for herself, alone inside this golden cone. When she opens her eyes she feels much stronger, and watches the rest of Barry's work without being overwhelmed or buffeted by emotions triggered by him.

If you are unwilling to do a meditation like this, you may still find that by centering yourself, sitting up straight, feeling your weight on the floor, being aware of your own strength and imagining that you are radiating positive energy towards the person who is working, you may be able to avoid picking up any unwanted energy or emotional charge from them. *Noticing* what it is about their charge that you don't want to deal with can also help you get on top of the emotion, rather than drowning in it.

At other times, feelings expressed in the group may affect you in a positive way. You may learn a lot about yourself by noticing how you respond to what is happening. Or you may find that other people's emotions stimulate and unblock you, bringing to the surface buried feelings which you can fruitfully explore in the group.

Claire is crying about a relationship which has finished. While she is crying one of the other group members, Petra, starts to feel uncomfortable, then sad, then suddenly finds herself crying about a relationship which finished for her over a year ago. Up to this time Petra had felt blocked and out of touch with her emotions about this lost relationship. Claire has helped her to contact and express these emotions. Petra asks one person in the group to sit with her on the other side of the room, and explores these feelings very fruitfully at the same time as Claire continues to work.

At all times be aware how other people's emotions affect you: then you can either 'sit with' that awareness and learn from it, or allow it to bring out feelings of your own, or decide to protect yourself against what may hurt or unbalance you.

'Therapy Is Stupid': Resistances to Therapy

A frequent problem in a self-help group is that an individual in the group expresses difficulties in relation to the therapy process itself. Her difficulty may range from 'I think the whole idea of therapy is stupid' to 'I want to do therapy, but I can't in this group because nobody knows what they're doing'. This kind of remark can seem very threatening. The temptation is to brush it aside and press on with the 'real work' of the session, or to lapse into an intellectual discussion. Both responses are a mistake. These problems can throw up much valuable material to explore in the session. Rather than thinking you should be dealing with something else ('My relationship with my mother', 'What happened at work today'), it is worth stopping to explore thoroughly what you are feeling about doing therapy and what is going on for you here and now in the group. These present feelings will be the most helpful and immediate starting point for you, and if you attempt to ignore them you will be distracted from effectively tackling any other topic. Here is an example.

Laura came to her group saying that she didn't feel like doing therapy and felt anxious. After some discussion the group decided she should work on her anxiety. She tried talking to a cushion but couldn't imagine it was part of herself. She said 'I think doing therapy badly is what it's about for me; not doing things well and worrying about them.' The group suggests she try to remember times in her life when she felt anxious. She runs back through various recent events (work project, marriage, moving) to exams at school and the group suggests she focus on this, as the earliest situation may have set the pattern. She talks about wanting to please her parents by doing well in exams, and how much she hated having to study the teachers' way, learning by rote instead of understanding. The only exam she enjoyed was Botany: she felt it didn't matter, answered two questions she liked instead of four, and did really well in the exam because she had been able to do it her own way.

Diane asked: 'What would be your way of finishing now?' and Laura asked for a stomach massage as she felt tense there.

Afterwards the group said that it was all right for Laura to go at her own pace with therapy and do a little at a time.

Here Laura's anxiety about doing therapy turned out to be linked with earlier anxieties about doing things to please her parents. In other cases, different emotions might be found to underlie the problems which individuals find in doing therapy. Here are some commonly stated difficulties, with some suggestions about how they could be explored in the group:

'I can't do therapy with so much attention on me from all the group.'

Many people experience difficulty in 'taking time' in the group. Most of us are unused to receiving so much positive attention from others and do not feel we deserve it. A woman who makes this objection could explore her fantasies of what will happen if the group does give her their attention ('You'll get bored with me . . .', 'You'll resent me for getting the limelight . . .') and notice what earlier situations this reminds her of ('Every time I got my father's attention, my sisters were jealous of me . . .'). Exercise **135** is also very useful to tackle this issue.

'I don't want to do all that crying and stuff, it's self-indulgent and phoney.'

Here the group could ask: 'Who will think you're self-indulgent?'

'My boyfriend . . . my mother . . . she always used to laugh when I cried and tell me not to be so silly . . .'

'Try acting your mother and then answering her back.'

Or the group could ask: 'What are you afraid will happen if you're self-indulgent?'

'I'll lose grip of everything. Things will become an amorphous mass, I'll lose my sense of who I am . . .' and so on.

'I've got *real* problems, I can't work them out in a therapy group with cushions like you can.'

There is often a note of moral superiority in this objection, and the woman might be asked to go round the group saying to each person in turn 'My problems are more real than yours'. This could be followed by feedback about how it felt to all concerned.

Alternatively, the woman might be asked deliberately to exaggerate in the group how great her problems are, or to tell the group what she gets out of having worse problems than anyone else. This is not to suggest that the woman does not have real problems (so, probably, does every woman in the group), but she may be using this argument as a rationalisation of her fear of doing therapy which might help her.

'I can't do any therapy in this group, because I feel nobody here likes me.'

In this case, it would be good for the woman to check out the reality of her fear by having other group members give her feedback about what they feel towards her. It may turn out that she herself has negative feelings towards other group members which she has projected and attributed to them. She might be helped by feedback from group members who appreciate her presence in the group. Alternatively it may emerge that her difficulty is in fact with one person in particular.

'I can't do any therapy in this group because I don't get on with Kate'.

If you feel a strong antipathy for someone you do not know particularly well, this is not usually a sign that you can't get on together. More often what is happening is that you set things off in one another, or each see in the other person things you don't like in yourself. In this case it would be useful to do together exercise **61** for exploring projections. You will probably find the antipathy very much defused as you separate the real woman from your fantasy of her.

It is a different matter if you are involved with another group member in a close emotional relationship which has become very difficult or hostile. In our experience such women have been able to work productively on their difficulties in the group, but it has sometimes also happened that they have decided to stop coming to the group at the same time, because they found that when in the same group they were so preoccupied with each other they could not give attention to anyone or anything else. These two people may need to take time to work things out between them individually at their own rhythm. After a few weeks or months they are usually able to start attending the same sessions again.

'I don't really want to be here. I feel I've been dragged into this therapy group'.

Here the women could be asked to act out the part of the person who has dragged her to the group ('You really need to go to a therapy group, you know you're in a terrible state, you'll get a lot out of it . . .') as well as the part of the unwilling dragged one ('I don't want to go, I'm frightened, I don't want to change, I don't want to be upset . . .'). She may find from this dialogue that these are two conflicting parts of herself, two voices inside her own head, and this may help her to take responsibility for bringing herself to the group. She might also feel unsure whether other group members want her there.

'I daren't let go into expressing my feelings in this group, because nobody here knows what they're doing.'
This woman might be asked, 'What would happen if you let go?'
'I'd be helpless and vulnerable . . .'
Or she might be asked, 'Who said it is so important to know what you're doing?'
'My father, he always said . . .'

This way of exploring problems with therapy is much more helpful than allowing the session to become a discussion about the advantages and disadvantages of therapy. This is not to say that these objections to doing therapy are always imaginary, or are merely defences. One woman might have a housing problem more urgent for her to resolve than anything she can do in a therapy group. One woman might need a break to incorporate what she's learned and concentrate energy into organising the practicalities of her life. Another woman might be right in feeling that she needs more experienced help: some crises *are* too difficult for a self-help group to cope with. Another woman might find she cannot function within any group as it reminds her too painfully of her boarding school. Another might be right in feeling this is not the time for her to do therapy, or that she is not liked enough in this group to make progress. It is good to set aside a clear time for these issues to be discussed and decided by the woman and the group as a whole. But any resulting decision will be made far more effectively if you can first clarify, using the methods we describe, any past, irrational or displaced feelings which are being projected into the present situation.

Chapter Ten offers several structures to help you clarify whether you need to leave your group, switch to individual or led therapy, or whether there are good reasons for you not to do therapy at all.

None of the Known Techniques or Structures Seem Right for Our Situation

In this case, don't be afraid to improvise freely. You may find you need to break the rules, or need to break your session for a non-therapy activity, for example, to do an hour of consciousness-raising or to go outside and run together. You may find that you need to create a new exercise, using a guided fantasy structure to cover a new topic, using sharing in pairs in a different way or inventing new words for a milling or movement exercise. You may find you need to follow your intuition and imagination to try a new way of using people and props, for example:

A woman who is feeling over-responsible carries another group member on her back to exaggerate the feeling.

A woman who is encumbered by griefs from her past finds a large black plastic sack to drag round the room and finally breaks it up and discards it.

A group where several people are irritable puts a big cushion in the middle for them all to shout at and trample on.

A woman whose husband left her after she had spent three years raising the family and supporting him financially so that he could write his thesis, takes a large newspaper and gains enormous satisfaction from tearing it to small pieces in the group: 'This is the footnote I looked up for you in the library . . .', and so on.

A woman who dreams of a giant penis blocking her path feels that a cushion is not large enough to work with and builds a construction with chairs, cushions and curtains. She makes a connection with her father, and after shouting at the monolith she gently dismantles it, talking to each item as a part of his personality and stating how she would like their relationship to change.

It is your therapy. It is important to see all the techniques in this book as tools to adapt, choose and use in your own way.

What Should I Do if Someone Really Breaks Down?

Most people in therapy situations will expose themselves only as much as they feel safe, and bring up buried material only at the rate they feel they can digest and assimilate it. On very rare occasions someone may go too far in therapy and may then adversely react. More often, people who are not doing any therapy may hit an emotional crisis without any outlet for their feelings. Both these situations can result in a near-breakdown or psychotic-type state where the person is very distressed and their contact with reality is disturbed. Though you may never need it, it is good to have some idea how to help someone experiencing this kind of crisis.[4]

1   *Don't try to 'do therapy' with her.* She will probably be feeling terrified of losing control, and will need calm, support and protection rather than questions to 'get into her emotions'.

2   *Treat her with respect.* Don't be in a hurry to give advice. Listen to her and be accepting. There will always be a part of her which is aware of reality; speak to that part and she will respond.

3   *Stay in touch with yourself.* Be honest and real with her. Be aware if you feel sad or frightened. If you feel out of your depth or cannot cope, admit it.

4   *Get help if you need it.* Talk to her about what her options are. Find out

what is available in her area. Some therapeutic communities are human or caring. Though medicines are abused, they may be needed to keep her out of hospital. If necessary bring someone with more experience to see her, or think about a hospital. Don't feel guilty about this, sometimes we cannot do it all for one another.

After Doing a Lot of Therapy, How Do I Put the Pieces Back Together Again?

When starting self-help therapy, many people are tightly defended against recognising or expressing their own emotions or problems: 'I don't really need therapy, I'm perfectly all right', 'I can cope with life quite well', 'I am not aware of repressing anything'. Discovering you can contact your pain and sadness is an important part of therapy and there is often a phase where you feel worse before you feel better. But if you begin to feel you are sinking forever into a swamp of emotions you may need to reassess what is happening in your group.

It may be that the group has an unspoken morality which says: 'It is good to suffer. The more you suffer, the more you will be liked'. Pain is sometimes more familiar and less frightening than pleasure. Reich pointed out that we need to increase our tolerance for pleasure as well as going deep into our pain. It may be easier to wallow in suffering than to take responsibility for healing yourselves and moving into positive changes in your lives. It is important to remember that therapy is basically about learning to lead a richer and happier life. As David Boadella puts it, '. . . neurosis is the crucifixion, not therapy. Therapy means getting down off the cross and being able to walk and see the sun again; not the passion of wounds forever. It means living and one day dying in your own time and space . . .'[5]

If you feel your group needs more practice in walking in the sun, there are various steps you could take. You might devote some sessions to pleasurable body exercises or positive meditations. You might spend some time discussing how each of you has changed through therapy and what further changes you might like to make. You might decide to meet socially, to go swimming or dancing, bringing your relationships out of the emotional atmosphere of the group and finding you can enjoy doing things together in the world too.

You might also find that you have over-emphasised certain therapy approaches at the expense of others. For example, doing regression work can leave people lost in feelings of pain and impotence dating from their early childhood, if it is not balanced with work in the here-and-now which helps them to say goodbye to the past and experience their power and joy in the present. It is good to achieve an overall balance in the kind of techniques you use. The process should not just be one of taking apart and dissecting, but also of making connections. There must be contact as well as release: making contact with the person or people you do therapy with can be very integrating and relationships between group members in the present should never be ignored.

It is a common tendency for a self-help group to over-emphasise the *release* of emotions. In our enthusiasm for reclaiming our lost language of feeling, we sometimes swing too far the other way, becoming a bundle of raw emotions and expressing feelings all the time, everywhere. Part of the process of re-integration is to recognise that once we have learnt to 'let go', that also gives us the power to decide when we want to 'let go' and when we don't. Alexander Lowen calls this self-possession:

> I have talked about letting go. Containment is equally important and is equally stressed in bioenergetics . . . The containment is conscious and voluntary which presupposes an ability to get go. If one can't let go because the holding is unconscious and structured in the body, one can't speak of containment as a conscious expression of the self. The person doesn't contain; he is contained.[6]

Much of this book has been about how to let ourselves feel, how to let others reach us. But in our lives we need to be able to choose when we don't want another's emotions to affect us, when we don't want to get distressed about something, when it is too painful or dangerous to express our feelings directly. It is important to be in control of our lives in this way. Practising our power to 'contain' is an important part of the process of putting the pieces back together.

It can be helpful to remind ourselves that in any case therapy deals with only one part of our lives. There are many other areas: our material surroundings, financial situation, our spiritual life, political activity, creativity and relationships. Therapy may be a very useful *tool* for helping us deal with those other areas, but it is not a *substitute* for them. The group may need to correct an over-emphasis on the centrality of the emotions. Within each person as a whole organism, our feelings need to be kept in perspective with other aspects of our being: our physical health, our thoughts and understanding, our basic sense of self and identity.

As we have tried to re-integrate ourselves after doing a lot of therapy, it is this last which has been important to many of us: the development of our sense of identity or core. Perhaps the process is not so much one of 'putting the pieces back together' as of finding something at the heart of all the pieces which gives us a sense of sureness and strength, from which we can grow back outwards. Having been conditioned to please and play roles for others, to be a subsidiary and accessory, we often lack a very basic sense of self and self-worth. In our group we moved toward this in a variety of ways. Some of us found we needed to look outside the group and enter a period of individual therapy. Some of us have been helped by Psychosynthesis and other spiritual approaches which emphasise the whole person, integrating the emotions and finding your 'centre', 'essence' or deeper sense of who you are. During therapy many behaviour patterns are challenged and if you are to let go of them you need to have something else to fall back on. It seems to us that a sense of self-worth grows with love, whether the love comes from an individual therapist, from the rest of your group or from a sense of spiritual identity. It is only by each person establishing this basic self-acceptance that she will be able to stop torturing herself and walk in the sun.

Below we list two exercises which may help with this process of balancing the emotions and integrating the therapy experience.

140 Chakra Meditation

This can be helpful for balancing out different areas of your life. It works by leading awareness through the chakras, or body centres, related to different aspects of our being which we described in Chapter Five. One person should read aloud, with sensitivity to what the others are experiencing, and allow several minutes pause between each instruction.

Sit comfortably on a cushion or on the floor. Let your hands be relaxed resting palm upwards on your lap or on your knees. Close your eyes and go inside yourself.

Be aware of your weight on the ground. Be aware of your breath moving in and out of your body. Let yourself relax any tightness you are aware of in your body.

Now send your awareness down your body to your legs and your genital and pelvic area. It may help to imagine breathing out through that part of your body. (*Pause*) Be aware of sensations and memories there.

This is the part of your body which connects with your sexuality, your grounding and the material basis of your life. Ask yourself, now, what do you need in these areas? What does your body need physically? What does your sexuality need? What do you need in other ways in your physical environment – your housing, finances, the food you eat? The answers may come in terms of diet, exercises, information, or social action you need to take towards changing your situation.

Now let your awareness move upwards into your stomach and heart area. It may help to breathe into this part of your body. (*Pause*) This is the area which relates to your emotional life. Be aware of what you find there. Ask yourself again, what do you need in this aspect of your life? Are you too cluttered up with feelings and personal history? Do you need to let them out more? Or make a change in a relationship? What are your main problems in this area of the emotions? Ask what can you do for yourself? And what can another do for you to give you what you need?

Now send your awareness into your head. This is the base of your mental activity: thinking and intellectual occupations. It is also the seat of your intuition and of your spiritual connection. (*Pause*) Ask inside about these areas – the mental, the intuitive, the spiritual – ask what blocks you from expressing yourself freely in those areas? And ask what you need?

Now consider your whole person. How do these areas – the physical, the emotional and the mental – harmonise in you? Do they work together or pull you in different ways? What do you need to do to bring them more into balance with one another?

Now become aware of your breathing again and gradually let your awareness return to the room.

After this meditation it is a good idea to write down the main points which came up for you: the needs you recognised and how you could answer them in your daily life. Then you could share what was most important, in a pair or in the group.

141 Exercise in Disidentification

Although we have reservations about Psychosynthesis, we find this exercise useful to put the emotions in perspective and contact a sense of self which lies beyond the turbulent feelings and the questioning of your personality which you may experience during therapy. You could try doing it every day for a week. It would be a mistake to do it before you have done a lot of therapy, before you have learned to connect with, and identify with, your body and feelings. You really need to 'get into' them before you can start to 'get out' of them and put them in perspective in this way.

Sit in a comfortable relaxed position. If you are alone, read the text through *aloud* slowly to yourself. If you are in a group, one can read it while the others close their eyes. Allow a short pause after each paragraph.

I *have* a body but I *am not* my body. My body may find itself in different conditions of health or sickness; it may be rested or tired . . . My body is my precious instrument of experience and of action in the outer world, but it is *only* an instrument. I treat it well; I seek to keep it in good health, but it is *not* myself. I *have* a body; but I *am not* my body.

I *have* emotions, but I *am not* my emotions. These emotions are countless, contradictory, changing, and yet I know that I always remain I, *my-self*, in times of hope or despair, in joy or in pain, in a state of irritation or of calm. Since I can observe and understand my emotions, and then increasingly direct and utilise them, it is evident that *they are not myself*. I *have* emotions, but I *am not* my emotions.

I *have* an intellect, but I *am not* my intellect. It is more or less developed and active; it is undisciplined but teachable; it is an organ of knowledge in regard to the outer world as well as the inner; but *it is not myself.* I *have* an intellect, but *I am not* my intellect.

What am I then? What remains after discarding from my self-identity the physical, emotional and mental contents of my personality, of my ego? It is the essence of myself – a centre of pure self-consciousness and self-realisation. It is the permanent factor in the ever varying flow of my personal life. It is that which gives me the sense of being, of permanence, of inner security. This centre not only has a static self-awareness but also a dynamic power; it is capable of observing, directing and using all the psychological processes and the physical body. *I am a centre of awareness and of power.*[7]

NOTES

1   Frederick S. Perls, *Gestalt Therapy Verbatim*, Real People Press, Lafayette, California, 1969; Bantam Books, New York, 1971, p 171.
2   Described by Hogie Wyckoff in Claude Steiner (ed), *Readings in Radical Psychiatry*, Grove Press, New York, 1975, pp 87–9.
3   From 'Red Therapy', Red Therapy Group, c/o 28 Redbourne Avenue, London N3 2BS, 1978, p 44.
4   These notes are indebted to *The Radical Therapist*'s advice sheet on 'Handling Psychiatric Emergencies'.
5   David Boadella in Jenny James, *Room to Breathe*, Coventure, London, 1975, p 227.
6   Alexander Lower, *Bioenergetics*, Coventure, London, 1976, p 298;reprinted by Penguin, Harmondsworth and New York, 1976.
7   Based on Roberto Assagioli, *Psychosynthesis*, Turnstone Books, London, 1975; Penguin, New York, 1976, pp 118–19. We have adapted and altered it slightly.

Chapter Ten
Getting What You Need from Therapy

Here we answer some common questions about choosing the therapy you need. Our answers come from discussions in our own group and with many other women. Where we compare the relative merits of different forms of therapy we keep the descriptions brief as you will find fuller accounts of the theory and practice throughout this book. Here we concentrate on how to match a woman's specific needs to what is available.

Although we have our own views as to which therapy may be most effective, we recognise that the fluid state of knowledge about therapy is such that, ultimately, the choice will be made on grounds of personal preference and availability. An important dimension will be your feelings about how you can work most securely, whether it is in a self-help therapy group, a led group or with an individual therapist.

CHOOSING THE RIGHT KIND OF THERAPY

If you often find your emotions getting lost in words, or feel flat and depressed rather than being aware of experiencing particular emotions such as anger, fear, joy or neediness, then it may be good to start with an expressive therapy.

Encounter and Bioenergetics
Both Encounter and Bioenergetics offer ways to learn to contact and experience your power and energy and can be used as a direct attack on blocks when you feel dead in your body or in your relationships.

If you want to look at your social relationships, Encounter is more useful.

Jean felt lifeless and unable to relate to people. She found the gentle pace of her self-help group left her untouched and decided to go to a forty-eight-hour Encounter marathon. This frontal attack on her resistances showed her that she *could* feel and gave her confidence to change herself emotionally.

If you want to focus on self-awareness, especially body awareness, try Bioenergetics: you will need to check what sort of Bioenergetics you are going to use. See Chapter Five for a description of the difference between blockbusting work, which is the sort we are discussing here, and the more subtle forms.

Susan found a six-week bioenergetics group helpful when starting therapy as she felt too split off from her body and the possibility of expressing emotions physically. She was so aware of the ways in which she hated her body and saw it only in relation to other people's use for or awareness of it that she couldn't let herself feel any pleasure – or much pain – in her body. Bioenergetics helped her in a concentrated way.

Both Bioenergetics and Encounter can feel too drastic, can leave you feeling that you have too little control over what is going on. This is a problem for women as it reflects what we often feel in the rest of our lives. In Encounter the group process can appear to take over and we can get too focused on the emotional dynamic between ourselves and others. In Bioenergetics, where the work is in the body and less in the conscious world of choice, the control is more with the therapist or group leader who understands what is happening in your body. The intense emotional and physical experience may feel too far removed for you to relate them to daily experiences and conflict.

It is always a mistake to feel you 'should' do any type of therapy. Sometimes women say 'I feel I ought to do Encounter' and this may follow a pattern of 'shoulds', of being over-conscientious, which brought the woman into therapy in the first place. In our group we made a mistake when we persuaded Janet to go to an introductory encounter group. At that point in her life her husband had just left and she was faced with the emotional and practical difficulties of coping with two small children on her own. The Encounter group, far from being a safe place to discharge some emotions and get some relief, made her freeze up, fearful that involving herself in the group would tip her over the edge and make her lose what control she did have left over her life.

If you want to work on increasing your self-awareness in a more gentle way, Co-counselling or Gestalt may be more suitable.

Co-counselling

A good starting point as it involves working in pairs, which some women find easier than coping with the attention of the whole group. (Also, this is an excellent technique if you don't have a group but do have a friend interested in working with you.)

The woman who is being the client is in control, which can be a new experience for many women who have always felt controlled in relationships. It gives clear time to each person. Again, this is important for women as we often feel our need for time and space comes last.

It helps to focus on what is positive about yourself and its techniques are designed to help you discharge emotion. It helps you to *listen* in a positive and accepting way.

Co-counselling does not, however, really allow for confrontation, and the emphasis on discharge has limitations, just as the emphasis on the positive can feel mushy and unreal. Yet Co-counselling remains the most accessible form of self-help therapy as it requires only two people to work at a time and recognises the value of the simplest therapeutic technique: giving concentrated attention.

We have found it useful to use Co-counselling amongst our group members, particularly when someone is in crisis and wants immediate attention.

Gestalt

Gestalt concentrates on feelings and body awareness in the *present*. It does not work by confronting resistances, as Encounter does, but makes you aware of your resistance and helps you feel your 'stuckness'. Gestalt can help a woman who may have got stuck in discharging a particular emotion while co-counselling.

Gestalt has the advantage of combining the verbal with the physical and can be used for working on interpersonal relationships.

It can clarify the emotional meaning of dreams and fantasies.

Gestalt is one of the simplest therapy techniques to learn to use in a self-help situation (and much subtlety can be developed) but in spite of its emphasis on body language as well as talking, it is easy to get lost in words. Also sometimes women who are feeling in severe crisis find that Gestalt emphasises their splits to the point where they feel terrified of disintegrating. Again: *do only what feels comfortable and right*. Speak up if you become frightened while doing Gestalt or any other kind of work.

Pysychodrama

Not the easiest way for a self-help group to work, but it can be used in time. Psychodrama puts a premium on sensitivity to your own and other people's feelings so you are unlikely to get lost in intellectualisation. If you want to go to a professionally led group, Psychodrama may be a good starting point as it encourages direct expression of emotion through verbal and bodily means which allows the therapy to relate clearly to everyday experiences.

All of these approaches seem far too frightening to me. I want to be more self-aware but don't feel ready to launch into the kind of emotional exposure you describe. How can I start?
You may find it easier to increase you emotional awareness by giving some time and attention to your body first. You could do this through dance, by joining a dance group; through massage if you feel you could get pleasure from a massage and learning to massage others, or even from one of the more formalised Eastern bodywork approaches like T'ai Chi or Yoga.

The Alexander Technique is also based on a theory which combines bodywork with emotional understanding. This technique, which works with relaxation, posture and alignment, is based on the work of Frederick Matthias Alexander earlier this century.

Some women find bodywork most terrifying of all since many of their deepest fears are tied up with trying to ignore their bodies as much as possible. If you feel this, don't push it.

Which forms of therapy have a spiritual aspect and how would I choose between them?
We think it is important to have a grounding in work on your emotions and body before you get very involved in psychic or spiritual work, so that you avoid a situation where you are dealing with more esoteric experiences without having much awareness of how you feel or interact with others.

Jungian analysis and Psychosynthesis both approach spirituality through the emotions, using symbols and symbolic representation as part of their tools for reaching spiritual awareness. While Jungian analysts use talking and artwork, Psychosynthesis also uses guided fantasy and other types of meditation.

Another approach to spirituality is through bodywork. Intuitive massage and healing use the ability to tune into another person's bodily energy as a healing agent. There are also the oriental body disciplines like T'ai Chi and Yoga which combine the physical and spiritual and can balance emotional therapy.

I want to do therapy which takes me further than increasing my awareness of what I am feeling. I want to explore the roots of my present day patterns which I seem to be stuck in. Maybe this will mean going back to look at my childhood. What sort of therapy will help me to do this?
The therapies which are most appropriate for this kind of exploration are Bioenergetics, Primal therapy and the various forms of psychoanalytic therapy, though you may also be able to do relevant work using Gestalt,

Psychodrama or Transactional Analysis. Practitioners and theorists of all three of the main regression therapies have made claims that theirs is the only way to work at what is often described as 'the deepest level'. This makes it difficult to select, particularly as people often take a strong partisan line. We have described all three approaches fully in Chapters Five and Eight. Here we will try to compare them.

Bioenergetics and Primal therapy are similar in that both encourage a person literally to regress and relive a childhood experience in the belief that reexperiencing early childhood pains will increase our capacity to feel in the present. Both use body work; both can be used effectively in self-help groups and both can also lead people into strong and painful emotions which they may have difficulty integrating or understanding unless special care is taken to help the person who has regressed to understand what has taken place and to relate it to her current experience. Such a direct approach can both unblock feelings which have lain dormant for years and have an energising and positive effect on people who have felt hopeless about themselves. Bioenergetics has the particular strength of working through the body and is thus able to tap emotions which are incredibly hard to reach in any other way.

The psychoanalytic therapies are somewhat different. They rely on verbal communication and the structured relationship between the therapist and client or patient. This means that although psychoanalytic *insights and theory* may be important for self-help groups, the approach itself cannot be applied. Psychoanalytic therapy involves talking about childhood and only re-experiencing it in the present through the transference relationship with the therapist; does not use bodywork; uses the relationship between the therapist and client as a way of keeping constant contact between past and present realities; can also unblock feelings but in a far slower and less dramatic way than Primal or Bioenergetics.

The experience of starting with the more 'expressive' forms of therapy and later turning to therapy which uses talking and the transference relationship, seems to be quite common.

I felt I needed therapy which involved talking and communication. I can regress and have a primal in an almost solipsistic way and this does not touch on the real difficulty I have in being close to people. I chose to do individual therapy with someone whom I felt I could trust to stay with me through all my withdrawals, outbursts of anger and silences: someone who uses our relationship to explore my difficulties in relating to others.

Often women are most distressed in the area of intimate relationships. Therapies which use the relationship between therapist and client as a basic tool for exploring the client's emotional and fantasy life can offer the possibility for a woman to find a different resolution for her inner conflicts within the process of exploring this relationship. This is not something which can be done in self-help therapy.

What guidelines can I apply to my choice of which approach to start with, whether in self-help or professional therapy?
There is no simple way of knowing which form of therapy will be the best starting point for you. People who have a great deal of therapy experience and who have seen many women in the process of change may sometimes have a good sense of what an individual needs. Unfortunately many professional therapists who might have the experience to make this kind of assessment are partisan to one form of therapy, making it difficult to rely on their judgement. Here are some guidelines which come from our experience and will help you to assess for yourself where you can best start therapy.

1   Think about your own life history, or do an exercise which charts your life history. See how far back your distress seems to go. If you find your problems appear to be fairly recent, associated with a particular crisis for instance, you will not want to start off with one of the regression-focused therapies. Of course, you may discover more about yourself when you start doing therapy, but you can always change your approach then.

2   Try to distinguish whether you first need help in learning to experience your feelings. If so you will want to start with one of the 'expressive' therapies such as Bioenergetics, Encounter, Gestalt or Psychodrama.

3   Try to decide if you will respond best to a full-blast direct approach (Encounter) *or a more subtle one* (Gestalt).

4   Are you already bursting with feelings? You may be someone who has trouble controlling your feelings or you may have been through a crisis which aroused emotions you do not normally express. Try to decide whether you would find it threatening to do therapy which actively encouraged you to release strong emotions. Perhaps your emotions are so near the surface anyway that you need a form of therapy which helps you to contain them. Try Gestalt, or a psychoanalytically based therapy.
Others who tend to feel overwhelmed by their emotions find it a relief to be in a therapy situation where expressing emotions is a 'norm'. They find they can accept the strength of their emotions more easily when they see others doing the same thing. It can help them to have self-control in other areas of their lives if they know that they can use therapy as a place to release feelings. If you identify with this you might find doing an encounter group, Bioenergetics or Psychodrama appropriate.

5   *If you find the idea of any particular form of therapy threatening, ask yourself what it is you are trying to avoid.* Don't feel you have to push yourself into whatever is more difficult for you.

6   *Do you really want to change?* If you choose a particular form of therapy, try to look behind your choice and see how it might be collusive with your *not* changing.

7   *Have you changed types of therapy often?* If you find yourself frequently changing therapies, groups or therapists, ask yourself whether you are really looking for the right sort of therapy for you, or are you attempting to avoid something you do not want to face?

CHOOSING BETWEEN INDIVIDUAL AND GROUP THERAPY

Group Therapy
A group can have the advantage of breaking down taboos about being expressive in public, can give you valuable feedback on how you relate to others, can show you how your feelings are not as extraordinary and shameful as you feared since they often seem to be shared by other women in the group. Watching other women in a group can enable you to work through similar feelings, or can spark off previously hidden emotions.

> Caroline found that she could confide safely in other group members who were not her intimates and that her feelings were sometimes similar to theirs. It took some of the fear out of her closest relationships and was a new experience for someone who had been brought up to believe that expressing feelings in public was laughable.

In a therapy group you work on two levels, both on individual issues you bring into the group from the outside, for example, events that have troubled you during the day, a crisis in a relationship, childhood experiences, and also on the issues that come up through the actual experience of *being in a group*. For example, in one group a woman sat silently through two hours then burst out, resentfully, that she felt there was never enough time for her problems. There was always someone whose problems were worse. As she talked it emerged that she was feeling in the group exactly as she had felt in her family where her role had been that of stable elder sister and she had had to deny her own unhappiness.

You may be interested in group therapy precisely because you have difficulties in coping with group situations. Group therapy seems particularly appropriate for women who spend a lot of time in groups, for example, in their work place, but find groups emotionally difficult.

Sometimes we feel we *ought* to be in a group, rather than doing individual therapy, to avoid keeping our emotions private and repeating the patterns of an intense couple relationship within an intense one-to-one therapy relationship. Feeling you ought to be in a group does not seem to us to be a good reason for choosing group rather than individual therapy. Individual therapy means acknowledging that you are important enough to be given time each week and this can be taking as much of a stand against your conditioning as sharing your private emotions in a group. It is misguided to think that a woman who chooses to do individual therapy rather than joining a group is abdicating her sense of social responsibility or sisterhood.

You don't necessarily have to choose between a group and individual therapy. You can do both. For some women a group may feel like the safest place to do therapy while others may feel they want to try a group after they have had some time in individual therapy. The important thing, again, is to avoid 'shoulds' and to *take what you feel you want.*

Individual Therapy

You may feel that you have satisfactory work, activities and relationships with friends but that it is in the area of intimate, often sexual, relationships that you feel blocked. If this is so for you, an intimate one-to-one relationship with a therapist, though it may sound frightening, may also seem the appropriate place to explore difficulties with intimacy.

Another common feeling for women which may direct you towards individual therapy, is a lack of identity, or sense of self, which may go along with the belief that other people's feelings are always more real and important than your own. A woman who felt like this said, 'When I was in a therapy group my emotions were always stimulated by someone else. In individual therapy I am left with myself for company. It is very uncomfortable but it brings me face to face with how little I feel there is of me.'

In individual therapy *you provide the input* and in that sense you do have control over what happens, although it often feels, as a strong transference relationship develops with the therapist, as if she is directing you along certain paths and tabooing others. And of course it is always possible that she is working badly and *is* doing this. The only check is to confront her and see what emerges. *Trust your instincts.*

How Do I Choose Between a Self-Help Therapy Group and a Professionally Led Group?

We have written this book because our own experience of being in a self-help group has been so important for us. A self-help group can be more than a place to do therapy: it can provide a small section of the community, a social grouping, in which normal taboos on showing what you are feeling do not apply. This has felt very important to us as one of our criticisms of society is that it constantly crushes our emotional lives. We needed to know that we were not alone in wanting to change this but, equally, we recognised that we could not assume it would always be acceptable to show what we were feeling. The knowledge that we needed one another inside and outside the group, and were not held together by a paid leader, gave us the sense that group members really *wanted* to help:

> In the group I felt a lot of healing energy. There were a lot of people helping me. I really felt this help and knew it would continue.

> I've done a lot of work in therapy. I can feel myself changing and it hasn't cost me a penny. Also, I feel that my therapy is in my control. It's my therapy and I can stop it when I want to. We have an agreement in my group that if someone wants to stop working she just says 'gooseberry' (that's the word we've chosen) and the group will stop pushing her.

It is important that in self-help therapy we are not having to pay for access to specialist knowledge. It is immensely valuable to find that knowledge in ourselves. Self-help therapy is a way to demystify the expertise of a professional therapist and to validate people's collective power when they co-operate with a common aim. We discuss this further in Chapter Eleven.

In some ways *going* to a led group is easier than *doing* a self-help group. In a led group the organisation and responsibility is carried for you. You are unlikely to develop a supportive network outside the group, as with self-help; nor will you have the satisfaction of feeling it is your group which you run for yourselves. The dynamics of the two groups will be different. In a led group there is an obvious authority figure, while in a self-help group one or two may emerge from among the 'siblings'. What you will get from a led group, though, is skill or particular expertise and sometimes we have found this very valuable. Some approaches, such as Bioenergetics and Psychodrama, are learned more easily in this way. This can also be true for understanding the group process which is made easier in a group which has the security of a leader to take responsibility while group members explore feelings between themselves. We found that we took the approaches and techniques used in led groups back to our self-help group and gained from combining both experiences.

You may feel that you don't want to have the responsibility that a self-help group demands. You may be holding a family together and want a therapy situation with a stable structure that you can rely on. You may worry about giving and not getting and feel more sure *your* needs will be met in a led group. For you a led group could be better. Ask for recommendations or try out a one-day group or workshop before committing yourself. Unpretentious leaders who are clear about their responsibilities and limitations have always been most helpful to us. There are some therapists, working with groups and/or individually, who are sensitive to what is happening in a person's body or can intuit what a person is feeling in a way which comes from experience and this is rare in self-help groups, but can be achieved with time and confidence.

How Can I Choose Between Co-counselling and Individual Therapy?

We have found that Co-counselling and individual therapy have quite different things to offer, even though both involve an individual rather than a group relationship.

Co-counselling does not usually mean that you will co-counsel exclusively with one other person. If this is what you want, Co-counselling is probably not for you. However, it does give you the possibility of having one person's undivided attention and has the advantage that you will reciprocate. This can feel very safe for women who have difficulty taking time in a group and feel they don't want to deal with this issue within a group until they have consolidated the experience of having their own space. It is an equal relationship, which means that you do not have to deal with the issues that arise in a power relationship of the kind that inevitably exists in individual therapy. It is also free after the initial training group. These are the reasons you may find Co-counselling a good starting point for your therapy.

As well as being a good starting point, Co-counselling can be useful as a continuing resource: an easily accessible form of therapy to use when you need it. If you have to face a difficult situation you can co-counsel on your fears and, having discharged some emotion, feel able to face the real situation employing the strengths you have at your command. The Re-evaluation Counselling network also has the advantage of being international and having workshops for particular groupings, including men, women, and groups based on class and racial background, among whom you can find Co-counselling partners.

Choosing to do individual therapy means choosing a relationship in which you do not reciprocate equally, in which you take but do not give back similar attention. For some of us this has been a crucial part of working on our conditioning as women/mothers/givers and developing our capacities for taking without guilt.

WHAT IS FEMINIST THERAPY?

Women frequently think there is one particular school of therapy based on a feminist theory of women's psychological development and using techniques which are different from other forms of therapy. In reality, feminist therapy has not reached this state of coherent development.

There are feminists like ourselves who have come into therapy through our involvement in the women's liberation movement. There are women who are trying to integrate their training as therapists with their understanding, as developed within the women's movement, of women's role in society. This is further complicated because among the feminists involved in therapy, as in other areas of the women's movement, there are different analyses of the roots of women's oppression. As socialist feminists we believe that a fundamental alteration in women's emotional lives will be possible only when there has been a basic change in the social structure into which girls are socialised and which determines the nature of our emotional lives. We recognise that this assumption is not shared by all feminist therapists, some of whom have goals more in line with the views of the growth movement.

The assumption which is shared by all feminists involved in therapy, however, is that as women we are brought up to be second-class citizens in a male-defined world, and that this deeply affects our emotional lives. It follows that the role of a feminist therapist, or a feminist self-help therapy group, is not to *adjust* us to being second-class citizens but to help us to explore how this experience has affected us, what a struggle it is to have our ways of seeing the world validated, and how we can make ourselves stronger.

At the simplest level, feminist therapy will understand that a woman who is unresponsive sexually in heterosexual relationships may be adopting this as her unconscious strategy in a power struggle, not as a form of 'sickness', and will try to find ways of enabling her to struggle directly which do not involve her own self-denial. Feminist therapy will recognise that a woman who is a lesbian does not come to therapy to be cured of her lesbianism any more than a heterosexual woman comes to be cured of her heterosexuality, but rather that both women may have many painful experiences, inside and outside the sexual arena, which they wish to explore.

Beyond these basic assumptions you will find feminists involved in all types of therapy. Broadly speaking there are *three* tendencies we have distinguished.

1   Some feminist therapy has consisted of combining approaches developed in the growth movement with an understanding of women's oppression and its implications for our present experience. This has been how we have worked in our self-help group and this book most strongly reflects that.

We have recognised the value of bodywork, Gestalt, Encounter, Psychodrama and other therapies for women, while rejecting some of the assumptions of the growth movement and being critical of some aspects of all these therapies. For example, in this book, we explain how Encounter can teach us how to confront one another more directly but recognise it can be harmful when it exacerbates the problems many women already have in separating their own and other people's feelings.

The techniques of feminists who practise as professional therapists probably differ little from those used by non-feminist therapists. However, the way they use those techniques is different, their assumptions about women and their understanding of the contradictions posed for women in our society will be shaped by their feminist consciousness.

2   *Radical therapy:* The techniques used in Radical therapy, as it has been developed in San Francisco, are taken from Transactional Analysis and the groups are called 'problem solving' rather than therapy groups. In the groups, women make contracts about how they want to change. The group encourages women to be explicit, assertive and supportive while breaking into each other's games and collusions. They tend to emphasise the ways in which women deny themselves power in the present and aim to encourage them to behave differently. They focus on a woman's *conscious* experience. In most therapy used by feminists the assumption is that for us to regain our power we need to look at our histories and our unconscious conflicts. We would see radical therapy groups as being helpful in a limited way. Gaining control over a particular aspect of your life can be strengthening, but for many women who seek therapy the need is for a deeper exploration of what it is inside us that *prevents us from changing*.

Problem solving groups in the USA are each run by a leader who is a member of the Radical Therapy Collective. In Holland feminists have set up a network of self-help radical therapy groups which use a modified form of the American technique, combined with Co-counselling. Experienced members attend a new group for a limited period to start the group off. In other countries this form of therapy has not been used extensively but there are groups, such as those centred on assertion training for women, which work at the same conscious level. In our self-help group we found some of the ideas useful and have explained these in Chapter Eight.

3   Feminist therapists have also been working psychoanalytically, using the transference relationship between the therapist and client as the basic vehicle of the therapy. They are attempting to develop a feminist theory of emotional development of women from what they are learning in their practice. Neither of the previously described tendencies in feminist therapy are oriented towards doing this; the growth movement therapists because they do not work on the basis of assumptions about developmental psychology; the radi-

cal therapists because they are not primarily interested in unconscious processes. The theory and practice of feminist therapy of this kind are discussed more fully in Chapter Eight.

CHOOSING A THERAPIST

Although this is primarily a book about self-help therapy we have suggested that no single form of therapy excludes others, that some people may be unable to work in a self-help group; others may find that they want a period of individual therapy after being in a self-help group. So we also see this book as a guide to professional therapy and recognise that the first difficulty may be knowing where to look for a therapist. Obviously we cannot give specific recommendations, but here are some guidelines.

Finding a Feminist Therapist
If you want a feminist therapist, or at least a therapist known to have been sympathetic to other feminists, use the women's liberation movement for contacts. In the USA now there are feminist therapist referral agencies in many large cities. If no such agency exists, or in Britain where at present only London has a Women's Therapy Centre which can act as a referral agency, contact the local Women's Centre for information about therapists working in the area. If they have no information, have they got contacts with individual women who have done some therapy or do they know of any feminists working in an allied field, such as counselling or social work? Use the women's movement network of contacts and feed your own information back into it.

Therapy Institutions
Remember you can do individual therapy in any of the approaches we have described such as Gestalt, Psychosynthesis, Psychoanalysis, Intuitive Massage and so on. Most have their own institutes or centres, for example, Centre for Bio-Energy, Institute of Psychoanalysis. There are also 'growth centres' which offer a programme of groups within the range of the growth movement therapies: often the group leaders work as individual therapists and can be contacted through the centre.

Free or Low Cost Therapy
In Britain it is sometimes possible to get free individual therapy either through the National Health Service or through specific counselling agencies. This is worth exploring through your own doctor or even through the local social services office. Make it clear that you are looking for therapy or counselling as doctors tend to resort very quickly to drugs, treating you as if you

had an attack of 'depression' a bit like an attack of 'bronchitis'. There are some centres which offer therapy to 'young people' (usually defined as under twenty-five). There are also places like the unpromisingly titled Family Welfare Association which give free psychoanalytic-type therapy.

Some therapy institutes offer reduced rates with students who are training under the supervision of experienced therapists. If you can cope with making enquiries it is worth exploring these possibilities.

Trust vs Technique

We have found that liking and trusting a therapist may be as important as whether she is a bioenergeticist or primarily uses Psychodrama. It is worth keeping an open mind. One woman in our group was committed to Bioenergetics and cynical about Psychoanalysis. She ended up choosing a feminist therapist who worked psychoanalytically. Another woman who also wanted a Bioenergetic therapist could not find one she liked and compromised by finding a woman therapist she felt she could trust, and doing some bodywork separately in a group situation.

A Man or a Woman Therapist?

Many women will feel that only a woman therapist will be able to identify with their experience. They will not trust an unequal relationship with a man. For many women their relationship with their mother is a central issue and this can usually be best worked through with a woman therapist. Some women have chosen to work with a male therapist for specific reasons. Two women in our group explained why they made this choice.

I feel I have been very destructive in one-to-one relationships with men and I need to work through this in therapy with a man.

I knew I needed to do therapy with a man because my relationship with my father was so problematic and so were my relationships with men, but I chose a woman first. Maybe I needed mothering first and then I was ready to do the most difficult thing. I think if I'd started with a male therapist I'd have cut off and resisted.

Interviewing a Prospective Therapist

It is hard to tell whether you trust someone you do not know to engage in what could be a very important and close relationship. If the therapist you are interested in runs groups it is certainly worth going to a group or workshop to see how you feel about working with her. The normal practice is to have an initial interview when you can tell the prospective therapist about yourself and ask her about how she works. It is very easy to feel intimidated in this interview situation, to imagine that the therapist can see right through you and is interpreting your every movement and sniff. Remember that you are choosing someone to help *you*. *Your* feelings and *your* need for information about her are of primary importance. Try not to worry about hurting her feelings. You will want some practical information about when the therapist can see you, how often she will expect to see you and what she charges. Some therapists like to see you once a week, some prefer twice a week or even more often (this is usually in the more psychoanalytic types of therapy) while some start with once a fortnight: often this will be a bioenergetic therapist who feels that you'll need two weeks to deal with the emotions stirred up in the therapy. Arrange a time which is comfortable for both of you. If you agree to a time which is awkward for you, does this fit a pattern of not meeting your own needs? If you can, choose a time when you don't have to rush away immediately afterwards, but can digest what has happened in the therapy session. Ask how long sessions will be. Some are fifty minutes, some an hour, some longer. Most therapists give you your time, no more and no less, so being punctual can be important. Ask about this too.

Get the financial arrangements between yourself and your therapist straight. We can't really give you an indication of what is *reasonable* to expect to pay for individual therapy since we do not believe we should have to pay for therapy. You can work out what you can afford and have some sense of going rates, which will vary from place to place and over time. The therapist often has, in her terms, good reasons for charging what may seem like high fees: usually to do with insecurity of being a private therapist (no guaranteed income, no holidays or sick leave with pay) and the high cost of her own training, supervision and therapy. Some therapists ask you to pay for the initial interview (which makes it harder for you to shop around for a therapist you like) but most don't. Check this out beforehand. Some therapists operate a sliding scale of charges, either having a fixed scale according to your income, or telling you what the sliding scale is and asking you to decide what you should pay.

The practical questions are easier to deal with. Questions about how she works, her training, her views on therapy and on women are often more difficult to be straightforward about. *Prepare yourself beforehand.*

Here are some points you can raise:

About her background:
What kind of training has she had?
Is she affiliated to any group or institute or does she have any other form of contact with people with whom she can discuss her work?

The nature of the therapy:
Ask her to describe a session to you.
How does she see the therapy relationship?

Does she work with transference?
How does she think the therapy she practises works?

Her views on women:
How does she think women get fulfilment in life: mainly through home and children or does she recognise the validity of seeking other kinds of satisfactions?
What does she think about bisexual and lesbian relationships?
Ask her how she feels about/relates to the women's liberation movement.

There are no correct answers to these questions, in the sense that they will guarantee you a good therapist. You may find that her readiness to answer these sort of questions is as important to you as the content of the answers. You may also find that what matters to you most is whether or not you feel understood: the relationship between therapist and client can be a very strong and loving one.

I need help badly. Will the therapist's politics make any difference?
We have put so much effort into developing a feminist and socialist perspective on therapy because we believe that therapy and politics are *not* separate issues. This book, and our work in feminist and self-help therapy, is our contribution to the project of developing a politically conscious approach to therapy. We discuss this more specifically in Chapter Eleven.

Much of the skill and experience available in therapy is in the hands of men or women who have not had much contact with the ideas of the women's liberation movement and may not have much sympathy with them. If you do work with a therapist whose political views are different from your own, you will have to work out whether she has sufficient integrity to treat you like a person rather than a patient and will, therefore, respect the differences in your viewpoints.

One woman who was looking for some help for her child rejected one clinic because they did not seem to be treating her or her child as people. They failed to tell her in a straightforward way what the possibilities were of her actually being offered any therapy; they ignored a long letter she had written trying to explain the nature of the problem and the kind of help she was looking for; they applied a rigid formula interview without considering its appropriateness to the situation. There was no discussion of political principles, though this kind of treatment reflects a clinic's underlying social and political biases.

We think that where we have worked successfully with therapists who do not share our political perspective this has been possible because:

We have been supported in our views of the relationship between therapy and politics by our self-help group and increasingly by the development of ideas within the women's movement.

We have clarified our differences with the therapist before starting work so that we know each other's assumptions. There may even be an agreement not to infringe on certain areas.

We have done enough therapy to have a clear idea of our need for particular skills which may not always be available within a feminist context. (Part of the point of our own work is to encourage other feminists to develop these skills.)

WILL I FEEL WORSE BEFORE I FEEL BETTER?

Behind this question lies the fear that if you start doing therapy you may discover all kinds of horrible or frightening things inside yourself that are best left alone, or you may open the floodgates of a torrent of emotion which you will not be able to contain. Women are often quite conscious of these kinds of fears. 'If I start expressing my dependency I will never stop', 'If I show my needs no one will ever be able to meet them'. There are other fears too. 'Will I be able to continue in my present life style, doing my job, looking after my family?', 'Will I lose something precious, such as my drive or my capacity to do creative work?'

You will probably feel relieved when you start doing some therapy. Getting over the hurdle of making the decision is a relief in itself, but also having a safe place to take these feelings, or discovering that you can feel something other than stuck and confused, will give you confidence.

Some people are so frightened initially they freeze up and can't do anything in the first few sessions. This is an unpleasant experience but if it happens to you don't despair. There is nothing unusual about being scared in a new situation. Stay with your fear and try to talk about it.

You are more likely to start feeling worse after you have been doing therapy for a few months. It can help you to get through a bad patch if you know what is happening and can see that it is a sign you are changing.

You may feel worse because you are giving up your old ways of protecting yourself. This may mean giving up a symptom (for example, tension pains), an addiction (cigarette smoking) or a former level of inner deadness and depression.

You may have hit a block. Experiencing your confusion and resistance, what Perls called 'going down the black hole', can be excruciating. You may feel better when you actually experience the pain you've been resisting.

You may be experiencing some past pain (reliving intense jealousy at your younger brother's birth) and have not yet found a way of integrating it, living with it amicably, or recognising that your childhood fears were wrong.

HOW LONG DOES THERAPY TAKE? HOW WILL I KNOW WHEN IT HAS ENDED?

We see therapy as a continuing process. You may want to work on yourself in different ways throughout your life. This is likely to mean that at different times you may want to work on pressing conflicts or distress, or explore a new aspect of yourself: perhaps massage if you have never done any bodywork, or by going to a group for new mothers if you are about to have a baby.

Self Help
People were often surprised to find that after five years we were still active members of a self-help therapy group. This is probably because they see therapy on a medical model where a sick person enters treatment and leaves when she is 'cured'. In our group we all felt that we had more control over our lives and more satisfying experiences than five years previously, but we still found that we could use our group for discussion, support and for doing therapy together when we needed to. A self-help group can change in this way to suit the members' needs.

Professional Therapy
The question of leaving or ending therapy is more pressing where you are working with a therapist individually or in a led group. When you are starting therapy it can feel quite daunting to enter a process not knowing whether to expect a six-week or a six-year involvement, especially if you have heard stories about people who have been 'in analysis' for years. Equally it can feel scary to start opening up to someone, or in a group, if you are afraid that the therapy will end before you are ready for it to stop.

If you start therapy with a particular problem it is worth looking carefully at your own life history and trying to assess honestly whether this problem is really part of a continuing pattern. For instance, in 'compulsive eating' therapy we often find that a woman who remembers having problems with eating or being fat since early childhood is *likely* to take longer to work through her compulsive eating problem than a woman who has only recently started eating compulsively, possibly in response to an obvious change in her circumstances such as a move to a new country, a marriage or the birth of her first child.

However, there are no hard and fast rules about how long therapy will last, or how to know when you are ready to end it. Common sense might indicate that therapy ends when the problems which brought you to therapy in the first place have been resolved, but you will probably already be aware that therapy is not that sort of process. Here are some indications which you may find helpful.

1   If you want to leave therapy, first check out whether or not you feel stuck. If you do, see 'Being Stuck' immediately below in this chapter and try some of the exercises we suggest there.

2   If you feel more confident that your perceptions of people and situations are based on what is happening in the present, rather than using current events as a sort of jumping off point for your fantasy life, then you may feel ready to stop therapy.

3   If you feel that you are able to recognise more easily than before when good things are happening for you, and organise your life so that your experience corresponds more closely to what you claim to want for yourself (obviously within the limitations of social reality), you will probably be feeling less in need of therapy.

4   If you are someone who has difficulty in experiencing feelings of dependency, learning to do so in therapy may be an indication that you have made a major change. Other women who quickly feel dependent and childlike in therapy may be ready to leave when they begin to experience themselves as an adult in relationship to their therapist.

Even professional therapy is not a once and for ever process with a final ending. For some women it may be more helpful to do a period of therapy and return later when they feel the need.

I have done quite a bit of therapy but I still feel stuck in some ways. What should I do now? Should I leave my self-help group (or my therapist)?
This happens to everyone who is doing therapy. You will need to discover whether your being stuck is part of a therapeutic process which you can work through in the therapy situation, or whether you either need to leave therapy or work on your problems in a different way.

Try to make some assessment of your present emotional position. Ask yourself how you felt when you started to do therapy, what has changed or moved for you, and what aspects of yourself you feel are not changing. It can be helpful to do this on your own *and* in your current therapy framework (with your self-help group, led group or individual therapist). If you feel that part of the problem is your mistrust of the group or the therapist see if you can find a friend to work with you, as well as airing your feelings within the therapy situation. However, a word of warning here: we have found that it is very easy in talking to a friend to justify yourself rather than explore your contradictory feelings, so do try to set up a structure with your friend. Here are some suggestions for structures which you can use with a friend or in a group.

142   Use writing, drawing or dancing to delineate the movement from your starting point in therapy to the present time. Then talk about what you have expressed and ask for feedback.

143   Set up a role play in which you start by playing yourself and then switch to being the group or the therapist.

Alternatively, have a dialogue between two parts of yourself: the one that wants to stay in the present form of therapy and the other part that feels stuck and wants a new group or therapist.

You can develop these ideas to suit your own situation and include other people by asking them to play different parts or to 'double' for you. If you are not in a therapy situation, try to find someone to co-counsel with so that you can express some of your stuck feelings and get some feedback.

Here is an example of two women trying to decide whether they should stay in their self-help groups or move on to a new form of therapy.

Doreen began to feel less and less safe in her group. She could not trust the group with any of the things that were troubling her. After being almost silent for several weeks she told them she was leaving because the group was no longer any help to her. Several of the women said how sorry they would be if she left, and Doreen began to cry. Gradually it emerged that she was feeling in the group much as she had felt in her family: that if she told the truth she would be seen as mad and feel invalidated. When Doreen realised that she was projecting her feelings about her family onto the group she felt greatly relieved and was able to see how this happened in other places too.

Staying in the group was the right thing for Doreen to do. Had she left she would have repeated and reinforced one of her most problematic patterns.

Mary had been in our self-help group for a year and a half and became increasingly aware of how her childhood experiences influenced her in the present. She worked on her childhood several times in the group but felt that she needed more time, space and consistent attention than the group could give her. We all supported her decision to do some individual therapy while remaining in the group.

CAN I DO THERAPY ON ONE PARTICULAR PROBLEM?

We have found that doing therapy which focuses on a particular problem can be very helpful, not because that problem is isolated from the rest of the woman's experience and personality, but because by dealing more effectively with that one problem, such as overcoming her fear of travelling on the underground or of not having orgasms, she may gain confidence that she will learn to control other parts of her life more effectively in the future. It can also remove the particular problem from acting as a focus and open the way to a more general self-exploration.

One very successful form of feminist therapy focusing on a particular problem is the 'compulsive eating' therapy started by a self-help group of women in the women's movement in the US and brought to Britain by Susie Orbach, who describes it in her book *Fat Is a Feminist Issue.*[1] In 'compulsive eating' groups the aim is for each women to see how she has used eating as a way of trying to deal with problems which cannot, in reality, be mastered by eating another packet of biscuits or by being larger. For example, a woman who eats compulsively (that is, not because she is hungry and really enjoys her food) each time she feels in conflict with her children, may realise that she is doing this to make herself feel bigger, more grown up and therefore more able to exert her authority. When she realises that being fatter does not make her more powerful she can learn to break this link and will not need to eat to deal with conflict situations. She can re-educate herself to assert her authority without literally making herself bigger.

We can see how a theme-centred therapy of this kind does not aim to deal with all the underlying unconscious feelings which have made it difficult for this woman to exert her power. What it does is to unearth these feelings and to allow her to use her new knowledge to give her control over the eating.

Self-help therapy groups based on a shared problem, such as compulsive eating, can be very successful, probably because having the same difficulties and working out how to deal with them can have a binding effect on the group. Equally a group based on common life experiences can be effective: for example, separated and divorced women, women with fertility problems, new mothers.

Two other forms of therapy, focused on a particular problem, which women have found very helpful are pre-orgasmic groups and assertion training. But sometimes the problem can feel too frightening to work on directly. For example, Lana decided that she needed therapy when she found that her inability to travel on the underground system was seriously affecting her life. Her phobia had driven her to therapy but she knew that there were years of unhappiness and unsatisfying relationships which she needed to look at. When her therapist offered her the opportunity of working directly on her phobias she realised that she was too afraid to do so. Later as she became less afraid of the more general feelings she found that the phobias gradually subsided. She never worked on the phobias as a separate issue in therapy. There is no easy way of discovering if you feel able to work on a particular problem or if it is too frightening for you, except perhaps by trying it out or fantasising what it would be like to do so. You could try Co-counselling for this.

Another guideline is to notice if you are avoiding doing therapy on a particular issue that causes you a lot of pain. You may feel bad about your lack of control around food and do not like the way you look, but avoid any discussion about 'compulsive eating' groups. This may be because you do not yet feel ready to tackle the problem directly. You might feel safer starting with some general therapy.

Sometimes women want to do therapy to enable them to deal with a particular crisis. Examples of this might range from dealing with an abortion, to bereavement, to adjusting to a new and more responsible job. The therapy is of limited duration and focuses on the particular crisis.

Judging whether short term or focused therapy will be helpful for you, or whether it will only scratch the surface of your problems, is difficult. If you tend to be a person whose life goes from crisis to crisis working on any one situation may give you insight into the pattern but it may be that the crises are symptomatic of some more fundamental issues. Similarly, if you sense that your present dilemma or situation is part of a pattern of relating that you have had for years, short-term therapy may be clarifying but is unlikely by itself to change something which is a basic part of your personality. If, on the other hand, this seems to be a unique crisis for you, a short-term focused look at your feelings may be all that you need.

WHAT KINDS OF CHANGES CAN I EXPECT TO MAKE THROUGH DOING THERAPY?

You can expect that therapy will change your attitude towards your feelings. You may feel more pain, more sadness, but you will also be more able to feel joy, love and happiness. You will start to befriend your feelings instead of rushing for a cigarette, drink or sleeping pill each time you feel a twinge of emotion. You will find that some symptoms such as fear of enclosed spaces or headaches disappear when the feelings can be expressed more directly. You will feel more alive in the present and less controlled by feelings you don't understand and perhaps even fear.

Often people think that the change will mean a complete transformation, which is something they both hope for and dread. Really changing your basic emotional or psychic structure involves a complex and lengthy process of working through your resistances until you feel safe enough not just to re-experience early pain, but also to establish new ways of dealing with the world. In this way you can hope to use therapy to break old emotional patterns and establish new and more fulfilling ones. As David Boadella puts it, 'We are all crooked trees . . . but the twists don't dominate so much, and the spaces may be enlarged.'[2]

WHAT PROBLEMS AM I LIKELY TO HAVE IN RELATING THERAPY TO MY EVERYDAY LIFE?

The problem comes up perhaps most frequently in personal relationships. People often have difficulties sharing what they are learning with friends or workmates who have no experience of therapy and may be openly antagonistic, as one woman in Red Therapy described it:

> At first I found it difficult that none of the people I was closest to went to groups. People's reactions ranged from interest to antagonism. Some people wanted to have intellectual arguments about it, often attacking it on political grounds. I'm no good at arguing, and usually felt that I couldn't win those arguments because they often came from an emotional position.

In this situation some people react by withdrawing, keeping the therapy experience completely separate from the rest of their life, sharing it only with those who are involved or sympathetic. Others respond in the opposite way and adopt a crusading spirit, trying to win the arguments and to persuade friends they should be doing therapy too. Another temptation is to express powerful feelings you have contacted through therapy with, or even against, others who have no therapy experience or understanding of the process. This may mean shouting and shrieking at an unprepared friend over the breakfast table, or deciding after you have worked in therapy on your negative feelings towards your mother that the only honest thing to do is to visit her to tell her you hate her and never want to see her again.

None of these ways of tackling the difficulty is helpful. It is arrogant to assume that because we have decided to do therapy, other people should get involved in it too. Other people do what is right for them in their own time. They may reach many of the same insights by a completely different route. It is a shame to withdraw into a ghetto of people who are all doing therapy: therapy does not give us all the answers and other people outside that world continue to have a lot to teach us. It is often very hurtful to pour undigested feelings onto someone who is not willing or ready for this experience. It can be a form of emotional bullying, misusing the power and energy which therapy has brought to light. Inappropriate dramatic displays of feeling showing how loudly you can shout, how daringly you can swear, communicate little and can block relationships rather than clear them. Physical warmth and closeness grow in therapy groups but to try to impose that closeness on others, for example, hugging people when they don't want it, is insensitive and exhibitionist. The power we contact in therapy is the power to be and to do, not the power to tyrannise other individuals with our new-found emotions.

A common mistake is to believe that therapy has revealed 'what I really feel' which must then, in the name of honesty, be directly acted on or shown to the person concerned. In fact what therapy reveals are not our 'real' feelings so much as that part of what we feel which is usually suppressed. We have many ambivalent and contradictory feelings at different times. Therapy is specifically designed to allow the exploration of difficult, irrational or child-like feelings, but we need to think carefully how we want to translate these feelings into daily life. In any situation our feelings may be only one factor affecting our behaviour. For example, a woman might explore ways in which her living situation restricts her, but might still feel that given the choice it is the best place for her to be at the moment. At the end of a session it is good to discuss how you can put what you have learned in the therapy session into practice. This might mean having a long talk with your flatmate about difficulties with her, or it may mean compromising less with your mother's demands in your next meeting with her – or even deciding not to see her for a while until you feel calmer about her and can judge what is the best way to share with her your changes and insights.

There is very often a time lag in digesting the therapy experiences: one woman in our group worked many times on her anxieties about leaving her job, imagining what she would do with her day if she had nothing to get up for, saying goodbye to her friends at work and so on. Two years later, she finally handed in her notice. Another difficult situation is where acting on your feelings would hurt another person. For example, a woman might express in the group how much she hates being woken by her child every night – she might imagine putting the child on a cushion and shout 'No!' and 'Shut up!' at the top of her voice – but this does not mean that she will immediately decide to leave the child to cry from then on. She would not react crudely to this feeling, but would base whatever action she takes on careful consideration of the many different factors and possibilities involved.

Can I Use the Therapy Skills I Learn in a Self-help Group in My Everyday Life?

With friends who are also involved in therapy, it can open up many possibilities in your relationship. You can use therapy techniques to explore any tensions or difficulties between you, though in any confrontation it is still very important that you both agree to it, and that one is not just bullying the other in some way. In our experience it is also very important to remain clear when you are doing therapy and when you're not:

'I'd like to do an hour's co-counselling with you later'
'I'm feeling really upset, could you give me attention for ten minutes so I can have a moan and a cry'
'I'm furious about work. Don't speak to me or you'll get it. I'm going to beat up some cushions in my room.'

Therapy can actually become a valuable tool in avoiding unnecessary conflict. If you're feeling bad you may be able to ask for time instead of having a dreadful fight with your lover. You learn to recognise when you are acting uncontrollably out of irrational feelings which are not caused by the person present, and you learn not to rub them off on that person.

It is also possible to bring therapy skills into your daily life in many different kinds of interaction. For example, the ability to *listen* to others, to ask 'how' and have them fill out their experience rather than trying to interpret it for them, to notice their bodies and react to them physically as well as verbally, all these can help you to be more sensitive to others whether they are involved with therapy or not. It is also possible to experiment creatively with therapy exercises. We have found this particularly true with children. Here is an example.

We were on holiday with four children cooped up in a small house on a rainy day. They were getting increasingly tense and bad-tempered. We asked them if they would like to do a 'Therapy game' and took them all upstairs to lie on mattresses. Then we showed them a bioenergetic exercise where you drum hands and feet on the mattress while shouting 'No! No!' They did it for about ten minutes and really enjoyed it, let off a lot of energy and returned in better tempers.

In another situation, one woman's children walk into a therapy session where someone is exploring claustrophobia through being squashed by the group. When this is over, the children want to try it themselves. The mother finally agrees.

I lie on Tania and the rest of the group encourage her to get out. I say: 'Keep still, Tania, you know I'm bigger and stronger than you' and 'Time for bed, Tania'. I am using both my strength and my reasoning to keep her down. She wriggles, struggles, pulling herself with great strength and finally gets free. My other daughter wants a turn, and when I refuse both children climb onto my back. How have I got so deeply into this situation? There's no way I can't behave how I feel like behaving. I want to shake them off

... I shake and wriggle, they're still there. I reason with them. The group encourages them to stay on. I pull at them with my hands but can only get one off at a time and in the meantime the other one gets on. This whole scene could go on for hours. Right, another attempt. Stand up. Another pull. OK, you've been warned.' Now I pick one off me and throw her on the ground, followed by the other. They're getting back on ... Two children hurtling back onto the ground. And now we're all laughing. They're not getting back on again. Collapse.

I couldn't have set up the situation. It happened because the children were there anyway. Right up until the end, although I was involved and acting on my feelings, I didn't feel carried away and I could have stopped at any point ... The group helped. Their support and encouragement to the children equalised our physical strengths and neutralised my word power. I realised very forcibly how differently I treat my two children. The whole experience was very physical. Later the children repeatedly said they wanted to 'do therapy' again.

This was a good example of using therapy to explore relationships with children: the way the mother suppresses her older daughter and the child's rebellion against that; the mother's struggle to get the children 'off her back', and their determination to stay on.

We ourselves have found that therapy understandings help us to be more open with our children, for example, allowing them to cry when they need to instead of telling them to 'Be quiet' or 'Cheer up'. In turn they seem to regard it as an illuminating game. As Sheila's eleven-year-old daughter wrote:

I think therapy is a good idea because it helps people to understand their feelings and because I know how difficult it is to understand them on your own.

Sometimes I get very miserable but I don't know why. Therapy helps you sort out your problems which makes you feel better.

Some grown-ups I know need to go to therapy, one of them because he gets depressed about writing, and the other because he gets depressed about everything.

NOTES

1   Susie Orbach, *Fat Is a Feminist Issue*, Hamlyn Paperback, London, 1979; Berkley Publications, New York, 1979. This is one of the few books about therapy written by a feminist. It includes a very helpful section on running a self-help group for compulsive eaters. Others may find the approach can be adapted: for example, similar techniques have been tried in a group of people giving up smoking.
2   Jenny James, *Room to Breathe*, Coventure, London, 1975.

FURTHER READING

Joel Kovel, *A Complete Guide to Therapy*. Pantheon, New York, 1976; Penguin, London, 1978. The author is clear on his own position which he describes as being conservative about therapy and radical in politics. He writes best about the therapies he is most sympathetic to: the psychoanalytic approach. Includes a section on common queries about therapy. Not particularly sensitive to women's issues.

Susan Stanford Friedman et al., *A Woman's Guide to Therapy*, Prentice Hall, New Jersey, 1979. A good critique of the dangers of psychiatric treatment and labelling for women but disappointing in that it reflects the earlier period of feminist understanding of mental health: criticising the status quo without suggesting how to get what you want from existing services or the provision of alternatives. Don't read this book if you are feeling desperate and want to know how to sift out some useful therapy for yourself.

Bridget Proctor, *Counselling Shop*, André Deutsch, London, 1979. A series of sensitive interviews with counsellors and therapists who use different approaches: intended for students it actually gives the prospective client a good picture of what the experience of professional therapy is like.

Jerome Liss, *Free to Feel*, Wildwood House, London, 1974. Enthusiastic descriptive guide to the growth movement.

Room to Breathe (see above). There are very few graphic accounts of an individual's therapeutic experience. Though we do not feel sympathetic to the confrontational approach Jenny James seems to have reached by the end of the book, much of what she writes conveys the texture of therapy beautifully. An additional bonus is her correspondence with David Boadella, her Reichian therapist who is supportive of her developments towards self-help therapy.

Chapter Eleven
The Inner and the Outer:
Politics of Therapy

It is no accident that the links between the personal and the political, and therefore between therapy and politics, have emerged as issues in the women's movement:

> ... every form of subordination suppresses vital understandings which can only be fully achieved and communicated through the liberation of the oppressed group itself. For example, no such organisation (a vanguard left-wing political organisation) had any real understanding of the subjectivity of oppression, of the connections between personal relations and public political organisations, or of the emotional components of consciousness until the women's movement had brought these issues to the surface and made them part of political thought and action.[1]

In our own activity we found it possible to use therapy as a part of a rich and inclusive political practice. For example, when we were involved in a food co-op with women on a local council estate, it emerged that many women came to the meetings looking for more than just cheap food. In a separate therapy group women were able to explore feelings of loneliness, lack of confidence, anger, exhaustion in the struggle to establish any independence; this activity ran parallel to the more outward looking activities of the food co-op and the community issues raised there. More recently when a sister was imprisoned, our struggle to support and defend her took many forms. The circulation of information and propaganda for her cause, the confrontation of bias in the legal system, the organisation of demonstrations and pickets, the close contact of friends who were able to relate to her on visits and help her stay in touch with her feelings and cry when she needed to, the conscious sending of loving energy from friends in the back of the courtroom when she was in the dock, all these were needed and made up a total political response to her situation. The more personal and feelings-oriented support seemed as essential as the rest.

The significance of the women's liberation movement is that it enables us to see the ways in which capitalism invades and attempts to control all areas of our lives and thus necessitates a response, a struggle, not just in the factory but also on the playground, in schools, at home and in bed. The women's movement's insistence upon opening out emotional and personal issues arises out of the particular responsibility that women in a patriarchal society have for emotional life.

Women's Realm: the Privatised World of the Emotions

In her book, *Towards a New Psychology of Women*,[2] Jean Baker Miller sees women as having the unenviable role of 'carriers' for society of certain aspects of human experience: those aspects which we understand least and over which we have least control. Women, as carriers of uncontrollable frightening experience, can then be regarded by men as emotionally disordered. Sally Berry expressed such an experience very succinctly in her poem.

I scream
You read your book
I scream again
You turn the page[3]

A familiar way of dealing with aspects of ourselves that we don't like is to attribute them to some other, usually less powerful, group. The radical feminist interpretation of patriarchal society sees that it is based on men using women in this way:

The fact is that we live in a profoundly anti-female society, a 'misogynistic civilization' in which men collectively victimize women, attacking us as personifications of their own paranoid fears, as the Enemy.[4]

Mary Daly is suggesting that this view of women is perpetrated in every fibre of the culture: that 'mind/spirit/body pollution (is) inflicted through patriarchal myth'. Not only is it around us but 'the ghostly gases . . . have seeped into the deep chambers of our minds.'[5] In *Purity and Danger*, Mary Douglas explains the ways in which a society separates out what is seen as clean and safe from what is seen as dirty and polluted as a means of maintaining order.

Ideas about separating, purifying, demarcating and punishing transgressions have as their main function to impose system on an inherently untidy experience. It is only by exaggerating the difference between within and without, above and below, male and female, with and against, that a semblance of order is created.[6]

In our culture one of the ways that system has been imposed is through the separation of rational, external, political male, and irrational, emotional, spiritual female. The latter then being seen as dirty and polluted:

'Don't touch me', she said to her young lover
'There is an old woman rotting between my legs and I cannot wash the smell away'[7]

To understand why our society imposes order in particular forms we have to remember that we live in a patriarchal society whose forms are dominated by capitalist economic organisation. This has profound effects on every aspect of our lives.

THE GROWTH OF THERAPY

The growth of psychology in general and therapy in particular has been used to contain a major contradiction within capitalism: that increasing material wealth (for some) has been created at the expense of great personal stress. As society's emotional carriers, women have had to cope with this stress. We see evidence of this in the dramatically higher rate of admission of women to mental hospitals. The drug companies recognise it and push – through the medical profession – the use of tranquillisers and anti-depressants for over-burdened, isolated women.

Since the 1950s there has been an unprecedented development of therapy and counselling. From the 'growth centres' of California to the casework done by social workers in Britain and the pop pyshcology meted out in the media, the idea has spread that dealing with feelings is something which requires special and often specialised attention. A consumer society raises peoples' expectations of life beyond that of basic survival. It must do so for people to have the motivation, money and leisure to consume its products. Ironically this new production/consumption process can lead to a more alien-ated life both at home and at work. The dissatisfactions are harder to recog-nise. People may feel unsure and anxious in ways they find difficult to define. It is easier to know that what you need is a holiday or an indoor toilet, harder to understand why you cannot sleep at night or wake in the morning feeling distressed and vulnerable. We know of a ninety-one-year-old woman who told us that she had worked twelve hours a day, five days a week, and half a day on Saturday, and all for six shillings a week. She must have known what she needed: a rest and more money. She did not need expert help in understanding what was bothering her. Nor would she have had much time for therapy.

At the same time as people are expecting more from life and are confused by their own discontents, the old social forms of daily control and cohesion are weakened. The family does not stay together: children can escape from their parents. The community, whether village or street, no longer provides the combination of support and moral censure which could hold people in a just tolerable level of misery. Yet an orderly society depends on orderly psyches. Psychiatry and its offshoots, therapy, counselling and social work, provided officially, aim to control people when other means fail. Psychiatry can be used as a way of victimising or getting rid of people who carry their family's distress[8] or are awkward in other ways for the people around them. For women this can mean being labelled or contained for behaving in ways which do not conform to feminine role models, or because they are no longer able to service others and so can be assigned to the waste bin of a mental hospital if they make life difficult for others. This does not mean that such women would be fine if only they were left alone. Often they are deeply unhappy. The point is that the so-called treatment does not even begin to identify or tackle the causes of their unhappiness. This is not a book about mental hospitals and psychiatric treatment but some facts about them are significant for us.[9] Mental patients who are committed involuntarily have fewer civil rights than prisoners. Women are much more likely than men to spend some part of their life in a mental hospital. Mental patients know that the way to get out of a mental hospital is to behave well:

I finally figured it out. You weren't supposed to be angry. Oh no! They lock you up, throw away the key, and you're supposed to smile at them, compliment the nurses, shuffle baby, so that's what I did to get out.[10]

The school or marriage guidance counsellor, the doctor prescribing just a few tranquillisers to get you through a bad patch, the social worker visiting her client, all seem benign by comparison, but there are similarities. There has been a great increase in the number of people involved in the 'helping professions' in the past decade. Counselling and casework can be used to make their recipients accept situations which they justifiably resist or resent. The school counsellor may be more concerned to get a recalcitrant student to conform than to help her express her criticisms of the school more effectively. Similarly marriage guidance can be a way of shoring up a relationship which is harmful to all concerned and may be based on a view of women's role in marriage which, as feminists, we would reject.

Of course there are some people working in these institutions who act from a feminist and socialist perspective. A school counsellor we know commented that the most significant thing she had done in her job was to make the administration aware of the supercilious way in which they communicated with parents, thereby ensuring that working-class and black parents would feel alienated from the school. She actually managed to get them to address these parents with respect, which she saw as a minor victory. Similarly, in a day centre for former mental patients a feminist was concentrating on developing women's groups and using assertion training techniques. We need to fight for therapy and counselling centres which are financed by the state but controlled by us where feminists can devote their energies to helping women, rather than fighting the administration. In the meantime we have to recognise that therapy has been largely used in reactionary ways: we will now analyse how that has happened.

USING THERAPY TO REINFORCE SOCIAL AND SEXIST NORMS

To write about the difference between radical, anti-sexist therapy and reactionary sexist therapy is to explain why we have written this book.

From the beginning men have been the therapists and women have been the main group of patients/clients. Now we find a strengthening strand of feminist therapy developing. There is a real difference between 'straight' therapy and therapy which is radical and done within the context of the women's liberation movement. This difference is not so much in technique (as you will have seen from this book we have felt free to take what we find useful from many different types of therapy) as in the ways we relate in the therapy situation, the assumptions we make, the way we understand women's psychological development, the issues we address, the social context in which we work and our overall goals.

Basically, if a therapist or a group leader lives in accordance with the values of a patriarchal capitalist society then he/she will perpetuate those values in some way. As Phyllis Chesler wrote, 'Traditionally the psychotherapist has ignored the objective facts of female oppression. Thus, in every sense, the female patient is still not having a "real" conversation – either with her husband or with her therapist. But how is it possible to have a real "conversation" with those who directly profit from her oppression?'[11] And yet it is more complex than she suggests, for we have been helped in some ways by orthodox therapists who have participated in élitist forms of training and sometimes charged 'élite' fees. The problem is to identify which aspects of therapy reinforce sexism and authoritarianism. We have to be constantly vigilant and self-critical both in our own self-help groups and in professional therapy: 'We all find it hard to tolerate not having an answer in the chaos of our culture; hard not to make a whole truth out of a half truth; hard not to look for a leader and hard to live on a knife edge of ambivalence without becoming cynical or passive.'[12]

Through our own experience we have begun to identify some of the aspects of therapy which are reactionary. It is not easy to do this when you participate in therapy in isolation. Thus while we recognise the very real value of certain kinds of individual therapy, we know that the women's liberation movement, women's groups and self-help therapy groups have a particularly important function in maintaining a critical attitude.

Who Are Therapists?

I (Sheila) have found it useful to look at my own experience in psychoanalytic therapy which was pre-women's movement. My analyst wore a suit, lived in a large house in a middle-class suburb with a neat garden, had a wife who didn't work and a spotless child who went to private school. I still don't know what his assumptions were about women's role or what he thought about my attempts to combine being a student with taking most of the responsibility for the house and my small step-son, and being a trade union activist. I never talked to him about the level of organisation I sustained to do all this as well as to come to therapy two or even three times a week.

I never really understood what was going on in my therapy, although at the time I was studying child psychology in a theoretical way. I didn't read anything about the process of therapy because I wanted it to be an emotional and not an intellectual experience. (This, I now think, shows how I saw my intellectual life as something I could do in a male province, but not something that I could really own.) The result was that I had no perspective on the power relationship between the analyst and myself and instead felt threatened by him as analyst and me as patient. Given that I'd gone to therapy because I saw myself as 'frigid' it was an oppressive situation for me. Yet he was obviously a kind man, he never told me what to do, or what I should think, or laid interpretations on me. He was not oppressive in the blatant ways that feminist writers on therapy have documented. He didn't try to seduce me, tell me I should use make-up or dress differently, accuse me of being incapable of real love because I didn't have orgasms. I have no doubt that overt oppression of women does go on in therapy,[13] but I think what happened to me is equally common and perhaps more difficult to particularise. The oppression lay in *who he was*, the questions *he didn't ask* and the material *I didn't present*. It lay in the way I felt when I arrived at his house on my bicycle and he drew up in his large car; the sense that I had that he must see his wife and family and home as normal and my household as a sign of my abnormality. To be cured would be to be capable of living like him.

Problems similar to those I encountered can arise when there are even more marked class, racial or sexual differences. There are not enough feminist therapists, let alone black feminist therapists or lesbian working-class therapists. Feminist therapists are also susceptible to the conditioning and the effects of the society we live in. They too can become élitist or modify their views to keep a job. We can never discount what the therapist or the supporting institution signify for their clients. The growth movement leader who is obviously making a lot of money conveys an implicit message to her politically active and impoverished client. She does not need to tell her client that she sees her choices as neurotic; the client will assume it. The process works in reverse in a feminist situation. Women come assuming the therapist will validate their struggles towards independence and their moves to reject female stereotypes. In fact, sometimes it is assumed that the therapist will be critical of them for overdependence on men or for taking anti-depressants. But we also need to be vigilant against new 'shoulds' coming to us from feminist theory and practice.

The Training of Therapists

That therapy training is strictly controlled, incorporates some of the worst aspects of academic learning and is usually very expensive, are all factors which play an important part in determining who therapists are and leads us to criticise the way therapeutic skills are passed on. Therapy training is hierarchical and in the more traditional institutes one of the major mechanisms of academic control is to interpret any criticism or demands for democracy by the students in terms of their personal pathology. There has been less time for tradition to ossify the training programmes within the growth movement. Its freer and more informal tone is reflected in the training. However, it is still very expensive and one of the dangers of informal hierarchy is that it can encourage a personality cult around certain more experienced or colourful therapists.

The pre-selection of people who can even contemplate training in terms of their class, education and race is obvious. Trainees are likely to be pushed in the direction of the values that such a system embodies. We don't think it's useful to dismiss all professional therapy training but instead to try to infuse it with a political self-awareness: for women who are training or working as professional therapists to support each other, for instance in peer supervision groups. Courses on particular therapy techniques are beginning to be run in more democratic ways and at more realistic prices. So too are counselling courses. Moves are being made to develop feminist therapy training. A development of training which is feminist in orientation and accessible to women from a variety of backgrounds would, in time, produce therapists with a wider outlook and experience.

THE OPPRESSIVE CONTENT OF SOME THERAPY APPROACHES

Here we concentrate on the ways in which the structure and content of different kinds of therapy can be oppressive to women while apparently offering insight and the possibility of changing unwanted behaviour and of expressing repressed feelings.

Behaviour Therapy

The aim of Behaviour therapy is not so much to explore the reasons *why* a woman acts as she does but to help her change her behaviour. The most obvious danger of Behaviour therapy is that it may be used to make women conform to norms which do not benefit us or which harm us and which we are not encouraged or supported to challenge. An example is aversion therapy for lesbians. Behaviour therapy misses one of the main potential values of therapy for a woman: the opportunity to explore and reclaim herself. Instead if offers behavioural change which is inevitably limited, not just in effect but in the perspectives or new awareness that it can offer. (You will not find it mentioned elsewhere in this book, though we do borrow techniques to be used selectively along with 'insight' giving forms of therapy.)

Psychoanalytic Therapy

There are several feminist critiques of psychoanalytic theory[14] so here we will concentrate only on the effects of the theory when it is put into practice. At worst the Freudian view that little girls want to be boys, and the subsequent assumption that the role of therapy is to help a woman adjust to a conventionally defined position in life, can lead to interpretations of a woman's desire to be independent, her rejection of childbearing, or difficulty with male bosses, as clinical symptoms, thus failing to deal in any real way with the woman's social or psychological experience. Nor does it allow for women's desires to express themselves creatively and to be respected for so doing. For example, women involved in feminist therapy were described by one male analyst as having unresolved relationships with their fathers. This kind of reductionism is ludicrous and easy to spot. Often a failure to perceive it is at the more subtle levels we describe earlier in this chapter. The other tendency in Psychoanalysis is to refer everything back to childhood, which means ignoring the effects of current social and economic realities. A woman on her own with two children, having difficulty surviving economically and neglecting her children, may find that her therapist is looking for an unresolved Oedpial conflict which may have led to the breakdown of her relationship with the children's father and her problems with them. The truth is more likely to be that there is a complex interaction between her own childhood, the fact that maintaining family life is objectively difficult and maintaining a one-parent family is, in many respects, even harder.

The transference relationship, which is the crucial and valuable part of psychotherapy if properly used, can reinforce a woman's wish to please the therapist and therefore to conform to what she sees as the therapist's norms.

(This is hardly surprising as this is bound to be part of her conditioning.) As those norms are more than likely to be sexist, her real problems will again be compounded. The combination of this dependent relationship and the therapist's role as the interpreter of the unconscious can give the therapist a great deal of power. How is this used in sexist ways? Supposing a woman tells her therapist that she is angry with her because she does not take her frustration at work seriously. This may be interpreted in terms of the woman's feelings towards her therapist and the way in which she identifies her therapist with her mother. Again, the therapist is ignoring current social reality but this time is interpreting entirely within the transference relationship. Issues over payment for therapy can also be 'interpreted away' so that a woman's real financial difficulties in paying high fees, and a valid political objection in having to pay for therapy at all, are subsumed under the therapist's view that not wanting to pay reflects a wish to continue infantile dependency. It does not seem right to us to accept such an interpretation from a therapist whose earning capacity may be several times that of the client in question, though this doesn't necessarily mean that the issue of unsatisfied infantile dependency is irrelevant to women.

The Growth Movement

We think that without a socialist and feminist perspective, growth movement therapy easily falls into modes which support authoritarianism and sexism in our society. The growth movement emphasises personal responsibility and ignores social constraints. The emphasis is an understandable response to several important factors in the 1950s when Encounter and Gestalt were being developed. The denial of personal responsibility under fascism was still fresh in people's minds. Some response to the classic excuse, 'I was only obeying orders' was required. At the same time the daily reality of people's lives tended to make them feel more helpless, whether because of the development of nuclear power, the 'cold war' or their lack of control over the machines on which their existence depended. This in turn was somewhat contradicted, particularly in the United States, by a consumer society in which gratification (of certain sorts) was promised immediately. Alongside consumer gratification went a loosening of sexual mores: an apparently increasingly libidinal society.[15] The growth movement therapists spoke directly to the times, offering a quicker form of therapy, encouraging immediate demand and gratification. (est has recently been described as the 'MacDonalds of therapy'.) Ironically the growth movement offered an individualistic solution to the powerlessness of individuals.

The assumption that it is up to the individual to know what she wants and to own her own feelings is coupled in the growth movement with the prescription that when you know what you want you should follow through to try to achieve your own goals. In a therapy group where there is a limited amount of time available the growth movement ethos is that whoever asks first gets the time. In a group one of us attended the leader said, 'Whoever gets their clothes off first and gets into the centre of the circle works.'

The competition for time and space can encourage people to behave in sexually stereotyped ways. Men are more used to demanding and competing for time while women may either use their attractiveness to gain the group leader's attention or do so in other familiar ways like crying, being pathetic or solicitious to others: if a woman can't get space to work for herself in a group perhaps she can get space by being chosen to be someone else's mother.

Group goals reflect the personal orientation of many group leaders: to make participants more successful in a capitalist, sexist society. So, we have seen groups entitled 'Your Career: are you expressing yourself fully in your work?', 'Are you in the career that is right for you?' That group was offering a straightforward exercise in doing better under capitalism. Similarly, in a group on 'Ending a relationship' there was no suggestion of criticising a society dependent on the maintenance of couple relationships but also making it incredibly difficult to sustain them. Following a fairly realistic part of the blurb about 'discovering how past experiences affect current relationships' participants are offered 'three keys to establishing satisfying future relationships'. Again, the myth of the quick easy answer. Sales talk: 'if only you use X brand of toothpaste you'll be the most popular girl on the block'. Fortunes are made as therapy becomes the ultimate commodity to make you happy. If feelings are the only things that really count, and each individual is responsible for her own feelings, then any question of social responsibility or political determinism goes out of the window. Too bad if you happen to be born working-class, female or black. No limitations on our 'potential' are recognised except those we supposedly place there ourselves and which, in principle, we could remove.

How do growth movement groups deal with the issues of sexism?

They are not explicitly based on sexist theories of personality development. Perhaps the fairest thing we can say is that much depends on the leader's own personal awareness. We have seen a male group leader working sensitively with a woman who is experiencing new difficulties in her family, resulting from her activities in the women's liberation movement. On the other hand we have found some leaders who assumed that nonconformity to feminine norms was neurotic. Group leaders have felt at liberty to make such sexist remarks to women as, 'You could be attractive if you tried', 'Do you want to grow breasts?'

The general insensitivity to women in groups within the growth movement comes out clearly over the issue of touching. Permission to touch is often seen as one of the more liberating aspects of the growth movement, as compared to traditional therapy. Like the so-called permissive society, and the sexual revolution, it has largely been developed on male terms and in male inter-ests.[16] In groups which are based on touch, such as massage, and also in Encounter, touching each other is positively encouraged. Permission to hug, hold and touch is needed for people brought up to restrict such contact to sexual encounters or family rituals. However, the fact that these are the norms means that when a group leader feels free to put his arms around a woman, or when men in the group hug her, this is not necessarily going to be experienced straightforwardly by the woman herself. Being hugged by some-one in authority, or by strange men, has a particular meaning for most women. Some men do use groups as a way of having sexual contact with women. Most men, however well intentioned, have certain conditioned responses to touching women. These are factors which must be carefully considered when making a decision whether to work in a mixed or single-sex therapy group.

Questions of leadership are also crucial within the therapy situation. In spite of the more egalitarian style of the groups which have everyone on first name terms, and leaders socialising with group members, the issue of leader-ship itself is rarely challenged within the growth movement therapies. There is still a great tendency to defer to the expert: to someone who appears to have a clear theory and experience. This happens even in groups whose structure is consciously anti-authoritarian (such as women's and some left-wing groups). It is not surprising as we are all conditioned to function in a hierarchical and authoritarian society and it takes more than statements of good intention to alter that conditioning. In growth movement groups we often see individuals who are not overtly being coerced into imitating the group leader, miming and aping a leader in order to gain approval. In a group where there is no recognition of the dangerous aspects of the authoritarian role it will not feel safe to expose your own complex needs, and resistance to, authority. Yet if these are not clarified, opposition to authority can become as inflexible or dogmatic as the authority itself.

This lack of respect for, or understanding of, the significance of the group process is reflected in some leaders' lack of respect for the group as an entity. They see the group as a series of individuals without recognising the significance of their relationships with each other. Even where the group is primarily brought together to work on other issues we know that relation-ships between group members are extremely important. This lack of respect can also be reflected in the way that a leader may arbitrarily alter group membership without consulting the group.

The significance of all the fragments of criticism we have put together lies in what they reflect about the assumptions, often implicit or unconscious, of the therapists, the therapy and their institutions. These assumptions do not simply reveal intellectual interest: they reflect the power interests of those who perpetuate them.

313

HOW CAN THERAPY BE DONE DIFFERENTLY?

Feminist critiques of therapy recognise that social oppression affects women at the deepest levels and show how this is often unrecognised in traditional and growth movement therapy. In this book we attempt to go beyond this to suggest that there are ways of using therapy to make our deepest experiences of oppression conscious and therefore less undermining. We are beginning to see how therapy which is within our control, and which embodies feminist and socialist values, has a role to play in this process.

Recognising the Reality of External Oppression and the Need to Counteract It

We do not accept that people have simply chosen their pain, their situation or their bad experiences. If a woman has been sexually insulted in the street and brings her distress to a growth movement group she may be told, 'It's only because you feel bad about yourself that this incident bothers you.'

In a feminist setting she would be encouraged to express her feelings of anger and humiliation and to explore the self-hatred that may underlie the humiliation triggered off by the man's insults. The self-hatred may prevent her from responding effectively. When other women are encouraged to express their identification her feelings are validated. She does not have to add shame about her inadequate responses to what has already been a bad experience.

We are talking about several stages here:

1   Exploring the woman's experience and relating it to the real obstacles or objective difficulties she is facing.
2   Recognising that a lifetime of similar experiences affects a woman's view of the world, her self-perception and self-esteem and the way she interacts with others.
3   Trying to help her to tackle the obstacles she encounters, knowing that she will be better able to do this if she understands and can express what she is feeling.

We do not imagine that the next time she is insulted in the street that she will automatically feel fine, but rather that she will feel better able to act in full knowledge of her feelings and with the support of knowing that she is involved in a movement which is strengthening women. In Britain women have organised 'Reclaim the Night' demonstrations literally to reclaim our capacity to walk through the city streets at night in safety: marching through the streets of Soho at night with other women is a collective way of expressing women's resistance to this aspect of oppression and is an extension of the sort of therapy we are talking about.

314

Just as we recognise the realities of sexism and the ways it affects us emotionally, so in our therapy we try to recognise the ways in which class and race have affected us. In a feminist setting we will try both to discriminate positively in favour of those whose class or racial background makes it harder for them to feel confident and also to make sure they have the time and space to work on their feelings about their specific oppression. It is no use just being nice to an Asian woman in an all-white group. We have to face with her what her experience means. This is often difficult because it may bring up feelings we would rather conceal under liberal acceptance of our differences.

In some growth movement groups any mention of political activity is seen as neurotic and as an avoidance technique. We would see political activity, when done by people who are in contact with their emotions and motivation, as a healthy sign of acting in the world, taking responsibility for ourselves and others, a sign of love in the widest sense.

Self-Nourishment

Political activity for women, if it is not questioned, *can* come to substitute as a form of duty for being a wife and mother. In our society, women are expected to be nurturers of others and even when we consciously reject this role we find that we have internalised aspects of it so deeply that we cannot undo those aspects by an effort of will alone. Part of our therapy must emphasise our need to nourish ourselves and to seek nurturance from others. This can mean learning to ask for nurturance from other women, and to ask for emotional support from men rather than perpetuating the traditional model where women depend economically on men but where most of the emotional caring is done by women. We do need to recognise that we are worth taking care of. Our low self-esteem should not be covered by vague attempts at pretending it isn't a problem but should instead be altered through understanding its roots, which can provide a basis for a new attitude of self-acceptance and love. In our self-help group we found that we slowly began to ask each other for support rather than restricting those demands to our most intimate relationships:

> I'd been very together all week getting a job and looking for a place to live. I'd had a stiff neck for days and it took a few hours of being in the women's group to feel safe again, safe enough to feel sad, to feel weak. Then the group held me and supported me while I allowed myself to give up – not to hold my head up – to let it rest on someone else's shoulder and to cry.[17]

There is no simple ruling about women being encouraged to be stronger or to be weaker. In that last example, the woman had been very strong all week. She needed to be able to function with strength and yet maintain and increase her capacity to ask for support. In other situations women will need to work

315

in therapy on developing their strength. This is a very ambiguous area for women because while we are being defined by society as 'weak' we are also required to carry the burden of supporting others, which usually requires a great deal of consistent strength. In our group we did not find it easy to encompass the contradictory feelings of weakness and strength which emerged so clearly. We also found reflections of these contradictions in the process of writing this book together. Within the women's liberation movement women are often encouraged to act strong, but if we don't *feel* strong or can't express our weakness when we feel weak, this strength is paper thin and can be yet another lie to our real experience.

Allowing Our Contradictions

In some women's groups a kind of puritanical feminist consciousness develops which makes it unacceptable to admit to 'non-feminist' feelings, whether these are to do with dependency on male approval, jealousy and competitive feelings towards other women or fears of acquiring 'male' skills or attributes. Feminist therapy has to allow these feelings to emerge and to be explored in order to work towards real change. A woman needs to feel free to explore her motivations for political activity, or to be allowed to express her anger at a man, or her protection of him without being judged.

I think the women's movement doesn't have much of a sense of individual contradiction either, and I think therapy does . . . Since doing therapy I have felt specially impatient with the mass psychology that the left *and* the fucking women's movement come up with. Therapy helps you understand that each individual's history is specific to her as well as being part of the social history or role; that an individual's needs or choices are going to be different from yours, and probably internally inconsistent at times . . . and that inconsistency is in no way recognised by the rather sociological model of motivation put forward within radical political movements. And until political movements can actually meet the complexity of individuals' experience, they *aren't* going to mean very much except in a rather self-denying and moralistic subculture.[18]

Using Therapy To Clarify Our Politics

The deeper challenge to political activity seems to come from the clarification therapy gives to our *motives* for political activity. For example, a woman in our group who had volunteered to sew up hundreds of bags to be sold in aid of the abortion campaign explored in one session her dread at having to do so much extra work on top of a taxing job. She found that what was driving her to do it was the internalised voice of her mother telling her she should be working harder. Political activity can become just a new work ethic, or a new form of masochism, a new form of competing, or a new form of guilt or dogma. It sometimes emerges that the 'acting out' of unresolved childhood feelings lies at the very heart of an individual's political motivation. For example, it may emerge during a session that a generalised hostility towards authority is motivated by that individual's continuing anger against her parents. Activity motivitated by these kinds of unrecognised emotions of anger or guilt from the past can be self-defeating in a number of ways. It may take the form of obsessionally working on irrelevant tasks, of domineering others within your group, of acting like a 'wilful child' or adopting tactics which inevitably lead to defeat (thus re-creating a childhood situation where the child is powerless in relation to her parents). Or it may also be expressed in uncontrollable physical outbursts, for example, physical assault on a policeman when nothing is to be gained by this and the only person to suffer will be yourself. As one woman in Red Therapy put it, 'A lot of politics, and I only care about the left, is disguised personal fuck-ups, and being a revolutionary would be much more effective and much more enjoyable if that was acknowledged.'

Recognising these sources of our motivation does not in fact undermine our political activity, but can help us to be clearer and more conscious in our actions. Another member of Red Therapy said:

> I began to see more clearly the emotional basis for my intellectual commitments. However, realising that a deep-rooted desire to hit back at a Tory father whom I felt didn't want me, and a religious mother who told me I was basically and inevitably wicked, may well have been my original motivation towards political activity. Realising and working through this did not remove my political commitment but rather served to make it clearer. I became less likely to fall into the role of the wilful child, demanding to win at any cost, and more likely to make my judgments on the basis of the reality of the situation I was dealing with.

Reich draws a distinction between 'irrational' and 'rational' anger. Irrational anger, as he describes it, is anger from the past, often long repressed anger at parents or siblings deriving from distant childhood hurts. This anger may motivate us over years, or it may come out in uncontrollable explosive bursts, but either way it tends to express itself inappropriately in the present. Reich differentiates this kind of anger from 'rational' anger which is the clear, conscious and appropriate response to things which happen in the present, a response free of any distorting charge deriving from other experiences. Reich saw that there is enough injustice and suffering in our world to motivate a response of powerful rational anger and its expression through social and political action. He saw therapy as a means of clearing away irrational anger and other debris from the past, freeing us to act with greater power and consciousness in the present. He also believed that each person has in them love and an impulse towards freedom and self-expression which, if neurotic holding and repression is cleared, will express itself in rebellion against the life-hating norms of our society. In our group we found that therapy could be potent in helping us contact our power to act and our impulses to behave in less conventionally restricted ways.

Encouraging Goals That Transcend Sex-role Stereotypes

As one description of feminist therapy puts it:

> Feminist therapy explores with clients the inner contradictions in the pre-scribed social roles for women . . . It encourages the process of individual goal-setting and supports those client goals that transcend traditional sex-role stereotyping. It encourages the exploration of various life-styles and sexual orientations and supports the acquisition of skills for self-directed and inter-dependent living.[19]

As feminists our ideas of what constitutes a problem will also be somewhat different from those working without any kind of feminist consciousness. We would not be asking the women in work collectives why they don't go out and get regular jobs that pay well but would instead respect their motivations and try to work through the complications that inevitably arise in such a situation. If a lesbian works on her difficulties we would not be asking, 'Why are you a lesbian?' but rather we would be looking for the ways in which she may be being oppressed because she is a lesbian. We may also be open to less usual solutions to difficulties. Thus we might see celibacy as positive for a woman whose sexual relationships had so dominated her that she had never been able to deal with other aspects of her life adequately.

New developments within the women's liberation movement produce their own emotional contradictions for women. In all-women work collectives we have found that women, no longer having to deal with male authority and leadership, have instead had to confront the ways in which they were driving themselves, motivated by guilt towards women worse off than themselves. In a therapy situation they could focus on their own difficulties in nurturing themselves and learning to draw boundaries. Here we see how feminist therapy, while exploring the inner experience of the individual, is always working at the interface of the inner and the outer and can never simply take the individual situation or solution as a frame of reference.

Therapy Which Encourages Co-operation and Solidarity

We need to acknowledge positively the value of solidarity in changing and improving our lives; therapy alone is not enough. This may mean engaging in political organising or doing things in our private lives which give us the experience of emotional closeness and identification with other women.

Consciousness-raising groups have exactly this function, drawing out the similarities in women's lives. Therapy allows us to be as different as we are while recognising our common emotional experiences. A self-help therapy group is complementary to other activities which encourage solidarity and co-operation.

In self-help therapy the group will fall apart if people don't help each other. We have to try to work together rather than turning one person into the leader. We also have to try to make sure that if someone is shy, or afraid to take time or make suggestions, that we encourage her and recognise the reasons for her difficulties. She may be less articulate than others in the group. She may feel disadvantaged because she is the only lesbian or single person in a group which is predominantly heterosexual or made up of women in couples. This does not happen just through goodwill. It means that issues of leadership and passivity, competition and inequality, will have to be raised in the group rather than being denied:

> There are issues here of group dynamics which certainly can't be over-looked. If six people want to work it is often true that not all of them will have time to do so. It is possible to divide the time equally between people, but it may well take one person the whole evening to work through what they are feeling so we have to try and be sensitive to what's going on and watch for rigidities developing and try to bring these out into the open. If the same person starts crying at the beginning of every group, for instance, it is possible to confront the person with that perception and work through the inter-personal issues which that may bring out.[20]

As women we struggle between learning to recognise and fulfil our own needs while knowing we are inter-dependent with others. Disappearing into 'what we want' does not resolve this contradiction. This is a particularly difficult dilemma for women. There is a danger of moving from our traditional position of allowing everyone else's needs to come first to becoming aware only of our own needs and asserting these, unaware that they can be satisfied only within a social context.

Self-help therapy must deal with the recurrent tension between personal and group interest or the group cannot function. The process of self-help shows not only how we share our oppression but also how we have the power to co-operate to undo some of the effects of that oppression. Within the self-help group we know that there are no individual solutions for oppressed people and that we will not fight oppression successfully with an authoritarian structure. The egalitarian form of self-help therapy itself challenges authoritarianism.

By sharing what we have learned about self-help therapy we hope we have also been able to share our enthusiasm, our conviction that we *can* do our own therapy, and our vision of the power that can be released by doing therapy in socialist and feminist ways.

NOTES

1 Sheila Rowbotham, Lynne Segal and Hilary Wainwright, *Beyond the Fragments*, Merlin Press, London, 1979. Important book clarifying the contribution of feminism to a revolutionary movement. Expresses our own views of how therapy can be an integral part of politics and gives a fuller account of the political ideas we touch on.
2 Jean Baker Miller, *Towards a New Psychology of Women*, Beacon Press, Boston, 1976; Penguin, Harmondsworth, 1978.
3 Sally Berry in Lilian Mohin (ed), *One Foot on the Mountain: an Anthology of British Feminist Poetry 1969–1979*, Onlywomen Press, London, 1979, p 206.
4 Mary Daly, *Gyn/Ecology: the Meta-Ethics of Radical Feminism*, Beacon Press, Boston, 1978; The Women's Press, London, 1979, p 29.
5 *Gyn/Ecology*, p 3.
6 Mary Douglas, *Purity and Danger*, Penguin, Harmondsworth, 1970, p 15.
7 Valerie Sinason in *One Foot on the Mountain*, p 242.
8 R. D. Laing and A. Esterson, *Sanity, Madness and the Family*, Penguin, Harmondsworth, 1970.
9 See Phyllis Chesler, *Women and Madness*, Avon, New York, 1973; and Susan Stanford Friedman et al, *A Woman's Guide to Therapy*, Prentice Hall, New Jersey, 1979.
10 *Women and Madness*, p 169; see also, Janet Frame, *Faces in the Water*, George Braziller, New York, 1961; reprinted by The Women's Press, London, 1980; Marge Piercy, *Woman on the Edge of Time*, Alfred A. Knopf, New York, 1976; The Women's Press, London, 1979. These two novels vividly illustrate the punishment the so-called mad receive from the so-called sane.
11 *Women and Madness*, p 110.
12 Michael Rossman, *New Age Blues*, Dutton, New York, 1979. Some interesting articles giving a political critique of the growth movement from an insider's viewpoint.
13 See: *Women and Madness* and *A Woman's Guide to Therapy*; also most issues of *State and Mind* (PO Box 89, Somerville, MA 02144, USA) have relevant articles.
14 For a variety of perspectives and critiques of Psychoanalysis from a feminist perspective see: Shulamith Firestone, *Dialectic of Sex*, reprinted by Bantam, New York, 1971; The Women's Press, London, 1979; Kate Millet, *Sexual Politics*, Alfred A. Knopf, New York, 1970; reprinted by Virago, London, 1979; Jean Baker Miller (ed), *Psychoanalysis and Women*, Brunner/Mazel, New York, 1973; Penguin, Harmondsworth, 1973; Juliet Mitchell, *Psychoanalysis and Feminism*, Pantheon, New York, 1975; Penguin, Harmondsworth, 1975; Jean Strouse (ed), *Women and Analysis*, Dell, New York, 1974.
15 For a deeper discussion of the implication of these contradictions see: Herbert Marcuse, *Eros and Civilisation*, reprinted by Sphere, London, 1969; Beacon Press, Boston, 1974; Herbert Marcuse, *One-Dimensional Man*, Beacon Press, Boston, 1964; reprinted by Sphere, London, 1979.
16 See Barbara Ehrenreich and Deirdre English, *For Her Own Good: 150 Years of the Experts' Advice to Women*, Doubleday/Anchor, New York, 1978; Pluto Press, London, 1979. This book gives an historical account of how women have been

(mis)treated by medical experts and shows how authoritarian attitudes of nineteenth-century gynaecologists towards women are continuous with the psychological advice meted out in the forties and fifties, and the growth movement approach of the sixties and seventies. Unfortunately, while the authors recognise the need for women to take control of their own health services, they do not appear to include mental health in this.

17   'Red Therapy', Red Therapy, c/o 28 Redbourne Avenue, London, N3 2BS, 1978, p 40. Includes interesting ideas from activists on the links between therapy and politics.

18   Ann Scott, unpublished article, 1976.

19   'Feminist Therapy: A Working Definition', paper produced by the Feminist Therapy Referrals Committee, Penn Women's Center, c/o 115 South Beechwood Street, Philadelphia, PA 19103, USA.

20   'Red Therapy', p 31.

FURTHER READING

Apart from the books referred to in the notes, we can suggest:

Wilhelm Reich, *What Is Class Consciousness?*, Socialist Reproduction, London, 1972.
Wilhelm Reich, *The Mass Psychology of Fascism*, reprinted by Farrar Straus & Giroux, New York, 1970; Penguin, Harmondsworth, 1975. Fundamental to our developing the perspective we have on the relationship between politics, society and character structure. Still relevant to current politics and exciting to read.

Eli Zaretsky, *Capitalism, the Family and Personal Life*, Pluto Press, London, 1976; Harper & Row, New York, 1976. Worth reading if you are interested in following up the ideas we have referred to on the links between the changes in the mode of production and their effect on the structure of personal and family life.

Michael Schneider, *Neurosis and Civilization*, The Seabury Press, New York, 1975. Explores the relationship between Marxism and Psychoanalysis, suggesting both have contributions to make to the other discipline's understanding of the world. (Marxism needs a psychology and Psychoanalysis lacks a social and material framework.) Also shows how such a synthesis might be started by looking at ways in which contemporary personality forms reflect the economic structure of a consumer society.

Bruce Brown, *Marx, Freud and the Critique of Everyday Life*, Monthly Review Press, New York, 1973. Self-explanatory title. A less academic book than Schneider's and although in some ways less interesting, it does try to relate theory to people's experience of changing their lives in the student movement and subsequent period.

Claude Steiner (ed), *Readings in Radical Psychiatry*, Grove Press, New York, 1975. Theoretical and practical account of the Radical Psychiatry movement in the US. Well worth reading in spite of the limitations we have referred to elsewhere in this book.

Index of Exercises

Under the exercise numbers you will find some page references which may give you further *practical* ideas about how to tackle these topics.